ORIENT-EXPRESS
A PERSONAL JOURNEY

ORIENT-EXPRESS
A PERSONAL JOURNEY

JAMES B. SHERWOOD
WITH IVAN FALLON

The Robson Press

First published in Great Britain in 2012 by
The Robson Press
An imprint of Biteback Publishing Ltd
Westminster Tower
3 Albert Embankment
London
SE1 7SP

ISBN 978-1-84954–187-9

10 9 8 7 6 5 4 3 2 1

A CIP catalogue record for this book is available from the British Library.

Set in Caslon by Namkwan Cho
Cover design Namkwan Cho

Printed and bound in Great Britain by
TJ International, Padstow, Cornwall

To Shirley, who was my great supporter throughout the Orient-Express adventure.

CONTENTS

Acknowledgements

Building a successful business such as Orient-Express Hotels is not achieved by a single person. It has been my good fortune to have been helped by many others along the way.

Colin Bather headed the leisure division of Sea Containers from its inception in 1976 when I bought the Hotel Cipriani in Venice. Colin convinced Dr. Natale Rusconi to take charge of the hotel in 1977 and for thirty years Rusconi set the standard of five-star luxury for the entire group. Simon Sherwood became chief executive of Orient-Express Hotels in 1994 and served until 2007 with me as chairman. The company came of age under his leadership.

Jean-Paul Foerster managed the European hotels 1990–2001 and Adrian Constant ably succeeded him. Dean Andrews looked after North America 1997–2007. Paul White managed the hotel business in the southern hemisphere before being promoted to chief financial officer in 2005, succeeding James Struthers in the CFO position. White became chief executive in 2007 when Simon Sherwood stepped down. He continued in that role until mid-2011. Maurizio Saccani has deftly overseen all eight Italian hotels since Natale Rusconi retired in 2007.

Nicholas Varian took over as vice-president for trains and cruises in 1989 and developed this division into six luxury tourist trains, a cruise ship and five canal cruise vessels.

The success of the Venice Simplon-Orient-Express owes a great deal to the Swiss hotelier Claude Ginella who has run it since its launch in 1982, assisted by the outstanding chef Christian Bodiguel. Raymond Blanc of Le Manoir aux Quat' Saisons came into the group in 2002. He has made an enormous contribution to the world of French cuisine and the Manoir has held two Michelin stars since he opened it in 1984.

The food and beverage manager Vitorio Dall'O and the executive chef Attilio Di Fabrizio deserve special mention for creating one of the great dining experiences at the Villa San Michele near Florence, Italy. They often oversee the dinners served at my Capannelle wine estate in Tuscany.

The company has always depended upon its promotion to attract guests and Billy Hamilton, who died in office, was brilliant at it. He was followed by Nadia Stancioff and then Pippa Isbell who were both stars. Alison Booth was managing editor of *Orient-Express Magazine* under Shirley's leadership. It was published for twenty-four years and was an invaluable promotional tool. Vernon Stratton created many of the company's logos and brochures. He was an excellent photographer and one of his pictures is on the cover of this book.

David Williams has overseen sales and marketing while Roger Collins has skilfully managed the company's technical services. Ned Hetherington has served as general counsel both for the company and Sea Containers, keeping us all on the straight and narrow. Chresten Bjerrum, Sea Containers' regional manager for the Far East, was key to acquiring and developing all eight Orient-Express Hotels properties in Southeast Asia.

The board was greatly strengthened by James Hurlock, managing partner of the White & Case law firm, J. R. (Bob) Lovejoy from Lazard Frères, John Campbell, our representative in Bermuda and Danny O'Sullivan who was chief financial officer of Sea Containers until his retirement in 2004. Georg Rafael of Rafael Hotels and Adrian Zecha, founder of Aman Hotels, both brought their vast hotelier experience to the board at various times. Prue Leith, the restaurateur and novelist, joined the board in 2006.

I encouraged the hotel general managers to treat their properties as their own businesses and many superb managers served the company in the years before my retirement as chairman in 2007. I'd like to single out Philip Carruthers of the Copacabana Palace, Paul

Stracey of Charleston Place, Nicholas Seewer of the Mount Nelson Hotel, Bryan McGuire of '21' Club, Filip Boyen, our regional manager in Peru and his successor Laurent Carrasset, Patrick Griffin of the Observatory, Tom Evers-Swindell of the Eastern & Oriental Express, Anton Kung of the Ritz in Madrid, Tony McHale of the Windsor Court and later Keswick Hall and Jacques Hamburger of the Hôtel de la Cité in Carcassonne. Glen Michaels did a fabulous job with PeruRail after its privatization, assisted by my old colleague from Sea Containers, Romulo Guidino, on the freight side.

Sea Containers would not have come into existence had it not been for the support of Maurice Pinto, my classmate from Yale, and his cousin Joseph Pinto. Michael Gellert of Burnham & Co. put in substantial capital when it was needed. Philip Schlee was also a founder investor and worked in the company for several years. Our great mutual friend, the hugely talented designer Gerard Gallet, provided decorative inspiration for our trains and hotels. Franco Delle Piane, the Sea Containers regional manager for the Mediterranean, gave us invaluable assistance with the *m.v. Orient-Express* cruise ship service and in the acquisition of several of the Italian hotels. More recently he arranged for my purchase in 1997 of the Capannelle wine estate in Tuscany and he oversees its operation.

Finding and selecting the 161 images which we have used in this book was no small task, and I particularly want to thank Orient-Express Hotels for giving us access to its extensive picture library, and to Alison Booth for guiding us through it. I have also drawn heavily on the excellent Shirley Sherwood picture archive, the result of many years of intrepid work by a first-class photographer. My thanks to Compagnie Internationale des Wagons-Lits in Paris for the posters used on the first two pages of the first picture section. Ian Lloyd travelled with us on the inaugural trip of the Eastern & Oriental Express and we have used a number of his photographs. Some of the early pictures come from the Sherwood family photo albums, lovingly compiled and maintained by my mother; I took the Far Eastern shots myself as a young officer in the U.S. Navy. Dr. Natale Rusconi gave us access to his own private collection compiled in his years of running the Hotel Cipriani in Venice. Bill McAlpine gave us the photograph of him with his beloved Flying Scotsman, and Maury Pinto also found a picture of his own handsome visage. Fritz von der Schulenburg gave us permission to use his picture of Harry's Bar in London. My thanks to Vernon Stratton and to everyone else who contributed to our picture sections. My thanks to Vivienne Schuster at Curtis Brown for taking on this project and to Jeremy Robson, the publisher, who produced the final result.

Last but not least, special thanks go to my collaborator Ivan Fallon, the journalist, biographer and newspaper executive, who skilfully researched and enlarged my original draft into this book and greatly assisted me at every stage of the publication process. He is a true professional.

James B. Sherwood

CHAPTER ONE

The World's Most Celebrated Train

I bought my first train in October 1977. Or rather part of a train: two shabby pre-war first-class sleeping carriages without an engine. But they weren't just any old carriages – they were part of the fabled 1920s Orient-Express train, and had been used in the film of Agatha Christie's *Murder on the Orient Express.* They were to launch me on an entirely new phase of my life that would not only see the resurrection and relaunch of the Orient-Express, which had first carried passengers across Europe in 1883, but the creation of the luxury hotel group I would develop over the next thirty years.

The Orient-Express, then operated by SNCF (the French National Railway) had made what was reported as its last trip in a blaze of publicity a few months earlier. It was a sad affair, just three scruffy modern-day coaches and a sleeping car, the remnants of the most famous train in railway history, chugging mournfully into Istanbul five hours late. Although I had liked trains all my life I was no fanatical railway enthusiast, but the huge interest in the train's demise caught my attention. I could see there was still enough magic around the Orient-Express name for me to use it for a project that was beginning to take shape in my mind.

In 1976 I had purchased the Hotel Cipriani in Venice and reading and hearing the stories about the old train had given me a thought: why not buy the Orient-Express, refurbish it, and operate it along part of its old route from Paris to Venice, encouraging passengers to stay at the hotel? Venice had always been a favourite destination for tourists travelling by train, and I was convinced that passengers would be thrilled to re-enact the experience of travelling on the fabled Orient-Express in truly first-class conditions, also staying at one of the best hotels in the world.

So here I was at the freight depot of Monte Carlo station where the auction, to be handled that Saturday morning by Sotheby's, was to take place. Five cars from the original Orient-Express train, a restaurant car and four sleepers, were standing in the station ready to be sold. Sotheby's was taking the sale seriously: its legendary chairman, Peter Wilson, a tall, buccaneering James Bond-type character who had been connected with espionage during World War II, had flown in from London to preside personally over what must have been one of the more bizarre auctions in his long and distinguished career. Trains have an extraordinary romantic aura about them, and the Orient-Express conjured up an image of the lost era of luxury train travel, when elegant and beautifully dressed passengers journeyed across Europe on mysterious missions to exotic destinations. Its magic had even brought me to Monte Carlo that morning.

The hype around the sale was enormous. Princess Grace of Monaco (the former actress Grace Kelly) had obligingly travelled in the cars to Monte Carlo the previous day, and the pictures she had posed for went around the world. The Sotheby's publicity people had made sure that all the major networks, from CBS and NBC in the U.S. to the BBC and even a few Japanese crews, were there as well as what seemed like the entire world press. I had to push my way through the massed ranks of cameramen, reporters and spectators to reach the front row where plush red chairs had been reserved for the bidders.

There were three of us: a Swiss rail enthusiast called Albert Glatt; a mystery French buyer who was later identified as a representative of the King of Morocco; and me. We had all walked through the cars before the sale started and, to be frank, they weren't up to much. The restaurant car turned out to be a second-class one that had been dressed up for the film, and the four sleepers, while still grand in their own way, had seen better days.

Wilson briskly called the auction to order and started the sale, doing his usual trick of apparently pulling bids off the wall until the figure got to the region where it was getting serious. I dropped out of the bidding for the first two, which the French mystery man bought for the equivalent of $100,000 each. This was more than I wanted to pay and I began to feel I had wasted my trip. Then came the next two sleepers, identical to the first two and suddenly I was in the game. The Frenchman had got what he wanted, and Glatt, it turned out, was only interested in the restaurant car. I got the next sleeper for $72,800 and the fourth, which was the same quality as the others, for $41,000. I also managed to buy a number of marquetry panels that had been stripped out of original cars and some delightful René Lalique art deco glass reliefs of frolicking bacchanalian youths (which were subsequently stolen from a German workshop and had to be recast). Suddenly I was in the train business.

A few minutes later I discovered I was also a media celebrity. I was surrounded by a throng of journalists who showered me with questions: what was I going to do with the carriages, was I a railway buff, was this a boyhood dream fulfilled, and more in the same vein. Perhaps the real question they should have asked was: 'Are you mad?' but even they were too polite for that. I fended them off by saying that in the short term the cars would be sent to a covered warehouse in Bordeaux owned by agents of my company, Sea Containers. Then I would ponder what to do with them.

I had persuaded my old friends (Sir) Bill McAlpine and (Lord) David Garnock, both of them passionate railway enthusiasts, to come down and give me moral support, and after the auction Peter Wilson took us all to a celebratory – and splendid – lunch in the village of Eze, on the corniche between Monte Carlo and Nice. They were even more excited than I was. Bill had bought and restored the famous Flying Scotsman locomotive, and had even built himself a railway on his estate at Fawsley, west of London, which included a signal box, ticket office and, of course, his own steam locomotive. David also had a collection of lovingly restored steam engines, including the Great Marquess, taken out of service by British Rail in 1961. There were no better men to advise me on what I planned next.

However, that day I had something else on my mind. I had rented a car and after lunch intended to drive myself to Venice for a late dinner with my wife-to-be, Shirley Cross (we were married a few months later on 31 December) who to her considerable disappointment had missed the auction. The Monte Carlo sale was the only part of the entire project she was not directly involved in, but that day she was entertaining our guests, the Nobel Laureate Sir John Vane and his wife Daphne, at the Hotel Cipriani and we had agreed that she would hold the fort until I got there. But soon after I left Monaco the heavens opened and a viaduct collapsed on the road to Milan, forcing me into a long detour. There were no cell-phones in 1977, and it was 2 a.m. before I could call her in Venice to let her know I was still alive – and, almost as important, had bought the cars.

Shirley, in the meantime, had been doing her research and soon became as captivated by the Orient-Express project as I was. The train had a rich, romantic history that we both became intrigued by. Until cheap air travel had begun to replace it in the 1950s, it had been a vital link between western Europe and the Middle East. From 1919 until the SNCF finally stopped the service in May 1977, an Orient-Express train had left Paris for Istanbul every night, except in the war years, stopping at Venice on the way. And what trains: the LX (for de luxe) sleepers and restaurant cars, lovingly built for the grandly named Compagnie International des Wagons-Lits et des Grands Express Européens, were masterpieces of design and craftsmanship. The best of them were built between the wars, the high point of luxury train travel, when Lalique's art deco walls of lighted glass epitomized the hunger for elegance and novelty of the 1930s. Rail passengers had never travelled in such style before, and, if this train disappeared, they never would again.

I was determined to resurrect the Orient-Express but had no real idea of how to go about it. I had acquired the first two carriages of my train, which was at least a start, but where to find the others? It turned out that Wagons-Lits, which by then was an international hotel and catering company, still owned some old rolling stock which was scattered in marshalling yards all over Europe. At our request, they located a number of original Orient-Express first-class cars in Spain and Portugal, where they had been ignominiously sent when they could no longer meet the more rigorous technical requirements of the higher-speed railways to the east.

And so we went to Irún in Spain to inspect some decommissioned hulks of LX-sleepers and restaurant cars which looked, to my untutored eye, well beyond saving. Underneath the layers of dust and grime, the elegant Wagons-Lits lines were still there, but the windows were smashed, doors broken or gone altogether, there were missing floorboards and the beautiful marquetry had been covered over with linoleum. Over the years almost every carriage had been modernized in some way; I remember a poor old bar car, which had been gutted and redecorated with plastic trimming.

These cars, we were informed, also had another problem: the rail gauge in Spain was wider than in France, Switzerland and Italy, where we planned to use them, so the wheel sets would have to be changed to the so-called English Standard Gauge of 4 feet 8½ inches. Like many countries in the nineteenth century, Spain had adopted a different gauge as a protection against invasion, presumably by the French; the Russians had done the same for fear of being overrun by the Germans – not that it did them much good! We eventually got around the problem by buying wheel sets from 1920s standard-gauge cars which were being scrapped, and we swapped them.

Someone remarked that it would be easier to build entirely new carriages rather than attempt to restore this little lot but that never entered my head. I had decided that the Orient-Express was going to consist entirely of genuine first-class cars, built between the wars, which would be refurbished, restored and repaired to their original perfection. If there was no alternative but to replace something, then it must be made by craftsmen employing the same materials and techniques used in the 1920s.

That of course was more easily said than done and restoration turned out to be a much more complicated and costly process than I had bargained for. Bill McAlpine and other railway enthusiasts pointed out that what we were attempting had never been done before. Restoring old steam engines and carriages as museum pieces was one thing, but creating an entire vintage train capable of maintaining a scheduled service, day-in and day-out, on modern track and meeting health and safety standards in at least four different countries, was a very different matter. Obviously we had to meet modern safety standards but we were also determined to retain the integrity of the old train. Shirley would later become highly indignant when she overheard a passenger suggest that the carriages had been built brand new and 'antiqued'.

In the end we bought twenty-five original Orient-Express cars and split them between the Wagons-Lits workshop near Ostend, Belgium, and Bremer Waggonbau at Bremen, Germany, where they began the long and exacting task of restoration. Ultimately we were to restore eighteen cars, seventeen being the maximum length that could be accommodated on the track, plus a spare, and cannibalized the others. When attached to a locomotive, the whole train – or 'rake' as we learned to call it – would be almost half a kilometre long.

Finding and buying enough cars was only the first stage, and it was beginning to dawn on me what a daunting task I had so light-heartedly taken on that day in Monte Carlo. For a start the project had become larger. Our original plan was to operate the train only from Paris to Venice, but the British were the most frequent visitors to Venice going back to the Grand Tour days, and they were also lovers of historic trains. I felt we should re-create the entire journey starting in London.

In these days of the Channel Tunnel this would not have been such an issue. But with ferries the only cross-Channel connection, in effect it meant rebuilding two trains, one to run from London's Victoria Station to the English Channel, and the other to go the rest of the way, starting from the French side. The Folkestone–Boulogne route had rail connections on to the piers at both ports and at one stage we considered using a historic train made up of British Pullman cars, loading them onto a ferry, and then continuing with them to Paris where they would be linked up with the main Orient-Express train going all the way to Venice. However, we quickly hit insurmountable problems: regulations relating to brakes, buffers and even vestibules were different on either side of the Channel, and some of the wood-framed old Pullmans would not have been allowed on French railways which insisted on steel-framed bodywork. So we decided to have the British Pullmans run to the docks at Folkestone, the passengers would then walk off the train, much as they did in Graham Greene's *Stamboul Train*, embark on the Sealink ferry (then still owned by British Railways but which I would buy for Sea Containers in 1984), and then board the Orient-Express train at Boulogne which would be waiting alongside the ferry on the quay.

Now we needed two trains. This was a task for Bill and David, without whom I don't think I could have put together the train I envisaged: authentic British inter-war first-class cars to transport Orient-Express passengers between London and Folkestone.

All this time I was still doing my day job running Sea Containers, of which I was the founder, president and CEO. I had started the company in 1965 and by now it was a substantial international organization, operating in eighty countries and listed on the New York Stock Exchange. I was spending nine months of the year travelling around the world on its business, but as the trains took shape, so our enthusiasm for it grew. Shirley and I read everything we could find on the history of the Orient-Express and found there were dozens of books either about the train or which mentioned it. Shirley later turned this research into a beautiful book, *Venice Simplon-Orient-Express: The World's Most Celebrated Train*, which is now in its fifth edition and has sold over 500,000 copies.

The train had attracted the attention of Hollywood too. The action in Hitchcock's 1938 film, *The Lady Vanishes*, takes place on the Orient-Express as it travels through the Alps to Paris; in *From Russia with Love*, James Bond, played by Sean Connery, steals a 'Lektor' decoding device in Istanbul and boards the Orient-Express for Venice, along with some very sinister characters; and of course we all know about Hercule Poirot and his star-studded cast of suspects in the 1974 film *Murder on the Orient Express*. The more I got to know about it, the more convinced I was that we would get a return on the money we were investing, now getting into the millions.

As an American, I was interested to discover that luxury train travel was actually started by an American, George Mortimer Pullman, who built the first plush railcar, with seats that converted into beds, in Illinois in 1864, the year before Abraham Lincoln was assassinated (his body was later carried on a Pullman). The concept was picked up in Europe, and Pullman began shipping American-built carriages in knock-down form to England in 1882. But across the Channel an enterprising Belgian called Georges Nagelmackers, who had travelled on one of Pullman's trains on a visit to the U.S. in 1869, was ahead of him. He founded Wagons-Lits (which simply means 'sleeping cars') in 1876 and was the real father of the Orient-Express, quickly coming to dominate the luxury train market with his beautiful carriages, which were used in a network of international expresses steaming across Europe. The most famous of them was the Express d'Orient (later renamed the Orient-Express), inaugurated with much fanfare at the Gare de l'Est in Paris in 1883. Five years later the through-run from Paris all the way to Constantinople was established, a journey of sixty-seven hours and thirty-five minutes – a major breakthrough for those days.

By the turn of the century the pattern for the super-luxury railcar had developed. The new sleeping cars had all-steel suspension which smoothed the ride considerably, as well as enclosed vestibules and concertina gangways. Some compartments even had built-in wash-basins and commodes, a great luxury in those days, and passengers dined in exquisitely fitted dining cars with the best crystal and linen, fine food, good wine and immaculate service.

By the end of World War I, the Allies considered the train so strategically important that they introduced Articles 321–386 into the Treaty of Versailles, requiring it to operate without touching German soil. They also wanted to open up speedy communications with the Balkans, particularly the newly created country of Yugoslavia, which meant using the twelve-mile-long Simplon Tunnel which had been opened in 1906. And so the Simplon-Orient-Express train was born and inaugurated in 1919, running from Paris through Dijon, Lausanne, the Simplon Tunnel, Milan, Venice, Trieste, Zagreb, Belgrade, Nish, Sophia and finally Constantinople. The trip took fifty-six hours. The next twenty years, before it was suspended with the fall of France in 1940, were the Orient-Express's greatest, and it was this era of super-luxury travel I sought to re-create.

The fall of France was also marked by the most notorious event in the history of these great trains. The Armistice which formally ended World War I was signed at 11.11 a.m. on 11 November 1918, at Compiègne in Car 2419, in a ceremony presided over by Marshal Foch, deliberately designed to humiliate the Germans. When they entered Paris in 1940, Hitler's troops located the same car in a museum and transported it back to the exact same spot, on the same railway line, in the same woods, and Hitler personally made Foch's fellow World War I soldier, Marshal Pétain, formally sign France's surrender. Hitler then ordered the car to be taken to Berlin, but as the Russians advanced in 1945 the SS blew it up.

The British train proved the easier of the two trains to put together, as railway enthusiasts had preserved more of the first-class Pullman cars from trains such as the famous Brighton Belle which ran from Brighton to London, and the Golden Arrow which connected with its own cross-Channel steamer (the *Canterbury*) and then a fast train to Paris in the 1930s. We acquired them from all sorts of unexpected sources, including a master at Eton College, railway historic societies and restaurant owners who were using the cars to serve their guests. In France we found General de Gaulle's private car, which he had used in Britain in the war. We bought it, only to be informed the French government was about to impose an export ban on the following Monday. So over the weekend we got a road-haulier to transport it to the Channel, load it onto one of the Sealink ferries and spirit it out of France. There was a tense moment when the truck got stuck under a bridge but the resourceful driver let enough air out of his tyres to get through. That car is now in the British Pullman train. So are two cars from the special Pullman that carried the body of Winston Churchill from Waterloo station to Oxfordshire, where he was buried on 30 January 1965.

Two of the best cars were owned by a gentleman in Ashford, Kent, who had preserved all sorts of old buses, vintage cars and trucks which he rented to film-makers. He stored all these in a building owned by British Rail, which now wanted it back. When he claimed squatters' rights, British Rail had his electricity and water cut off, but he brought in oil lamps and trucked in his water. When we went to see him we found his bedroom was in one of the cars we wanted to buy and he made us take our shoes off before we could even enter. He reluctantly sold us one car at the time and the other a couple of years later and they are now in the Pullman train. Then we needed an original baggage car and eventually tracked one down in the north of England where it had been fitted out as a transporter of racing pigeons, a popular pastime in that part of the world. The outside was in a terrible condition but when we had replaced the panelling with beautiful varnished teak the railway authorities insisted we cover it over with steel cladding.

All this time the costs were mounting. We had originally budgeted $5 million for the Orient-Express project but when we decided to bring in the British Pullman the costs doubled to $10 million. We discovered we had made a fundamental mistake in our calculations, thinking the cars needed refurbishment and not major upgrades. How wrong we were. The work required by the SNCF to bring the Orient-Express cars up to the latest continental railway standards was exacting and expensive: complete rewiring, new air-brake systems and lots more. Rusting was particularly bad around the toilets, where water had sloshed around for decades. British law required that we strengthen the horizontal integrity of the U.K. train to ensure it wouldn't concertina in a collision.

There was no railway workshop in Britain prepared to take on the job of restoring a historic train, so Bill McAlpine came to the rescue and suggested we build a shed at his Steamtown Railway Museum at Carnforth, near Lancaster. A major furniture factory, Waring & Gillow, had recently closed nearby so there were excellent craftsmen only too willing to work and soon we had our own woodworking and French polishing shops and repair yard. We installed electric heating in the carriages, and when I went through the train before the ceilings were put back it looked like a spider's web. Even the original glass had to be taken out and replaced with shatterproof safety glass.

There are always surprises, good and bad, when you set out on a venture like this, and one of the good surprises was finding Bob Dunn. Bob's father had done the elaborate marquetry on three of the original carriages, including the restaurant car, and Bob himself was still in the business. Bob and his wife, who worked on the project with him, have since passed away, but we shall always be grateful to them for the superb and loving craftsmanship they put into the cars. Shirley went to see them and I can't do better than use her description of their work:

> They begin by washing the veneer free of the accumulated dirt of years. After drying, any loose bits are stuck back on again. The panels were originally supported on blockboard, which has often rotted over the years, so this has to be replaced. Missing pieces of veneer have to be matched, if possible, with old veneer. Bob had some of his father's original design patterns to work from and could use these templates when replacing the missing pieces. He also had some of the original veneers in his stock and so could get a perfect match.

It was painstaking work and the matching of grain and colour tone was a real artistic achievement. It took these craftsmen three weeks just to make one of the missing flower-spray ovals lost over the years. After that the panels went to Carnforth for French polishing and finally installation in the carriages they had first graced fifty years before.

We had hired Gérard Gallet, the French designer, to oversee the decoration of both trains, and he had to re-create or source literally hundreds of objects and fittings, from chairs and fabrics to authentic art deco lamps. He copied the original Wagons-Lits cutlery and the china was an 1820s design modified with our own logo. Even the towels and linen were replicas of the original. When it was complete, passengers would be surrounded by glittering mirrors and crystal, polished woods and brasses, exquisite marquetry and 'Sapelli Pearl' inlay, all flawlessly restored or replaced. There would be plush upholstery and heavy draperies, cotton-damask sheets, fine linen and designer tableware. The cars would also smell good because of the dozens of fine woods in the marquetry, which in some of the cars would groan when the train leaned into a curve, just as the old transatlantic liners did at sea.

By now our plan was coming together. The restored British Pullman would take the guests from Victoria station to the Channel, providing a superb lunch as it travelled through Kent, the 'Garden of England'. At Folkestone the passengers would board the Sealink ferry where a special lounge would be reserved for them. The main Orient-Express train would be waiting alongside at Boulogne's Maritime Gare and would arrive in Paris at 8 p.m., take aboard Paris-joining passengers, and depart towards Switzerland, eventually arriving in Venice the afternoon of the next day.

The northbound trip would be the reverse, departing Venice in the morning, arriving Paris early the following morning, Boulogne in late morning, Channel crossing, then the British Pullman to London in the afternoon over a substantial tea.

The weak link in all this was the uncertain Channel weather which could delay the arrival of ferries and, if train slots were lost on the continent, journeys would be delayed. I also worried that passengers would get seasick on the ferries, spoiling their trip, so we prayed for calm crossings. Today, with the Channel Tunnel, the trip is seamless, always punctual, and no one gets seasick.

I also had a very clear idea of the image I wanted for the whole venture. The train and the trip had to suggest an experience of special quality, unusual, exclusive and luxurious, evocative of a time when travel was glamorous and service was perfect. The motto I set was: 'We have restored the art of travel' and we gave this message to Vernon Stratton, whose promotion company was busily preparing the brochure. The carriages were not quite finished when they did their photoshoot and it was freezing, so the poor models had to be thawed out every so often (one of those photographs is on the cover of this book).

All this time costs continued to rise and the revised budget rose to $15 million. I'm afraid we sailed through that and in the end the total bill was $31 million. Sea Containers was making excellent profits in this period so the board let the project proceed. It was the right decision – and a very important one for the future of the company, as events were to prove.

New problems kept cropping up which required time and energy to deal with. One of the biggest was the battle over the rights to the Orient-Express name, which could have derailed the project late in the day. We needed permission to use it and there was a tussle between Wagons-Lits and SNCF as to who owned it, which was never fully resolved. SNCF wanted to hang on to it because they felt they could earn money by licensing it to various non-train operators, but Wagons-Lits had invented it and had operated the train for the best part of a century.

In the end, with the consent of the SNCF, we decided to call our train the Venice Simplon-Orient-Express, which would distinguish it from any other Orient-Express and would highlight Venice, which was the main point of it for us. It would also emphasize the fact that the route through the Simplon Tunnel was the same one established by the Allies at the end of World War I.

As it happened we changed the route a year later, no longer using the Simplon Tunnel, but the train had already got its sobriquet, VSOE, which I rather liked because of its similarity to VSOP, the finest of French brandies. In practice of course the train just got called the Orient-Express, which is what it is.

People tend to think of trains by the name of the locomotive that pulls them, as in the Flying Scotsman or the Great Marquess. But neither the British Pullman nor the Venice Simplon-Orient-Express had its own locomotive, as the railway companies over whose tracks the trains ran would supply them. Negotiating these contracts was another tortuous task. Because the railway line dead-ended at Folkestone Harbour, two engines were required, one to pull the train in, the other to pull it out. On the continent the loco changes were numerous. Two diesels hauled the train from Boulogne Maritime to

Amiens, and an electric one pulled it into Gare d'Austerlitz (later switched to Gare de l'Est). A different engine pulled it out of the station again, but near Beaune there was yet another switch from electric to diesel. Then at the Swiss frontier a Swiss loco took over, but swapped to an Italian one as it crossed the Italian border. In the steeper parts of the Alps, more than one loco was required. Today, the train operates via Austria and four red Austrian locos are needed to pull it over the Arlberg Pass to Innsbruck, and two to pull it up the Brenner Pass to the Italian frontier where Hitler and Mussolini had their historic meeting in 1943, each of them arriving by train.

All this consumed time as well as money and our timetable slipped by another six months. But finally we were able to set the end of May 1982 as our launch date, four and a half years after the Monte Carlo auction. In order to stoke enthusiasm, we decided to show off some of the British Pullman cars at Victoria station in London, from where all boat trains to the continent historically departed, and to display some of the exquisitely restored Orient-Express cars in Europe.

We greatly underestimated the public interest. In London, the idea was that visitors would enter one end of the train, walk through the restored cars, and out the other end. When I went to see how the visit was going I discovered that the queue of people snaked out of the station, across the road and up Buckingham Palace Road almost as far as the Palace itself. Working class and aristocracy rubbed shoulders along the pathway. I recognized an elderly duchess who said she just wanted to see the cars in which she had travelled as a young lady. The police had to be called to maintain order when it looked as if the normal operation of the station might be disrupted.

When we showed some of the Orient-Express cars in Brussels, the crowds spilled over the platform onto the tracks, bringing the whole station to a halt until order could be restored. In Venice we had two cars loaded aboard barges which were towed to the Hotel Cipriani where we had invited 300 friends to come to a luncheon and view the train. Five hundred people turned up, but the imperturbable general manager, Dr. Natale Rusconi, had catered for that number, suspecting there might be a rush.

Finally, on 25 May 1982, we launched the new Orient-Express service on platform 8 at Victoria Station, ninety-nine years after its first journey. There was a battery of cameramen and reporters present and we had invited celebrities and dignitaries to be there, including the Duchess of Westminster, Liza Minnelli and Alan Whicker, the BBC TV journalist who made an hour-long documentary of the first trip shown on prime-time television a few weeks later.

I gave the inaugural speech in which I said that although the Orient-Express 'had the intrigue and the glory' in fact British passengers had always been carried on the first part of the ride in the same cream-and-brown Pullman carriages which were now waiting at the platform. I remarked that my favourite car was Ibis, which was also the oldest (built in 1925), because the marquetry panels squeaked as the train went round bends. 'I was not allowed to ride in her today,' I said, 'because the TV people said it squeaks too much for their sound recorders.'

After singling out Bill McAlpine and a few others for special thanks, I cut the ribbon and the British rake of the Venice Simplon-Orient-Express left the station. It was a great moment. I found myself wondering what my Sherwood ancestors back in the American Midwest would think of it all.

CHAPTER TWO

A FAMILY OF TOBACCO FARMERS

I was born on 8 August 1933 into a family that had been farm-ing tobacco in America for nearly 300 years. My parents lived in Lexington, Kentucky, which I still regard as my home town, but my mother actually gave birth to me in New Castle, Pennsylvania where she had grown up and where her parents had a large house. She was not too impressed with the medical treatment in Kentucky in those days so she decided to go home to her family to have her baby. I was an only child.

My father, William (or Bill) Earl Sherwood, was a lawyer in Lexington, specializing in patent law, but his father and grandfather, both alive well into my childhood, still owned tobacco farms in north-ern Kentucky, and had branched out into banking and railways where they had prospered. They were born, grew up and died in northern Kentucky, and generations of Sherwoods are all buried in the same churchyard. My father was the first of our particular line of Sherwoods in 300 years who never lived on his own tobacco farm. He was also the last to own them – when his mother died years later he inherited four tobacco farms, which he offered to me. I declined and the farms were sold. And there endeth this particular line of Sherwood endeavour.

I sometimes try to imagine what it must have been like for the Sherwood family at the time I made my entry into the world. The Great Depression, which had by then lasted for four years, hit its bottom in 1933, with unemployment across the country at 25 per cent, but much higher in the rural areas where farming was devastated as crop prices fell by as much as 60 per cent. There had also been a severe drought in the summer of 1930, which ravaged the agricultural heartland of the country. Farm exports, notably wheat, cotton, tobacco and lumber, collapsed, and across the nation farmers defaulted on their loans, leading to runs on small rural banks, which in turn toppled some of the bigger financial institutions. In 1930 alone, fifteen banks closed their doors in Kentucky. The sub-prime banking crisis doesn't even begin to compare with what was happening then, at least in terms of its impact on ordinary people.

But the Sherwoods had survived turbulence, revolutions, wars and natural disasters in their time, and would pull through this crisis. World War II brought boom times again for the tobacco industry, and by 1944 cigarette production in the U.S. hit a new record of 300 billion, 75 per cent consumed by servicemen. By that stage tobacco companies such as Philip Morris and American Brands were among the largest companies in the world, and the big advertising agencies on Madison Avenue grew up on the back of them. It was quite an industry.

When times were good, they were very good, and when they were bad – well, they were horrible. In the years they had farmed in Maryland, my branch of the Sherwood family had not only the elements to contend with, but fought in the Revolutionary War (or War of Independence) of 1775–81, after which the British Navy blockaded Chesapeake Bay, adding to the misery of planters by preventing sea commerce. In Kentucky, where they moved in 1790, they lived through the devastation of the Civil War of 1861–65 when the state became of critical strategic importance to both sides. Abraham Lincoln, born in a log cabin only seventy-five miles from Lexington, once prayed: 'I hope God is on my side, but I must have Kentucky'.

It was officially a neutral state at the beginning of the war but, after a failed attempt by the Confederates to take it, Kentucky came under Union control. Many of the farmers had drifted up from the Deep South over the years, and for a while the loyalty of the state teetered. The Sherwoods, like so many families, fought on both sides. There are seven Sherwoods listed in the Kentucky Civil War Soldiers index, five of them Unionist, the other two Confederate. Two of them, one a cavalryman, the other a foot-soldier, were called James. They both fought for the Union.

For some reason I had never really thought about the history of the Sherwood family until I was in my sixties, and I now regret not talking more to my great-grandfather, who would have been alive during the Civil War. What little I did know came from my father, but he was away in the war until I was thirteen and after I left home to go to Yale and then the Navy, I had other things to think about.

It was only in May 1999, when I bought the Inn at Perry Cabin in St. Michaels, Maryland for Orient-Express Hotels, that my interest was really sparked. I remembered that we Kentucky Sherwoods originated in Maryland, and that the family first arrived from England sometime in the seventeenth century and planted tobacco. But I didn't know much else. Only some time later did I discover that the first Sherwood had landed in North America in the year 1645 and by an extraordinary coincidence had laid out his farm only a mile from the Inn. Richard (Rick) Lidinsky, who had managed the Sea Containers office in Washington, D.C. for some years, took up the search for the Maryland Sherwoods with great enthusiasm (President Obama later appointed Rick as chairman of the Federal Maritime Administration). I also remembered that my great-uncle Clarence, a Princeton graduate who lived in Orange County in California, had traced the family tree back to Maryland. I used to visit him when passing through Los Angeles when I was in the U.S. Navy. In 1956, when my ship was sent back to California for a refit, I went out to his house only to find it had been sold. He had died when I was in the Far East and no one had told me. When I enquired about his papers I was told they had disappeared, apparently taken away by one of the family. Then some time later one of my Sherwood relatives contacted me to say he had the papers, and they actually took the history back to the arrival of the first Sherwood in Chesapeake Bay.

As I pulled together more of the Sherwood family history, a fascinating tale emerged – at least for me, as a member of the family. In 1632, King Charles I granted 11 million acres of land on the east coast of Chesapeake Bay to Cecil Calvert, 2nd Baron Baltimore (he was actually an Irish peer). Historians believe that this land, which would later become the state of Maryland, had originally been promised to the first Lord Baltimore, Cecil's father, by King James I, but James, who died in 1625, later changed his mind when Baltimore declared himself a Catholic. In a gesture of reconciliation, Charles gave it to his son and the first English settlers in Maryland, many of whom were Roman Catholic, landed on St. Clement's (then Blakistone) Island in 1634.

Francis Sherwood, my first American ancestor, arrived eleven years later (three years before the ancestors of George Washington). He paid £4 for his passage to the New World, thankfully leaving behind an England then in the midst of civil war, which had been raging for the past three years and would continue for another six. Poor King Charles lost his head in 1649.

Francis travelled under what was called the 'headright' system, a legal grant of land made to settlers which was widely used to populate the thirteen colonies of North America. He landed in what is now St. Mary's in the Maryland Province and took the 'Oath of Fidelity' to Lord Baltimore on 2 January 1646. Francis had to

faithfully and truly acknowledge the right honble. Cecilius, Lord Baron of Baltimore, to be the true and absolute lord and proprietor of this province and country of Maryland, and the islands thereunto belonging; and I do swear that I will bear true faith unto his lordship and to his heirs.

Having sworn this feudal and subservient oath to Baltimore, Francis was given his promised 100 acres of land near St. Michaels as reimbursement for his passage. It was there, on the edge of the beautiful Chesapeake Bay, that he was finally able to build his house and establish the very first Sherwood tobacco farm.

In England one weekend I happened to mention all of this to Sir Reresby Sitwell, a historian and owner of the great country house Renishaw Hall in Derbyshire, who immediately declared that my family would almost certainly have had its roots in the nearby

Sherwood Forest, famous for its association with Robin Hood (or Robin of Loxley as he preferred to call him). Reresby, by yet another odd coincidence, was a big Robin Hood enthusiast and actually possessed what he believed to be Robin's original bow. Although there have probably been almost as many genuine Robin Hood bows (and Robin Hoods for that matter) as there have been Jesus of Nazareth crosses, he made a persuasive and eloquent case, and for the sake of our friendship I was prepared to believe him.

Reresby put me in touch with the Nottinghamshire historian, whose thesis was basically this: there is only one Sherwood Forest in Britain, most Sherwoods originated there, and the first written record of a Sherwood dates from 975. Until the thirteenth century, men living near the forest were called, for example, John of Sherwood, but over the centuries the 'of' was dropped, and they became plain John Sherwood.

Francis Sherwood did well in Maryland. In the years after he arrived, and for generations afterwards, tobacco was a pretty good business and he prospered. Tobacco was the main source of money for the earliest settlers in North America after they arrived in Jamestown in 1607. By the middle of the seventeenth century, when Francis produced his first harvest, the British and European markets would take all the tobacco America could produce. The bigger issue was finding the labour to farm it. Francis would have employed what were called 'indentured servants', basically poor Englishmen who traded years of labour (usually four) in exchange for their passage. Later, Irish and Scottish rebels were also transported to the Maryland colony and provided another source of cheap labour before they moved on to the developing industrial areas in the north.

By 1661, Francis was sufficiently well off to send for his son Hugh Sherwood, then twenty-eight years old, who travelled to Maryland from England and claimed his land grants. Hugh was already well educated when he arrived, and in his long lifetime he commanded the local garrison, represented Talbot County in the Maryland government and laid out the county capital, Easton. Unlike the early Maryland settlers, who were Catholic, and the next wave who were Quakers, this branch of the Sherwoods were Church of England, later Episcopalian – Hugh was a vestryman at the St. Michaels Parish Church.

They say Hugh always planned to go back to England again, but the land he was granted pleased him so much that it 'crook'd his intention'. In 1670 he built a house which he actually called 'Crook'd Intention', suggesting an interesting sense of self-deprecating humour. Shirley and I visited the house, which is listed as the oldest building in the Maryland Historical Register and stands on Francis Sherwood's original Maryland farm. There is a village called Sherwood near St. Michaels, and Sherwood's Landing, from where tobacco was moved by boat to the larger port of St Mary's for transportation across the Atlantic, still exists.

They are all situated in Talbot County, Maryland, which was to play a significant role in the Sherwood family history. Talbot is a fascinating and beautiful place: it has 600 miles of coastline, more than any other county in the U.S., and the east shore of the Chesapeake where St. Michaels is located is a series of low-lying islands and bays. It is one of the oldest centres of European settlement in the New World, where for more than a century tobacco was so important that it was actually used as a currency. Ships anchored in the bay and traded English manufactured goods for tobacco. St. Michaels became a significant shipbuilding centre, developing the fast Boston clipper privateer, which successfully ran the Royal Navy's blockade in the war of 1812. One of my favourite authors, James Michener, wrote his best-selling novel *Chesapeake* when he lived in St. Michaels, and it provides a fascinating perspective on the history of the region. Sherwoods would be born, multiply, and mostly prosper in Talbot County for the next five generations.

Tobacco played a big part in the Revolutionary War, which began in 1775, when British tobacco taxes were a cause of bitter grievance. It became a vital source of finance for Washington's Continental Army, as the 'rebel' army was called, and was even used as collateral for a loan which Benjamin Franklin negotiated with the French (the security was 5 million pounds of tobacco). At a low point in the war, a desperate General Washington sent out a plaintive cry to his countrymen:

'If you can't send money, send tobacco'. After the war the British, who were sore losers, enforced an embargo on American tobacco, and even France, which had been a staunch ally during the war, cut its imports by two-thirds. During his presidency Thomas Jefferson, who, like Washington, was a Virginia planter, attempted to sell his tobacco to France, but they wouldn't take it.

It was this crisis that caused the fifth generation of Maryland Sherwoods to stage their own private diaspora. The Sherwood that interests me is John Sherwood, who would have been about my six-times great-grandfather. He moved from Maryland to northern Kentucky in 1790, bought land and did what he knew best: planted tobacco, which he shipped down the Ohio and Mississippi Rivers to New Orleans where it was loaded onto ships for transportation to European ports. Successive generations farmed there until my great-grandfather branched out into railroads and banking and my father finally broke the mould altogether.

Like every other farmer in the South, the Sherwoods owned slaves, but in 1865 my great-great-grandfather gave them the land where they lived and let them stay there as free men. Over the years they drifted away, many of them north into Ohio and Illinois. My father, when he was visiting his clients in those states, developed a habit of looking up the local Sherwoods in the telephone directory and calling them up for a chat. Many of them could trace their ancestry back to the Sherwood farm in Kentucky from which they took their name.

By the time my father was born in 1905, the family dependence on tobacco was already weakening. My great-grandfather was something of an entrepreneur, and had invested in the Louisville & Nashville Railroad which ran along the edge of one of his tobacco farms, carrying freight and passengers from Lexington to Maysville on the Ohio River (Daniel Boone was one of the founders). He built a station on his land beside the hamlet of Ewing, which has been preserved to this day. During World War II, when petrol was rationed, there were twenty-two trains a day calling at Ewing, and passengers frequently boarded at his farm to go to Maysville or Lexington. He also owned the small Ewing Bank.

My great-grandfather was quite a character: I remember him buying the local fairground, which had gone bust in the Depression, pulling down the stand, and attaching the land to his farm. He kept the track, which was used for trotting, a popular sport in Kentucky. My friends and I used to dig for coins in the dust of the old fairground, sometimes finding nickels and dimes.

His son, Robert Hildreth Sherwood, my grandfather, went to Transylvania University in Lexington, the oldest university west of the Appalachians, and worked for the Louisville & Nashville Railroad until he retired after the war, although he retained his tobacco roots and the family farms. He was working in Covington, about 100 miles from Lexington, when my father was born.

My father grew up in Ewing and went to the University of Kentucky to study engineering. The head of the engineering school, Professor Charlie Anderson, would come to have a big influence on him, and from early on he took a particular interest in my father's career. This was the Roaring Twenties, when the United States was in the biggest boom in its history, and the large manufacturing companies were crying out for qualified engineers. Innovations, inventions and developments were tumbling out of every factory and laboratory across the country: air-conditioning, talking movies, passenger planes, electrical devices, gadgets and machines of all shapes and sizes, and much more.

It was a great time to be a young engineer, but Professor Anderson persuaded my father to go a step further. All of these developments, he pointed out, were going to need documentation and patenting – and the need for patent lawyers could only grow. It was a very specialist field, and to qualify my father would have to take a law degree on top of his engineering degree – which meant a total of seven years' study, a daunting prospect for any young man, particularly in times when his fellow students would be climbing up the promotion ladder in the big companies they would have joined on graduating.

But Charlie Anderson was obviously convincing, because that was what my father decided to do. He remained close to Charlie for years afterwards, and I have memories of the old boy, by then in his nineties, regularly coming to dinner at our family home in Lexington. He had a

wonderful 1920s Rolls-Royce, which he insisted on driving himself. My
father regarded him as such a menace to other drivers that he would
call the police, who knew Charlie and his car very well, and they
would clear the road for the short distance between the two houses.

Bill was an excellent sportsman at college, particularly keen on
baseball, which was the national sport, and which he played for the
university. But his real passion was horse riding. Lexington, the heart
of the rich Bluegrass Country, is the centre of America's thoroughbred
breeding industry (although the famous Kentucky Derby is run in
Louisville) so he could not have chosen a better place. While still at
university, Bill's love of riding caused him to volunteer as a cavalry
cadet for the U.S. Army Reserve Officers' Training Corps (ROTC), a
college-based, officer commissioning program. He took the view that
as a cavalryman he at least got to ride the horses. Many years later, I
followed in his ROTC footsteps by enrolling in the Naval ROTC
program when I attended Yale University during the Korean War.

To qualify as a patent lawyer you had to have actual work experience as well as academic qualifications, and when he graduated in
the mid-1920s my father took a job in Pittsburgh with Westinghouse
Electric Company, which in those days vied with General Electric to
be America's number one electrical manufacturer. Westinghouse had
introduced the first continuous-filament tungsten light bulb in 1909,
made fridges and other electrical appliances and developed the first
automatic elevator, as well as very early air-conditioning systems. It
was in Pittsburgh that he met my mother, Florence Balph, a student
at Pittsburgh's Carnegie Mellon University. Her father was the president of the biggest bank in New Castle, Pennsylvania, important in its
day but now just another branch of one of the big Wall Street giants.
But her mother, said to have been a very strong-willed woman, died in
the flu pandemic of 1919 when she insisted on going to Pittsburgh at
the height of the epidemic. Her brother, my Uncle Bill, was a banker
with Mellon Bank, and his son Bill was my only first cousin. Bill Jr.
died in the 1990s.

Although my father was still some way from qualifying as a
patent lawyer, in 1929 he married Florence and they went to live

in Washington, D.C. where he continued his studies at The George Washington University. Both of their families were happy enough to support the young couple, and could afford to do so, so I don't think they lived as penniless students. As part of his law studies, Bill also worked in the Patent Office, one of the grand old buildings of Washington, which covered an entire city block between F and G streets (the Patent Office moved in 1933, just after Bill left, and today houses two of Washington's institutions, the National Portrait Gallery and the American Art Museum).

After graduating, my father came home to Kentucky where, except for the war years and early 1950s, he stayed for the rest of his long life (he lived to ninety-three and my mother to ninety-nine), first in Louisville and then, in the late 1930s, in the rich, prosperous town of Lexington where I feel my roots are still. He and a friend set up their own legal practice specializing in patent law, and over time he would come to have clients all over the Midwest. He was a good father and husband, a cultivated man who loved his opera, and listened religiously to the live broadcast from the Met every Saturday afternoon – a great institution in those days, sponsored by Texaco – which kindled my own love of opera. He was a slim, erect man who retained his army posture through his life, and I remember him as genial and good-natured. The family house, which was in one of the better districts of Lexington, was pleasant but not showy, and all his life he abhorred any display of wealth. Years later I bought my mother a Cadillac and had it delivered to the house. My father was horrified and sent it back, saying 'lawyers and their wives can be seen driving Buicks but not Cadillacs'.

My mother was a talented musician and it was always said in the family she was good enough to have been a concert pianist but was too nervous to perform in front of an audience. She was also reckoned to be strikingly beautiful. Interested in literature, she used to write poetry and essays for the Monday Club in Lexington, a group of twenty-four women who each had to present a paper every two years (Shirley once went to one on 'Kentucky and the Slave Trade', which certainly opened her eyes).

Unfortunately, when I was seven, my mother and I essentially lost my father for the best part of six years. Because of his reserve status in the U.S. Army, he was unexpectedly called up for active service in 1940, two years before Pearl Harbor and America's entry into the war. The army urgently wanted engineers, and Bill was sent to Detroit to work on the development of the tank-destroyer, which was a kind of cheap tank with a large gun and no turret, later used (with mixed results) to knock out German Panzers in Normandy. Then he was sent to Texas to test the new vehicle on the ranges there. By the middle of the war he became frustrated by the lack of action and his distance from the shooting and, probably without telling my mother, he persuaded the army to send him to the Pacific where he could do some real fighting. He got more than he bargained for. In 1945 he was at the Battle of Okinawa, the last major battle of the war, where the Americans suffered 50,000 casualties and the Japanese garrison of 100,000 was basically wiped out. Bill served with distinction and ended the war with the permanent rank of Colonel.

The Lexington that I grew up in was a quiet, prosperous community of about 100,000 people (it's 300,000 today), 25 per cent of whom were black. Like many towns in the South, it was still effectively segregated in those days and blacks had to sit in the back of the bus and in the balcony in the cinema. They used different toilets, went to different schools, and there was very little mixing of the races, a situation which as a young boy I simply accepted. However, there was none of the racial hatred that boiled over where the Ku Klux Klan was active in the Deep South.

But life in Lexington ended for me in 1946, when I was only thirteen. After the war my father, now in his forties, came home expecting to resume his law practice, which had been kept running by his partner. Before he could start however, he was asked by the U.S. Atomic Energy Commission to document the development work of the atomic bomb, the biggest technological advance of the age. We moved to Berkeley, California, where some of the vital scientific work on the bomb had been carried out at what is now the Lawrence Berkeley National Laboratory at the University of California.

My father never talked about his work, some of which is still top secret today, but I developed an interest in the bomb then and in how it worked. The first splitting of the uranium atom occurred in Germany in 1938 and the scientists there – and elsewhere – were convinced that a bomb with incredible destructive force could be built if enough fissionable material was available. This material had to be either U-235, an isotope of uranium, or plutonium.

The race to build the bomb was mostly about finding a way to produce these elements, and a team of American scientists under Ernest Lawrence was convinced that U-235 could be produced by an electromagnetic system. A gigantic installation was built at Oak Ridge, Tennessee, where there was a plentiful supply of electricity, to carry out this process. In layman's terms, a rapidly moving uranium gas was passed through magnets, which diverted the U-235 isotope on to a different pathway where it could be collected, but the process was enormously difficult and inefficient.

Better results were obtained in the rival process, the production of plutonium at Hanford, on the Columbia River in Washington State, which was masterminded by Enrico Fermi, a Nobel Prize winner from Italy. The plutonium was produced by a controlled nuclear reaction, which required large amounts of water for cooling. In the end two bombs were produced, one using U-235, the other plutonium.

The actual bomb itself was developed by Dr. J. Robert Oppenheimer, a controversial scientist who set up the first test at a site in Los Alamos, in the New Mexican desert. The test was successfully conducted on 16 July 1945, with a plutonium bomb. But the first bomb dropped, code-named Little Boy, which destroyed Hiroshima on 6 August 1945, was the U-235 version. Three days later a plutonium bomb, called Fat Man, was dropped on Nagasaki and the war in the Pacific ended a few days later.

Little Boy was basically a gun made by the U.S. Navy gun factory, which shot a projectile of U-235 into a block of U-235 to create the critical mass and explosion. Fat Man contained two hemispheres of plutonium surrounded by conventional high explosives which, when set off, drove the two hemispheres together to create the critical mass and consequent atomic explosion.

Germany began developing its own atom bomb early in the war, and it is frightening to think that if Hitler had pursued the project and built it first, the outcome could well have been very different. Hitler's hatred of the Jews drove many of the top scientists out of Germany and Italy (Fermi was an Italian Jew) and a number of them ended up in the U.S. working on the project.

Because the production of both the U-235 material and plutonium was basically an engineering exercise, as was the bomb itself, my father's skills as a patent lawyer were well used. I never learned anything directly from him, but I was interested to know what he was actually working on, and most of my knowledge came later from a book called *Manhattan Project* by Stephane Groueff, published in 1967. My father did say later in life that he was surprised greater use was not made of nuclear energy, which he argued was a cleaner and less expensive source of energy than fossil fuels.

California was an eye-opener for a teenager from the Midwest. From the moment we arrived in Berkeley I loved it, and have loved California ever since. I was enrolled in Berkeley High School, which had magnificent facilities and every one of my teachers had a Ph.D., not common for secondary school teachers in those days. Photography and movies were enormously in vogue, and I developed a lifelong interest in both, making my first documentary film on San Francisco's cable cars, which even today provide a unique means of transport. I was inspired by the great photographer, Ansel Adams, whose black-and-white photographs of the American West today sell for tens of thousands of dollars.

I also made some good friends there, including Wendell Stanley, son of the Nobel Prize winner of the same name who was the first man to isolate a virus (the mosaic disease in tobacco). Wendell remains a good friend to this day. Unfortunately we were not destined to stay in California for long, and three years later we were off again, this time to New York.

The University of California, Berkeley, where Oppenheimer was Professor of Theoretical Physics, was only one of the development centres of the bomb, on which 130,000 people were working in 1945. The entire project was driven by Brigadier-General Leslie Groves, a U.S. Army engineer, and his office was on 270 Broadway in New York City – hence the Manhattan Project – close to Stone & Webster, which was the principal project contractor, and to Columbia University. So, in 1949, the Sherwood family moved again, this time to the rich New York suburb of Bronxville, which in those days was said to have the highest real estate values in the world. It was a great shock for a sixteen-year-old only child who had to leave his many friends in sunny California.

I was used to friendly, open Kentuckians and Californians, and was not prepared either for the weather on the East Coast or for what I saw as the unfriendliness of New Englanders, whom I found stiff and formal. I remember promising myself that one day I would live in California, a promise I never kept, although one way or another I have spent a lot of time there, particularly when I was in the Navy. However, I soon made the adjustment and found a new group of friends, including Stewart Tucker, later my room-mate at Yale, and Bob Riggs, who would serve on the Sea Containers board for several decades.

It was at Bronxville that I first developed my skill as a bridge-player, which was to feature strongly in the next phases of my life. My friends and I played other card games too, particularly poker, but I found I was good at bridge and was often asked to make up a table.

My father meanwhile was busily documenting his bomb, ploughing through endless records and files in his office in Columbus Circle in Manhattan. He had originally accepted a six-year contract, three years in Berkeley, three in New York, and once he had completed the documentation, his job was done. He always planned to go back to Lexington and take up the practice he had been forced to abandon more than a decade before, which of course he finally did, working well into his eighties, walking about two miles each morning to his office and home later. Of all three of us, my mother took to Bronxville best. She began writing again, and found friends with shared cultural interests.

The school I attended, Bronxville Senior School, was an excellent establishment with very high academic standards, and at the end of the year my grades were good enough for me to be offered a place at both Yale and Princeton. Half the entire senior class was accepted into the elite Ivy League universities. I talked it over with my parents, and in the end I chose Yale, where I started an economics degree in the autumn of 1951. I found New Haven, Connecticut a dreary, cold town in winter after the sunny Californian climate, and I can't say I enjoyed Yale as much as others did, and as I should have done. But there were many bright spots too. Yale was an all-male university, the nearby Smith College was all-girls and there was much fraternizing between the two.

Because of my California-inspired interest in films, I was quickly elected as chairman of the Yale Cinema Club and served in that position until graduation. We showed famous films in a large lecture hall, preceded by a relevant speaker. Robert Penn Warren spoke about *All the King's Men*, his story of Huey Long, the charismatic and corrupt governor of Louisiana. Tennessee Williams spoke about *A Streetcar Named Desire*. He was staying at the Taft Hotel while one of his Broadway plays was being trialled in New Haven. I remember Warren being tense and nervous while Williams was effervescent. We sold season tickets to the students in the college dining halls, but never had enough money to engage in any film production work. The chairman of Time Inc. was a 'Yalie', so I wrote to him asking for financial help and he sent $5,000, a huge amount in those days. It allowed us to experiment in a modest way with filming techniques. I was also a member of the Yale radio station, WYBC, and it was here that I met with my future business partner, Maury Pinto, a member of a distinguished Spanish family which had emigrated from Morocco just before the war.

I also played a lot of bridge at Yale, often well into the night, and usually for money, and my fortunes certainly prospered. Despite this, when I finally left Yale I had some large outstanding bills at my tailor, J. Press, and the club, Mory's. Mory's is one of Yale's great institutions and was the inspiration for the Yale Whiffenpoof song made famous by Rudy Vallée in the 1920s and later recorded by everyone from Bing Crosby to Elvis Presley:

To the tables down at Mory's,
To the place where Louis dwells,
To the dear old Temple Bar we love so well...

It would take me a year in the Navy to pay off my debts, as I did not want to admit to my father that I had overspent my allowance.

I was not an outstanding scholar at Yale. I started strong but finished weak, regretting more and more that I had not majored in history, which I loved and which I won a prize for in my first year. But there were some great moments too: I have wonderful memories of the great scholar of Latin American history, Samuel Flagg Bemis, pompously ejecting several Latin American students when they objected to his interpretation of their country's history. When we were studying modern European history, we came to the Russian Revolution and my professor said he was stepping down from this part of the course and the lectures would be conducted by Alexander Kerensky, the man who led the October 1917 Revolution before being overthrown by the Bolsheviks a month later. Today, I suppose, Kerensky's equivalent would be Tony Blair, who often lectures at Yale.

During much of my time at Yale, the U.S. was yet again at war, this time in Korea, and the draft was in place. Theoretically even students could be drafted, but I never knew anyone from Yale who was. However, we were all aware that when we graduated we were going to have to do two years minimum in the armed services, and we expected that to be in a war zone. Although the Yale curriculum called for four courses at a time, we were offered the possibility of becoming a member of the Naval Reserve Officer Corps by taking a fifth course, which had two advantages: you could not be drafted while still at college; and you started in the forces as an officer. I was steered towards the Navy by my uncle, Vice-Admiral William A. Glassford, who was married to my father's only sister. He had a brilliant career in the war, where he commanded a task force in an attack against Japanese forces in the Battle of Balikpapan; after Germany surrendered, he went to Hamburg to take charge of the destruction of what remained of the German fleet.

And so I signed up for the Naval ROTC where I learned the theory of naval warfare as well as some other useful stuff – like how to handle small-arms, which I confess I have not put to much use. The head of the Naval Warfare History Department was Professor Thomas Mendenhall, the first occupant of the academic chair at the United States Naval War College, who lectured at Yale and was Master of Berkeley College. He was a brilliant teacher and I learned a great deal from him. I spent a whole year on naval engineering, which would later be very useful to me, learning the mechanics of how ships function. There was even a course on how to behave as an officer, which was no bad thing for a young man to learn. On one afternoon a week we had to march around the square, but the navy was never like the army and there was a limited amount of square-bashing.

One summer, in my junior (third) year, I was posted to Norfolk, Virginia for training at sea, the highlight of my time in the ROTC. We had several weeks of exercises before we docked in Havana, Cuba and a group of us young officers were allowed shore leave. I went immediately to the Hotel Nacional de Cuba which in the days before Castro was one of the great hotels of the world (Sinatra had recently performed there, and it was said to be the haunt of Hemingway and Winston Churchill when they were in town). These were the great days when Havana was wild, dangerous, noisy and fun. It was also ruled by the Mob, and Meyer Lansky, known as the 'Mob's Accountant', controlled the gambling in Havana – although I don't suppose any of us cared very much about that.

Rather cheekily, I marched up to the reception desk at the Nacional and asked for a suite, which we used as our base for the rest of the trip. It was a habit I have followed for the rest of my life and it has invariably been worth it: whatever city I have been in, long before I could afford it, I always took a suite in the best hotel in town and it was always worth it just in terms of enjoyment.

I wasn't a big beer drinker in those days (or ever), and in Havana my chums and I discovered the frozen daiquiri, which is a potent concoction of local rum and limeade served up in slushy ice in a champagne glass. One morning in Havana we started drinking daiquiris at Sloppy

Joe's at nine in the morning and I decided to count how many we drank. I lost count at forty-two.

My naval experience at Yale was a turning point in my life. The four years in the U.S. Navy that followed set me on a path for a business career in shipping, and eventually to trains and hotels.

CHAPTER THREE

BRIDGE AND THE NAVY

In the summer of 1955 I was awarded my B.A. degree from Yale and then, still wearing the same mortar and gown, I walked down the stage to be given another award: my commission as an officer in the United States Navy. I was now Ensign James Sherwood, the lowliest commissioned officer in the entire navy, but that didn't stop me swaggering proudly off the stage. I was assigned to an amphibious ship based in the Far East, and was ordered to report first to the Naval Amphibious Base in Coronado, California in September for a three-month training course. I went home to Lexington briefly that summer to see my parents, then, complete with my new white naval uniforms, I flew to San Diego and life in the navy.

The Korean War, which had overshadowed my early student days, had ended in a ceasefire two years earlier, but the world was a tense place and I fully expected to see action somewhere before my two years' service was up. The Communist threat was on everyone's lips and McCarthyism was at its height, with accusations of disloyalty, subversion or treason thrown around at random. There seemed to be Reds under every bed. The U.S. was developing bigger and more powerful nuclear weapons, but the Soviet Union had unexpectedly tested its own atom bomb and the common wisdom was that nuclear war, causing destruction on a scale the world had never yet seen, was highly likely.

This was the period of the Cold War, with the Soviet Union making hostile noises in Europe, while in the East, the even more sinister Mao

Tse-Tung and Communist China loomed large. The French forces in Indo-China had been defeated at Điện Biên Phủ in May 1954, and the Communists were now pushing south in Vietnam. All through the Far East the influence of the Chinese and Communism was seen to be spreading: in Indonesia, through Laos, Cambodia, Burma, and even Thailand. The British were fighting rebels in the jungle in Malaya and other danger spots were simmering; we weren't aware of it at the time, but 1955 was the year President Eisenhower stepped up the number of American military observers in Vietnam, and China and the Soviet Union pledged additional support to Hồ Chí Minh and his Việt Minh forces in Hanoi.

But that all seemed very distant when I turned up at Coronado, which is on a spit of land on the west side of the bay, opposite San Diego, not far from the Mexican border. It was a huge sprawl of buildings and equipment, with its own practice landing beaches, covering several square miles and housing more than 5,000 military personnel, students and reservists. It had been set up during World War II when the Navy realized the importance of amphibious landings in the Pacific War, waged through a series of island hops, and of course in the landings in North Africa, Italy and D-Day in France. We officers, new and old, were there to learn all about it.

I had studied basic naval skills at Yale, including navigation and even the wonders of steam turbines, but they weren't much help to me in Coronado where we went through rigorous training in new disciplines. I learned how to survive in the water for long periods (never lift your arms above the water when swimming, to conserve energy), and we studied the latest hardware and tactics used for landing men and equipment onto beaches at night. We were taken off the coast and expected to conduct a landing in the right spot, under fighting conditions, in the dark – all our exercises seemed to be conducted in the dark, but then most landings in real wars are too.

My course was attended by all ranks of officers, from mere ensigns like me to captains and even admirals who had come for training in the latest amphibious techniques. I was surely the most junior, having only been commissioned a few weeks earlier.

It didn't take long to settle into naval life: several chums from Yale were also at the school, and new friends were quickly made. Our routine was a combination of exacting training practices interspersed with some pleasant relaxation. The Navy was reasonably well paid when you took into account free housing and food so, despite having to pay off my tailor and other debts from my Yale days, I was able to buy a car. Crossing into Mexico was a simple matter, with no border delays to worry about, and at weekends a group of us would drive over the border to Tijuana, which was only fifteen miles away. I have very fond memories of Caesar's Restaurant in Tijuana, the home of the Caesar Salad, and the wonderful mariachi guitarists who played so beautifully there. This was before Herb Alpert & the Tijuana Brass made the mariachi popular in the 1960s, and even today when I hear the mariachis and Tijuana Brass belting out the old songs it brings tears to my eyes.

I had been at the base only a few weeks when, out of the blue, I got an invitation to dinner at the base commander's house. None of my colleagues got one, and there was much speculation in our mess as to why I had been singled out. I had still not the slightest idea of what to expect when I arrived, smartly dressed in my whites, at the appointed time.

The commander greeted me cordially, took me aside and disclosed that he had been reading my Yale record where he discovered I was an 'accomplished' bridge-player. I modestly admitted this was probably true, if a bit exaggerated – I had certainly wasted enough hours playing bridge at Yale to be at least competent at the game but I didn't think of myself as in the top rank.

I am still not sure today why my bridge-playing abilities were even on my Yale report, but I am very pleased they were. One way or another, my reputation as a reasonable hand at bridge proved to be of considerable benefit to me in the Navy and led afterwards to my career in shipping – without which I could never have bought the Orient-Express. So, in a way, it all began that evening at the bridge table.

The base commander enquired politely if I might be interested in making up a four, and of course I leapt at the chance. Bridge soon became a regular feature of my evenings at Coronado and I found myself playing opposite some of the most senior officers in the Pacific Fleet, who were also attending the school. This was only ten years after World War II, and many of these officers had seen action against the Japanese. One of them, Captain Leon Kintberger, who at the time was en route to Japan to command an amphibious squadron, became a particular friend. He was a very interesting man with a fine war record – in 1944 he led a destroyer division into action off Samar Island in the Battle of Leyte Gulf, taking forty hits from Japanese battleships and cruisers before his ship was sunk. His action turned the tide of the battle, causing the Japanese to retreat, and Commander Kintberger, as he was then (he later became an admiral), was awarded the Navy Cross, second only to the Medal Of Honor or the Purple Heart. No one minded that I was a mere ensign who had been in the Navy for only a few weeks. Bridge is a great leveller.

At the end of my three months at Coronado I graduated from the school and set off to join my ship, a Haskell-class attack transport whose function was to carry large numbers of troops and equipment and get them ashore under fighting conditions. I don't even remember being told her name at this stage – just her anonymous number, which was *APA-212*, and I was to join her in Subic Bay in the Philippines, half a world away. So I packed my uniforms and belongings, and took off from Oakland, California, on a propeller-driven U.S. Navy passenger plane.

The trip would take five days, as there was only one flight crew on the plane and they had to rest each night before carrying on the next day. On the first day we flew to Honolulu, where we were all nicely accommodated in the Bachelor Officers' Quarters; then we stayed at Johnston Island for a night, and the next day we flew to Eniwetok, an atoll in the Marshall Islands where the Navy had fought a major battle in 1944; then Guam, and finally into Clark Air Base in Luzon, not far from the Subic Bay Naval Base. It had been an exhilarating trip, long flights interspersed with comfortable sleepovers. The Navy looked after its own.

The Subic Bay base was vast, with its own major ship-repair, supply, and rest and recreation facilities inside a big sheltered bay at Zambales. There were ships everywhere, coming and going, and the bay itself was still littered with the wrecks of Japanese ships that had been sunk there.

The *APA-212*, when I finally found her, was bigger than I expected: 453 feet long with a beam of 62 feet, a maximum speed of 19 knots, and a crew of over 500 officers and enlisted men. She was capable of carrying – and landing – 1,500 men. And she did have a name, the *Montrose*, which those who sailed in her were fiercely proud of, affectionately calling her 'The Rose'. She had been built in 1944 when the naval yards were mass-producing amphibious ships which could carry landing craft as well as troops and tanks, desperately needed for the war in the Pacific. She had seen action in the Leyte Gulf, and took part in several amphibious landings where she claimed at least two Japanese kamikazes destroyed. In April 1945 she arrived, loaded with troops and equipment, off the coast of Okinawa where she and her sister landing ships came under their most ferocious attack yet.

Several of the sailors aboard the *Montrose* left accounts, which give a flavour of what it was like:

> The second Betty (Japanese aircraft) began to roar on the *Montrose*'s starboard side, so the gunners switched their sights to the new target. Fire was opened with the 40mm and after the five-incher at 4,500 yards. At 4,000 yards a shell from the big fantail rifle struck the diving plane squarely midships and it burst into flames but continued falling in a long and steep glide directly toward the Montrose. All of our guns now followed the stricken Betty, riddling the fuselage and wings until she flew apart and smashed with a geyser of spray into the water 200 yards off the stern of the *Montrose*.

The *Montrose* was one of the lucky ones that day. While she was busy shooting down the kamikazes, four of her sister ships were hit, one of which blew up, killing 200 troops.

My father arrived in Okinawa during the eighty-two-day battle for the island and went ashore probably from a ship just like *APA-212*.

By that stage he was in his forties, a bespectacled and very senior engineer, who was sent in as an administrator of the island. Goodness knows what horrors he found there.

When I joined her, the *Montrose* had just completed another operation, this time a humanitarian one. After their defeat at Điện Biên Phủ the French agreed to withdraw from Indochina and hundreds of thousands of Vietnamese refugees fled frantically for the south, clogging the roads, which were impassable. The U.S. sent transporters, including the *Montrose*, to Hải Phòng to pick them up and take them to Saigon, and *APA-212* alone took 9,060 refugees in what became known as 'Operation Passage to Freedom', said to be one of the biggest evacuations by sea in history. Commodore Winn sent a telegram to all hands on the *Montrose*, congratulating them for carrying 'the Mostest the Fastest'.

Memories of this operation were still fresh when I joined, and the crew were clearly moved by the plight of the refugees. 'They came aboard the ship tired, hungry and frightened and with what little hope they could muster,' a crew member recorded. 'They were driven by a great fear which caused them to abandon their villages, their properties and their belongings.' The ship was on high alert, ready to go back for more, and the stories from my fellow officers were mostly about how insensitive the French were in handling refugees.

We spent a lot of time at sea, where I was kept busy carrying out manoeuvres and exercises with the fleet. Although it had placed many of its big ships in mothballs after the war, the U.S. Navy was still a mighty force with 1,500 ships in service, the massive Seventh Fleet controlling all the important Pacific sea lanes, particularly the tense Taiwan Strait between China and the island of Formosa (Taiwan), which China continually threatened to cross.

The downside of this was that many ships were under the command of World War II veterans who had mostly returned to the Navy reluctantly for the Korean War and couldn't wait to go home again. There was a serious shortage of senior officers. The upside, as far as I was concerned, was that junior officers could expect to have more responsibility than in a normal peacetime navy. Ensigns were required to play their full part from the moment they stepped aboard, and I stood watches and generally took a full part in the running of the ship. I rapidly learned the ropes, translating the theory I had studied at Yale into the real thing. We didn't have GPS in those days and navigation was a challenge, but I knew how to use an old-fashioned sextant and I improved my navigational skills at sea. Probably because I was a university graduate, I got stuck with running the ship's office, something that seemed to happen to me throughout my sea-going career.

My first trip out of Subic Bay was to Hong Kong where, as the most junior deck officer, I was given the worst watches: midnight–4 a.m. and noon–4 p.m. The executive officer, responsible for discipline aboard the ship, laid down strict rules while in harbour: no boats or sampans to be allowed to tie up alongside, sentries to be on the alert to stop vendors coming aboard 'in unauthorized places', and a fire hose to be rigged on the forecastle and fantail 'to ward off persistent vendors and merchants'. Liberty was restricted to the island of Hong Kong and Kowloon, a narrow strip of land on the mainland. We were solemnly warned that crossing the Chinese border, even by mistake, 'would probably be a one-way trip'.

On my first night on watch in harbour, one of the sailors returned around one in the morning, quite the worse for drink, and announced that his girl was waiting for him – whereupon he jumped into the sea. In those days there were no piers in Hong Kong and the ships all anchored in the fairway, where there was a strong current. I had to think fast and quickly rousted out a boat crew to go after him as he was being carried across Hong Kong harbour. We managed to get to him in time, but it was a close-run thing.

We remained in Hong Kong for several days more than were strictly necessary. Ships always tried to linger there, partly because a formidable Chinese lady called Mary Soo would come aboard with an army of cleaners to descale the decks and paint the ship from stem to stern, taking their pay entirely in waste materials which would otherwise have been thrown away. They were particularly interested in expended brass shell casings from gunnery practice, which could be turned into lamps and sold in the markets and shops in Hong Kong. The boatswain's mates always kept the shell casings carefully, knowing they were a useful trading currency. One day a senior officer spotted casings going off the ship and there was hell to pay. 'Don't you realize', he said to the hapless officer of the deck, 'that those casings will be taken by the Communists, turned into shells again and then fired against us?' Since every ship stopping at the fleet anchorage in Hong Kong was flogging its shell casings to Mary Soo, we spread the word to lie low.

Hong Kong was probably even more romantic in 1955 than it is today. It was a British colony, bubbling with energy and excitement, one of the busiest ports in the world. There were people everywhere, in the hundreds of junks and sampans in the great harbour (on which whole families lived), on the crowded ferries and in the perilous shanty towns which appeared to hang off the hillsides. Kowloon was bursting at the seams with refugees who had poured over the border as the Communists tightened their grip in China. There were hawkers, markets and stalls on every street, and in the Central District at noon there were so many people on the streets that the only way to walk was in the footsteps of the person in front. There was nothing you couldn't buy there, from expensive (and fake) watches and cigarette lighters to uniforms, which the tailors would knock up in a day at a fraction of the price back home.

But the colony was also clearly beginning its economic miracle, as the big British trading houses (or 'hongs') as well as the Hong Kong & Shanghai Banking Corporation (HSBC), which more or less controlled the colony between them, moved their base of operations from Shanghai to Hong Kong and Japanese and American banks moved in. It was a real entrepôt, the entry point for the Western world into the mysterious and closed China, and the hub for trade in the Far East. Cheap labour from immigrants, low taxes, sensible government, sophisticated financial markets, foreign expertise and plenty of capital provided all the ingredients needed for the economy to take off. In later years when I returned, as I have done often, the wharves had given way to giant buildings, the shanty towns had become blocks of apartments but the hustle and bustle which make it such a special place was still there. Today Hong Kong, now owned by China, which operates it very successfully on the principle of 'one country, two systems', has one of the highest living standards in Asia.

We often dined at the Foreign Correspondents' Club, the backdrop for the film *Love is a Many-Splendored Thing*, starring William Holden and Jennifer Jones, or on the terrace of the Repulse Bay Hotel on the other side of the island, and danced at Gaddi's in the luxurious Peninsula Hotel in Kowloon. I joined the Hong Kong Club, in those days housed in a magnificent colonial building overlooking the famous cricket pitch, which, bizarrely, was right in the centre of the crowded city occupying the most valuable real estate in the colony. The club had dormitories for visitors, a billiard room, a wonderfully colonial atmosphere, and was filled with members who had been forced to leave the mainland when the Communists swept through China in 1947. We were sorry to leave.

The *Montrose* was back in Hong Kong some weeks later, and one evening a couple of friends and I decided to go ashore for dinner and a film. Although the wind was up, there was no storm warning. However, when we got back to the fleet landing at about midnight, the wind was really up and all boating had been suspended. A typhoon was headed our way and we were just in time to see our ship steam out of the harbour without us. I said 'no problem', and off we went to the Hong Kong Club, which gave us a nice dorm under the eaves.

I assumed we would return to the ship the next day, but the full force of the typhoon hit the city, and day after day passed with no sign of the *Montrose*. Unless you are in a storm like this you don't realize how ferocious it can be: the rain travels horizontally and the wind is so strong you can't keep your footing even by leaning into it. We had left our ship without much cash, and while we could put our expenses in the club on the tab, we couldn't go anywhere else even when the rain slackened.

Lee Chong Tai, a tailor in Johnston Road, came to the rescue. All Asia sailors had their uniforms made in Hong Kong, and Lee became my regular tailor. I went to his shop and explained our predicament and he advanced several thousand Hong Kong dollars, which kept us in the style to which we were accustomed until our ship returned after a week at sea. It was a good move by Lee, as we gave him all our custom for years afterwards and recommended him to others. Lee has long passed on and today my favourite tailor in Hong Kong is A-Man Hing Cheong in the Mandarin Oriental. I have bought all my shirts and suits there for decades, as do many of the old China hands.

In 1956 the *Montrose* returned to Long Beach for a refit, and was berthed next to a smelly fish-meal processing facility. It was a frustrating, tedious period for me, as I wanted to be actively doing something rather than looking out at the ship-repair yard all day. There were a few incidents which broke the tedium, not all of them pleasant: at roll-call one morning, my entire department was standing at attention when a cloud of noxious fumes from the fish factory swept across the ship, leaving the men gasping and some prostrate on the deck. California's environmental laws were not as strict then as they are today.

The ship was scheduled to remain on the West Coast for a year after refitting, which sounded pretty boring to me, so I applied for a transfer to a smaller vessel which I thought would be more challenging. As luck would have it, although she did stay in California for the next six months, the *Montrose* was sent to the Bay of Siam where she berthed in Bangkok, and from there to Hawaii, where she participated in the filming of the musical *South Pacific*. I would like to have been there for that.

By that stage I had been assigned to *LST-1080*, which had only been given a name the year before, ten years after she was built: *U.S.S. Pender County*, named after a county in North Carolina (many LSTs, like APAs, came off the production line so fast they never got a name, just a number). LST stands for Landing Ship Tank, and that's pretty much what they did: carry tanks and trucks which they could load and unload through a ramp in the bow, similar to a roll-on ferry. *LST-1080* was just over 300 feet in length with a top speed of only 10 knots, and a crew of seven officers and 200 enlisted men. Oddly enough, I discovered she had a lot in common with the *Montrose* – she was launched the same year, served in the Pacific at the end of the war, and she had participated in 'Passage to Freedom' in Hải Phòng.

While I was kicking my heels in Long Beach, she had sailed from her base in San Diego to Japan in October 1956, and I was to join her at Yokosuka, Japan, the former headquarters of the Japanese Imperial Navy. My duties on the *Montrose* included running the ship's office, which prepared all the orders, and I was able to turn this to my advantage. The obvious route from California to Japan was straight across the Pacific, but I cut my own orders and decided to go the long way round, via Europe and India. I had some accrued leave, and planned to spend as much time as possible in London and Paris.

I proceeded first to Lexington to see my parents, then to an air base in New Jersey where I caught a military plane for England. The propeller planes of 1956 didn't have non-stop range to England, so we landed at Goose Bay and Shannon en route. London in 1956 was still very visibly recovering from the war years and the damage done by the Blitz, with gaping holes in elegant Georgian terraces and bomb craters everywhere. The docks and the City (the financial area) had been particularly heavily bombed, but the dome of St Paul's stood unharmed and majestic against the landscape of what had been the financial centre of the world. Rationing had only ended two years earlier and London seemed to me, after the light and cleanliness of California and Lexington, to be a gloomy city, the air thick with smog.

I stayed at the Park Lane Hotel in Piccadilly, which overlooked Hyde Park: one of the best views in central London. Across the street, right in the heart of the most respectable part of the city, I was surprised to see prostitutes gathering in the evening and openly plying their trade. There were few restaurants and the food was of poor quality, but to a 23-year-old from Kentucky it was a great experience to be there and I thoroughly enjoyed my stay.

Paris, by contrast, sparkled with life, and the food and wine were delicious. I made a mental note to return to live in Paris one day, which I did some years later. I then went on to Frankfurt to stay with an old friend from Lexington and Yale, John Hays, who was doing his military service in the U.S. Air Force. He stayed in Germany and became a musician, got a job in an opera orchestra and married a German lady.

I was still in no great hurry to get to the Far East and was determined to see as much of the world as I could while I had the chance. From Rhein-Main Air Base, near Frankfurt, I hopped on another plane, this time stopping in Delhi. I stayed in Maidens Hotel, a beautiful old colonial building set in a large lush garden. I ventured into the old city, where the poverty shocked me, and made the classic tourist mistake of giving a few annas to a boy who was begging. Within minutes, I was surrounded by so many beggars that they stopped the traffic. The next morning I took a guide and we went to Agra by train to see the Taj Mahal. I was enchanted by the magical place, but I remember one corner of the building was covered with a vast swarm of bees. I left Delhi very early for the airport and for a moment, before reality dawned, I thought the parks were covered with snow: tens of thousands of sleeping people, all dressed in white, lay there. The poverty of India was crushing, but the colourful costumes, sacred cows meandering down the streets and the Moghul forts and architectural remains of the Raj were fascinating sights, and I returned to India many times in the following decades.

I finally reached Japan, via Bangkok, a few days later and joined my ship at Yokosuka, which is located at the entrance to Tokyo Bay, forty miles from Tokyo itself and just south of Yokohama. My title was First Lieutenant, in charge of the deck operations such as cargo loading and unloading, moorings, boats and so forth. I was also gunnery officer and, as usual, I ran the ship's office. The captain turned out to be an alcoholic shoe salesman from Seattle, who disappeared in the evenings and drank his dinner but seemed reasonably alert during the day. At least he left the running of the ship to me and my fellow officers. Over the next few months we made four trips to Okinawa and Iwo Jima, where we participated in amphibious operations. LSTs were designed for grounding, and on one of our first voyages to the east coast of Korea we ran aground on a falling tide. Far from being worried, we sat there until the tide was right out, then amused ourselves running around the ship in the mud until we refloated.

But we had a more serious grounding off the jet-black volcanic beach of Iwo Jima, when the shoe salesman dropped the stern anchor too soon and the cable ran out, exposing the ship to broaching in the heavy surf. We radioed for help and another LST quickly came up, we took a line and they towed us to deep water. I then lowered a boat with a grappling hook, and for the next twelve hours we trawled for the cable, found it and recovered the anchor. The captain damaged his ankle getting into a boat in the heavy sea, was taken to a shore hospital, and we never saw him again. He was not replaced, and my colleagues and I took over.

One night in the Straits of Formosa, when our squadron of LSTs was proceeding to Hong Kong, I was on watch and I saw what seemed to be a city of light straight ahead where there should have been only water. After an hour it became clear that it was Hong Kong's junk fleet heading for the open sea, which was a sure sign of an impending typhoon. We got a belated signal to turn round and head north, keeping within the north-west quadrant of the typhoon's expected track. The LST was so slow we couldn't outrun the storm, so we battened down and were hit by the full force. First, the radars wouldn't turn in the wind, so we couldn't tell where the other ships in our squadron were. Then the force was too great for us to steer and when we tried to use the engines to head up into the wind, that failed too. From the trough at the bottom of a wave to the next crest was more than 100 feet. To get from the bridge to the accommodation, you had to take an outside ladder and I can recall hanging on to the rails for dear life with my feet swinging over a huge drop into the open sea as the ship rolled. Eventually the storm passed and we arrived in Naha, Okinawa, where there was not a light to be seen as the typhoon had passed right through the city.

Our squadron was assigned to Naha for Christmas 1956. Okinawa had been levelled in the war, and Naha was widely regarded in the Navy as the pits, so we were dreading it. But as we steamed into Naha Harbour, a signal came through detaching our ship from the rest of the squadron, and ordering us to Sasebo, Nagasaki for the holidays. Sasebo was a paradise for sailors, with friendly girls, plenty of alcohol and great clubs. I already knew it well: my friend Dick Blodget, the son of the actress Cornelia Otis Skinner, had developed a great affection for champagne, which we could buy at the Officers' Club for a pittance, so great quantities were consumed.

No one could understand why we were singled out for such a treat, but as soon as we steamed into Sasebo Harbour I saw the flagship of the amphibious fleet flying the pennant of (by now) Admiral Kintberger. Immediately I knew he wanted to play bridge over the holidays and had learned where my ship was to be and then ordered her to Sasebo. When the crew found out, I was a hero.

In early 1957 we were assigned to move a U.S. Marine air wing from Kurong po-ri, a small port north of Pusan in South Korea, to Hiroshima. This was my first visit to Hiroshima, which had been completely destroyed by the atomic bomb in 1945, and to get there we travelled through Japan's beautiful Inland Sea, an extraordinary contrast with the desolation of Hiroshima. That part of the trip was calm enough but over in Korea there was chaos. With the war over, the U.S. was pulling back its forces and handing over a number of its bases to the South Koreans. Our job was to bring out all the equipment we could, but it proved to be a far from simple task. The waste was appalling: there were trucks overturned on the roads and expensive equipment scattered everywhere, abandoned by the Marines. Nothing was accounted for, and no one seemed to care. We moved what we could back to Japan, but large quantities were just left there. We made forty crossings of the Korean Strait, each one twenty-four hours' steaming time.

The *Pender County* didn't possess her own jeep, so on one crossing I commandeered two of the abandoned Marine jeeps and got the lads to repaint them in Navy grey and write the ship's name on the hood. From then on we spent our free time in Japan driving around the countryside, visiting places of interest. In those days no military person was allowed ashore out of uniform, so we were never questioned.

I found Japan intriguing, and was always surprised at how courteous the Japanese were, given the ferocity with which they had fought the war against us and the defeat they suffered at American hands. I made a number of trips to Kyoto, which I thought to be a most beautiful place and where I discovered the joy of Japanese art for the first time. I also developed a respect for the achievements of General MacArthur, not just in the wars against Japan and North Korea, but for what he achieved after the war as administrator in Japan. As with Hong Kong, Japan was beginning to get off its knees to become the economic superpower it would be twenty years later and that was a direct result of MacArthur's benign rule and organizational skills. MacArthur was remembered in Japan for two other achievements: he saved the Emperor and introduced baseball, which today is Japan's most popular sport.

My two years' military service was up in mid-1957, and the *Pender County* was heading for San Diego when I got a call from Admiral Kintberger for me to report to the office in Yokohama of the Military Sea Transportation Service, headed by Admiral 'Dutch' Will. When I duly appeared I was told they needed someone experienced with LSTs to undergo six months' training in Yokosuka, and then go to Manila to manage a group of six Japanese-manned and flagged LSTs designated for 'special duties'. They were a bit unspecific about what the 'special duties' were exactly, but I was told enough for me to understand that the U.S. was supporting the anti-Communist forces in Indonesia with arms and materiel, and some of these would be delivered by the six ships straight into the port of Surabaya, where the Indonesian military would collect them. The U.S. did not want to be seen to be directly involved, hence the Japanese crews and flags. Kintberger had recommended me for the role. I would have to sign on for another two years but for a 24-year-old lieutenant (j.g.), six months ashore in Japan, followed by a year or so in Manila seemed very appealing. I took the job.

'Support for anti-Communist forces' in Indonesia turned out to be support for President Sukarno of Indonesia and, reading the intelligence reports, I began to wonder if we had got the right man. No one liked Sukarno or trusted him, with good reason: his only saving grace was that he had successfully defeated a group of Communists, without support from outside, and seemed to offer the best chance of producing a stable, non-Communist government in this critical part of Asia. Sukarno had collaborated with the Japanese in the war with devastating consequences for his country, where millions died of famine or in slave labour camps in Japan. When the Dutch came back to reclaim their former colony after the war, Sukarno was briefly imprisoned. But after his victory over the Communists in 1948, the U.S., strongly opposed to the brutal colonial war the Dutch were waging, threatened to cut off Marshall Aid funds to the Netherlands if they continued military operations. The Dutch, under enormous international pressure, finally granted Indonesia its independence in 1949 and Sukarno became president of a deeply divided and desperately poor republic. Now we were helping him stay in power.

Thankfully I didn't know much about the tangled politics and dynamics of the area as I settled into my new role. The idea was that I would spend six months in Japan being trained to take responsibility for the handling of deliveries coming in from the U.S. for the Navy in Manila. I would report to a senior officer in Subic Bay, 100 miles north of Manila and very close to the giant Clark Air Base, which was completely destroyed by a volcanic eruption some years later.

I took a beautiful house in Kamakura, just above the Great Buddha, a monumental outdoor bronze dating from the thirteenth century which inspired Kipling to write:

> *O ye who tread the Narrow Way*
> *By Tophet-flare to Judgement Day,*
> *Be gentle when 'the heathen' pray*
> *To Buddha at Kamakura!*

The windows of my bedroom looked straight on to Mount Fuji, Japan's highest mountain (3,776m), and on a cold winter's morning its extraordinary symmetrical cone was perfectly framed against the crystal-blue sky. It was an idyllic spot, made more so by the fact that I had found a very attractive Japanese girlfriend who spoke perfect English and lived in a pretty house behind Yokosuka. She was my excellent guide and interpreter, and taught me a great deal about the customs and culture of the Japanese.

While I was at Kamakura I started the collection of Japanese art which I have gone on building all my life and which gives me great pleasure today. I became friendly with a distinguished retired Japanese admiral, who was an expert on both Chinese and Japanese art, and often entertained me in his home, a singular honour for a foreigner. He acquired art from the rich families of Kamakura, who had hit bad times after the war, and then sold it on to the dealers and collectors. I was able to persuade him to let me buy some fine pieces at good prices. I wished afterwards I had been able to spend more, but a lieutenant's salary had its limitations.

I had also been inspired by a book James Michener wrote about Japanese prints, called *The Floating World*, and I started collecting these as well. Michener won a Pulitzer Prize for his book of short stories based on his experiences in the Pacific during the war, and the musical play *South Pacific* by Rodgers and Hammerstein is based on one of them. Much to my delight, he unexpectedly appeared in Manila to visit one of my ships and give an award to a Japanese sailor who had saved his life in the South Pacific.

I frequently went to Tokyo for the weekends and always stayed at Frank Lloyd Wright's Japanese masterpiece, the Imperial Hotel. After the original Imperial burned down, Wright was asked to design a new structure which would withstand an earthquake, a big concern for architects in Tokyo long before recent events in the area. Wright designed it in what was called the 'Mayan Revival' style of architecture, with a tall pyramid-shaped structure and Mayan motifs, giving the building a dramatic visual effect. He incorporated a series of innovations intended to protect its staff and guests in an earthquake: the iconic reflecting pool which could be used for fire-fighting, cantilevered floors and balconies to provide extra support, seismic separation joints and much else. The building survived several earthquakes, including a major one in 1923 (magnitude 8.3 – the 2011 earthquake in north-east Japan was measured at 9.0), although it was damaged more than Wright ever admitted. It somehow managed to escape the American carpet-bombing in the war, after which it was taken over by the occupation forces. When I went there a new tower wing had been added, but the grandeur of the old building was intact. Unfortunately,

Wright's foundations were shallow, and in later years the hotel began to subside, and became very run-down. When Tokyo property values shot up to absurd levels in the 1970s, the owners knocked it down to make way for a modern high-rise building. However, some of it survived: the central lobby wing, the heart of the hotel, and the reflecting pool were disassembled and rebuilt in the Museum Meiji-mura, and are open to the public. I have always thought it would be special to rebuild the old Imperial and make it into an Orient-Express hotel.

All this time I was receiving instruction in ship management, and learning how to handle the cargoes coming into Manila on the big American-flagged ships, some of which would be heading out again to Surabaya on my LSTs, bound for the Sukarno forces.

I moved to Manila early in 1958, where I lived in the Army and Navy Club on the Luneta, which is the national park in the centre of town. The club was next to the American Embassy, where I had the use of their beautiful pool and which was the centre of expatriate life. After a few months, I took a beautiful apartment near the club, which I shared with Bob Manley who headed the CARE charitable relief organization in the Philippines. On the floor below lived Mike Simmons and his wife Pat, who would later play an important role in my life. Mike headed the Dodwell & Co. shipping agency, and a lot of military cargoes arrived in the Philippines on United States-flagged ships, some of which Dodwell represented. Mike loved to play the guitar and when I was in town we spent many evenings at Guernica's, a bar owned by a Basque guitar player.

Someone described Southeast Asia at this time as a 'tinder box on the point of incineration'. The Philippines themselves were a dangerous place, as the Huk guerrillas, originally peasant farmers who had fought the Japanese even when their Filipino landlords supported them, degenerated into violent gangs and murderers. On some weekends we had to drive through Huk country to get out of the heat of Manila to the cool mountains of Baguio in the north. We always stopped halfway to have a San Miguel beer at a place the Huks had raided on more than one occasion. We never actually encountered them or had a problem, but we always went prepared. My lasting memory is of a group of us sitting around a table with coasters on top of our beer glasses to keep out the flies, and each one of us with his .45 pistol lying ready on the table behind his glass. Baguio, cool enough to have open fires in the evening and heavy blankets to sleep under, was a dream after the heat and humidity of Manila.

To give you an idea of the wild and woolly nature of the Philippines in those days, one night I was awakened by a popping noise coming from the Luneta, which I thought was firecrackers. The next day I learned that there had been a shoot-out between an armed gang and security guards in the harbour. Apparently the crew of a ship owned by Lykes Lines had tried to smuggle in a large cargo of cigarettes, which were subject to a very heavy duty. The crew of the ship were in league with the gang, and in the middle of the night they secretly removed the contraband and took it across the harbour to the President's jetty at the foot of the Luneta. But then the guards on the jetty decided they would hijack the cargo for themselves, and there was an almighty gunfight. The gang, presumably better armed, shot and killed all the guards and got away with the loot. It was the gunfire I had heard.

By the end of 1958 my mission and my navy career were coming to an end, and I began to wonder what to do next. I had enjoyed an exhilarating four years in the Navy, with its unique blend of hard work and peril at sea, and great fun ashore. I had early exposure to the responsibilities of command, and learned a great deal about life and culture as well as maritime affairs. I was fortunate in that I was too late for the Korean War and too early for Vietnam, so I never had to endure the horrors of war which so many, including my father, did. But I had been in some hazardous situations, had learned to rely on my own judgement and wit, and was a far more mature person than the raw ensign who set off from Yale what seemed like a lifetime ago.

I was demobbed at the naval base in Treasure Island in San Francisco Bay, and went home to Kentucky, ready to begin the next stage of my life. I was looking forward to it.

CHAPTER FOUR

FATHER OF CONTAINER LEASING

When I left the Navy in January 1959 I was twenty-five, equipped with a degree from Yale and a reasonable naval record, which opened up a lot of doors in 1950s America. My father, who had a number of large industrial concerns among his clients, had been urging me for some time to think about an M.B.A. from the Harvard Business School, and I decided that was good advice. I was aware I needed to have at least a year's experience in business before starting, so I headed for New York, got a job as a trainee banker at American Express and started in the banking hall at its head office in lower Broadway, consoling myself with the thought that this was never going to be my long-term career.

I had only been there three days when I got a call from a former colleague of my old boss in Manila, Admiral 'Dutch' Will, about Admiral Giles Stedman, now the European vice-president of the United States Lines shipping company. Stedman was looking for someone to take over its commercial operations in France and Switzerland, and Will, who must have been pleased with my work in the Philippines, had recommended me for the job, which would be based in Le Havre.

This sounded pretty interesting. United States Lines was probably the grandest of American shipping companies at the time, the successor to the United States Mail Steamship Company, and had lucrative contracts with the U.S. government for carrying mail, troops and military cargo to American bases in Europe and the Far East. It owned two of the great ocean liners of the age (or any age), the ss. *America*, generally regarded as the most beautiful liner ever to fly the American flag, and the *ss. United States*, which had been built on an aircraft carrier's hull and had achieved a recorded top speed of 42 knots, making her the fastest passenger liner in history. Her real top speed was even greater, 48 knots, but was kept a closely guarded secret for fear she would one day have to carry troops through submarine-infested waters.

Stedman turned out to be another one of those tough navy veterans with an extraordinary war record, which included the evacuation of 1,400 people from Singapore aboard an American passenger ship just before the Japanese arrived in 1942. I discovered later he was also involved in one of the stranger rescues of World War II when a U-boat torpedoed a British freighter off the coast of Ireland in 1939. The U-boat captain first allowed the crew to get into the lifeboats, then fired rockets to attract the attention of the nearby *ss. Washington*, flagship of United States Lines, which was commanded by Stedman, before finishing off the freighter.

After four years in Asia the thought of spending some time in Europe was more appealing than my Broadway banking hall so I accepted. I booked my passage to Southampton on the *America*, and was packed and ready to leave when I got a call from Stedman's office in London to say that the manager of the company's 'Mercy Service' had contracted hepatitis, and I would be required to fill in for him during the winter of 1959/60. I presumed this was something to do with American aid abroad and, a little puzzled by this turn of events, proceeded across the Atlantic. I took the train up to London and reported to the United States Lines' European headquarters in St. James's, still wondering about this 'Mercy' business. There I was told that I was to continue north to the company's Liverpool office, which was on the river Mersey – not 'Mercy' as I had thought.

It wasn't quite what I had in mind when I accepted the job in New York, but I was assured it was only for a few months, and then I could go to France. So I took the train to Liverpool, which initially struck me as even gloomier and grimier than London had been on my visit there a few years earlier. On my first day in the city I was told not to walk on the sidewalks because the gargoyles on the buildings were so corroded by the grime that they often fell onto the streets, and a number of people had been seriously injured, so for days I kept carefully to the middle of the street with cars passing dangerously on either side of me.

But the city had something special and historic about it too, epitomized by the Royal Liver and the Cunard buildings on the waterfront, relics of an era when Liverpool was one of the wealthiest and busiest ports in the world (it actually handled 40 per cent of the world's entire trade in the early nineteenth century). It had taken a real pummelling in the war, with some eighty German air raids, and there were bomb craters everywhere and what seemed to be miles of slum dwellings, although there were some fine streets and buildings too. The Cavern Club was open, but this was a couple of years before The Beatles made it famous and I never discovered it.

I had got used to warm weather and planned to find a nice apartment to protect me from the elements in the northern winter, but I soon discovered that Liverpudlians had never heard of central heating, and all the apartments I looked at were cold and damp. So I took a suite in Liverpool's grand old Adelphi Hotel, which was well heated and within walking distance of the office. I was given a temporary membership at the Royal Liverpool Golf Club, but there was never a weekend when it wasn't raining, so I never went.

The United States Lines business in Liverpool was fairly straightforward: its cargo ships brought in cotton for the Manchester textile mills, military supplies for the U.S. bases and a variety of other items termed 'general cargo', all packed into the ships by hand and then removed again by hand in a slow process called 'break-bulk cargo handling', which was hugely labour-intensive. Once unloaded, the ships normally proceeded to Glasgow, where they took aboard full cargoes of Scotch whisky, around 300,000 cases per vessel as I recall, and carried them back to the U.S. The big passenger liners never came to Liverpool and our business was entirely general cargo. Although I had not worked in the shipping business before, my experience in Manila and Subic Bay had taught me the principles, which I was now able to apply on a commercial basis. The staff in the large office knew the routine well, and they were friendly enough to this young American who had been parachuted in as their temporary boss.

Glasgow was also part of my area of responsibility and I went there often to see our agent, Graham Ackerley, a former British Army colonel who was the head of the family shipping agency Benjamin Ackerley & Son. He was well connected to the local gentry and distillery owners, and my lasting memory of him is of a windy and wet evening when he took me to the estate of the Duke of Montrose, where we dined in great state in a large, eerie, candle-lit dining room with the thunder and lightning raging outside, like a scene from *Wuthering Heights*. The main course consisted of 'haggis and neeps', a truly disgusting Scottish dish made of minced meat in a sheep's stomach and turnips, over which our hostess related the fate of the first duke, who was hanged, drawn and quartered. The family had recovered the bones and placed them in a glass case, which I considered was all too visible on the sideboard. Fortunately the whisky flowed freely, as it always did in Scotland.

On one of my early visits to Glasgow I discovered an interesting industrial practice, which had apparently been going on for years. As the whisky was stowed aboard the ships, a small number of cases, maybe one per cent of the total, was carefully put aside from the others and stowed separately. When I asked about this, I was told that these cases were a present (or bribe if you like) for the stevedores and customs officers in New York City, who regarded them as a perk of the job, and heaven help the ship that withheld this little offering. It was all too easy for a net-load of cases to land too hard on the pier or for cargoes to be held up by suddenly over-zealous customs officials. The cost to the shippers was tiny – the price of a bottle of Scotch in a New York liquor store consisted largely of excise duty, and the whisky itself was worth only around fifty cents a bottle.

I wasn't about to disturb this little custom but there were all sorts of customs and practices among the heavily unionized dock workers, particularly in Liverpool, which were more difficult to ignore. One of the worst was 'the lump', which was a carry-over from the war when gangs worked four-hour shifts but worked around the clock.

After the war, the shifts were changed to eight hours, but the dockers continued to work only four at normal rates, and insisted they got paid for the other four at double-time. Dockers would go on strike at the drop of a hat, often when a perishable cargo was to be unloaded, and a ship could often sit there for weeks. Even when the dockers did work, it was incredibly slow and labour-intensive to load or unload a cargo, putting it into slings item by item, which were then hoisted and stowed aboard or ashore. Containerization, a decade later, would expose the inefficiencies in the system – by which stage many of the dockers had priced themselves out of a job.

It was a long winter, but by the spring of 1960 I was at last allowed to take up my assignment in Le Havre on the mouth of the river Seine. Le Havre is not far from the D-Day beaches; it had taken a hammering in the war and been shabbily rebuilt. It was a regular port-of-call for the *ss. United States* and *ss. America* who were competing head-to-head with Cunard's *Queen Mary* and *Queen Elizabeth* in the race across the Atlantic, the most profitable sea route in the world. After the war, United States Lines had built cathedral-like offices in the town, paying for them with 'blocked francs', which were freight revenues that could not be repatriated because of French exchange controls. United States Lines had built up significant quantities of the blocked currency, but when I suggested we use it to buy prime real estate in Paris I was told 'we are not in the real estate business'. I'm afraid that was rather typical of the spirit of the company at the time. It would have made them a fortune.

Le Havre in the spring was a more agreeable place than Liverpool in the winter and I took an apartment in the pretty little town of Étretat, a beach resort with high cliffs and a natural arch where Monet liked to paint. Le Havre was only ten miles away and there was no traffic so I could drive there in no time.

One of our big passenger liners arrived in Le Havre from New York once a week, embarked and disembarked passengers to and from Paris, and left again a few hours later. Freighters arrived several times a week primarily carrying military cargoes for the big U.S. bases in France and Germany. The routine was similar to the one I had got used to in Liverpool and Glasgow. Once the cargo ships were discharged, they moved to the French 'outports' of Bordeaux, La Rochelle and St. Nazaire. At St. Nazaire, on the river Loire, they loaded champagne, at La Rochelle they loaded brandy and at Bordeaux they took aboard the great cabernet sauvignon wines from the Médoc and the merlots from St. Émilion, and shipped them back to the U.S. market.

Pleasant a place as it was, Le Havre had little night-life and at the weekend it was dead. It was lonely for a young bachelor, so I began going to Paris, three hours away by train, whenever I could get away. On my first few trips I sat uncomfortably as the old steam locomotive pulling the Paris train out of Le Havre laboured agonizingly up the long hill outside the town. After that, I used to drive to the top, leave my car, and wait for the train in a typical French café, which was full of Gauloises smoke (I was a heavy smoker in those days) and farmers having their breakfasts, which they washed down with large quantities of Calvados, an apple brandy I grew to appreciate. It made the journey go much more quickly.

My boss in France was an Englishman, Michael Edwards, ten years my senior, who was based in the Paris office of United States Lines. Michael was one of the great fun-lovers of his age, with highly sophisticated tastes and exquisite manners. He taught me a great deal about good living as well as about shipping, and came to have a big influence on my life. He had graduated from Cambridge University after the war, having been called up as a seaman when he was a teenager. His father, who had once owned the India Steamship Company, had been enormously wealthy and Michael had been brought up to appreciate the finer things in life. He used to relate, very amusingly, the story of how his father spent £5 million of his fortune buying artifacts from King Tutankhamun's tomb, which he kept in a special wing of his country house near that of Lord Carnarvon. It was of course illegal to remove artifacts from Egypt, so he never let any expert near them. After he died, Michael's mother decided to sell them, but the experts at the auction houses said they were fakes. They must have been very good fakes, because the Louvre had also acquired some from the same source.

I had learned some French at school and although it was rusty I was improving, and could get by reasonably well. Michael, who was fluent, introduced me to his wide circle of friends, and through the Navy and Yale, I had a number of other contacts and friends in Paris. It didn't take me long to become part of a group which tended to congregate at cafés on the Rive Gauche or Montmartre at the weekends. Most of the time we drank, ate and talked for hours, but there were some interesting parties too, and I remember one on the Rive Gauche when the hostess appeared wearing only a hat and gloves.

Michael was insistent that I get to know all the wine shippers and took me around some of the best vineyards in France, introducing me to the owners and winemakers, all of whom welcomed him as an old friend. Switzerland was also part of my territory and, as Michael considered the Swiss pretty dull, he left it to me. Once a month I went to Basel and stayed at the (then) wonderful Hotel Euler. Our agent, Hans-Peter Maeder, invited me to dinner at his home, and we ate off gold plates with gold utensils, the first time I had done so. Clearly being a shipping agent in Switzerland was a profitable profession.

Switzerland's biggest exports were high-value goods such as watches, cameras (before the Japanese took over the market), aniline dyes and cuckoo clocks. They were generally flown to the United States at huge expense because the cargo ships were too slow and pilferage and damage were rife in the French and American docks. Transporting this precious cargo to the U.S. was potentially worth a lot of money, but United States Lines got only a fraction of it. I thought if I could offer a speedy, reliable and secure journey aboard our fast passenger ships from Le Havre, we could pick up the business. However, I had a particular conundrum with the *America* and *United States* which arrived on alternate weeks in Le Havre from Southampton at about 6 p.m. on Saturday night. They had to leave by midnight to make their morning arrival in New York four and a half days later, taking into account possible weather delays. Both ships had large cargo holds and could comfortably have taken the Swiss cargo, but there was never time to load it because of the slow manhandling process on the docks.

I had been thinking about this for some time, and so had the Swiss agents, and we discussed various solutions. They wanted to save transport costs, and I wanted their business. Finally we came up with the idea of building a number of steel containers which could be loaded with the valuable Swiss export goods at Basel railway station on Fridays, with the train departing that night to arrive alongside our passenger ship in Le Havre by 6 p.m. the following evening. There were large shore cranes on the pier which could easily lift the containers into the cargo holds and complete the loading process before the midnight departure. The steel containers could be securely locked to prevent pilferage, and there would be no issues with go-slow dockers who would never get near the containers.

Because of the speed of the great ships, the goods would arrive in New York almost as fast as by air services, which were neither frequent nor, in the days before jets could make the trip in one leap, very fast. We had some containers built and gave it a trial run, and it worked perfectly. Over the next weeks and months we made a number of improvements and it quickly became a regular service, with the Swiss agents offering us more and more goods. We had found a new revenue source for United States Lines, which generated millions of dollars every year using cargo space which otherwise would have been empty. Unwittingly, we had invented one of the first container services.

The idea of 'containerization' was not really new, but at this time was still at the experimental stage, and many shipping companies were highly sceptical of it. It had been pioneered by a remarkable man called Malcolm McLean, a farm boy from North Carolina who became a truck driver and ended up revolutionizing the world shipping industry. One obituary writer later said of him: 'McLean made a contribution to maritime trade so phenomenal that he has been compared to the father of the steam engine, Robert Fulton.' Another said his vision 'gave the industry the jolt it needed to survive for the next fifty years'.

McLean, who later became a good friend, remains one of my heroes and his life story, so critical to mine, is worth spending a moment over. In the 1950s, McLean, by then one of the biggest truck-operators in

America, took an ordinary truck trailer and redesigned it into two parts, one a truck platform on wheels, and the other an independent steel box, or container, which was pilfer-proof and strong enough to withstand the roughest conditions at sea or on land. In 1955 he patented a steel-reinforced corner post structure, which could be gripped by a specially designed crane, lifted off the wheeled platform and stacked in the hold – or even on the deck – of a cargo ship.

McLean's containers quickly changed the way goods were transported on the roads and railways, but he made some powerful enemies. When the big railway companies, seeing him as a serious threat to their freight business, tried to close him down in 1956, McLean sold his trucking business for $6 million. He believed the potential for sea containerization was much larger than trucking, and offered a way to speed up loading and unloading as well as breaking the stranglehold of the unions. Stevedores in the east coast ports wouldn't work when it rained, demanded extra wages whenever they considered a cargo 'dirty' or 'smelly' and had long ago adopted all the bad practices I had encountered in Liverpool. Pilferage was endemic, and cargoes were often damaged, adding to the cost of transportation.

McLean started by converting a World War II oil tanker into the first container ship, called the *Ideal X*, which made its maiden voyage in April 1956 carrying fifty-eight steel containers from Port Newark, New Jersey, to Houston. The unions, the railroad authorities, rival ship owners and government officials watched the voyage with bated breath, hoping – praying – for a disaster, and when the ship docked and unloaded its cargo, it was immediately inspected by the authorities. To their great disappointment, it was found to be dry and secure – and the container industry was underway, ushering in the biggest change in shipping since steam replaced sail. Today the volume of containerized traffic exceeds 100 million units annually, and 90 per cent of all international general cargo is carried in containers.

As McLean's business grew, the big shipping companies, including United States Lines, belatedly decided they must fight back. The top management in United States, suddenly jittery, asked who in the company knew anything about containerization, and my name came up. I found myself promoted, offered a big leap in salary and transferred from France to the head office on Lower Broadway, Manhattan, to help develop containerization for the company. This was a very useful experience for me as up to this point I had only seen the shipping industry from a local, operational point of view in Liverpool and France. Now I could study the bigger picture, analyse the global trends and form an educated view of where the industry was going.

I could see, even if senior management couldn't, that the advent of containerization, offering cheaper, safer and more reliable cargo transportation, linking sea seamlessly with road transport, threatened the very existence of United States Lines, and other shipping companies like it if they didn't convert to containers. The jetplane was killing their passenger liner business: *America* would be sold to Chandris Lines a few years later, and the *United States* was withdrawn from service in 1969. The *Queen Mary* and *Queen Elizabeth* suffered a similar fate. I actually tried to buy the *United States*, and offered $3 million for her but was topped by a guy from Seattle who offered $5 million. Unfortunately he never did anything with her and she sat in Norfolk until she accumulated so much in port dues the banks foreclosed. She was sold at auction, stripped of all her beautiful fittings, then it turned out she was full of asbestos. She was towed to Turkey, where safety rules weren't so demanding, for her removal. Today she is just a rusting hulk somewhere in Norfolk, and I grieve for her. She deserved better.

Back in New York I took charge of the relationship with United States Lines' largest customer, Container Transport International Inc. (or CTI), which was also located in Manhattan. CTI's business was forwarding U.S. military cargo, including the household goods of military personnel moving to and from overseas postings, mostly to the big bases in Europe and the Far East. A considerable quantity of these cargoes went on our ships, and CTI and its competitors (the largest was North American Van Lines in Fort Wayne, Indiana) were now building small steel containers to transport them. When the containers were emptied in Europe, they often went to Volkswagen's

Wolfsburg plant. Here they were loaded with spare parts, which were sent to the U.S., where the VW Beetle was making serious inroads into the car market. The problem was that there was more military cargo moving east than spare parts coming back, so the steel containers piled up in Europe, or were returned empty to the U.S. at high cost.

I became close to the owners of CTI, Tom Newman, Jerry Slater and Ben Bernstein, and we developed a plan to benefit both companies. United States Lines had enough high value general cargo booked on its ships coming back from Europe to fill the surplus CTI containers, so we leased them, filled them with the cargo in European ports and shipped them back to the U.S. where they were unloaded, emptied and passed back to CTI to begin the whole cycle all over again. In this way we had military cargo booked by CTI going one way and our own high-value general cargoes coming back. As a result CTI shipped even more cargoes on United States Lines ships, we made more money out of it, and the relationship grew.

United States Lines was an old-fashioned, traditional shipping company, co-founded by President Theodore Roosevelt's son Kermit, and the management was having difficulty adjusting to the new era. It depended largely on U.S. government subsidies, and there was no appetite to spend the capital required to upgrade the fleet. There were some good shipping people there, like my boss John Griffiths (who later left and ran a major shipping agency in New York), but I was getting very frustrated with the way it was run: the chief executive was the chairman's son-in-law, played golf every afternoon and was simply not fully engaged in the business.

At a social occasion one day I made a proposal to CTI that they should start a new business which would build or buy containers to lease to other shipping operators, rather than operate them themselves – really a development of the United States Lines/CTI arrangement which worked so well. A 20-foot container cost $1,000 to build and if CTI leased it out for $2 a day, which I calculated it could, it would get its money back in eighteen months. It would work much like the aircraft or car leasing business does today, with shipping companies renting a container for a fixed period and giving it back – or extending the lease – when they had finished with it, after which it would be rented to someone else.

I suggested that if they went for the idea, CTI should hire me to run the business and I would receive a carried interest in the profits. They agreed immediately and in the middle of 1963 I moved back to France, this time to Paris, the city I had come to know and love more than any other. I had never really enjoyed living in New York City, which was an impersonal concrete jungle to me, and I understand today why New Yorkers travel so often to Florida and the Caribbean. I had a walk-up apartment on 12th Street, and after Étretat in Normandy I found it small and uncomfortable. But it also seemed to me that the new leasing business should be based in Europe where most of the world's shipping companies were located. To be honest, I could equally well have gone to London, which was still clinging to its position as the centre of world shipping and of course the Lloyd's insurance market was based there, but at that time of my life I preferred Paris (my opinion would reverse a few years later when I came to know London, where I moved to).

Michael Edwards had been promoted to the United States Lines' European headquarters in London on the death of Admiral Stedman, and he rented me his beautiful apartment on the Île Saint-Louis, where I stayed for several years. I took a suite of offices in the Rue du Cherche-Midi, hired a secretary and a small staff, and began work. The first task was to set up a network of agents in Europe to handle and lease out the steel containers, and this was soon achieved. I was constantly on the road, visiting all of the big liner-ship operators, who were fascinated to hear about the latest container developments. They wanted to know what Malcolm McLean was up to in the U.S. and what other shipping companies were doing about containerization, and I was able to persuade them to dip their toes into the container business, if only to gain practical experience.

My CTI leasing business was highly profitable from the start and went from strength to strength as the container trade boomed and more and more shipping companies used our services. We were able to lease every container we could get our hands on, and were constantly running behind demand, which was rising exponentially. We were the only people doing it, but it was only a matter of time before others entered, and it was important to press on as hard and fast as possible.

Then we came abruptly to a halt. The company had no more containers. The entire fleet had been leased out and the banks were demanding personal guarantees from the company's owners against loans to buy more. The largest shareholder, Ben Bernstein, refused to give his guarantee, even though we had customers waiting for more containers. It was the biggest financial mistake he ever made, and it was to cost him millions. But it worked hugely to my benefit, although I did not feel that way at the time.

My good friend from Yale, Maury Pinto, and his two cousins Morris and Joseph, were now managing Pinto & Cie., the family investment company, which was based in Paris with a branch in Madrid. They also had close ties with Burnham & Co. in New York, ultimately Drexel Burnham Lambert (which many years later would be dominated by Michael Milken, master of the 'junk bond', and forced into bankruptcy in 1990; Milken and his associate-in-crime, Ivan Boesky, both went to jail). The Pintos were active investors and on the lookout for the next big thing to come along – which I hoped might be container leasing.

Container leasing is essentially a financial rather than an operational shipping business, and when I explained the mechanics of it as well as my predicament to Maury, he immediately saw the commercial opportunities. He proposed that we form a new container leasing company, to be called Sea Containers Inc., which his company would back. One of Maury's associates, Philip Schlee, whose family tea business in China had been nationalized, also agreed to invest. We raised a total of $100,000, of which I contributed $25,000 in return for a 50 per cent stake.

I left CTI in early 1965 and moved into the Pinto offices in the Place Vendôme, beside the Paris Ritz Hotel, where I worked all hours to get the new business off the ground. It was a delightful place to be, but nice as it was, I was gradually forced to the conclusion that Paris should not be the headquarters for this operation, and it needed to be based in the City of London, where we moved a few months later. Philip very generously put his office in Old Jewry, near the Bank of England, at our disposal, and he transferred to London to administer the business.

Now we needed both containers and customers and I hit the road again, meeting potential clients and shipping companies and building a new team of agents. I had the advantage of being well-known from my CTI connection, and soon we had plenty of customers – but not enough containers to service them. Luck favoured me in the shape of the German recession of the mid-1960s, which resulted in factories facing low order books and short-time working. Unlike British or American companies, Germans never wanted to lay off skilled labour, and were prepared to take on unprofitable work just to keep the factories open. A chum of mine in Hamburg, Hans Grosse, had contacts with Mannesmann, the German industrial giant in Karlsruhe. He reckoned we could get a good deal from them on steel containers, which they might build just to keep their factories open. The problem was that we were desperately undercapitalized to take on such large obligations.

Hans and I travelled to Mannheim to meet the management, and I presented a cheeky proposal under which the containers would be built by Mannesmann to the new international standard of 20 feet in length, and they would keep title to them until they were paid for. If we defaulted, their recourse would be to recover the containers, which might be anywhere in the world, but lease contracts would also be assigned to them as additional security. It was a big risk on their part and in normal circumstances they would not even have considered it, but they went for the deal and the arrangement worked beautifully. Mannesmann was eventually paid in full, and we took over the ownership of the containers.

That gave us one supply of containers, but we desperately needed more. I knew that North American Van Lines were sitting on a mountain of smaller steel containers in Europe which they had been unable to employ. They were not ideal for our purposes, but they would do at a pinch. I went to Fort Wayne, Indiana to meet the chief executive, and convinced him to let me take over his idle containers and lease them out. My proposal was that whenever a container was on lease they would get a percentage of the revenue. They also went for the deal.

I knew the smaller Van Lines containers would be difficult to lease on the open market, but I had a different plan for them. I went to Occidental Petroleum who were building a pipeline in Libya and persuaded them to lease 1,000 of the containers to be used to protect their equipment from the scorching desert sun, particularly the tape they used to lag the pipe. They were delighted with the proposal.

When I travelled to Libya a few months later, Occidental flew me over the pipeline, where I saw our containers dotted across the landscape. This was in the days of King Idris and the Italians, who had ruled the country as a colony up to the war, still dominated business life. The whole country only had a population of 2,000,000 and it was a pretty godforsaken place, although in Tripoli, because of the Italian connection, you could at least get a decent plate of pasta. The U.S. Air Force base, Wheelus, was in the middle of Tripoli. I have reflected often about what might have happened if a few daring soldiers had been sent in to grab Colonel Gaddafi when he seized control of the country a few years later, while the King was overseas on a state visit. Forty-two years of tyrannical rule might well have been prevented.

We now had two sources of containers and some good customers and Sea Containers was prospering, but we needed more capital to cope with a market that was exploding. The Pintos convinced their Wall Street friends Burnham & Co. and one of their partners, Michael Gellert, to invest several million dollars in 1967 and we were able to step up our activities considerably. Containerization had become one of the growth industries and was catching the attention of the financial press and investment companies, and Sea Containers was riding the crest of it. Shipping companies were laying down purpose-built container ships, and harbours and ports were investing in special container cranes and facilities, much to the anger of the trade unions. There were now international standards for the size of containers, based on what are called in the trade a TEU, for 20-foot equivalent, and a height of 8 feet, further streamlining the business. All the shipping companies were moving into containers in a big way, but no one outside the U.S. had yet seen the potential of container leasing. In Europe I was on my own and had a clear run at the market.

It was an exhilarating period for me, as I watched the company expand at a faster and faster rate, outgrowing its City of London offices. We had to move twice over the first few years, once to an office behind Park Lane and then to bigger premises in Mayfair. By 1968 the stock market was in one of its bull markets not dissimilar to the dot-com boom thirty years later, and investors were hungry for new growth situations. Burnham recommended we take advantage of it and float the company on the U.S. market. We had only been in existence for four years, and the New York Stock Exchange required a five-year record, so we listed instead on the over-the-counter market at the extraordinary multiple of sixty-nine times earnings. We got a NYSE listing a year later.

I sold part of my holdings and suddenly, aged thirty-six, I was a multi-millionaire, free to move my life forward any way I wanted, without financial worries.

I was much more fortunate than Malcolm McLean, the man who had made my success possible. His company, Sea-Land Services, Inc., forged ahead after that first trip of the *Ideal X*, and in 1969 he sold out for $160 million of stock to the R. J. Reynolds tobacco company, with a five-year non-compete agreement. He lived well and often invited us quail hunting on the old Dupont shooting estate in Alabama which he had acquired. He was a generous host in the old-fashioned southern style to which I had been accustomed from my youth in Kentucky.

When his five years were up, he cashed in his R. J. Reynolds shares, which had risen substantially in value, making him one of the richest men in America. He then bought my old company United States Lines, which by then was a shadow of its once-mighty self, and against my advice built a fleet of very slow but economic container ships called Econships, and entered new trades in which he had no experience. He vastly overexpanded, got caught when the market turned down, and lost his shirt. The company was forced into bankruptcy in 1986, and Malcolm had to sell everything, including the Alabama estate. He lived on in the Pierre Hotel in New York for years and I saw him often.

Malcolm was a great man, and has always been recognized as the 'father of containerization'. I have been described as the 'father of container leasing', which has grown into a multi-billion-dollar industry and is an essential cog in the machinery of international trade today.

CHAPTER FIVE

SHIRLEY CROSS

I first met Shirley Cross, as she then was, in the village of Codicote, in Hertfordshire, in 1960. The connection was Mike Simmons, my old guitar-playing friend from Manila, who headed up the Dodwell shipping agency (later taken over by Inchcape) in the Philippines handling, among others, some of the ships which had carried my precious military cargoes. In my days in Manila, Mike and I became good friends, particularly when I moved out of the Army & Navy Club and took an apartment above him and his wife Pat, and we spent many evenings together.

We stayed in touch and every two years, when Mike and Pat travelled to England for home leave, I met up with them. Mike introduced me to his sister, Sue Turner, and her husband Donald, who lived in the same village of Codicote, and we in turn became good friends to the point where I offered Donald, who worked for ICI, then Britain's biggest and most prestigious company, a role at Sea Containers where he became vice-president of sales and marketing. Mike eventually also came to work for us as regional manager of the Far East, based in Hong Kong, and in the years that followed both of them became important members of the Sea Containers team.

Well before that, however, in 1960, I was invited to Sunday lunch by an attractive young couple the Turners knew well. Michael and Shirley Cross lived in a converted pub called The Old Bull in the middle of Codicote, with their two little boys, Charles and Simon. They had met at Oxford where Michael had qualified as a doctor and

Shirley read botany. I had always assumed that botanists were those odd people who worked at Kew Gardens or sailed with Captain Cook in search of rare species, but Shirley gently put me right, explaining they were actually scientists, and she herself specialized in genetics, which, she said, was now the 'big thing' in the scientific world. She was well ahead of her time – a decade or so later, genetics became a 'big thing' on world stock markets too, with companies such as Genentech commanding huge premiums. Michael, several years older than Shirley, had been in the Royal Navy before going to Oxford, and had actually served in Palestine after the war, ruefully relating his role in the British blockade which tried to stop the Jews from Europe getting into Israel (the subject of the film *Exodus*). He was a charming man, and I remember thinking he would have needed all his maturity and his good looks to have ensnared the beautiful, black-haired Shirley.

I was based in Paris at this stage, building up Sea Containers, and over the next few years I saw them occasionally on my periodic visits to England. When they told me they were going to Buffalo to work on some scientific projects I suggested they meet up with some friends of mine who lived there. I didn't see or hear of them for some time after that until one day Donald told me the shocking news that Michael Cross had been killed in a plane crash and Shirley was returning home to the house in Codicote with her two children. It was one of those freak accidents you believe can't happen – the plane caught fire in mid-air and everybody aboard was killed, probably before they hit the ground.

The next time I met Shirley was in 1967, over the baptismal font at the christening of the Turners' new baby, Catherine, to whom I was a godparent. The other godparent was the recently widowed Shirley. We chatted later and she told me that, with two young children to support, she had taken up a career as a research scientist working at the Smith, Kline & French laboratories in Welwyn Garden City. The boys went to private school nearby. I began seeing a bit of her, taking her out to shows and restaurants, and I got to know her two boys who were fun-loving youngsters and generally well behaved. I had bought a

Maserati Ghibli and we used to pile into it on a Sunday and have a spin through the countryside – to their enormous delight and their mother's equally enormous worry. There were no seat belts in those days.

By now I had moved my office to London and, flush with a bit of cash from the Sea Containers flotation, I bought a house in The Boltons, between the Fulham and Old Brompton roads, in Chelsea. It had been divided into flats and was in a terrible state, completely uninhabitable, and I set out on the long task of converting it into the comfortable house I still live in today. It took several years and I can remember taking Shirley there for the first time to show her the garden. She had to teeter along wooden planks to get to it. The garden was worse than the house, an utter ruin, but she looked calmly around and remarked: 'You know, this could be a lovely garden,' before throwing off ideas about what to do with it. Even then, she was a superb gardener.

When the house was finally finished, I moved there on a permanent basis, keeping a small flat in Paris, and Shirley and I started taking our holidays together, sometimes with the boys. Along with the house, I also bought a boat, an 85-foot ketch called *Barinia* (it's Russian for 'mistress'), and took Shirley and the boys sailing in the Mediterranean, which they loved. We sometimes sailed it into Venice, mooring at the Arsenale, and staying at the Hotel Cipriani, even then one of my favourite hotels.

I was now approaching forty, was comfortably off, and although my thoughts (and Shirley's too) began turning to marriage, I felt I wasn't ready for it yet. Ours was to be a long courtship – ten years to be precise – but we had some fun in those years.

But as Sea Containers continued to prosper it took up most of my attention. I was putting in long days and weeks, travelling nine months of the year, visiting every major port in the world, setting up operations in Australia, designing and ordering new ships and running a publicly listed company with outside shareholders who demanded my attention. I felt I had to visit every new client personally, and established ones regularly, and because I was reasonably well known in the business it was me who ship owners wanted to see. For all of these reasons, I felt Shirley and I should wait until things stabilized (of course they never did), and I could spend more time in London.

Sea Containers had started with a clear lead over the market, but as time went on we had to run harder and harder to retain our reputation as innovators and stay ahead of the game. In 1968 we introduced the Coldwrap refrigerated container, our first venture into specialized containers, which caused widespread comment throughout the industry. We launched it with an advertising campaign which ran:

> *What if a container could provide precise, total control of refrigerated shipments, over any distance, at any temperature?*

And we answered our own question thus:

> *It would open up the possibility of distant new mass markets for delicate perishables.*

Actually it did more than that, virtually eliminating the 20 per cent spoil rate which shippers were used to, and proved a big money-spinner.

We followed that up with other innovations and we were the first leasing company to embrace the 8-foot-6-inch-high container unit which eventually became the industry standard. We embarked on a major building program, ordering six Hustler-class container ships, offshore gantry cranes, refrigerated tank containers and ventilated and side-door units. We designed and constructed a range of lightweight, easily erected, shoreside gantry cranes and set them up initially in Lisbon and Oporto, where they became an immediate success. By 1972 we were designing the first 'deckship', basically a self-propelled barge which carried all its containers on the open deck.

There were always new opportunities and new challenges to be dealt with, and the oil crisis of 1973–4 provided both. The price of oil quadrupled from $3 a barrel to $12 when Arab members of OPEC, led by Saudi Arabia, cut their production by 5 per cent, ushering in an era of recession, high inflation and crashing stock markets. Motorists queued at petrol stations, interest rates soared and there was a serious economic and banking crisis in the U.K., which brought down the Conservative government of Ted Heath in March 1974. The Sea Containers business took a dip, but our investment in container ships and container cranes held up much better than the rest of the shipping industry, which hit one of the worst times in its post-war history. Many shipping companies went out of business, and the great Burmah Oil, which had expanded into tankers and liquefied gas carriers, went spectacularly bust, taking the London Stock Exchange to a new low in January 1975.

The other side of the coin, however, was the vast transfer of wealth from the Western countries to the Middle East, which brought some interesting opportunities. The Persian Gulf was booming and I was determined to take advantage of it. We started with two large container cranes in the small emirate of Sharjah and were actively hunting for new business when our agent in Dubai, George Chapman, called to say that the ruler, Sheikh Mohammed bin Rashid Al Maktoum, wanted to see me urgently. I took the next plane out, and was met by a man with a Rolls-Royce who took me to the only decent hotel in town, the Intercontinental, and told me to wait until Rashid was ready to see me. Demand for hotel rooms in the Gulf in those days far exceeded supply, and I was used to slipping the reception clerk a $100 note to get my confirmed room, but not on this occasion – this time I was the guest of the ruler and they bowed and scraped.

The next afternoon the Rolls called for George and me, and took us to the Sheikh's Palace where we were ushered into a long room full of old men in white robes who lined the wall, flicking their worry beads. Rashid sat at a desk at the head of the room, and rose to greet George like an old friend, which I felt was a good sign. He was an imposing man in his early sixties, his trim grey beard and hawk-like face instantly bringing to mind his love of falconry and hunting in the desert. He was the eighth Maktoum to rule over Dubai, but the first to embrace the modern world, and he was said to tour Dubai twice a day to see for himself the progress on the many construction projects taking place.

After the usual ceremonial cup of tea, he gracefully steered me to a vantage point which looked out on to the Gulf itself. When he gestured in what I understood to be the direction of Sharjah, I saw that his smile was gone and he was now bending his full penetrating gaze on me.

'Don't you know, Mr. Sherwood, that Dubai, and not Sharjah, is the port for this part of the world? It has always been so, and always will be. So why do you supply cranes to Sharjah and not Dubai?'

This took me aback, and I could only mutter something to the effect that 'we would be delighted to offer our cranes to Dubai'. In fact there was nothing we would have liked more. The new Port Rashid, a key part of the Sheikh's massive modernization program, had opened the year before, construction was well advanced on a tunnel under the Creek, and there were plans for an even bigger port, Jebel Ali, some twenty miles down the coast.

'When can you supply Dubai with the same cranes you provided Sharjah?' he asked. Clearly he was annoyed that his little neighbour had stolen a march on him.

'Within ninety days,' I replied.

'How much?' I increased the price that Sharjah had paid, and he shook my hand and said a 40 per cent deposit would be lodged with The British Bank of the Middle East the next day – which it was.

Back in the hotel I asked George Chapman how he knew Rashid so well. George explained that when he came out to Dubai after the war, he lived in a house-trailer which had air-conditioning. Rashid lived in a tent nearby, but when the summer heat was unbearable he would often drop in on George. Dubai only discovered oil in the 1960s, and it has long since run out, but Rashid was a visionary and his sons, the Maktoum brothers, have developed Dubai beyond all recognition from those days in the 1970s. Rashid's great phrase was: 'My grandfather rode a camel, my father rode a camel, I drive a Mercedes, my son drives a Land Rover, his son will drive a Rolls-Royce, but his son will ride a camel.'

Given the financial crisis in Dubai a few years ago, he could yet be right.

While all of this was going on, I had taken on another project, this one for my own personal amusement. Although I was a frequent visitor to London, I didn't know the city well enough to be confident of my restaurant choices, and frequently had indifferent meals in overpriced establishments recommended by one of the restaurant guides. Nor did I really know where to go to shop for antiques, clothes or even fishing rods. London's museums were a mystery to me and whenever I went to the British Museum or the National Gallery I found myself wandering aimlessly in search of what really interested me. Other people I met, even those who lived in London, were having similar experiences and the guides were no help, recommending restaurants which might have been good a decade ago but had gone downhill since.

So I devised my own guide: *James Sherwood's Discriminating Guide to London Fine Dining and Shopping – with a special section on museums and art galleries.* I appointed a wonderful lady called Susan Blackburn as editor, and we engaged a group of men-about-town, including Simon Jenkins, Anthony Sampson and others who knew their city well, and sent them out to dine in restaurants incognito. The Editor's Note in the guide set out the context:

> This guidebook is not an omnibus. It is a highly selective guide to the best restaurants in London, to the shops which sell the best of what you are looking for, and to the finest works of art. It is the result of a thorough search for quality, written for people who are able to recognize it but may not have the time to spend on the quest.

We included a section, which no other guide ever did, called NOT FOR US. It listed all the restaurants 'whose fame might lead you to their tables' but where you would now get a god-awful meal. My intention was to create a guide for busy, well-off people, mostly visitors, who did not want their time – and money – wasted. Some of the restaurants we rejected were famous ones: for instance, À l'Ecu de France in Jermyn Street, once regarded by many as the best restaurant in London; nor did we rate highly Bentley's, the seafood restaurant chain, Bertorelli's, Le Boulestin, l'Etoile, Madame Prunier, the Ritz, the Ivy, J. Sheekey, and even Wiltons, then probably the biggest power restaurant in London. Only four restaurants got two stars, our top category: Le Gavroche, then in Lower Sloane Street, run by the Roux brothers (dinner for two, without wine: £16, and you could get a bottle of Blanc Pouilly-Fumé for £2.85); Waltons (£14 for dinner, £1.50 for a reasonable bottle of wine); the restaurant in the Capital Hotel in Knightsbridge (£11 for two), and Carrier's in Islington, where a discerning couple could partake of a superb dinner for £11 with a decent bottle of wine for another £3. Claridge's, the Connaught, the Café Royal, Scott's and Le Coq d'Or only merited a single star; the Savoy Grill, everyone's favourite, was closed at the time.

We had a lot of fun, much of it at the restaurateurs' expense, and included sections on restaurants to eat with your wife, your mistress, with your children, in blue jeans or even in the company of 'beautiful people'. Needless to say, publication brought howls of protest from the rejected restaurants, including the Hambro family who owned Wiltons, but considerable appreciation from everyone else. Soon the whole town was talking about it, and I found myself something of a celebrity, a hero to some, reviled by many.

It is interesting to look back at some of the prices we thought very fancy then: a Château Léoville-Poyferré '66 at Claridges was £5.75, while Le Gavroche wanted all of £11.60 for a Chambolle-Musigny bottled by Latour. Many wines on the list of even the top restaurants were under £2, main courses were under £1, and there was general indignation that dinner at Mark's, including drinks before and wine during, came to £30. But then a tailor-made suit from Huntsman of Savile Row cost £150 and James Purdey & Sons of South Audley Street would custom-make you a side-by-side shotgun but it would take four years and cost you £3,000 (£6,000 for an over-and-under).

The first edition sold 10,000 copies, the second 50,000, and I actually made money out of it, which came as a nice surprise. My intention was to update it every couple of years, but after two editions poor Susan developed terminal cancer, and after that I never had the heart to go on with it. I interviewed a few other potential editors but none seemed to me to have her particular gift for painstaking detail, judgement and organization. The guide never appeared again, although people still come up to me to tell me they have a copy, which now sells on Amazon at far more than the original price.

All this time I was becoming more and more involved with Shirley and the boys, and it was clear, even to a bachelor like me, that I was going to have to do something about it. She was busily making her own way in life, and had written the definitive text on the subject of autoradiography, a sophisticated technique whereby scientists can determine where drugs go in the body. She was now working on a D.Phil. on the subject. But her proudest achievement was her contribution to the development of Tagamet, or cimetidine to give it its more formal name, which became one of the most successful beta blocker drugs of all time, and has made stomach ulcers a thing of the past. It is now regarded as so safe it is sold over the counter. Her team leader, Dr. James Black, later won the Nobel Prize for Medicine for his research on beta blockers.

By the mid-1970s Tagamet was almost ready for the marketplace (it got U.K. approval in 1976 and FDA approval in the U.S. three years later) and Shirley abandoned me for the best part of a year, travelling to Melbourne and then Los Angeles where she gave a series of lectures. When she came back her reputation was such that she was offered some fairly fancy jobs by the big drug companies, and this finally brought things to a head. One day she told me she could not go on being with me, bringing up her children, running a household and doing a demanding job properly. 'I want to be with you more, Jim,' she said, 'in fact all the time, travelling with you and doing all the things you do.'

A week later I took her to dinner at Mark's Club, asked her to marry me, and she accepted. So all in all, 1977 turned out to be a bit of a watershed for us: I bought the first cars of the Orient-Express train, Shirley completed her thesis to become Dr. Shirley – and on New Year's Eve we were married in St. Mary's Church, opposite our house in The Boltons, which was full of beautifully scented mimosa. My parents came over and Shirley's parents were there, and they got on like a house on fire. Shirley's son Simon was best man and Charles gave away the bride. Both boys, without even telling their mother, went down to the post office and changed their names from Cross to Sherwood. I have always loved them for it.

CHAPTER SIX

VENICE AND THE CIPRIANI

When I first started visiting Venice in the early 1960s, everyone knew Giuseppe Cipriani, founder of Harry's Bar and the Hotel Cipriani, two of the best-known establishments in the ancient city. I frequented both, tasting my first-ever Bellini, a delightful blend of fresh white peach juice and Prosecco sparkling wine from the Veneto, in Harry's Bar, then taking the beautiful Riva-built launch across the lagoon to the Hotel Cipriani on the island of Giudecca for a swim in the pool, which was bliss on a hot summer's day.

Giuseppe was something of a genius when it came to food: not only did he pioneer the Bellini, but he also invented Carpaccio and named them both after Venetian artists. My favourite of his dishes has always been the Taglierini Verdi al Prosciutto Gratinati (thin green noodles with béchamel sauce, cheese and ham, baked). His Venetian risottos with fresh vegetables or shellfish, always of soupy consistency, were outstanding by any standards in the world.

On my first visit I missed out on the Hotel Cipriani and stayed instead at the Gritti Palace, a wonderful old palazzo facing the Grand Canal. It was built for Doge Andrea Gritti in the sixteenth century, and turned into a hotel after the war when it became a favourite haunt of Ernest Hemingway (he certainly got about). Nothing was expensive in Venice in those days, and I recall the gondoliers outside the Gritti offering their services at a rate equivalent to $10 for a whole day. Today $10 won't get you ten minutes, but at least the *vaporetti*, or public water taxis, are a very efficient and inexpensive way of getting around this beautiful city.

I didn't meet Giuseppe Cipriani until a few years later, but when I did get to know him I found him a most engaging and fascinating man, and because his story became intertwined with mine, it is worth relating a little bit of it here. He came from a poor family in Verona, the son of a bricklayer, was brought up in Germany and immediately after World War I, aged eighteen, he started work as a waiter in France, Belgium, Palermo and finally Venice, where he got a job at the Hotel Monaco, just a few yards from the old rope warehouse that he would later convert into Harry's Bar.

In those days all the successful bars were in the plush hotels: the Europa, the Bauer or the Grand (the Gritti hadn't yet opened). So he hit on the idea of creating his own elegant bar to cater for well-off Venetians and visiting European aristocrats, where customers didn't have to go through imposing lobbies and past intimidating porters. But he had no money – which is where young Harry Pickering enters the picture.

Harry was a sad young man from Boston, taken to Venice by a rich aunt in the hope of curing his incipient alcoholism. This he did by spending entire days at the bar of the Europa, where the peripatetic Giuseppe had moved, downing large quantities of alcohol with his equally hard-drinking aunt and her companion (there was also a dog but history doesn't record if it drank too). Harry and the aunt fell out, she and the dog went home, and Harry was left stranded and penniless. It was probably the best thing that ever happened to him: he quit drinking, borrowed 10,000 lire from his obliging barman Giuseppe, and took off. This was just before the Great Crash of 1929 and Giuseppe lost hope of ever seeing his money again.

A couple of years later Harry suddenly reappeared, repaid his 10,000 lire and, according to Harry's own account, added another 30,000 (some versions say 40,000) 'so that you can open a bar of your own for high society. I think they'll call it Harry's bar. Not a bad name.'

Harry's Bar duly opened in the old rope works in May 1931 and was immediately swamped by visiting aristocrats, celebrities and just ordinary drinkers. Giuseppe later remarked that if all the people who told him they visited it on opening day were actually there, they would

CHEMINS DE FER PARIS-LYON-MEDITERRANÉE
SIMPLON-ORIENT-EXPRESS

LONDRES
PARIS
DIJON
BORDEAUX   LAUSANNE   TRIESTE   BELGRADE   BUCAREST
         LYON   VENISE   NISCH   SOFIA
              MILAN   SALONIQUE
              TURIN   CONSTANTINOPLE
                                                          ATHÈNES

ONDRES-PARIS-BUCAREST-ATHÈNES-CONSTANTINOPL

(*Previous page*) A poster from the 1920s showing the route of the original Simplon-Orient-Express. (*Above*) An advertisement for a French musical comedy reflecting the popular view of what passengers got up to on the Orient-Express train. Both images © Compagnie International des Wagon-Lits

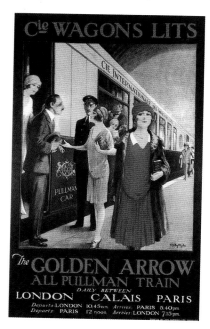

Fathers of the Orient-Express: Georges Nagelmackers, founder of the Wagons-Lits Company which inaugurated the Orient-Express in 1883; and George Mortimer Pullman, (*below*) the American who built the first luxury sleeping car in 1864. © Compagnie International des Wagon-Lits

Wagons-Lits' Golden Arrow all-Pullman service from London started in 1926 and linked up with the Orient-Express in Paris. © Compagnie International des Wagon-Lits

The Monte Carlo auction in October 1977 which started it all: Gerard Gallet is seated to my right (*in glasses*). Peter Wilson of Sotheby's is in front of the microphone. Mostly journalists packed the station. (*Below*) Sir William McAlpine who greatly assisted the venture; and one of the Lalique glass panels purchased at the auction.

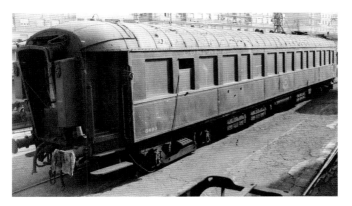

We found original cars in all sorts of strange places: a Wagons-Lits car in a dreadful state which we tracked down in Spain (*left*); General de Gaulle's private car (*centre*) was spirited out of France to form part of the British Pullman train – and got stuck under a bridge; and (*bottom*) a Brighton Belle car in the English garden of a railway enthusiast.

Refurbishing the British Pullman (*above left*) to its finished state (*above right*). A carpenter makes a new window to accommodate the original glass (*centre left*) while the exquisite Art Deco marquetry panels are French polished. (*Bottom left and right*) Marquetry medallions for the Pullmans, and (*centre*) one of the mosaic floors in the lavatories.

At long last the inaugural trip starts on 25 May 1982 from Victoria Station. Shirley is on my right and Colin Bather, who headed the leisure division of Sea Containers, is on my left (with glasses).

The British Pullman arrives at Folkestone Harbour where passengers transferred to the Boulogne ferry.

We sent a restaurant car and a sleeping car to the Hotel Cipriani in Venice, and invited 300 Venetians to inspect them. More than 500 people turned up.

The 1974 film *Murder on the Orient Express* had a star-studded cast. Here Albert Finney (Hercule Poirot) examines Richard Widmark's murdered body.
© Thorn-EMI Films
Ltd., London

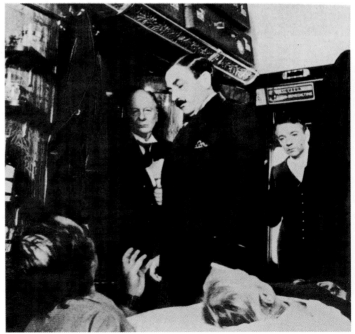

The Venice Simplon-Orient-Express glides through spectacular Alpine scenery on its way to Venice.

Chef Christian Bodiguel displaying some of the dishes from his kitchen aboard the train while passengers (*right*) are serenaded in the bar car.

Claude Ginella has been the general manager of the Venice Simplon-Orient-Express since the start.

Billy Hamilton, responsible for promoting the train and the company, shown here on an excursion to Vienna with Anne, Duchess of Norfolk.

Helena Bonham Carter, who accompanied her mother Elena on a trip to Venice with us.

The Inn at Perry Cabin in St. Michaels, Maryland (*top*), now an Orient-Express Hotels property, near where my first Sherwood ancestor Francis established his tobacco farm in 1645.

(*Above*) Crook'd Intention, in St. Michaels, the house built by Francis Sherwood in about 1670 for his son Hugh. The wing to the right is a later addition; and (*right*) my great-grandfather in Ewing, Kentucky built a new house in the late nineteenth century. He was a banker and railroadman.

(*Top left*) George Roland Balph, my mother's father who was president of the Citizen's Bank in New Castle, Pennsylvania where I was born; and my paternal grandparents (*top centre*), Catherine and Robert Hildreth Sherwood, who lived and died in Northern Kentucky. My aunt Henrietta (*right*) on her graduation day from the University of Kentucky. She married Admiral William A. Glassford immediately after the War. (*Below*) My parents, Florence and William Earl Sherwood, in the 1920s.

About 1943

My father, Bill, during the
Pacific War.

Me with my first bicycle.

(*Left*) As a teenager in California where I first developed
my lifelong interest in photography and the cinema.
(*Bottom*) A newspaper clipping from 1937 when my
father took me (*far left*) and some friends to the circus
in Louisville, Kentucky.

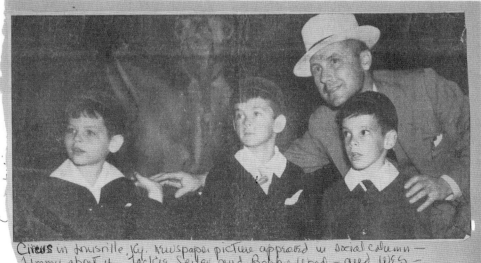

Circus in Louisville, Ky. newspaper picture appeared in social column —
Jimmy, about 4, Jackie Seiler and Bobby Wood — and WES —

Sloppy Joe's in Havana as a midshipman in 1954. I discovered the frozen daiquiri there.

Admiral Glassford who guided me towards the U.S. Navy.

Graduating from Yale in June 1955 before going to sea.

The Hong Kong Club where I sheltered very comfortably from a typhoon.

Ensign James B. Sherwood, the most junior officer in the U.S. Navy; and (*below*) my first ship, the *U.S.S. Montrose*, in Manila Harbour in 1956.

The Imperial Hotel in Tokyo designed by Frank Lloyd Wright where I often spent weekends in 1957.

By 1957, now looking more serious, I had been promoted to Lieutenant (j.g.). In the mid-1950s many of Hong Kong's residents lived in crowded sampan colonies (*right*).

The 'Pen', Hong Kong's most glamorous hotel was (and is) The Peninsula in Kowloon, controlled by Michael Kadoorie's H.K. & Shanghai Hotels. We went to their elegant Gaddi's Restaurant for dinner dances. Today the waterfront is covered with high-rise buildings.

Manila Harbour was still choked with sunken Japanese vessels in 1957 when I was based there.

have overflowed all the way to St. Mark's Square. He kept a visitors' book for a few years and in it are the names of Arturo Toscanini, Guglielmo Marconi, Somerset Maugham, Noël Coward, Charlie Chaplin, Barbara Hutton, Orson Welles and too many others to list. Peggy Guggenheim and her set were big customers. When the Germans occupied Venice in the war, Giuseppe had a hard time, but he loved to tell the story of being summoned by the American commander after the city was liberated in April 1945. 'Cipriani, you are not a good Italian – you have not yet reopened Harry's Bar!'

His most famous customer was of course the ubiquitous Hemingway who installed himself at a corner table in the winter of 1949–50 and became the only client Giuseppe ever drank with, breaking his own rigid rule. Hemingway didn't like to drink alone. He was working on his latest novel, *Across the River and Into the Trees*, which mentions Harry's Bar a number of times, turning it forever into a 'must visit' for every American tourist and student of literature. Giuseppe, however, always maintained it was he who made Hemingway's reputation rather than the other way around: 'They gave him the Nobel Prize *afterwards*, not *before!*' Out of interest I recently looked up the reviews of the book when it came out, and many of them were scathing. But here is the great Tennessee Williams reviewing it in the *New York Times*:

> I could not go to Venice, now, without hearing the haunted cadences of Hemingway's new novel. It is the saddest novel in the world about the saddest city, and when I say I think it is the best and most honest work that Hemingway has done, you may think me crazy. It will probably be a popular book. The critics may treat it pretty roughly. But its hauntingly tired cadences are the direct speech of a man's heart who is speaking that directly for the first time, and that makes it, for me, the finest thing Hemingway has done.

But Giuseppe's greatest contribution to Venice was creating the Hotel Cipriani, which is where I come into the story. Among the glitzy crowd who frequented Harry's Bar in the 1950s were the three daughters of the Earl of Iveagh, the head of the Guinness brewing and banking family, all very grand ladies: Viscountess (Patricia) Boyd, Lady Honor Channon and, the youngest of the family of five, Princess Brigid of Prussia. The Guinness family had been fixtures in Venice ever since Rupert Guinness, the second earl, bought a villa in Asolo, not far from Venice, allegedly to house his mistress who was a famous opera singer.

In 1956 Giuseppe, by then Commendatore Cipriani, persuaded the Guinness sisters to back the project he had been dreaming about for years: a new hotel which would provide lodging for his clients and other rich guests, and which he reckoned Venice, rapidly recovering from the war, sorely needed. He already had a site in mind: an old boatyard on a three-acre site on the island of Giudecca, directly across the lagoon from St. Mark's Square, well away from the madding crowds of Venice in the summer. The Guinness family agreed to put up the money on the condition that he name it after himself. Giuseppe got a stake, and the Hotel Cipriani opened in 1958 to great acclaim, offering simple but superb food and high quality service. Each of the Guinness girls designed suites for themselves: the Lady Honor, Lady Patricia, and Lady Brigid Suites, which are still there (although they have been redecorated since). I am told that a room cost $10 a night in those days; today it is likely to cost $1,000.

Giuseppe wanted to go a step further and offer something no other hotel in Venice could: a decent swimming pool. A few years after the hotel opened, he convinced the Guinness girls to build one on what had been the adjacent boatyard slipway, but they were by now cautious of his grandiose ideas and insisted on having the drawings prepared by a London architect. When they returned to Venice the next summer they looked in astonishment at the huge pool Giuseppe proudly showed them. 'But it's much bigger than we agreed to,' one of them remarked. 'It is exactly in accordance with your architect's drawings, 25 by 50 metres,' replied Giuseppe disingenuously. 'Oh,' the Guinnesses said, 'we thought the measurements were 25 by 50 *feet*.'

He had done it deliberately of course, building a pool more than ten times the size the architect had designed, probably at ten times the cost. But it was an inspired thing to do. The Guinnesses were not stingy but they would never have agreed to such a giant undertaking, and Giuseppe was quick to take advantage of a deliberate 'lost-in-translation' episode – and he was right. The pool has added greatly to the attractions of the Hotel Cipriani and is much appreciated by guests and locals alike. There will never be another like it in the historic centre of Venice.

The Hotel Cipriani became increasingly popular in the 1960s and 1970s, especially after the pool was built. Giuseppe Cipriani managed the hotel as well as Harry's Bar until he was too old to continue (he was born in 1900), at which point he sold his 20 per cent interest in the hotel to the Guinnesses and brought in his son, Arrigo (Harry in Italian) Cipriani, to manage Harry's Bar. The Guinnesses replaced him with a new general manager, and when I arrived on the scene the man in charge was Enzo Cecconi, who would later become a well-known restaurateur.

By then the boom times had gone, and the great Italian 'economic miracle' was over. It had transformed the country from a poor, agricultural nation with mass emigration into one of the world's industrialized powers (the sixth biggest economy in the world). The Italian economy had grown at 8 per cent a year through the 1960s and into the 1970s, but that came to an abrupt halt with the oil crisis in 1973 which hit Italy, totally dependent on imported oil and gas, particularly hard. There was a financial crisis, the lira fell through the floor, and the authorities – such as they were – were forced to bring in exchange controls and higher taxes. For several years the country was basically ungoverned, with a breakdown of the political system and an attempted coup by a group of neo-Fascists, which was only narrowly foiled, followed soon after by an attempt by the Communists to seize power from the hapless Christian Democrats. The anarchist Red Brigade and the neo-Fascists competed to carry out appalling acts of terrorism and atrocity, and for several years kidnappings, murders, assassinations, riots, bombings and mass arrests were the order of the day. It culminated in the kidnapping and murder of the former Prime Minister Aldo Moro by the Red Brigade and, in 1980, the bomb at Bologna Central Station which killed eighty-five people and wounded

200. In short, Italy was not a great place for tourists, and Americans in particular chose more peaceful countries for their holidays.

Although Venice was generally regarded as the safest city in Italy, the Hotel Cipriani couldn't escape the downturn, and by the mid-1970s it was losing money. The Guinness sisters, alarmed at what was happening across the nation, got cold feet and decided to sell while they could, quietly putting the hotel on the market. Shirley and I had become frequent visitors, and I had held a Sea Containers management conference there, so we had got to know Enzo Cecconi fairly well. I think I may even have mentioned to him, almost as a throwaway line, that the hotel would be a good buy for somebody in its depressed state and that I might be interested.

One day in 1976 I got an urgent call from Cecconi to tell me that Arrigo Cipriani, son of Giuseppe, was about to buy the Cipriani. Arrigo and Cecconi apparently did not get on, and he told me they'd had a row the previous evening when Arrigo informed him that the first thing he was going to do when he took over was to fire him. The gist of the phone call was to propose that I should buy the hotel to save Cecconi's job.

It so happened that he got me at a good moment. Sea Containers had shrugged off the recession of the mid-1970s and in 1976 chalked up its best net profit yet, $15.1 million, and its share price had risen from $7 to $25 in the year. The company, which I had started just twelve years before in Paris, was now valued at $95 million, but I could see trouble looming over the horizon in the shape of the big international companies, with much greater resources than ours, moving into the marine container leasing industry which up to that stage we pretty much had to ourselves. Despite its success, Sea Containers was always heavily borrowed as it needed to raise more and more capital to pay for expansion, and I always worried, even when things were booming, that we were very vulnerable to high interest rates, an economic downturn or to serious competition which would eat into our margins – or even all three, which is what we got several years later.

I had been dwelling on this for some time. We had discussed it at our board meetings and strategy sessions – including the one in the

Hotel Cipriani – and I had concluded that it would be prudent to diversify. I had identified hotels as a business which could be managed side by side with marine containers and would not compete with our customers, who were the big ocean carriers, but my view was by no means unanimous and there were directors on the board who argued we should stick to the business we were doing so well in.

Sea Containers by then had offices and agents in eighty countries, all of which I had personally visited, always staying in the best hotels, so I felt I knew something about the business, if only as a customer. I had a pretty good idea where luxury hotels were needed, where existing properties could be upgraded and where profitable acquisitions might be made. I rated Lagos, Nigeria, as the city in most need of a luxury hotel when the water in my room consisted of a pail left outside the door in the morning (I quickly moved to our agent's compound in Apapa, the port of Lagos).

I had to move very fast to get the Hotel Cipriani out of Arrigo's clutches, far faster than a big public company like Sea Containers could do, so I decided to do the deal myself and buy the hotel as a personal investment. The next day, at Cecconi's prompting, I called Colin Bather, an impressive multilingual Englishman who lived in Venice and ran the Guinness sisters' European investments from an office in the hotel. Bather confirmed the hotel was for sale and put me in touch with the Guinness family office in London's St. James's, which was handling it. The Guinnesses were asking £1 million for the hotel but they also wanted to sell the Villa Cipriani in Asolo (the home of the opera singer) as part of the deal. I asked for the accounts of both properties and Shirley and I visited the sleepy village of Asolo, which is about an hour's drive north-west of Venice, not far from the studio and home of the great classic sculptor Canova. The Villa Cipriani had no pool, nor did it seem likely they could obtain permission for one, and with Venice so close by, Asolo was not a compelling location for a luxury hotel. So I informed the Guinnesses that I would not be interested in Asolo but was prepared to make an offer for the Hotel Cipriani in Venice.

Negotiating in Italy is an art form. Italians always ask for outrageous prices so one must not take the first price at face value. I countered their £1 million with an offer of £800,000 and a few days later the Guinnesses accepted. Lawyers were instructed to start drawing up papers. Then word of my offer reached Arrigo Cipriani and I got a call from the Guinnesses to say Arrigo had appeared in St. James's and presented a bank draft for £900,000 – which they had a mind to accept. However, the Guinnesses did give me the chance to match Arrigo's offer, indicating that if I did, they would definitely sell to me. After consultation with my lawyers, we agreed to convene a meeting consisting of me, the Guinness executive and lawyers from both sides. I reluctantly increased my price to match Arrigo's £900,000, the Guinnesses once more accepted, and the lawyers were instructed to get on with the documentation so that an early closing could take place. But Arrigo wasn't finished yet. In a last-ditch attempt to gain control of the Cipriani, he appeared again in the St. James's offices, this time (I was told) clutching an attaché case containing £100,000 in cash, bringing his offer to £1 million. Again, I wonder if the Guinness family might have gone for it, or at least forced me to match it, but their lawyers had attended the meeting at which my £900,000 offer had been unconditionally accepted. No lawyer wants to be in the invidious position of having to testify against his own client, which the Guinness lawyers would have to do were I to challenge the family in court (which I had every intention of doing), and they insisted that my offer go through.

So I had acquired my first hotel, the legendary Hotel Cipriani in my favourite city of Venice, and my mind was already buzzing with plans for what I might do with it. In the end I did the obvious thing: I sold it to Sea Containers at the same price I paid for it. It is a decision I often regretted afterwards, as I was under no obligation to and I felt even at the time I should keep it as my personal investment. But I was wary of suggestions I might have a conflict of interest, and at the time I felt it was the right thing to do. When my board agreed – some of them, notably my old colleague Jim Hurlock, rather reluctantly – to buy the hotel, I insisted as part of the deal that I be allowed to buy my own apartment in the hotel, and be given an option to buy the hotel at appraised value should the ownership of Sea Containers (later Orient-Express Hotels) ever change hands, or to match an offer if the hotel was put up for sale. Sea Containers took possession a few months later. I asked Colin Bather to join us and take charge of the new Sea Containers hotel division, and he immediately set about making changes at the Cipriani to increase profitability.

In the meantime Enzo Cecconi, the *casus belli* of the whole affair, decided to leave the Cipriani and set up his own restaurants in London and Paris, although we remained friends. Unlike most people who work in Venice, Enzo is actually from an old Venetian family and met his American wife, Sarah Coleman, at the Hotel Cipriani where her family were frequent visitors. To say they were an unusual family would not do them justice: Sarah's mother was from San Francisco and had been married three times, once to William Willard Crocker, chairman of Crocker Bank, and the third time to Alexander Montagu, the 10th Duke of Manchester, which made her a duchess. Duke, Duchess and their two daughters frequented the Hotel Cipriani and Shirley and I sometimes joined them for dinner. The Duke was a delightful if somewhat retiring figure who had left Britain to live in Kenya after World War II, but the Duchess had acquired a beautiful apartment in Casanova's old palace behind the Hotel Cipriani, with extraordinary views across to the Piazza San Marco where she created a superb collection of furniture and old master paintings. Orient-Express eventually bought half the palace from her.

As for her son-in-law Enzo Cecconi, after he left the Hotel Cipriani his new restaurants in London and Paris became big successes. I found a replacement who was to prove his weight in gold: Dr. Natale Rusconi had managed the Grand Hotel in Rome and the Gritti Palace in Venice and had also served as a senior executive of the exclusive CIGA Group (now owned by Starwood). He made an immediate impact on the Cipriani when he took over in 1977 and he stayed for the next thirty years. His first task was to turn around the losses, which he did remarkably quickly, and by the time he retired in 2007 the hotel achieved record profits of $14 million. Its value that year was many times the £900,000 I paid for it in 1976.

Of course, over those thirty years the company invested substantial amounts into the property, and new rooms were added in every location possible. In Venice in particular, and Italy in general, it is almost impossible to add cubic volume in a historic city. Smaller rooms were combined to make larger ones or suites and adjacent buildings were acquired and converted into rooms. The old 'Granaries of the Republic' in front of the Piazza San Marco on the tip of Giudecca, once used for storing wheat and corn for times of war in Venice, were purchased in 1990 and carefully converted into banqueting and conference space, which has proved an important addition to the hotel.

The back of the property, on the Zitelle quay, has to have one of the best views in the world: the campanile and cathedral in the Piazza San Marco, the entrance of the Grand Canal with its Custom House and the lagoon island of San Giorgio Maggiore with its striking sixteenth-century Palladian church. I thought this would be the ideal location for a restaurant, but planning laws were very strict in Venice and a new building was out of the question. Moorings, however, were permitted, and we designed a barge which could be moored against the quay, providing a platform on which we could construct our restaurant. This got us around the planning restrictions, but we hadn't reckoned on the fast current and the wash of passing ships, which caused the barge to wobble precariously and diners to feel queasy. Fortunately guests could also sit at tables on the quayside, so all was not lost and after two years of making do Rusconi was able to obtain a permit to build a permanent platform on which we built a fixed restaurant. We called it Cips (pronounced 'Chips') because the New York crowd who come every summer have developed the slang words 'the Cip' ('the Chip') to describe the hotel. It has proved a great success.

The Cipriani only has ninety-five rooms, but many of them are suites, and the hotel has become almost a club. Some 40 per cent of the guests are repeat visitors who have been coming year in and year out (some from long before I ever became involved), and many others are passengers on the Venice Simplon-Orient-Express who are given discounts at the hotel if they travel on the train as part of the same trip. The food, in the best tradition of Giuseppe Cipriani, is so good that many guests only dine in the hotel, one night in the main restaurant and the next at Cips.

My one big regret about the whole Cipriani experience is that I was never able to form an alliance with the Cipriani family, which would have benefited both of us. Giuseppe was great, and continued to visit the hotel years after we took over, greeting old customers, training new staff and generally behaving as if he still owned the place. His behaviour was faultless. Not so Arrigo who, from the day I bought the hotel, waged a war against me which went on for decades and which I found very personal and unpleasant at times. A low point was when he published a book branding me a 'hamburger-eating Texan', and accusing Natale Rusconi, one of the most accomplished hotel managers of my lifetime, of providing 'acid food'. I am not Texan and rarely eat hamburgers, and was irritated at the time but was prevailed upon, in the interests of peace and harmony, to let his frivolous allegations die a natural death – which unfortunately they never did. Rusconi had much greater cause for complaint: under his management the Hotel Cipriani appeared at, or very near, the top of every annual hotel ratings of luxury resort hotels throughout the world. You can't do better than that.

We weren't the only people Arrigo had issues with – there were some family disputes too. On the island of Torcello in the Venetian lagoon, where the city of Venice first began, old Giuseppe owned a small inn called Locanda Cipriani. It is basically a restaurant with a couple of rooms above, and when Hemingway was drinking heavily, Giuseppe installed him in the Locanda on a strict alcohol ration. The Locanda was inherited by Arrigo's sister when Giuseppe died and shortly thereafter a dispute broke out over the use of the family name. A similar sort of dispute subsequently developed between Arrigo and Orient-Express Hotels.

At the time of the Hotel Cipriani purchase we assumed the Cipriani family would continue to operate under the Harry's Bar and Locanda Cipriani names, or any other brand they liked, as long as there was no confusion with the Hotel Cipriani brand. We registered the name in Italy and the European Union. Deprived of the Cipriani name, Arrigo went ahead with other plans which we felt traded on the brand. In 1985 he decided to create a Harry's Bar-style restaurant in New York. He called it Harry Cipriani, which didn't worry us, and we let it pass. The restaurant was in the Sherry-Netherland Hotel at the corner of 59th Street and 5th Avenue, managed by the Forte group, whose founder Charles Forte and his son Rocco had impeccable Italian credentials. Then Arrigo and his son Giuseppe opened a restaurant simply called Cipriani in SoHo and we could no longer ignore it. This was our brand, we had paid for it, were entitled to it and we considered Arrigo was now abusing it.

I pleaded with Arrigo to make his restaurant name more clearly distinctive from the Hotel Cipriani – call it Harry Cipriani, Harry's Bar, Arrigo Cipriani or whatever, anything but just 'Cipriani' which was ours. He refused to make any accommodation, and eventually we had to take him to the Federal Court in Manhattan. The wily old judge, who was in his nineties, one morning called the parties into his office. He said he had carefully read the briefs and based on these documents he thought the probability was that the Ciprianis would lose the action if it came to trial (which was to start the following week) and suggested we settle out of court. I then suggested we sign an agreement, which allowed the Ciprianis to use the name but only in association with other words which would make it clear that there was no connection with the Hotel Cipriani. Arrigo reluctantly agreed and the judge said that we should meet after lunch and sign the agreement.

The lawyers worked through the morning and then lunch, but were unable to agree a wording and when we reassembled we had to inform the judge we still had no agreement. 'I thought that might be the case,' he said, 'so I took the liberty of scribbling an agreement over my lunch and my secretary typed it up. Would the parties like to sign?' Each side would pay their own legal expenses, and I could see Arrigo was not happy, but his lawyers prevailed and he eventually did sign. I was very impressed with this old judge who had saved us all a costly and time-consuming trial, and while the others were still closeted with their lawyers in the next room, I asked him how often trademark cases like this actually went to trial. He said, 'Not one has ever got into my courtroom.' I wish there were more judges like that.

I had hoped that Arrigo would have learned from this, but alas in 2004 he opened a Cipriani on Davies Street, opposite Claridge's, in London. Again we pleaded with him to call it Harry Cipriani but he wouldn't listen, arguing that Cipriani was his family name and he would use it if he wanted to. Our lawyers insisted we had to sue because if we allowed the name to stand it would be a precedent resulting in our loss of protection in the entire European Union. So we went to court and won. This case had an amusing and ironic twist to it. The restaurant, it turned out, was owned by the Cipriani holding company in Luxembourg, which licensed the name to its London subsidiary. When deciding on damages, the judge enquired whether Cipriani London had paid a royalty to the Luxembourg company for the use of the name, and they were forced to admit they had been paying a percentage of sales. Some £8 million had been passed to Luxembourg in this way, so the judge decided that if the Ciprianis felt the name was worth £8 million, then £8 million should be paid to Orient-Express Hotels, plus £1.5 million in legal costs.

The news came as a bombshell to Arrigo, who immediately put Cipriani London into administration, and we were faced with having to pursue our claim against the receiver, a long and arduous task. Fortunately, the Ciprianis found a backer who took the restaurant out of administration, and we were paid £3 million in cash and £6.5 million in promissory notes secured by Harry's Bar in Venice.

In 2009 Arrigo Cipriani, by then in his late seventies, eventually made a long-overdue apology to Natale Rusconi for remarks he made thirty years before. I am still waiting for mine.

I was made the fifteenth honorary citizen of Venice since the formation of the Italian Republic in a grand ceremony in the City Hall in November 1994. My two immediate predecessors were Peggy Guggenheim (I serve on the board of trustees of the Guggenheim Foundation) and ambassador Sir Ashley Clarke, who devoted his life after retiring from government service to Venice in Peril and other institutions responsible for helping to save the art and fabric of the unique city.

CHAPTER SEVEN

GROWTH – IN FITS AND STARTS

As the 1980s opened, Sea Containers still had only the beginnings of a leisure business: a train which was two years away from launch, a hotel in Venice we had bought for less than £1 million and not much else. It was growing fast but, compared to the rest of the Sea Containers group, now a major international concern, it was only a drop in the ocean. To be frank, I didn't have a lot of time to devote to it, as these were big years of expansion for Sea Containers and that occupied my attention night and day. However, I made sure that Shirley and I were in attendance at the Hotel Cipriani in June 1980 when the European heads of government met in Venice and Margaret Thatcher, Giscard d'Estaing and the Dutch Prime Minister all stayed at the hotel. I observed the different styles of the British and French leaders with some interest: the arrival of Margaret Thatcher, whose delegation consisted of Peter Carrington, her Foreign Secretary, Geoffrey Howe, the Chancellor, and Robert Armstrong, her famed Cabinet Secretary, was low key, and she was the only leader who thanked the staff afterwards. She left a nice message in the Golden Book and she later wrote a charming letter to us. Giscard was haughty and arrogant, and immediately insisted that the French flag we were flying, which was the same size as the Dutch and British flags, be replaced with a larger one on the grounds that he was not just the political head of his country, which is what the others were, but also the Head of State. Rusconi, the consummate professional, at first refused but eventually had to give in to pressure from the city and government officials. The

French officials then produced a flag at least three times the size of others. Rusconi had the last laugh, however: he instructed one of the hotel's seamstresses to sew the seams of the French flag together with invisible thread, and when it was duly hoisted, it hung inert in the breeze while the others flapped proudly.

A week later there was an even bigger event when the G7 leaders gathered in Venice for that year's Economic Summit, hosted by the Italian Prime Minister Francesco Cossiga. They were an interesting lot that year: Mrs. Thatcher of course, a year into her premiership, Jimmy Carter, Giscard d'Estaing, Helmut Schmidt, Pierre Trudeau and Roy Jenkins representing the European Community, the first time Europe was given an honorary seat. The Japanese premier, Masayoshi Ōhira, had died just a few days before, so there were six rather than seven leaders.

The venue for the actual meetings was on the island of San Giorgio Maggiore, just a stone's throw away from the hotel and this time the American delegation bagged the Hotel Cipriani for President Carter, and the hotel was thronged with security men and officials. A week before Carter arrived in Venice, the White House telecoms team set up a switchboard in the hotel and we were told that all calls, both incoming and outgoing, would henceforth pass via the White House. This turned out to be a good thing: the Italian phone company was instructed to add new lines into Venice, making international calls, almost impossible at peak times up to then, a great deal easier. Carter refused to use the hotel's launch to take him back and forth, insisting that he travel in the admiral's barge from a U.S. Navy warship, which watched warily over proceedings from its anchorage nearby. The barge's coxswain hadn't a clue how to negotiate the currents of the lagoon, and it took a very long time for Carter to travel the few hundred metres between the hotel and San Giorgio Maggiore, all the time being filmed by the world's TV. It was raining and when Rusconi saw the U.S. Secretary of State, Edmund Muskie, standing in the rain waiting for a launch, he lent him his elegant (everything about Rusconi was elegant) raincoat. 'It was never returned,' he told me sadly.

Thinking back to that summit more than three decades ago, I find it interesting to reflect on how little has changed since then. The main political item on the agenda, astonishingly, was Afghanistan, and I kept the official communiqué issued at the end of the meeting which stated:

> We therefore reaffirm hereby that the military occupation of Afghanistan is unacceptable now and that we are determined not to accept it in the future. It is incompatible with the will of the Afghan people for national independence, as demonstrated by their courageous resistance, and with the security of the states of the region. It undermines the very foundations of peace, both in the region and in the world at large.

Yes, this really was 1980! The great leaders of the Western world, including the U.S. and Britain, were of course referring to the *Soviet* invasion of Afghanistan, but it is astonishing how politicians and statesmen can turn themselves on their heads when it suits them. One has a terrible sense of *déjà vu* when one looks at the other topics so earnestly debated by the world's leading statesmen in Venice that week: 'The central problem that we discussed,' said Cossiga in his concluding press conference, 'was that of energy' (there was another oil crisis that year) and he went on to list the 'specific actions', including nuclear, the leaders had agreed to take in order to make the world less dependent on oil, which were supposed to have a major impact within ten years. Thirty years later they haven't made a bit of difference. The other topics look pretty familiar too: inflation, jobs, particularly for youth, and the gap between rich and poor countries. *Plus ça change...*

On a lighter note, there were always celebrities coming through Venice and when we were in residence, Shirley and I often greeted them in our best proprietorial manner, or offered them a drink on the terrace. When Elizabeth Taylor checked into the Hotel Cipriani in 1993, we invited her to join us for lunch by the pool, and she brought her little white dog called Sugar which she hugged to her legendary bosom. While she was stroking the mutt she suddenly looked at her fingers, and exclaimed: 'Oh, my god, where's my ring?' Shirley said,

'Did you just use the washroom before you arrived?' We sent someone off to the ladies' washroom and she came back a few minutes later holding this huge diamond ring. Taylor put it on her finger remarking: 'The Krupp Diamond, you know. I always wear it in Richard's memory.' It looked far too big to be real.

After she'd gone, we hastily looked up the Krupp Diamond, which turned out to be 33.19 carats, and was Burton's first present to her in 1968 (there were many more later, including the 69-carat Taylor-Burton stone). He paid $375,000 for it, the highest price ever paid for a diamond up to that point. We thought it might have been a copy, but it wasn't – she did always wear it, except of course when she casually abandoned it in the ladies' room of the Hotel Cipriani. That same ring fetched $8.8 million when it was auctioned, along with all the other Taylor jewellery, at Christie's in New York in December 2011.

We had met Elizabeth several times before in England. Her best friend from her schooldays was Lady Sheran Hornby who lived a mile away from us in the country, and Sheran and her husband Simon invited us to dine with Elizabeth on a number of occasions. I was always impressed by how informed she was and by her interest in politics and world affairs.

☞

Since buying the Hotel Cipriani in 1976, and the train a year later, I hadn't really made much progress in adding to our hotel portfolio until, one day in early 1980, I was skiing with Shirley and the boys in Colorado at the Lodge at Vail where we always stayed. The owners approached me to say they wanted to sell and because I knew the place so well and admired its location (right in the centre of the village, at the number one ski lift) I was immediately interested. The Lodge then had 417 rooms, mostly condominiums owned by individuals, which were rented out when the owners were not in residence – which was most of the time. The Lodge managed the process and provided other services, taking a management fee, which was how it made its profits. In December 1980 it became the Sea Containers leisure division's second acquisition, nicely in time for the peak ski season, when it made all its profits.

We had owned the Lodge for a few years when a far bigger deal came along. In those days the main Vail ski resort was owned by the wealthy Bass family from Dallas, Texas, and when they put it on the market we offered to buy it. The business wasn't very profitable but it owned large tracts of land in the mountains around Vail, and we negotiated a price of $50 million, steep for Sea Containers at the time, but we considered it good value in view of the potential. I sent a lawyer to Texas to draw up the agreement and I planned to fly out myself for the actual signing. The days passed, the lawyer said he was being ignored, and we began to feel something was wrong. Then it was announced that the business had been sold for $55 million overnight without us even getting the chance to match the offer.

The buyer was George Gillett, one of the more extraordinary dealmakers even by the standards of the crazy deals which were going down in the mid-1980s. From the most modest beginnings, he had built a billion-dollar business based on the unlikely combination of meatpacking and television stations, his acquisitions financed by the junk bonds of Michael Milken. Now he was adding ski resorts to his bizarre portfolio. As *Time* magazine described it, 'Gillett, a Wisconsin boy, loved to ski, and he loved to ski at Vail, a powdery paradise in the Colorado Rockies. So he bought the joint in 1985.'

I should have learned a valuable lesson from this abortive deal, which is that when negotiating a purchase, particularly in the U.S., one should always obtain an exclusivity period so that 'gazumping' is not possible. But, as an aside, I must confess to having made the same mistake again some years later when I was trying to buy the Carlyle Hotel in New York City. I discovered that our offer, which had only been verbally accepted, had been 'shopped' and the hotel was sold for a few million more to Wolff Maritz, a Los Angeles firm which invests in hotels. I would have liked to have owned the Carlyle, a great hotel, and it would have given us the prestige New York hotel I have always craved.

In the case of Mr. Gillett, the situation unravelled very suddenly in

1991 when he overpaid for yet another television station, the interest rates on his junk bonds spiked to 17 per cent, and when the notes came due, as he said later, 'we were dead'. But he did well with Vail. When he stole it from under my nose, profits were $5 million. When his company went belly-up six years later, they were $45 million. It was still not enough to save him, but it was a big lost opportunity for me. One learns the hard way – or maybe, in my case, you don't learn at all.

I still had the Lodge at Vail, which was turning out to be something short of a home run. It was enormously profitable in the ski season (Vail even today has the best ski trails in the world, set in groves of aspen), but we gave much of the profit back in the summer when there were too many beds on offer and prices were a fraction of the winter season. Eventually we decided the answer was to acquire more land around the Lodge, which we could develop to give us critical mass. We did a deal with the U.S. Forest Service, which administered the mountain land in Colorado, whereby we would swap a parcel of our forest land in return for a lesser acreage of their land at Vail. This caused uproar in the village, with residents loudly protesting that if we could swap land, then others could too, and the village would be overrun by developers in no time. We went to court, won, the village appealed, then we couldn't get a decision on the appeal, and eventually we went to Washington where, after two years and hefty legal costs, we got an order forcing the Denver judge to act. But it was not over yet. We had to close the land swap before the village again appealed the verdict, so we stationed lawyers at the Denver Federal Court and the moment the decision was handed down we swapped the land. Fifteen minutes later the village lawyers filed another appeal, but they were too late.

By this stage Mr. Gillett's company had run into serious financial problems and the Vail resort was acquired by Apollo Advisors, which bought up Gillett's debt at a deep discount and effectively got it for nothing. Vail Resorts, as the business is now called, approached us in the early 1990s to buy the Lodge because they wanted to expand their ski facilities on the land we had acquired in the swap, and to build new chalets. The price they offered was too good to refuse so we sold out, although as a family we still go to Vail every Easter for the fine skiing. It had been a frustrating but educational episode, where we eventually came out well ahead, but missed out on the big prize.

Looking back on the first half of the 1980s, I see them now as a steep learning curve in what was a new business for me. I was feeling my way into a highly competitive and crowded market, missing out on opportunities because we were not big enough to be on the radar, or simply being outbid for hotels which were worth more to someone else than they were to us. Mostly we were able to extricate ourselves from situations at a profit, but building the group of luxury hotels I had set my mind on was proving more difficult than I thought – with many a false step along the way.

In March 1983 we acquired five of the British Transport hotels, which were being privatized by British Rail. These properties had been built by the railways in the dim past when they were all privately owned, road transport was slow and passengers were encouraged to travel by rail for their holidays – and stay in the railway hotels. They were all very grand places but totally out of date for the modern traveller who no longer travelled much by train, and in the new fervour for selling off state assets in the Thatcher era, they were put up for sale.

The jewel in the crown was the Gleneagles Hotel, near Auchterarder on the east coast of Scotland, which was built by the former Caledonian Railway Company in 1924 with its own railway station and golf course. Golf and grouse shooting at Gleneagles had become part of the British social season, along with tennis at Wimbledon, cricket at Lord's, yachting at Cowes and polo at Deauville. We lost it to another investor but we bought five other hotels, including the golfing resort of Turnberry on the west coast of Scotland, an hour's drive south of Glasgow. It had 136 rooms and two championship links golf courses, and had staged the Open, which many golfers regard as the premier golf tournament in the world, in 1977. It's a beautiful place with sweeping views down to the sea and out to Ailsa Craig, a famous island landmark a few miles offshore. We acquired the property for £3.5 million and set about refurbishing it, a process we never completed.

In many ways the issues we had with Turnberry were similar to those in Vail: it was a very seasonal market, and the profit you made in the summer was given back in the bleak winter months. The prevailing weather in Scotland comes in from the west, often pounding this part of the coast for days on end, while Gleneagles is near the east coast and has a much more benign climate. By mid-October all the golfers disappear, not to be seen again until Easter or even later. The costs of keeping the hotel open in the winter far exceeded the revenue, and dragged the whole operation into losses.

The high point of our brief ownership was the Open in 1986. All the big names were there, including Jack Nicklaus and Gary Player, and it was won by Greg Norman. But we learned yet another lesson here: the organizers make all the profit from these events, and the hotel just about broke even, although it did benefit from the publicity. Ever since then, Orient-Express Hotels has always been cautious about making deals with event organizers who leave you with little or no margin. When we were approached by a Japanese company to sell Turnberry at a large profit, I agreed with some relief, and we did retain a management contract. The other hotels didn't fare much better. They all needed significant capital investment and, after our experience at Turnberry, we couldn't see how we could make a decent return. Again we sold at the first opportunity.

The Windermere Island Club in Eleuthera in the Bahamas, which we acquired in November 1984 for a small sum, wasn't a great success either. Again, although it couldn't have been more different to Turnberry, it was a stunning place and the pink sand was so beautiful that I used to carry a bottle of it around with me to compare with sand on other beaches. We bought it as an experiment, and although it proved a disaster, I consider the investment a learning exercise that aided me enormously when it came to acquiring other beach resort properties.

The sand turned out to be one of the few good points about the resort. First, there was the question of getting there: there was no dependable air service, no night-flying and the local unions required guests to take an ancient taxi at a cost of $100, even though the hotel was only minutes from the airport. Then there was the weather: the Bahamas is often cold and windy in the key months of January and February, and sun-seekers went elsewhere. We also had problems with the staff, work permits and an accountant who charged for the cost of lobsters but photocopied the same invoice from the supplier over and over. This was during the era of the Pindling government, when drug smuggling was rife and crime was everywhere. After a few years we had had enough and closed the club. It took several years to get rid of it.

Oddly enough in July 1984, as part of the much bigger acquisition of the Sealink Ferries company, we acquired an asset with the same name as the club in Eleuthera, the Windermere Iron Steamboat Company. The Lake District is a quintessentially English place, once home of the poet William Wordsworth, and visitors go there in the spring, summer and autumn to walk and ride the ferries that criss-cross Lake Windermere. The oldest of the ferries was a splendid antique relic called *The Tern* and we thought we might use her and her sisters to access a new hotel we would build on the south side of the lake. But the planners were determined that no new construction would be allowed – and they were probably right. We managed to sell the fleet of ferries at a decent profit some years later.

I put these setbacks down to experience, and tried to profit from them. The lessons of Eleuthera I have never forgotten. They were: firstly, only develop beach resorts which have guaranteed warm sun in winter; secondly, a hotel or resort must have easy access; and thirdly, keep a tight control on the staff. I would put these into practice later when we acquired the La Samanna resort in St. Martin, only fifteen minutes from the second biggest airport in the Caribbean, and Maroma on Mexico's Yucatan peninsula, an hour's drive south of Cancun, which has many international flights a day and lots of warm sunshine even in mid-winter. They have both been great investments.

———

CHAPTER EIGHT

HARRY'S BAR

I first met Mark Birley over lunch in 1977, a year after I bought the Hotel Cipriani. He was a very tall (nearly 6 feet 6 inches), very elegant Old Etonian, exquisitely turned out, speaking with that drawing-room drawl the English upper classes of his generation liked to cultivate. 'A towering, pampered monument to English style,' someone once called him, and it's how I remember him from that first meeting.

At the time he was best known as the founder of the legendary Annabel's, then at the height of its fame as the chicest nightspot in the world. I was a member of Annabel's, like everyone else I knew in London, and of its sister, Mark's Club, which he also owned and where I would propose to Shirley a few months later. I knew something about his background, as most people on the London social scene did, as he was constantly appearing in the gossip columns and society magazines: Eton, Oxford (briefly), then a spell in advertising with J. Walter Thompson, launched Hermès in London, and then converted the basement under the Clermont Club, the casino owned by the even more colourful John Aspinall, into the nightclub where everyone from Frank Sinatra and Aristotle Onassis to the Beatles went. He was equally well-known for marrying the beautiful Lady Annabel Vane-Tempest-Stewart, youngest daughter of the Marquess of Londonderry, and losing her to Aspinall's best friend, Jimmy Goldsmith, in spectacular circumstances. Nothing about him was ordinary.

Billy Hamilton, who I had employed to do the public relations work on the Orient-Express train, introduced us over lunch, and

Mark mentioned he was a frequent visitor to Venice, often stayed at the Hotel Cipriani, loved the food at Harry's Bar and had decided to open a new all-members club in London. He wanted to call it Harry's Bar, he said, and it would feature superb Harry's Bar Venice-style food and fine Italian wines and have a great atmosphere. He had done a deal with the Cipriani family, had the right to use the Harry's Bar name in London and had even located a perfect site for the new club, an old wine shop on South Audley Street, Mayfair, which could be leased and transformed into a club restaurant. Would I be interested in partnering him, even contributing some of the expertise and staff from the Hotel Cipriani to get it off the ground?

Flushed with the success of turning round the Hotel Cipriani I was up for it, responded with enthusiasm and we quickly agreed a deal. Although Mark's other clubs were doing well, he had little cash, so the agreement was that Sea Containers would put up 100 per cent of the money, half of which would be a loan to Mark's company, in return for a 49 per cent stake in the club. Mark would own the majority 51 per cent and we agreed – and this was a critical point, important to both of us at the time, and even more important later – that if either of us ceased to be personally involved with the club, the surviving partner could buy out the other's shares at appraised value. Our initial investment would be £600,000, half loan, half equity – a net £300,000 for us, assuming the club generated enough money for Mark to pay us back. That was the deal, translated into a legally binding document by the lawyers, signed and sealed by Mark and me. I never thought that one day I'd have to rely on it, or that it would be challenged.

It was a joy to watch Mark go to work and I learned a lot from him. He was an artist and perfectionist when it came to décor, with a brilliant sense of what would work, as well as great imagination and exquisite taste. He employed the talented decorator Nina Campbell to assist him and they made an impressively creative and practical team. Those two really did know what they were doing. The ambience of the club today, more than thirty years after opening, is still the same as when they designed it – and it still looks as fresh and undated as it did then, arguably the most elegant of all the elegant clubs Mark created.

He acquired a collection of original Peter Arno cartoons, many of which (the coloured ones) were covers of the *New Yorker* magazine which poked gentle fun at New York society. These lined the Fortuny fabric walls, creating a warm atmosphere very different to the minimalist style which had become the order of the day in New York. He was on top of every detail, down to how the napkins should be folded, selecting the plates, cutlery and even the pepper pots. Every silver pepper pot in Mark's Club was said to be worth $800, the mustard pots cost $1,000 each, and Mark spared no expense at Harry's Bar either. I didn't complain, as I was adopting exactly the same approach to the Orient-Express train then taking shape in the workshops. It was the right thing to do, and no one could do it better than Mark.

Someone remarked that if Mark Birley was not remembered for anything else, he would go down in history as the man who first wrapped a lemon in muslin to prevent the pips spoiling the fish. Just before the launch of the new club he added another little touch which became a talking point around London (I even heard it mentioned in New York) and somehow added to the legend of the new club: he insisted that the menus be written in Italian only, with no English translations, adding a subtle point of difference and culture. There were stories of club members actually learning enough Italian to understand the menu in order to impress their girlfriends over a romantic dinner. I am only sorry to see the new owners now include an English translation, although thank goodness it's only for the luncheon menu.

Mark already had two all-members clubs and an unrivalled address book, and his idea was to invite what he called the London 'A List' to become members with a fixed annual subscription, as he had done at Annabel's and Mark's. These members would pay the same subscription for life, but new members would pay more as they joined later. The original club had seventy-five covers (seats), but within weeks of opening demand was so great that we acquired part of the building next door and expanded to 125 covers. Even so, we had to limit the membership to 3,000 or members couldn't be assured of a table. Business during the London 'season', from the Chelsea Flower Show in late May to the end of Wimbledon in early July, was particularly hectic, with many members coming in from overseas for the Epsom Derby, Ascot or one of the other events on the social calendar. I suggested keeping the club open on Saturday evenings, but Mark vetoed it, remarking that 'our' kind of people usually spent weekends on their country estates and the place would be empty. Mark himself didn't like the country, preferring to create the English country house effect in his clubs and his beautiful London house and garden. He also pointed out that if we only opened Monday–Friday, the same brigade of waiters and cooks would be on duty right through, making it cheaper and more efficient.

There must have been a truce in my relationship with Arrigo Cipriani at this time, because he cooperated with us in setting up the club, and we sourced most of the furniture from his Harry's Bar Venice suppliers. Arrigo even proposed that his sister, Carla Brass, become the manager and we flew her to London to meet Mark and me. Mark met her at the airport, and brought her into town where he showed her to the apartment he had already rented for the new manager. Over dinner, however, she took him aback by advising him that her salary requirements were £150,000 per annum, a huge sum in those days, and the company had to pay for her to go home to Rome every weekend. Mark said she should discuss these issues at lunch with me the next day, but she never showed up and returned to Rome on a morning flight. We never found out why. Mark eventually hired a talented chef from Milan but his food, although imaginative, was quite different from Harry's Bar Venice food – although I did manage to persuade him to include some of my Venetian favourites on the menu. That was the extent of my contribution to the food at Harry's Bar – other than to eat a lot of it – but I'm delighted to say those dishes are still on the menu today.

The agreement between us provided for Mark to manage Harry's Bar for a fee of 5 per cent of revenue, which included maintaining the membership roster and all the accounting – cheap at the price. The problem was that although the club was packed and prices were high it couldn't make a profit. Costs seemed to me astronomically high, and after some months of watching the figures dive deeper and deeper into the red while revenues actually went up, I got in touch with my friend Albert Roux, owner of Le Gavroche, London's premier French fine dining restaurant. Albert had started his career as the chef to the distinguished Cazalet family, and he and his brother Michel rose to fame as London began to transform its eating habits from the quite ordinary to the trendy in the 1960s and 1970s. I gave the Harry's Bar accounts to Albert, and he ran his finger expertly down the lines of figures, looking at the percentages, and immediately pronounced that some of the kitchen staff were robbing us blind. It was a common phenomenon, he said, well known in restaurants which were not tightly controlled: the suppliers bribed the staff with free foodstuffs and then marked up their prices to the restaurant. There is a practice in restaurants of small tokens of appreciation to kitchen staff, but in this case it was major fraud. He also pointed out that Mark was spending £40,000 a year on flowers, but when I pointed this out to Mark he simply said flowers were important and they should continue. They did but the kitchen staff was changed, the club became profitable and we never looked back.

Once the kitchen staff had been sorted out the profits began rolling in, quickly allowing Mark to repay his loan, and over the years there were excellent dividend distributions. Mark had other clubs, including Mark's, Bath & Racquets and later George, but Annabel's and Harry's Bar were always his most successful ones financially.

Mark never remarried after Annabel left him, but he loved women and would join us in Venice or when we went skiing with a different lady each time. This sometimes led to tensions, because in Venice he would suddenly abandon his lady companion of the moment and go off in search of *objets d'art* to incorporate into Harry's Bar or one of his other clubs, usually assisted by Lady Romilly McAlpine, wife of Alistair. Shirley often had to console Mark's abandoned ladies and, although we were fond of Mark, we eventually found our trips together too stressful and called a halt.

One of our weekends with Mark in Venice was nearly our last. We were flying back to London on our company plane when, shortly after we took off and were heading north-west over the mountains which surround Venice, the plane was hit by hail stones the size of golf balls. The nose cone was ripped off, the wings were heavily dented and the landing lights were smashed. Fortunately, the key systems were still operational and we limped back to London, very relieved to land. Mark took the incident calmly, but Enzo Cecconi, who was on board, was convinced we were goners. We found a bottle of Scotch on the plane and quickly consumed it.

Harry's Bar became a fixture of the London restaurant scene, inhabited by the great and the good who came for superb Italian food, good wines and the club atmosphere. Everybody knew everybody else, and if they didn't, they introduced themselves. Mark didn't like business transacted over the tables, and waiters were sent to warn members who produced pens and paper to desist. But in fact many deals were conceived and agreed in Harry's Bar, and it was the favourite haunt of captains of industry and City bankers, as well as media people.

In 2005 Mark's health began to deteriorate, and the issue of the option came to the fore. Mark wanted his son Robin and daughter India Jane to inherit his clubs, including his 51 per cent shareholding in Harry's Bar, and brought them into the business, ostensibly to revamp Annabel's which was no longer attracting London's younger crowd. Robin had just achieved some success with his Birley's Sandwiches chain in the City, and India Jane was making a name for herself as a serious artist and decorator. I had no problem with either of them. But I did have a problem of a different kind: the club had become quite valuable, and if we gave up our option there was no assurance that Mark's successor, whether it be Robin or someone else, would maintain it to the required standard. In effect, our option, which was worth quite a lot of money, could become a wasting asset and I needed to protect that. So I thought the answer was for us to buy two per cent of the shares, bringing our stake to 51 per cent, and give Mark's company a new management contract which would be terminable if the club's performance declined.

Mark took exception to this proposal and brought in a publicist called David Wynne-Morgan to mount a campaign against me and my company on the theme of the corporate giant taking advantage of the small private family. I found myself depicted as a heartless American businessman, apparently described by some of my 'Wall Street peers' as 'one of the toughest businessmen in their midst' and 'very fiscally oriented'. The columnist Taki (Theodoracopulos) wrote an offensive article about me in his 'High Life' column in the *The Spectator* (although, as he acknowledged, we had never met). *Vanity Fair* published a seven-page article about the affair under the witty headline 'Wild About Harry's' in its October 2005 issue, which was clearly very sympathetic to the Birleys. I was more flattered than perturbed by it all, and never took it too personally, even when I began getting calls from mutual friends such as Sir Evelyn Rothschild, asking me 'to relent'. I replied that I had never wanted change at Harry's Bar, but change was being forced upon me and I had no choice but to protect my company and shareholders. My board took the view that if we could get a high enough price we should sell our shares. We appointed an appraiser who said our 49 per cent shareholding was worth £10 million and eventually we sold out to Mark's company. It was not a bad return on our original £300,000 investment. All of Mark's clubs were bought by Richard Caring for a reported £100 million shortly before Mark's death.

Since it was first launched in 1979, I have always enjoyed special privileges at Harry's Bar, and Caring has honoured them. He has also upheld Mark's traditions at all his clubs, and the food and service at Harry's Bar is as good as it ever was – so in a way there was a happy ending. I just wish he would take the English translations off the luncheon menu in fond memory of Mark.

CHAPTER NINE

EXPANSION IN ITALY

That day in May 1982, when the Venice Simplon-Orient-Express steamed out of Victoria Station and into history, was a sunny one on the English Channel. The sea was calm and the crossing was smooth. No one got seasick. We had all sorts of celebrities and dignitaries aboard, including Sir Peter Parker, then the chairman of British Rail, on whose tracks we were travelling. Billy Hamilton, our PR supremo, was intent on making sure the trip did not go unnoticed, and had invited a battery of journalists, including Nigel Dempster, the widely read gossip-columnist for the *Daily Mail*, and Eric Newby, one of my favourite travel writers who had a great passion for trains. Michael Demarest of *Time* magazine, another train buff, was also aboard and later gave us a two-page spread which reached 26 million readers.

At Folkestone, we disembarked from the Pullmans and boarded the ferry *Horsa*, where we were serenaded by a Palm Court orchestra, and so to Boulogne and our Orient-Express train to Paris and beyond. We had set off just before noon and by breakfast time the next day we were eating fresh croissants taken aboard at Lausanne, then through the Simplon Tunnel to Milan and after lunch the train pulled into Santa Lucia Station in Venice. The fabled Orient-Express had arrived home, and was back in business. It had taken us nearly five years and $31 million to get here, but as we motored slowly down the Grand Canal it all seemed worthwhile. We crossed the lagoon to our own apartment in the Hotel Cipriani, pleased to be home, but reflecting on a trip which no one who was on the train that day will ever forget.

It had been a flawless first journey, but the early years of the Venice
Simplon-Orient-Express train were not without their problems.
Because of the tight schedule we had to stick to, the route through the
Alps took place largely at night, and the guests complained they could
not enjoy the mountain views. By the time they were awake, the train
was trekking across northern Italy from Milan to Venice, which was
flat and boring. We had also scheduled three round trips a week, and
had done our sums on that basis, but that was proving too demanding
for the staff and maintenance crews.

After a couple of years of this I felt we had to make some changes.
Well before dawn on a freezing morning in January 1984, Shirley,
Billy Hamilton and I set off by train from Venice on a journey into
unknown territory, seeking an alternative route, which would inevitably take longer but would be a good deal more scenic. We were
headed for the Arlberg, with its wonderful ski resorts, via the Brenner
Pass and Innsbruck, but there was no direct route. We had to use five
different trains that day, all of them, amazingly, on time, proving that
Mussolini, credited with making the Italian trains run on time, had
left some legacy. We passed through St. Anton, where I had often
skied in nearby Lech, and on through the Arlberg Tunnel to Zurich.
Although this part of the journey was single track, it was also spectacular, with amazing views out over the Alps and valleys, which we
knew by now was what passengers wanted on their way to Venice. It
had a major disadvantage, however. It was 173 kilometres longer on
slower track, so it would lengthen the journey by several hours. That
meant that three trips a week would have to become two.

In the summer of 1984, we carried out a two-month experiment
and switched the route from the Simplon to the Arlberg and over the
Brenner Pass. It was an immediate success with passengers, but we
had many months of arguing with the railways about time-tabling
before we were able to change on a more permanent basis. By early
1985, the Venice Simplon-Orient-Express no longer used the Simplon
Tunnel. From Paris it went south-east to Basel and Zurich, and then
over the Arlberg into Innsbruck and on over the Brenner to Verona
and finally Venice. This is the route of the train today. The scenery on

the journey through Switzerland, Austria and the Italian Tyrol, which now takes place in daytime, makes up for the fact that we can only operate two round trips a week.

There were other issues which also required attention. We had originally set up our maintenance and warehouse base near Boulogne, which seemed at the time to make sense, but we soon found the French railways were overcharging us, and worst still, the cars were being robbed of contents when the train was out of service, despite having watchmen. We decided to move the base to Venice where the Italian railways offered us an excellent maintenance and storage base near the Venice station. We were worried that the French unions, who had never been very friendly, might vandalize the train if they discovered we were moving out, so we moved our stores and equipment bit by bit so as not to attract attention. Finally, over a single weekend, we pulled out completely, and when the train next arrived in Boulogne we took the precaution of having armed security guards aboard while the turn-around took place. They were never needed.

France, like Italy, had its social issues in those days, and on the way into Gare d'Austerlitz the train followed the track through Communist-controlled suburbs, where youths threw stones at it, breaking windows on several occasions. After we had some gunshots through the windows, we decided it was time to find a different route and we switched to the Gare de l'Est where the tracks ran through tunnels and cuttings which were more secure. We've not had trouble since.

Our move to Venice went smoothly and Maurizio Saccani, who now manages all the company's Italian hotels, skilfully organized the maintenance and warehouse facility with support from the Hotel Cipriani. Claude Ginella, a Swiss hotelier, took charge of the continental train in 1981 and the highly talented chef Christian Bodiguel joined in 1985. Together they provide a level of service and cuisine to three-Michelin-star standard. Colin Bather, who headed the company's leisure division, had overall responsibility for the train, but he died suddenly in 1996 and Nicholas Varian took over until his retirement in 2009. Varian's last major improvement to the train was to replace all the wheel sets with new high suspension ones. The original wheel sets, then seventy-five years old, had lasted remarkably well but they were showing signs of cracking. Today, the entire railway line all the way to Venice is welded steel and this combined with the new wheel sets means that the ride is incredibly smooth and guests can enjoy a peaceful sleep.

Each year the train makes one trip to Istanbul, taking five nights, two of which are spent in hotels in Budapest and Bucharest, where special daylight tours are provided. Several times a year the train goes northbound from Venice to Paris on a different route, passing via Vienna, Prague, Krakow and Dresden, with overnights in hotels in these cities and daylight tours.

Most of the great travel experiences of the past have vanished, including Concorde, which has come and gone without being replaced by another supersonic aircraft. Venice Simplon-Orient-Express is a truly authentic experience. Long may it last.

All the time we were sorting out the issues of the train the hotel operation, after some stops and starts, was starting to take shape. I was still wrestling with the problems of Vail and elsewhere when another opportunity emerged right on our own doorstep in Italy. Our third hotel acquisition could not have been more different from Vail. In 1981 we were approached by Lucien Tessier, owner of the Villa San Michele near Florence, asking if we would be interested in buying the hotel he had created out of an old convent. It was – still is – a wonderful little gem, which Natale Rusconi and I felt we could not pass up. The hotel is as old as the hills. The land registry shows that the Convent San Michele alla Doccia sotto Fiesole was built on land purchased in 1411, and the building was first occupied a couple of years later. But the history of the place goes back centuries before that.

Fiesole, overlooking the great cathedral of Florence, is one of the oldest towns in Europe, and was an early centre of Etruscan civilization, dating to the ninth century BC. The old Roman road from Fiesole to the River Arno, built more than 2,000 years ago and now just a path, passes through the Villa San Michele garden. The convent has a façade which has been attributed to Michelangelo, but the records suggest it was probably designed by the Florentine artist and architect Santi di Tito, perhaps inspired by Michelangelo's drawings, a number of which are remarkably similar to the villa's façade. The present façade is actually a restoration, and was completed on 6 October 1600, thirty-six years after Michelangelo's death (Santi di Tito died in 1603).

Tessier had converted the convent into a 32-room hotel in 1952 and now decided to retire to Positano with his charming Irish wife Moira. Natale Rusconi and I inspected the property and we both thought it was so special it would make a splendid hotel, provided we could increase the number of rooms, even if we had to do so gradually over a period of time. The purchase price seemed reasonable, but Tessier wanted to sell the contents as well at what seemed to me an exorbitant price, which he supported with a valuation from one of Florence's most reputable antique dealers. I called Peter Wilson at Sotheby's, the man responsible for selling me the Orient-Express cars in Monte Carlo, who referred me to Sotheby's in Milan. They sent an expert out to look at the contents, and then I heard nothing for weeks. When I finally called the valuer he told me, 'I cannot write to you about this matter because every item of furniture is a copy, even if the antique dealer in Florence claims they are originals. Sotheby's would not want to become involved in a dispute over authenticity.' I then confronted Tessier with this news. He didn't seem particularly surprised or upset, but he did agree to reduce his asking price for the contents by two-thirds, and we completed the purchase of the property and contents in 1982. To be fair, the copies were of very high quality and their only defect was that they were not the originals.

The town of Fiesole then had a Communist mayor who we feared would create difficulties with our plans for enlarging the hotel, but in fact the opposite proved to be the case. He felt, quite rightly, that an upgraded and larger Villa San Michele would improve the image of Fiesole and bring in more tourists, so he assisted us in submitting a new town plan that incorporated our proposed expansion. It then had to be approved by Rome and the region, which took years, but today the hotel has forty-six rooms, most of which are suites, and a magnificent pool, set in a tree-clad hillside with the city of Florence at its feet. It's a unique place.

Too late, however, we realized the old convent of San Michele wasn't called *alla doccia* for nothing. *Doccia* means conduit of water, which we only fully understood some time after we bought the property when an exceptional storm caused a torrent of water to wash away much of the historic garden.

We rarely had ugly incidents at our hotels, but we did have one at the Villa San Michele. In our early years of ownership, when Italy was still in its bad period of political unrest, the Villa San Michele was raided by an armed gang. The intruders assumed that the guests in the presidential suite would be the best targets for robbery, so they burst in on them in the middle of the night. The lady in the next door room, hearing shouts coming from the terrified occupants, considered quickly what to do. She picked up the company's brochure by her bed, which had the telephone number of the Hotel Cipriani in Venice, dialled the hotel, got the concierge on the phone and reported to him what was going on. The concierge called the police in Fiesole and the robbers were nabbed as they drove out of the hotel.

In this same period of unrest in Italy we also had a 'Keystone Cops' incident at the Hotel Cipriani. In the middle of the night a boat with three hooded thieves came alongside the main landing, which is closed at night so that boat engines do not disturb sleeping guests. The boat landing moves to the pool garden at that time. The thieves entered the lobby and woke up the night concierge, Mario, who was slumbering at his desk. They pointed a gun at him and demanded that he open the safe, which held the guests' valuables. Mario explained that this was impossible because he had only one key and the guests had the second keys, which were needed to open the boxes. At this point one of the robbers punched Mario, but did not notice Mario's assistant, who had heard the disturbance, rushing to the rescue. He was an ex-paratrooper and he picked up a glass table and smashed it over the head of the robber who had hit Mario. The robbers then panicked, ran back to their boat, started it up and drove off at speed. But they had forgotten their third accomplice who they left stranded in the front garden, so rushed back to collect him. By this time the hotel's resident manager had been alerted, grabbed a gun and ran into the garden, firing it wildly into the air. This had the effect of waking everyone up, including the guests. The police soon arrived and the situation was quickly brought under control. In Italy there are two police forces, the Polizia, who are the local police, and the Carabinieri, who wear colourful red and blue uniforms and consider themselves superior to the ordinary Polizia. The next morning the commander of the Carabinieri came to the hotel and demanded to see Rusconi. He said, 'Dr. Rusconi, the Carabinieri have been insulted. You know we are the superior police force. You should have called us when the robbery took place, not the Polizia.' The robbers were apprehended the next day, but I never knew whether they were by caught by the Polizia or the Carabinieri.

In truth Venice is, and always was, a very safe city. During the Red Brigades period many wealthy Italians moved their principal homes to Venice to avoid kidnapping, which was rife at the time. In later years our close friend Lord Alistair McAlpine, brother of Sir William who helped us with the British Pullman, moved to Venice when his beautiful home, West Green in England, was bombed by the IRA. Alistair was very close to Mrs. Thatcher, who regarded him almost as family, and he had served as a highly successful Treasurer of the Conservative Party. Two of his close friends, Ian Gow and Airey Neave, were killed by the IRA, and he was also in the Grand Hotel in Brighton when the IRA blew it up in 1984, narrowly missing Mrs. Thatcher but killing and seriously wounding a number of cabinet ministers and MPs attending the annual Conservative Party Conference. He decided to leave London for Australia, where he had important interests, but the security services advised against it, saying there were many IRA sympathizers even in the police force; the same was true of the U.S. where feelings about Northern Ireland ran high in the Irish-American community. So he moved to Venice and bought a beautiful house, which he and Romilly filled with an eclectic mixture of books, antiques, paintings and sculptures. To our great regret, his marriage to Romilly broke up and Alistair left Venice with his new wife Athena (who was actually born in Ireland) to create his own stylish hotel, also converted from an old convent, in Puglia.

Soon after we had added the San Michele to our burgeoning port-folio another opportunity in Italy came our way, this one in Portofino, a beautiful old fishing village on the Ligurian Riviera coast of north-ern Italy. The old town, which backs on to a national park, has been kept in its original state by strict planning laws, which have prevented historic buildings being modified or new buildings being constructed. I knew the village well because my container leasing business took me frequently to the nearby city of Genoa where most of the Italian ship owners were based. Portofino was a gourmet's delight: the best pesto in the world comes from the Ligurian hills behind it, and I frequently drove the short distance from Genoa in the evenings for one of the delicious pasta dishes with pesto sauce. Focaccia, a bread seasoned with onions or tomatoes, originates from Portofino, and there are seafood specialities unique to the area: moscardini (tiny squids) and bianchetti (baby white fish which are no longer sold legally). All of these are washed down with the local Gavi di Gavi wine.

However, I rarely stayed at the Hotel Splendido because most of my trips to Genoa were made in winter and the hotel was closed then. I had to make do instead with a dreadful small hotel on the sea-front, called the Nazionale, where the owner was a disagreeable lady who hated her guests – or maybe it was just me she hated.

When I became interested, the Splendido was owned by a Milan-based insurance company that had become subject to a hostile takeover bid. Its president was a legendary Italian power-boat racer, Carlo Bonomi, who started selling off assets to defend himself and his company, and to our delight and amazement we were offered the Splendido. We paid the equivalent of $8 million for the property, but it didn't save Bonomi who failed to fight off the predator and got taken over.

Of all the hotels we own, the Splendido is one of the most special and I still cannot believe how fortunate we were to acquire it. By rights the owners should never have sold it, because it has the enormous advantage of having no competition, almost unique in the hotel world. The only other hotels in Portofino are small inns, which operate to three-star standard, while the Splendido is truly five-star. One must head back inland from Portofino to Santa Margarita to find other luxury hotels, and then take a bus back into Portofino because there is very little car parking in the village.

Of course, as with so many of our purchases, we needed to refurbish and upgrade the hotel, and although we started immediately, the process took many years. We could only work when the hotel was closed for the winter, and there was a great deal to be done: many of the rooms were too small so they had to be enlarged by making three into two, or two into one, and even the manager's house became two suites. When we bought the hotel and started the refurbishment, we were assured we had all the necessary permits from the regional government in Genoa. We selected a Bergamo firm as the contractor but shortly after work started the permits were suddenly cancelled. The hotel's general manager enquired as to the reason for this, and was told that a local contractor had a right to the job, which of course they didn't. But to move things ahead a local contractor was employed who immediately sub-contracted the job to the original Bergamo contractor, taking a nice fee for doing nothing in the process. Such are the ways of doing business in Italy.

Then came the water crisis. The main water supply worked perfectly most of the time, but in the peak period of July–August, when the Portofino peninsula was filled with thousands of visitors and there wasn't much rain, we suddenly found the water supply had slowed to a trickle. Most of the water, we discovered, was diverted inland to the towns of Santa Margarita and Rapallo, and several times in our first summer the Splendido had completely run out of water. We had to run a pipe down to the sea and pump up salt water, which was used in the toilets and swimming pool, and fresh water was trucked in by tanker at great cost. For the following season we planned to build a large cistern capable of holding a week's supply of fresh water, which we thought could be augmented at night when there was a little water pressure from the main supply, or when it rained. However, we had reckoned without the village officials who limited our cistern to 50 cubic metres because otherwise the local water hauliers would lose business. We eventually got around the problem with the aid of a clever bit of scientific innovation: we installed a reverse-osmosis water purification system in a marine container, which we put on a trailer and parked in the hotel's garage. This allowed us to convert the sea water into fresh water.

The Splendido is some way back from and above the sea itself, but the Hotel Nazionale was right in the port, and I always reckoned it would complement the Splendido perfectly and give us a stranglehold on the five-star market. Some years later, through the assistance of the Sea Containers regional manager for the Mediterranean, Franco Delle Piane, I managed to buy it, after the Rome-based bank which owned it put it up for sale. The bank had a problem, not unusual in Italy at the time, in that it did not want to take a book loss on the transaction. We got around this by constructing a long lease, which paid out the purchase price over a number of years at a very low interest rate. We renamed it the Splendido Mare and converted it into sixteen rooms and a restaurant where guests could experience the village life and go up to the Hotel Splendido on the hillside to enjoy the pool, tennis and its restaurants. We could manage both properties from the main hotel, which meant the incremental cost of operating Splendido Mare was very low, and today the two Splendidos are among the most profitable hotels in the Orient-Express Hotels portfolio. In 2006 we added the final touch: we bought the ice cream concession in the main square, which had rights to a number of tables. Italian ice cream is a great delicacy but the ice cream produced by the concessionaire was disgusting. We replaced all the equipment and now offer wonderful ice creams and sorbets to the crowds which parade through the port every day.

CHAPTER TEN

CROSSING THE ISTHMUS

After this burst of activity and the excitement of the maiden voyage of the Venice Simplon-Orient-Express, it was time to sit back and consider where all of it was leading us. The leisure division of Sea Containers was now becoming significant, and we were finding that the investment analysts were confused by a strategy of having marine containers and luxury hotels in the same group. The leisure division also needed its own independent management and image, and after some debate in the group and with our advisers, we decided we should find a way of decoupling it from the main marine container business and spinning it off as a separate concern.

Our solution was to own the leisure assets in a U.S. company called SeaCo Inc., and 'pair' its shares with those of Sea Containers Ltd., which was registered in Bermuda and which owned the container assets. This meant that when you bought a share in one company, you also received a share in the other, a mechanism called 'stapled stock'. The marine container business was largely untaxed because containers had to be free to move from country to country without taxation interference by any government, while hotels and other leisure assets were always taxed in their country of location. In order to maximize investor interest, each company from now on would prepare its own annual report.

The two companies were 'paired' in 1976 and 'depaired' on 15 March 1984, and the shareholder rosters then gradually became different for each of them. In 1986 SeaCo got a new name, Orient-Express

Hotels Inc., and its own board of directors, each one carefully chosen for the contribution they would individually make to the success of the new concern. At this stage they were Mark Birley, our partner in Harry's Bar; Adrian Zecha, founder of the Aman Hotels Group; Sir John Bremridge, former Financial Secretary of Hong Kong (who pegged the Hong Kong dollar to the U.S. dollar at the same rate as exists today); Sir David Davies, a banker and former chief executive of Hongkong Land; Georg Rafael, a founder of Regent Hotels Group; Peter J. Pearson; and myself. It was Georg Rafael who gave the company its new name.

By 1986, the properties in the portfolio were the Hotel Cipriani, Villa San Michele, the Hotel Splendido in Portofino, the Lodge at Vail, the British Pullman and the Venice Simplon-Orient-Express trains, the Lake Windermere Iron Steamboat Company, Windermere Island Club, retail shops in Paris, London and on the trains and 49 per cent of Harry's Bar in London. The company also managed the Turnberry golfing resort in Scotland, although it had sold the actual property to Japanese interests. There were lots of other acquisitions and prospects in the pipeline and I felt Orient-Express Hotels, as it would be known from now on, was coming together nicely.

One of the first projects for the newly independent group was, suitably enough, a sea-going venture. The original concept behind the purchase of the Venice Simplon-Orient-Express train was to bring more visitors to our hotel in Venice, but even before its launch the publicity surrounding the train caused it to take on a life of its own. The train project became bigger than I ever imagined, driving the whole image and branding of the new company, which was beginning to emerge as a leading international luxury hotel company. In 1977 when I first bought those old carriages in Monte Carlo people thought I was either eccentric or slightly crazy, but now a mention of the train brought instant recognition almost anywhere in the world and opened up all sorts of opportunities which would never otherwise have been available to us. By the mid-1980s the Orient-Express train was considered so successful it was singlehandedly reviving luxury train travel around the world. The revivals met with mixed fortunes: Royal Scotsman trips to Scotland in post-war cars, and Palace on Wheels in India, a train made up of old maharajas' coaches, were relatively successful, but lots of others including the Southern Cross, which was to run between Sidney and Melbourne, flickered and died. It was not an easy business to get right.

However, the Venice Simplon-Orient-Express went from success to success and we began to think about how we could make more use of the brand. One idea I had been mulling over for some time was a cruise ship operating out of Venice, thus combining the train, the Hotel Cipriani and now the sea. One of the problems was that the coast around Venice was not ideal cruise territory because the great Po River silts up the shore and the region is flat and uninteresting. On the other hand, there were so many beautiful places further south that I felt, with a bit of imagination, we could construct a cruise which would complement both the train and the hotel to the benefit of all three.

I flatter myself I know these cruising grounds almost as well as anyone, having owned a sailboat based in the Mediterranean since 1969. The Greek islands are a sailor's dream, full of interesting villages, architectural ruins, deep blue sea and sandy coves and beaches. Even if the wind blows up a heavy sea, there is usually a sheltered bay to run into and I have explored most of them. In the early days I sailed a lot in the Balearic Islands and the South of France, Corsica and Sardinia, but these areas became progressively less attractive as tourism built up and spoiled the ports. In those days my boat *Barinia* was based in Palma de Mallorca at the Club Nautico, and we would often put in to Soller on the north coast of the island to visit friends who lived in the village of Deià, made famous by the poet Robert Graves. We eventually bought the famous La Residencia hotel in Deià from Richard Branson in 2002.

In the 1970s we shifted *Barinia's* winter base to the Cannes area of the Riviera, where the skipper and his wife lived, and where we still keep her. In those days I was usually able to get a berth on the quay at St. Tropez in the summer months, even though it was then at the height of its fashion, with Brigitte Bardot in her prime and tourists in their droves thronging the port. We liked to sit with a drink at the Café Sénéquier and watch the parade of fashionable people passing by but, frequent a customer though I was, I found it almost impossible to get a table at the quayside restaurants, and L'Escale was the most difficult of all. One day I was cruising in the area with my stepsons when we met one of my old shipping friends, Jean Panigeon, who lived in Belgium. We lunched aboard my boat, and as he was disembarking he enquired politely if he could assist us in any way. I asked, half-jokingly, whether he could get us a table at L'Escale, and he simply replied: 'What time?' I indicated that nine o'clock, which is when most French take their dinner, would be fine with us, and rather sceptically we showed up at the restaurant half-expecting to be fobbed off. The owner, however, rushed over, greeted us like royalty and ushered us to the best table in the window before saying: 'Monsieur Sherwood, this is your table every night while you are in St. Tropez – and there is nothing to pay.'

This was a rather astonishing turn of events, and in the days that followed I made enquiries as to the reasons for this largesse. It turned out that Panigeon's parents had owned a home on Tahiti Beach (the main beach for St. Tropez), and during the war Panigeon had been recruited by the Deuxième Bureau (France's Secret Service) to work with his childhood friend Joseph L'Escale, founder of the restaurant. As I was told the story, on a certain night of the week the restaurant owner would invite the Germans to enjoy his hospitality at dinner time, and at the same moment an Allied submarine would surface off Tahiti Beach and Panigeon would escort operatives ashore. Implausible as it may sound, there was clearly sufficient truth in it for the bond to remain strong enough to get us the best table in the house.

There are lots of other wonderful destinations on the west side of Italy and I have always loved sailing down past Portofino, Sardinia (where the Aga Khan's Costa Smerelda was achieving prominence) and the Aeolian Islands off Sicily with Stromboli erupting every few minutes. Sicily, where Orient-Express Hotels now has two hotels in the beautiful town of Taormina, under the slopes of Mount Etna, has always fascinated me. But none of these destinations fitted geographically with Venice and we had to think about Greece and Turkey.

Just as we had done when we planned the Arlberg route for the train, Shirley and I set out to sail the Adriatic, the Greek islands and Turkey from Istanbul to Antalya, trying to work out a schedule, which would include as many of our favourite ports as possible in one week. We plotted a dozen different routes but none of them really worked for us, until we hit on the idea of going through the Corinth Canal, which cruise ships seldom did but which would save the long trip round the Peloponnese and make the cruise possible. Eventually we designed a one-week cruise itinerary, which would start at Venice on a Saturday night, cross east through the Corinth Canal in the morning of the third day, stop in Piraeus in time for passengers to visit the Acropolis, reach Istanbul on the morning of the fourth day, arrive at Ephesus on the morning of the fifth day, Katakalon (for Olympia) on the sixth, and the ship would be back in Venice on the morning of the seventh day.

The key to this route was the Corinth Canal, which was too narrow for most passenger ships, so we had to find a rather skinny ship that could carry enough passengers to make the trip a financial success. The canal itself is of great historic interest, providing a dramatic passage between the Adriatic and the Bay of Athens (known as the Saronic Gulf), and we thought it would bring something extra and unusual to the cruise if we could include it. It is a brilliant bit of engineering and was dug at sea level so that, although it is nearly four miles long, it has no locks. It took a long time to complete: the crossing had been originally developed by King Periander in 602 BC, but was not a full waterway and boats had to be hauled out and dragged on sledges across the narrow isthmus. Julius Caesar planned to complete the canal but was assassinated before he could even begin; the emperor Nero brought in 6,000 slaves from Judea in AD 67 and actually broke the first ground himself, but then perished by his own hand the next year. The French had a go after completing the Suez Canal, but became distracted by building the Panama Canal and the French contractor went bust. Finally the great canal-builder of the age Ferdinand de

Lesseps stepped in and finished it off, with Greek help, in 1893, some 2,500 years after the project was first started.

We identified the perfect ship for our purposes, owned by the Finnish/Swedish company Silja Oy (interestingly Sea Containers bought Silja some years later, and I became chairman of it). It was a type of ship called a 'cruise-ferry', popular in the Baltic, with all the features of a pure cruise ship but also the capacity to carry cars. It had 330 cabins, four restaurants and two swimming pools and, most importantly for our purposes, it was long and lean with a shallow draft.

Before finally committing to the purchase, I took the precaution of asking Sea Containers to send a marine superintendent to the Corinth Canal to check she could actually pass through. He went down, did his measurements and reported back that she was too large, which I couldn't understand because, based on the charts I had been studying, it was possible for her to make it even if it was a narrow squeeze. This meant of course that the venture was dead before we had even begun. But in the summer of 1985 I decided to check for myself and sailed through the canal on *Barinia* pretty much with my own measuring tape. I invited the chief pilot of the canal to make the transit with me, and I spread out my charts on the main deck table and asked him to explain why the ship couldn't pass. 'But of course she can!' he exclaimed indignantly. 'This is what I told your marine superintendent. In fact a ship which is even a bit larger than this one already passes the canal once a week.'

When we reached the other side I immediately sent a telex to London saying: 'Buy the ship'. It seems the marine superintendent had decided to err on the side of caution, and to be fair, it was a tight fit: the ship's beam was 22.3 metres while the canal would only take responsibility for 21 metres. When the ship was actually in the canal, she had to have a tug in front to keep her in the middle, but fortunately the banks of the canal were mud so even if the hull touched, which it often did, there was no damage. The ship's draft was also an issue, but we calculated that if she bunkered in Piraeus for the round voyage back, she would be at her lightest at the time she actually entered the canal. We could never carry any freight on the car deck for the same reason.

Naturally we called the ship *m.v. Orient-Express* and encouraged passengers to take the train to Venice, spend a few nights at the Hotel Cipriani and then make the cruise. The maiden voyage, again with a large contingent of dignitaries and travel journalists aboard, left Venice in May 1986, and we did not get off to a good start. Venice had exceptionally low water that day, and a large number of fishing boats were stranded on the mud flats waiting for the tide to float them off. The ship was under the control of a surly port pilot who took her far too quickly through the lagoon, building up a stern wave, which spilled onto the mud flats with such force that it capsized one of the fishing boats. The pilot belatedly realized his mistake and slowed the ship, but it was too late – we learned later that a fisherman on board his boat had been killed.

The ship was a financial success from the first cruising season, and we made about $3 million profit during the summer months. The problem, as with so many hotels, resorts and cruise ships, was the winter when we chartered her out. Unfortunately some of these charters were to fairly dodgy people who didn't pay. I remember arriving in Antigua one February, primarily for a holiday but also to see the ship, only to be told that the charterer had not paid his bills and the ship was going to be seized on Monday morning. I immediately went to the master and suggested he might like to sail over the weekend. 'But the agents have all the ship's papers,' he protested. I ascertained that the ship had enough fuel and water aboard to make the crossing to Madeira so, after a hasty consultation with our marine department in London, I requested the master to sail immediately for Madeira. We had another set of ship's papers prepared and delivered to him there. In the marine world ships can be arrested for non-payment of debt, even if it is incurred by a third party. We had no idea how much the charterer owed and the thought of defending an arrest in tiny Antigua was not appealing.

In 1989, as I shall describe in the next chapter, Stena Line of Sweden made a hostile takeover bid for Sea Containers and in order to defend ourselves we had to sell off some non-core assets to raise cash. Silja Oy, which had originally sold us the ship, had in the meantime decided to expand its cruise operations and thought the *m.v. Orient-Express* would be an excellent addition. They offered $36 million for her, and Sea Containers, which had originally purchased her for $16 million and had invested several million in improvements, accepted, making a tidy profit and raising some very valuable cash.

There is, as there always seems to be, a sequel to this story. In 2001, as part of its regulatory reform program, the Greek government decided to privatize the Corinth Canal and Sea Containers bid for it and won. We calculated we could increase the transits, then 12,000 vessels a year, by 50 per cent through an effective sales and marketing program. We drew up plans for a major marina on the east side of the northern end, and a roll-on, roll-off ship berth on the other side. We also intended to develop a mixed leisure facility, including restaurants, shops and a hotel, offering *bateaux mouches* trips along the canal.

We started with high hopes, but the project went sour when we could not get the Greek government to honour the terms of the contract. We could not obtain permission to build the marina, and when the financial crisis hit Greece in 2008 the traffic through the canal, particularly yachts, dropped off dramatically. Sea Containers handed the keys back to the government.

In the years that followed the launch of the *m.v. Orient-Express*, cruising out of Venice grew enormously, and today it is not uncommon for ships carrying thousands of passengers to be seen moving through the Giudecca Canal between the Hotel Cipriani and the Piazza San Marco, the centre of Venice. These new ships cannot get through the Corinth Canal and they don't exactly follow the itinerary of the *Orient-Express*, but in a way we can say that she pioneered the concept.

CHAPTER ELEVEN

THE HOSTILE TAKEOVER BID

By the early 1980s Sea Containers had outgrown its third head office. We had started in that little office in Old Jewry in the City of London in 1965, moved to Park Street and then to Vogue House in Hanover Square, each time to bigger premises which quickly proved inadequate as the company grew. We never seemed to get it right, but I was determined that the next move must be our last, and we would find a large corporate headquarters which would reflect the size and standing of the company we had become – or rather companies; Orient-Express Hotels was now a substantial concern in its own right and required its own office space.

I was on the lookout for something larger and grander when, one summer's evening, I found myself taking a party of people by launch from Westminster down the river Thames to Greenwich, where we had moored our latest container ship for the admiration of clients, investors and anyone else who was interested in coming aboard for a glass of champagne. One of the guests on the launch was Nigel Broackes, co-founder and chairman of Trafalgar House, a large British holding company that owned the Cunard shipping line and its flagship, the *QE2*. Trafalgar also owned, among many other assets, the London Ritz, the *Daily* and *Sunday Express*, *Evening Standard* and major construction and property companies. Broackes had been a brilliant young entrepreneur, one of the brightest stars of Britain's financial world, but age and prosperity had made him rather grand and a tad pompous, and he languidly gazed out over the river as if he owned it.

Nigel played a critical role in getting the Channel Tunnel project underway, and he was a favourite of Mrs. Thatcher who had appointed him chairman of the London Docklands Development Board, responsible for developing the thousands of acres of wasteland in East London which had once been the biggest port in the world. Today the huge Canary Wharf, Rupert Murdoch's print-works in Wapping, London City Airport and many other large buildings and developments in London's docklands are testimony to his success in the role (which was unpaid, although he did get a knighthood a few years later).

As we were nearing Blackfriars Bridge, Broackes airily flapped a hand toward an unfinished building on the south bank of the river, remarking: 'There's a great buy for somebody. It would make a fantastic company headquarters – and going cheap.' He explained that it had originally been designed as a hotel, but the developer had gone bust and the receiver was about to put the building on the market.

Although it was surrounded by ugly scaffolding, its position and size – 600,000 square feet – looked perfect for what I wanted. I leapt into action the next day and contacted the bank which had pulled the plug on the developer, and the receiver who was dealing with the sale. We discovered that £15 million had already been spent on the building, but it still needed a hefty investment just to get it to a stage where it could be rented. After some haggling, Sea Containers bought it for £15 million, and converted it into Sea Containers House, one of the landmark riverfront buildings on the south side of the Thames. It had plenty of space for expansion and became the smart new headquarters for both Sea Containers and Orient-Express Hotels. As executive chairman of both companies I had my office on the thirteenth floor, with a superb view of the dome of St. Paul's and the great sweep of the river. It took until 1985 to complete it and cost £80 million in total, but it is an iconic building, familiar to everyone who lives in or visits central London.

One Monday morning a very large man strode into the building and announced to the receptionist that his name was Kerry Packer 'and I want to see Jim Sherwood'. I had met Packer once before in

Sydney, but really didn't know him. I invited him up to the thirteenth floor. He was no sooner in my office than he said: 'You know, Mr. Sherwood, the way I spend my weekends is I walk around London and look at buildings. Then I select ones I think I should buy, and I would like to buy Sea Containers House. And I am offering you £85 million for it.'

As the building had cost us £80 million and we had just moved in, I said I didn't find his offer irresistible. He glowered at me in that rather threatening way he had, and said: 'Mr. Sherwood, when I make an offer, and you don't accept it and then you come back to me later, I am always going to offer a lower price. This is going to be my best offer, and I think you should take it.'

I replied that it was simply not enough and I wasn't interested, so he left the same way he had come. I discovered later he had persuaded the security guard to let him look around the building on the previous Saturday, and he seemed to have arrived at his figure just by walking around it. When the building was completed and we had let all the space we were not occupying ourselves, we were able to sell it to an insurance company for £110 million, and take a £30 million profit as well as free up a lot of cash. When London property prices collapsed a few years later, I was very happy we had sold. Whenever I met Packer at social events after that I used to tease him about it and he took it in good part.

This was a golden period for both Sea Containers and Orient-Express, both of which were on a roll. Although the two companies had formally 'decoupled' in 1984, they were still closely inter-related and intertwined – not least because I ran them both from my new office in Blackfriars.

The mid-1980s were excellent years for Sea Containers, with the U.S. economic recovery causing a surge in world trade and therefore in demand for containers. We couldn't meet demand in our main markets and although we spent $139 million on new containers in 1984 alone, we were still falling behind. The Chinese export trades were being containerized, equivalent to half a dozen smaller nations containerizing at the same time. Revenues in 1984 hit a new record of $369 million and net earnings per share more than doubled. We were still the leader in the leasing of specialized containers, and across the group all divisions were going great guns. However, I may have tempted fate by forecasting a further improvement in 1985 (which we achieved) and an even better year for 1986 (which it definitely was not).

We had not quite completed the move into our new premises when Sea Containers took its biggest step yet. In 1984, not long after we had bought some of its British Transport hotels, British Rail was required by the Thatcher government to sell off its ferries, which had really been extensions of its rail network. The company, Sealink, operated ferries on the Dover–Calais, Folkestone–Boulogne and Dover–Dunkerque routes across the English Channel, as well as to the Isle of Man, Isle of Wight, and on three different routes to Ireland, north and south. A look at the prospectus revealed all sorts of problems but also a number of nuggets, such as the port of Newhaven in East Sussex, with a lot of developable land around it, the port of Fishguard in Wales and various other assets.

Originally Sealink had shared its routes with its French and Irish equivalents, but life had moved on and Sealink now faced tough competition from private sector operators, which were not carrying the excess baggage of a legacy state carrier. On the horizon was the real tiger in the forest: the Channel Tunnel, still struggling to get its act together and raise the huge sum required for the giant project, but none of us had any doubts it was going to happen, however long it took or how astronomic the cost. Mrs. Thatcher had decreed it would go ahead, so go ahead it would (and did).

We offered £50 million for Sealink and we were the only bidder. P&O would have liked it, but wouldn't have been allowed because of the monopoly rules, and others were frightened off by the poor trading record and the trade unions. The minister in charge, Nicholas Ridley, was deeply disappointed by this figure and to ease his pain we agreed to add the net cash in the business to the price, bringing the headline figure to £66 million. Ridley was able to save his face by announcing this figure and on 27 July 1984 we signed the deal. It was the biggest acquisition Sea Containers had made so far, and some members of the board were very uneasy about it, concerned about the level of losses we were taking on, and the fact that it was highly unionized. To my great regret, my original partner and friend from Yale Maury Pinto was so opposed to us entering the ferries business that he resigned as a director.

My appraisal of the Sealink business, however, was that there was a gold mine of assets to be unlocked if we could get in, reach agreement with the unions and turn the business around. I knew enough about state-owned businesses to believe they were always overmanned, usually had hidden assets and underutilized properties, and there were great opportunities to extract profits by reducing costs and increasing margins. And that's exactly what we did.

The first delicate task was to arrive at a working agreement with the unions, who we expected to be hostile and to oppose fiercely the lower headcount and changes in working practices we would be asking for. The National Union of Seamen had a reputation for militancy and I was warned to expect serious opposition and trouble from their Scottish leader, Sam McCluskie, widely regarded as one of the toughest trade union leaders of his generation. That may have been his reputation, but in my dealings with him I always found him a pussycat – or at least fair, constructive and realistic. He was a hulking nineteen-stone giant of a man, with a personality to go with it, and looked just like Burl Ives until he opened his mouth and spoke in what one interviewer described as the 'doon tae earthness of Leith's dockland' (Leith is a port near Edinburgh). He was the ultimate fixer, a master of behind-the-scenes wheeler-dealing and political machinations, with a contempt for ship owners who he was convinced were out to 'get' the union and its members.

But I liked him from the beginning and we got on, albeit from our very different standpoints. I needed to cut costs and modernize the business, and McCluskie understood that and wanted to protect as many jobs as he could. We agreed early on that if the management did not take a confrontational approach but were prepared to go 'softly, softly', we could all work to a plan which would achieve significant savings over a period of years while avoiding a major strike. A strike would have killed us both, and each of us acknowledged that at the outset.

I took the view that we were in the ferries and ports business for the long haul, so we needed to make comparatively minor staff reductions and incremental changes in working conditions each year, rather than all at once. McCluskie cooperated with this approach and was able to take his militant union with him, with the result that we avoided compulsory redundancies, partly by non-replacement of those who left or retired. If we had to withdraw a ship from service – and we started with thirty-five of them, many of them old – the seafarers were offered first option on other jobs within the fleet.

I greatly enjoyed observing McCluskie across the table during these interchanges, some of which were interminable. At times he was bullying and blazingly angry, when his language became as picturesque as it was unprintable, then a few minutes later he would be charming and cajoling. He employed all the negotiating skills he had learned in the rough-houses of trade union meetings and Labour party politics, and it was very easy to be lulled into a sense of false security. It was very effective, and it saved both the company and many of his members' jobs.

When our longstanding shipping executive director, Nigel Tatham, was forced to retire early with heart problems, Michael Aitken was recruited and soon picked up the reins. We turned the business around fairly quickly, were soon into profits and over the years we got our investment back from sales of surplus properties and other assets. We had taken a calculated risk in moving into the ferry business, but Sealink proved a good buy, and we came out well ahead. It confirmed my view that state-owned assets are usually undervalued and worth acquiring.

Sea Containers' net income dipped to $25 million in 1987 and Orient-Express Hotels made $12 million, but by 1988 Sea Containers' growth times were back again, and net income almost trebled to $68 million, while Orient-Express Hotels reported a record $22 million profit. They were both trading well, but I was ever watchful for trouble on the horizon.

It came from a most unexpected source. Sea Containers was still sorting out the ferry business and expanding the container operations when, out of the blue, we got an unwanted hostile takeover bid. On 13 March 1989, the Swedish ferries company Stena announced it had acquired an 8 per cent shareholding and was contemplating making a bid for the entire company. It had been quietly accumulating shares until it got to 4.9 per cent, the maximum before a stake had to be declared, and then did a classic 'dawn raid', mopping up any shares on offer before anyone realized what was going on.

Their intentions were clearly hostile, but that morning they indicated they wanted to sit down with the company and see whether we could agree a way forward. I had no intention of agreeing to anything, and foolishly Stena did not make a formal offer when they had the initiative. We were able to begin putting our defensive walls in place. I called Michel David-Weill, the legendary chairman of Lazard Frères and one of the most powerful men on Wall Street, who often stayed at the Hotel Cipriani, and asked him to act for us. We also appointed White & Case, the law firm whose managing partner, Jim Hurlock, had served on our board. David-Weill, although he was involved in some of the huge takeover battles then being waged in America, took a keen personal interest in our defence, often appearing late at night when we were in the midst of strategy meetings, offering some sage words of advice and encouragement. He delegated Jesse Robert Lovejoy to be the point man, and he was very effective; some years later I asked Lovejoy to join the Orient-Express Hotels board when we felt that we needed to have a director who could give us an expert perspective on U.S. securities. Lovejoy became the chairman of Orient-Express Hotels in 2011 and I became chairman emeritus at the same moment.

From the outset we had an advantage in that I owned part of the company and could count on others for support. But that still left a majority of the shares out there for Stena to buy. The Templeton fund management company owned 17 per cent, and it was clear from the start that this could be the decider either way. Our lawyers were aware that Bermudan law allowed subsidiary companies to buy shares in the parent company. If the purchases were made without financial assistance from the parent, the purchased shares remained outstanding and therefore could be voted by the subsidiary. Our advice was to go out and borrow as much money as we could, and use it to repay intercompany debt owed to the subsidiaries, thereby allowing the subsidiaries to buy out the Templeton stake, which would effectively close the door on Stena. As it happened I knew John Templeton, founder and chairman of the company, who lived in Lyford Cay in the Bahamas where I regularly met him, and had done shareholder presentations to him. I flew out to see Templeton and our subsidiaries bought his shares for $43 a share, compared to the average $18 he had paid.

Stena and its advisers went wild when they heard this news and announced they would challenge the validity of these purchases and voting rights in the Bermudan courts. The non-cancellation of voting rights would never have been allowed under U.S. or U.K. rules, and if Stena had made an offer immediately we could not have borrowed money and our subsidiaries could not have bought our shares. The bid battle was now becoming a very big affair in the newspapers, as everyone knew Sealink ferries, and in legal and City circles our defence was being studied with great interest. All sort of issues, points of law and principles were raised.

Stena joined forces with Tiphook, a British container lessor, and on 26 May 1989, through a joint company called Temple Holdings, launched a bid for Sea Containers at $50 per common share. The shares had been trading in the low $30s before Stena appeared on the scene. Their plan was to break up Sea Containers and on-sell the marine container leasing business to Tiphook. They also announced their intention to divest the shareholding in Orient-Express Hotels so it could remain an independent public company.

In response, we argued that Sea Containers had a much higher liquidation value, net earnings of $7.15 per common share and the directors could not recommend such an inadequate offer.

The second stage of our defence strategy was to embark on a major disposal of non-core assets, and we promised to deliver shareholders $70 a share in cash if they stuck by us and rejected the offer. Shareholders would still own a stake in the remainder of the company, which would include container leasing and the shareholding in Orient-Express Hotels, plus properties and parts of the profitable ferries business. So we began seeking bids for our assets, and it soon became apparent that we could raise at least $1.1 billion in cash, equivalent to the $70 a share we had promised to return to shareholders after payment of the underlying debt.

Stena and Tiphook responded to our defensive efforts by raising their offer twice, first to $63 in mid-August, and then again to $70. The Sea Containers board was aware that $70 was a premium of more than 100 per cent on the market price before the bid, the court case in Bermuda could go either way and there were uncertainties over completing our planned asset sales.

It was Jim Hurlock who saved the day, convincing the board to hold out, and the Stena offer was duly rejected (Hurlock joined the Orient-Express Hotels board in 2000, and served as chairman after I stepped down in 2007). Michael Stracey, the chief financial officer, was also a tower of strength at this time, holding the fort in London while I raced around pursuing our defence.

I couldn't have got through it all without our company plane, which I used to criss-cross Europe in order to sell assets and meet bankers and shareholders. In the middle of the bid battle, Shirley and I had been invited to Paris for the French bicentennial celebrations in 1989 and while we enjoyed a lavish party given by Michael Edwards the night before, we were looking forward to the parade down the Champs Elysées the following day and the finale in the Place de la Concorde in the evening when Jessye Norman was due to sing the *Marseillaise*. I had to skip the parade and fly back to London for a quick meeting, and then I was to join Shirley back in Paris in the evening. All went well until I got to Luton Airport in the afternoon only to be told that all the French air controllers had walked off the job in order to watch the closing ceremony on television. I returned home to London and watched it by myself. Shirley was staying at the Hotel Ritz in Paris, where I rejoined her the next day. Because of all the royalty and bigwigs in town for the ceremonies, I had not expected to be able to get our usual suite but Frank Klein, the Ritz's general manager, said, 'We are hosting seven heads of state who will never come to this hotel again, while I see you very often, so assuredly your usual accommodation will be available.'

It was a brief moment of relief in an otherwise tense time. Dan Sten Olsson, the son of the founder and chairman of Stena Lines, was a determined and resourceful man and refused to go away. He later told me that the logic behind his bid was that he had run out of growth in Scandinavia, and he believed there were better opportunities in Britain. He had missed out on the Sealink privatization, which he now regretted, and had set his mind on acquiring it second time around.

Everything now hung on the decision of the court in Bermuda, which would determine whether the shares our subsidiaries had bought from Templeton could or couldn't vote at the special meeting. The chief justice had decided the case was so important he would hear it himself, and every lawyer on the island seemed to be involved in some aspect of the affair. Things moved very slowly, with five-day breaks when there was a cricket match on, and long weekends. I was banned from going to Bermuda while the trial was on because I could be forced to testify and the lawyers didn't want that to happen.

Eventually the court handed down the decision, which was in our favour, and Stena threw in the towel. In the first days of 1990, ten months and many millions in fees after hostilities opened, Olsson made a peace offer. Stena's proposal was that they would buy our cross-Channel, North Sea and Irish ferries for $600 million in cash, which seemed a great deal to us. Because they had never been able to examine the books, they didn't know where the main profits came from and they paid us a huge price for parts of the business that had low profitability, such as the Fishguard–Rosslare route. They left us with the Isle of Man and Isle of Wight, the major profit-earners. We agreed to sell the older part of the container fleet to Tiphook for another $546 million, but retained the most profitable parts.

Stena cancelled its request for a special meeting of shareholders and we held our delayed annual meeting on 15 March 1990, almost exactly a year since Stena first appeared on the scene, at which shareholders approved the recapitalization proposals by a landslide.

The bid had been extremely disruptive for everyone involved in the company and I was determined we would not lay ourselves open again to a hostile predator. Part of the plan approved by shareholders was for Sea Containers and certain subsidiaries to make an offer of $70 for the company's shares, using the proceeds from the asset sales to Stena, Tiphook and others. Seven million shares were tendered, and four million of these were purchased by subsidiaries and another three million cancelled. This created a situation where 58 per cent of what remained of Sea Containers was now owned by its own subsidiaries. Orient-Express Hotels later adopted a similar arrangement where subsidiaries held outstanding and voting shares in their parent, giving the subsidiaries the ability to resist an unfair takeover bid. Of course, the directors of the subsidiary companies must exercise their fiduciary responsibilities, which meant that if a fair offer was ever made for the company, it could be accepted. No formal offer was ever made for Orient-Express Hotels.

Although we won the battle, it was all very messy and I cannot say I enjoyed the process. The unfortunate downside of a hostile bid is that the target company is in limbo, staff are worried about their jobs and it is impossible to recruit good people or start anything new. An even more unpleasant aspect is the public trashing of opponents, which the advisers regard as part of the game. We were advised to dig up dirt on Stena, and they tried to do the same with us. Stena's chairman had been accused of being involved in illegal metal trading with Germany in World War II, and we were accused of trying to avoid the consequences of the Falklands War by changing the flag of two of our British ships operating to Argentina to the Panamanian flag. When I produced a letter from Britain's Foreign Office requesting that we make the flag change that allegation was quickly dropped.

We discovered that appeals to shareholders were a waste of time because most of the shares had been snapped up by the 'arbs'

(arbitrageurs) in the early weeks of the contest. These are specula-
tors who buy shares on the assumption that the first bid is not the
final price and in our case they were proved right when Stena and the
company increased their offers to $70 a share.

But it hadn't been entirely a wasted year. We had made good
progress on a number of fronts – and there were some interesting
hotel prospects in the pipeline in some exciting parts of the world. It
was time to get back to work.

CHAPTER TWELVE

SOUTH AFRICA

Although the hostile bid probably set both Sea Containers and its associate Orient-Express Hotels back by a year in terms of our development, there were lots of things that had been in the pipeline and were either coming to fruition or were in need of attention. One of these was the Hotel Quinta do Lago, a major new development on an exclusive part of southern Portugal's Algarve coast, near Faro. Orient-Express Hotels had originally been approached in 1987 by Prince Khalid bin Fahd Al Faisal, a member of the Saudi royal family and a successful businessman in his own right, to build and manage a new hotel on a superb property he had acquired on the Atlantic Ocean overlooking the wildlife sanctuary of the Rio Formosa estuary. It had an enormous beach at the end of a causeway, housing one of my favourite restaurants, Gigi's, famed for its delicious fresh seafood with plenty of garlic, washed down with light Vinho Verde wine. Gigi, a Brazilian, charges outrageous prices but they are worth it.

We agreed to take it on and we supervised the building of the 141-room hotel, opened in 1988 to great fanfare. But we soon discovered there was a major problem: in the Algarve a hotel without a golf course is the equivalent of an Australian pub with no beer – and we had no golf course. We thought we had when we agreed the deal, and one of the attractions of the new hotel was that it was built in the middle of an exceptional golf course, the San Lorenzo, generally regarded as the best in the Algarve. Unfortunately Khalid had declined to buy it when he had the chance and the Trusthouse Forte group, which had its own hotel a few miles up the coast, nipped in and bought it instead. Of course they immediately cut us out and gave their own guests (plus those rich enough to be members) the exclusive right to play. There are ten golf clubs in the resort area, but none of them as good or as close to the hotel as the San Lorenzo and we had no guaranteed start times on any of them. The manager of the hotel, Jean-Paul Foerster, eventually cobbled together a solution, but had to settle for second best and the hotel laboured on under its golf handicap for years. Foerster did better than the hotel, later assuming the role of European regional manager for Orient-Express Hotels. His father had been a famous hotelier, serving for many years as the general manager of Reid's in Madeira, which we acquired some years later, and also as general manager of the Ritz in Lisbon.

In 1997 Prince Khalid eventually got tired of the hotel and its golf problems and moved on, so we bought the hotel from him for the very reasonable price of $27 million. We already had Reid's Palace in Madeira by then and were looking at other hotels in Portugal to get some critical mass.

But it was never a great success for us. The golf situation got no better, and with Portugal joining the euro, the outlook for the hotel and the Algarve in general became poor. Long before the current crisis within the European Union, membership of the euro caused considerable problems for countries like Portugal and Greece, making them uncompetitive against countries with weaker currencies, which can devalue. Even then it was possible to see that the imbalances and structural faults in the EU were inevitably going to lead to major difficulties for the poorer countries, and of course that it is exactly what has happened. Turkey has captured some of the Mediterranean market because of the strength of the euro, and South Africa now attracts many of the golfers who formerly went to the Algarve in the northern hemisphere winter. When we needed to rationalize Orient-Express Hotels and weed out the poorer performers, we sold the hotel at a small profit, but it was not one of our finest deals.

Our entry into South Africa, on the other hand, proved a very good deal for us, and we could not have timed it better. The low point in the country's fortunes was probably 1988, with the economy feeling the full effects of international sanctions and whites leaving the country in large numbers in what became known as the 'chicken run'. I knew the country better than most, as Sea Containers' business often took me to Durban, the shipping centre of South Africa, and I made some good friends there, including Murray Grindrod, whose family controlled the Grindrod shipping group. He became a member of the Sea Containers board where he served for twenty years. South Africans are pretty pragmatic people and natural optimists, but there was a pervading feeling of fear and foreboding about the future, and the expected end of a very comfortable and privileged way of life for the white population of five million people. By the late 1980s it was clear to all but the most blinkered that change was on the way, and the only question was whether it would be peaceful or bloody. At that stage none of us knew (not even the ANC leadership) that Nelson Mandela had been taken from Robben Island to the mainland and secret negotiations had already begun with President P. W. Botha. But one could feel the tensions mounting and it felt like sitting on top of a pressure cooker.

We always had our main meetings in Durban, where I usually stayed at the Beverly Hills Hotel in Umhlanga Rocks, the original family hotel of Sol Kerzner, who cut his teeth there before going on to create Sun City, several chains of hotels, and two of the biggest casinos in the world in the Bahamas and Connecticut. After Durban, we always tried to end our South African trips with a few days in the gracious Mount Nelson Hotel in Cape Town, which is truly one of the great hotels of the world, with an incredibly loyal clientele who come back year after year. We were as loyal as anyone else, and after weeks on the road, it was always wonderful to drive through the iconic Prince of Wales gateway, up the driveway with its lines of Canary Island palm trees, to the distinctive Mediterranean-pink walls of the familiar hotel and be greeted by name by all the usual staff. We greatly enjoyed the hotel's Edwardian elegance, down to the white-gloved, turbaned waiters in the dining room, the tail-coated *maître d'*, the potted plants and the air of tradition and permanence it generated.

Shirley loved the garden and liked to spend hours going through it with the head gardener, each of them learning something new each time from the other.

Although it looks directly on to the majestic Table Mountain, the Mount Nelson always felt like a little bit of old England, which is exactly what Sir Donald Currie, founder of the Castle Steamship Company, set out to create in 1899 when he built it on an eleven-acre site in the historic heart of the city. South Africa was an important destination for the two big shipping companies which plied the route, the Union Line and the Castle Line, and before they merged to become Union-Castle, they both built luxurious hotels in Cape Town to give their rich passengers somewhere decent to stay during the European winter. But within months of the Mount Nelson's opening, the Boer War started and it effectively became the rear headquarters for the British Army. The British commander Lord Kitchener (of Khartoum fame) based himself there, as did generals Buller and Roberts. They were the principal British commanders of the bitterly fought conflict in which the British at one stage had 500,000 soldiers in the field fighting a Boer population, including women and children, of half that number. For the three years the war lasted many of the key decisions, good and bad, were taken in the luxurious suites of the Mount Nelson, which was booked solid with senior officers, distinguished war correspondents, wives and sweethearts and even ordinary adventurers and sightseers. To prevent overcrowding, the Swiss manager, Emile Cathrein, introduced an 'officers only' policy in the hotel's facilities, which caused considerable resentment, particularly among the Canadian and Australian troops. A young Winston Churchill was nursed back to health in the hotel by his mother Jennie after his escape from a Boer prison camp, and he filed a number of his dispatches from what he described as 'this most excellent and well-appointed establishment which may be thoroughly appreciated after a sea voyage'. Rudyard Kipling, Arthur Conan Doyle and H. G. Wells all stayed in the Mount Nelson during the period. Cecil Rhodes was a familiar figure, and so were the other two men who did more than anyone else to carry on the war: Joe Chamberlain, the British colonial secretary, and Alfred Milner, the high commissioner and governor of the Cape Colony. The Afrikaner writer and philosopher Laurens van der Post (godfather to Prince William), first visited the hotel with his father in 1911 when he was five, and later wrote about the 'special magic' it always had for him.

The hotel became an institution in the years between the wars, a haven for wealthier English visitors who caught the same ship at the same time each year, stayed in the same cabin and the same suites at the Mount Nelson with the same servants and the same luggage. The Prince of Wales made a visit in 1925, when he opened the new entrance and the avenue created in his honour, and the hotel became high fashion in British genteel circles. In 1956 Union-Castle merged with Clan Line to form British & Commonwealth, and the Mount Nelson became part of the Cayzer empire. The Cayzer fortune, which is huge and very private, was created by an extraordinary man called Charles William Cayzer, the son of a Plymouth schoolmaster who ran off to sea at the age of fifteen and ended up building one of the biggest shipping companies of its day – or any other day. I had a lot of dealings with its container interests, Overseas Containers Ltd., of which it was one of the founders in 1969. The last Union-Castle passenger liner was taken out of service in 1977, but people continued to come by plane and the hotel remained a favourite wintering spot for the well-heeled British tourist.

I regularly met the Cayzer regional manager on my visits to Cape Town and usually enquired whether the family would sell the Mount Nelson. The answer was always 'no', but nothing is for ever. In the mid-1980s the Cayzer family, although it owed its great fortune to shipping, took the momentous decision to get out of the business altogether and by 1986 it had sold its last ship. By that time its main holding company, Caledonia Investments plc, had diversified into financial services, commodity trading and aviation and a year later in October 1987, it sold all its shares in British & Commonwealth to a consortium put together by its own management. It was Britain's second biggest management buy-out at the time, and it turned out to be a very good decision for the Cayzers – their successors backed Exco, a fast-growing and controversial money broker, which made a disastrous acquisition in the U.S., went spectacularly bust, and in 1990 the British & Commonwealth Group collapsed with debts of £1.5 billion.

Well before that the new owners decided to pull out of South Africa because of sanctions and their fears that the country would decline when the government changed – just the kind of opportunity I like. As the news got out that the Mount Nelson was to be sold, there was horror and indignation in Cape Town and among old clients the world over. South Africa was already feeling very nervous about the tense political situation, and this felt like another unpleasant threat to its fragile future. The columns of the *Cape Times* and *Argus*, the two local papers, were full of angry letters and the place hummed with rumours. Sol Kerzner was said to be interested if he could get a licence to turn it into a casino; Graham Beck, another very successful South African businessman, wanted to buy it to turn it into a complex of apartments; it was going to be knocked down to be replaced with high-density townhouses and so forth. No one mentioned me, although, unbeknownst to the outside world, I already had the inside track.

My Cayzer friend in Cape Town had given me a heads-up and I had every intention of using it to stay ahead of the game. I learned from him that the independent valuation was R25 million, or £5 million. I quickly contacted the new owners, offered the full price, and on 1 November 1988, Orient-Express Hotels took over the Mount Nelson just in time for the high season. Orient-Express's reputation went before me, and consternation in Cape Town gave way to relief when I announced we were going to keep the hotel as it was and invest in overdue improvements.

We didn't have long to wait for political change to come to South Africa, and thank goodness it was peaceful. Early in February 1990 the hotel was packed with journalists, camera crews and dignitaries who had rushed to Cape Town for the event the whole world awaited: the release of Nelson Mandela after twenty-seven years in prison. President F. W. de Klerk was expected to announce it in his Opening of Parliament address on 2 February but in fact, as he told me later, he had no intention of doing so that day. Nor did Mandela, who was part of the plot, want him to. Watched by the entire world press, de Klerk, in a historic thirty-minute speech, swept away all the restrictions, prohibitions and accoutrements of apartheid, announced the unbanning of the ANC, the Communist party and thirty other political parties, abolished the pass laws and other petty restrictions which were an integral part of the apartheid system, and promised to work with the ANC and other parties towards a fully democratic election that would involve all South Africans, whatever their colour. It was a historic moment, only topped nine days later when, on 11 February 1990, Mandela finally took his long walk to freedom and Cape Town – and the world – erupted in joy. There wasn't a spare garret – or a dry eye – in the Mount Nelson, suddenly the most popular hotel in the universe.

Mandela gets most of the credit for the miracle of the smooth transition to full democracy that followed four years later when the elections were finally held, and South Africans of every colour turned out to stand in the queues, often for hours, always in high good humour and camaraderie, to cast their vote. Mandela became president in April 1994 and appointed de Klerk as one of his two deputy presidents, a position he retained for two years before resigning.

In my view, de Klerk's role in the build-up to the election, and in the first critical years of the new government when he alternately chaired the cabinet meetings, was almost as important as Mandela's. He came from the most conservative and tradition-bound Afrikaner stock, and can trace his ancestry back to the earliest days of the Huguenots in South Africa and the later *voortrekkers* who took their wagons and families off to the Transvaal and Orange Free State to escape the British. His forefathers fought the Zulus at the Battle of Blood River and took on the whole British Empire in the Boer War. His uncle was Prime Minister under the apartheid system, his father was in the Verwoerd cabinet, and he himself served as a minister under Vorster and P. W. Botha at the height of the repressive regime. Yet he had the courage to end the system he had grown up under, defying the entire right wing of his party, ignoring the many death threats he received (he still gets them), and embracing the new rainbow nation with enthusiasm and energy. We often see him and his wife Elita when we are in Cape Town, where he lives, and I find it fascinating listening to him recount the events of those times. History will judge him more kindly – he deserved the Nobel Peace Prize he got with Mandela.

The election in 1994 and the elevation of Mandela to president made South Africa the most fashionable country in the world and everyone wanted to go there. Companies and trade organizations made up for the years of sanctions and bans, and held their meetings in Cape Town, Johannesburg or Durban, the three major cities. The Rugby World Cup in 1995, which South Africa won and which did a great deal to heal the wounds of the white population (as described in the film *Invictus*), brought in another influx of visitors. All of this helped make the Mount Nelson highly profitable in those years, and we urgently needed more room. Fortunately the Cayzers had bought up the surrounding buildings as they came up for sale, and we had the space to increase the room count, which was done progressively over a number of years under the leadership of Nicholas Seewer, the Swiss general manager who smoothly ran the South African operations from 1990 to 2010.

After the political transition and our success in Cape Town I looked around for further investment in South Africa. Johannesburg had a bad reputation for violence, but it seemed to me the city, by far the richest in Africa, would regain its prominence across the continent. The city centre had largely become a 'no go' area with a great deal of violent crime and poor policing, but I found it a bustling, energetic place with first-world infrastructure, one of the best climates in the world and the potential to become the major hub of South Saharan Africa, which it is today. The better hotels were located in the northern suburbs around Sandton, considered safe by the white community, which had largely deserted the downtown areas. Property values were extremely low and I became interested in a new apartment complex that was being built on a cliff-side overlooking the Johannesburg zoo, but was not yet completed. The views were spectacular and the district, called Parktown, was comparatively safe yet was much closer to the city centre than Sandton. I thought it would make a perfect hotel, and we approached the Prime Minister of Gauteng Province, Tokyo Sexwale, and got his backing for our application. We then contacted many of the neighbours to get their support for a zoning change. They were suspicious, but our credentials as owners of the Mount Nelson Hotel, as well as the hotels in Europe which a surprising number had been to, helped to assuage their fears and they did not actively resist.

We named the new hotel The Westcliff, after the district where it was based, engaged local architects to design it and Graham Viney, who had done work for us at the Mount Nelson, to do the interiors. The hotel opened in 1997 to much acclaim. We were especially pleased because it was completed on budget – an objective that, regrettably, we haven't always achieved. We discovered early on that our banqueting and meeting facilities were inadequate so we managed to acquire more land and built a large banqueting hall, which today is extremely popular for weddings and meetings.

For me, South Africa has always been the ideal destination during the northern hemisphere winter. Friends go to Florida, the Caribbean and Southeast Asia, but South Africa has superb weather, long days and a profusion of flowers and greenery when it is winter in the northern hemisphere. There is little time change from Europe, the climate is dry and daytime temperatures are in the 80s. There are more species of plant on Table Mountain than exist in the entire United Kingdom, and Shirley loves to spend time in the Kirstenbosch Botanical Gardens, one of the best in the world. We try to spend at least a month there every year, starting just after Christmas, and we always feel much better for it.

We now had a useful foothold in southern Africa and I began to think about how we could capitalize on it and expand further our interests in the region. Shirley and I had gone to Kenya on our honeymoon, and had found game-viewing there disappointing, with dozens of Land Rovers crowding in on any sighting of a few miserable lions. The Grindrods took us to a camp near South Africa's Kruger Park but it wasn't wild enough for what I wanted either. Then friends suggested we visit Botswana for a taste of 'old Africa'. We did and were fascinated

by the quantity and diversity of animals and the feeling that we had
the entire area to ourselves. We had been contacted by some California
interests who owned a business called Gametrackers Botswana with
leases on six camp sites in Botswana, all of which were accessible only
by air except in the very dry season when off-road trucks could get
through to supply them with building materials and heavy equipment.
Each camp had its own air strip. Gametrackers didn't have the necessary funds to upgrade the properties so they asked us to take them
over while they would act as selling agents in the U.S. The camps were
pretty basic and needed complete rebuilding, but they had fabulous
locations inside the national parks.

We ultimately developed only the three most important sites. The
northernmost was Savute, which is in the Chobe National Park, where
there are enormous herds of elephants, giraffes, zebras and innumer-
able buck. Then there was Eagle Island in the Okavango Delta, which
one visits by boat and where bird life abounds; and thirdly, the largest
of the camps, Khwai in the Moremi Park, which is on a river full of
hippos that grunt and groan all night.

The country, which is the size of France but with only 2.1 million
people, has an extraordinary abundance of game: an estimated 180,000
elephants compared to only 15,000 in Kenya. Shirley was out one
morning on a game-viewing with a young Prince Harry and they saw
a pride of thirty-five lions. I was sleeping in that day because getting
up at 5 a.m. for the daybreak excursion is sometimes a bit early for me.

Against my better judgement the management of Orient-Express
Hotels changed the name of the safari camps from Gametrackers to
Orient-Express Safaris. I rather preferred Gametrackers but then I
don't fill the camps with guests, they do. I preferred to be involved
with the acquisitions and delegate the day-to-day running to the
professional managers.

The Botswana government awards twenty-year leases to qualified
operators and we needed to get these renewed before we could invest
in the camps. I made a trip to Gabarone, the capital of Botswana, to
meet with the ministers involved in the lease process. Despite having
my appointments confirmed in writing, upon my arrival I was advised

that all the ministers had gone to Pretoria for meetings with the South African President Nelson Mandela. I asked whether it would be possible to meet any of them in Johannesburg, and was told they were all staying at the Sandton Sun Hotel where I was also planning to stay. As soon as we got to Sandton, we sent invitations to the ministers inviting them for breakfast, and much to our surprise the entire Botswanan cabinet showed up, still waiting to be called to Pretoria. We found them very pleasant and helpful and wound up spending most of the morning with them. A few weeks later we received our new leases.

I thought that it might be fun to carry on the tradition of having tented camps, but the tents had to be very spacious and luxurious and, because Botswana is very hot in summer and cold at night, they would need to have both air-conditioning and heating. Our Paris designer, Gérard Gallet, came up with an elegant design for tents which are as grand as any five-star hotel: set on plinths, they have air-conditioning and heating vents set unobtrusively above the bed head, a large shower-room, bathroom, desk, lounge area and an outdoor terrace deck, all in the most magnificent setting in the middle of the bush. At night you can hear the animals in the river or roaming through the camp, and lions sometimes chase their game right past the tents. Hippos come out of the water onto the lawns on Khwai at night, and can be extremely dangerous. There are some (not many) mosquitoes which carry a slight risk of malaria, but I've always found the best way to deal with that is to spray on insect repellent, especially at sundown, and I've never been bitten yet. It's all part of the thrill of being on safari in the bush.

We built swimming pools at each location, but elephants can literally smell water for miles so the challenge is to make the pools inaccessible to them. We tried putting 50,000-volt wires around the camps, but the elephants simply selected a brash young bull to smash his way through and the others followed behind. Water towers don't work because the elephants gather around them and push them over. In the end, we realized that the pools have to be sufficiently high off the ground so that the elephants cannot climb up the embankment.

With properties in both South Africa and Botswana, I turned to other places in the region. Back in the Portuguese days I once visited Lorenzo Marques in Mozambique with the Grindrods, where we stayed at the grand old Polana Hotel, the best-known hotel in the country. It was an interesting experience. As soon as we crossed the border the road became a single-lane ribbon of tarmac where the vehicles loved to play 'chicken', finding out who would be the last to turn aside before collision. Portugal at the time was fighting insurrection in both northern Mozambique and Angola and when the Salazar government in Lisbon was toppled, Portugal withdrew from both countries, resulting in economic collapse. Angola was probably the greater tragedy of the two because it had enormous oil resources, which could have been used to develop a high standard of living, but instead it fought a useless civil war dragging in the Cubans and South Africans. Mozambique also went through a dark period, but partially recovered under President Machel until he died in a plane crash, which has never been explained but which some of his supporters blamed on the South African security services. Both countries are now emerging from their past, and Mozambique, with its proximity to South Africa, is becoming a very interesting country to invest in.

Lorenzo Marques is now called Maputo and a few years ago when I heard the Polana might be for sale, I went back. I met with the Prime Minister, Pascoal Mocumbi, who seemed to be a very competent and unassuming person. I asked how he had become Prime Minister, and he said he was really a surgeon from Lausanne, Switzerland who had been co-opted to help with the administration. The Polana was 50 per cent owned by the government and I sensed it would be difficult to buy them out because a lot of the senior government people would lose their perks. The general manager said that board meetings could spend a large amount of time talking only about which flowers to plant in the garden. This did not seem to be a recipe for a successful property so we didn't pursue it.

We travelled on several occasions to Mauritius, which has a number of five-star hotels, all of them beach resorts, but I decided the island was too remote and too competitive, and most of the tourists are South Africans who do not spend as much as Europeans.

Our quest to know Africa and the nearby islands was greatly facilitated by our eccentric and lovable friend Christopher Bailey, a larger-than-life bearded Welshman with eclectic businesses in the maritime world, including the naval shipyard in Malta which he had bought when the government privatized it. Christopher kept a large yacht, *Welsh Princess*, based in Dar es Salaam, where he owned the Oyster Bay Hotel as well as a wonderful game park in the Selous Mountains, Beho Beho, also in Tanzania, which he regarded as his second home. We once toured the Seychelles together and another time visited the Camores and Madagascar. They were hilarious trips: the captain rarely drew a sober breath, and on one occasion we had to spend a couple of nights at the Oyster Bay while a sober Scandinavian skipper was flown in to take over. Christopher was a great practical joker, which might manifest itself when walking down a remote beach and suddenly being approached by a man-size penguin, which would turn out to be a crew member Christopher had dressed up. Sarah Bailey was very fond of lemurs, which are indigenous to Madagascar. While they are engaging creatures, they are very messy on a boat and Sarah insisted on keeping several aboard. We visited a reef off the north shore of Madagascar, which had the biggest lobsters I've ever seen, as well as enormous brightly coloured fish in the shallows.

Life at sea with Christopher was a great adventure, but the potential for five-star hotels anywhere other than the Seychelles and Mauritius was non-existent. I found the Seychelles the more interesting, and some excellent hotels have now been built there. There are some amazing sights: a valley on Praslin Island where the *coco de mer* grows (the enormous nut shell which looks like a lady's backside); Bird Island, which is blanketed with sooty terns at certain times of the year; and the island of Aldabra with its amazing array of tropical fish and giant tortoises, all contributing to make an exceptional travel experience.

Having explored the Indian Ocean and Africa south of the Equator, I decided it was time to move on. Another even more exciting market was emerging. We were off to Brazil.

CHAPTER THIRTEEN

FLYING DOWN TO RIO

My Rio, Rio by the Sea-o,
Flying down to Rio where there's rhythm and rhyme,
Hey feller, twirl that old propeller
Got to get to Rio and we've got to make time.

So sang Fred Astaire in that wonderful old black-and-white movie, *Flying Down to Rio*, as he helped to save the Hotel Atlantico from closing down because it hadn't got an entertainment licence. Made in 1933, the film marked the first screen pairing of Ginger Rogers and Astaire (who was not yet a star and only had a supporting role), and helped make Rio de Janeiro one of the most fashionable resorts for the well-heeled globetrotters of the time. There was, of course, no Hotel Atlantico in Rio in the 1930s – the real hotel that starred in the film was the Copacabana Palace Hotel, which overnight became the best-known hotel in all of South America.

Like most film buffs, I had come under the spell of the film and thought about it often as I flew down to this extraordinary city with its half-moon-shaped bays, giant granite bluffs coming straight out of the sea and its two spectacular beaches, Copacabana and Ipanema. The words of the song often echoed in my mind:

You'll love it, soaring high above it,
Looking down on Rio from a heaven of blue.

I had been flying down to Rio for years on Sea Containers business and did indeed love it as I soared high above it. Its energy and vibrancy reminded me of Hong Kong or even 1950s New York, and I enjoyed its night-life, its restaurants and of course the beaches (and what was on them in their bikinis of course). Unfortunately Rio was also crime-ridden, dangerously overcrowded and desperately poor, with huge favelas clinging to the hills on the edges of the city like giant anthills. Nothing prepared me for the poverty I saw in Brazil in the 1960s and it hadn't much improved by the 1980s as the population trebled to 150 million from 1940, mostly living in the cities. But Brazil accounted for half of the economic activity of all of South America, and as most of the big shipping companies were based in Rio, it seemed an obvious place to set up Sea Containers' regional headquarters, which I did in the early 1970s. We did well there for many years, manufacturing and repairing containers in the port of Santos as well as managing our container leasing and other shipping interests.

As I've mentioned before, my invariable habit in any city is to stay in the best hotel available, and my first call was the Copacabana Palace, which still had a reputation as the grand dame of South American hotels, invariably referred to as either 'legendary' or 'famous' in all the guidebooks (it still is). I expected something magnificent; what I found was anything but. The classic stucco façade, modelled on the great hotels of the French Riviera, the dark panelling, heavy drapes and some of the old furniture all hinted at its former grandeur, but it was shabby, run-down and looked to be on its last legs. There was inadequate air-conditioning, no soundproofing of the windows, making it hard to sleep, and the water from the taps either came out dark brown or a lighter shade depending on how long you let it run. Even Copacabana Beach itself looked dirty, particularly compared to Ipanema, which had become much more fashionable.

I gave it one go, left in disgust, and then worked my way through the other hotels in the city, all of them equally bad or even worse, until I reluctantly settled for the Intercontinental, a drab building way out of town but which at least had a pool and gardens and was in a quiet neighbourhood. I disliked it but it was the best of a bad bunch.

Rio simply had no half-decent hotel, a fact I stored in my mind for future exploration.

As Orient-Express Hotels developed through the 1980s, I began to think seriously about adding a South American property to our portfolio – which meant Rio and, in turn, the Copacabana Palace. With the Mount Nelson we now had the best hotel on the entire continent of Africa, and I could see that with money and time the Copacabana Palace could be restored to its rightful place as the finest in all of South America. When the Astaire film was made in 1933, it was a new hotel, only ten years old, and had been built with no expense spared by the Guinle family, then one of the richest in the world. The Guinles were of French descent, and their vast fortune was founded by Eduardo Palassin Guinle who in 1888 won the concession to build the port of Santos and operate it for ninety years. Santos was – and still is – the largest port in South America, the entrepôt for Sao Paulo, Brazil's biggest (and ugliest) city. When Eduardo died in 1912 he left an estate said to be worth $2 billion and the port of Santos continued to churn out profits until the lease ran out in the 1970s.

Along with a huge fortune, Eduardo's son Octavio inherited two luxurious hotels, the Hotel Palace in Rio and the Hotel Esplanada in Sao Paulo but decided to build something even grander, a hotel which would exceed in style and opulence anything yet opened on the whole continent of South America. He hired the French architect Joseph Gire, who is said to have been inspired by the lavish structures on the French Riviera, notably the Hotel Negresco (whose dome was actually designed by Gustave Eiffel) and the Carlton in Cannes, and instructed him to build him the finest hotel that money could buy. He had purchased a superb site, right on the unblemished Copacabana Beach then used only by a few fishermen, and now he desired a spectacular hotel to go with it. Gire gave him what he wanted: a palatial, white-fronted building with a sumptuous atmosphere of quality and elegance, looking as if it had been lifted straight from the Promenade des Anglais. He added a huge casino and a large swimming pool (not as large as the Cipriani's though), and when the hotel opened in 1923 it quickly became a favoured resort for the international set.

Visitors today like to say they can feel the spirit of Marlene Dietrich or Humphrey Bogart. Orson Welles lived there for more than six months after completing *Citizen Kane* – he was apparently making a docudrama on the Rio Carnival, but the main character, a fisherman, was killed by the film crew's boat and the project was shelved.

The great days of the Copacabana had long gone by the time I stepped through its art deco doors with the intention of buying it for Orient-Express. It was the late 1980s, and Brazil was in deep financial crisis, with massive international borrowings which it had no hope of repaying, high unemployment, a worthless currency and hyperinflation which at times reached 25 per cent a month. The IMF and the big banks had insisted on ferocious austerity measures, which failed to curb inflation but caused economic growth to grind to a halt, resulting in what the economists refer to as 'stagflation', the worst of all economic worlds, where you have inflation but no growth. The economic boom of the post-war years had come to an abrupt halt by the early 1980s, to be replaced by what became known as the 'wasted decade'. Brazil had become a basket-case, a veritable banana republic.

For the poor old Copacabana Palace this meant an accelerating rate of decline that had actually started when the Brazilians moved their capital from Rio to the brand new Brasilia in 1960 and forced government departments and nationalized industries (of which there were many) to move there. But for me this was the ideal background against which to take over the hotel – in normal economic times we would never have been able to afford it, even if it had been for sale. I have always been a believer in 'contra-thinking', doing the opposite of what others were doing, and it had paid off handsomely for me many times, notably in South Africa and relaunching the Orient-Express when the common wisdom was that luxury rail travel was dead. Buying the Copacabana Palace Hotel was perhaps an even bolder decision, but the more I thought about it, the keener I became.

I had just come through the year of the hostile takeover and the massive restructuring of Sea Containers, which had effectively halved in size. We were still left with a decent array of businesses, and the sensible thing to do was to expand in areas where we had expertise and a reputation. And so I was on the acquisition trail for classic hotels which had fallen on hard times and could be purchased cheaply, renovated and relaunched. The Copacabana Palace fitted the bill perfectly. Besides, I believed that Brazil, with its huge natural resources, population growth and proximity to the U.S. markets, was not going to be a basket-case for ever and, as it turned out, 1989 probably marked the nadir of its economic troubles.

Buying it, however, was not a straightforward task and, as with the purchase of many of Orient-Express Hotels' great properties, there is an interesting story behind it. I started by approaching the son of the owner, José Eduardo Guinle, with the suggestion that his mother, Dona Mariazinha Guinle, who had inherited the hotel in 1968 when Octavio died, might consider selling it to us. He tossed aside my proposal, saying dismissively: 'My mother gets an offer once a month to buy the hotel, and she refuses them all.' He made it absolutely clear that I should not pursue the subject further. I remember being very disappointed as it really was a magnificent structure on perhaps the world's most famous beach, and was crying out for renovation and relaunch. I could think of no hotel that would better suit our portfolio of great world hotels.

Then I had a stroke of remarkably good fortune. The Brazilian ambassador in London in the 1980s was a charming and very effective diplomat called Mário Gibson Barbosa, and Shirley and I had become good friends with him and his beautiful wife Julia after spending a long weekend together one Easter in the Extremaduran castle of Fleur Cowles and her (fourth) husband, Tom Montague Meyer. A few years later, in early 1989, Shirley and I were in Rio and the Gibson Barbosas gave us an elegant dinner at their home on Leblon Beach. Seated next to me was a small elderly lady who identified herself as Mariazinha Guinle. The placement was obviously deliberate because the Gibson Barbosas knew of my interest in the Copacabana Palace. I could not let a chance like this go by, and told Mariazinha that I knew she got all sorts of offers for her hotel and was not interested in selling, but if she ever changed her mind I would be most interested to acquire the property on behalf of my company. She looked astonished. 'But

I've been dying to sell it for years,' she exclaimed, 'and I've never even had an offer!' Clearly her son José Eduardo, for reasons best known to himself, had decided not to pass on my interest.

When I had recovered my breath sufficiently, I asked her how I might pursue a purchase, and she told me I should meet with her lawyer, José Bulhões Pedreira, who had an apartment in the hotel. Next day I contacted him. He confirmed that he had recommended she sell the hotel and she was keen to do it while it still had some value. We began negotiations immediately. I made an offer and we quickly agreed a price for the Guinle majority shareholding, which was reported as being $23 million, but which was somewhat greater because we had first to restore the depleted capital in the company, as well as buy out some minority shareholdings.

We took possession in September 1989, which happened to coincide with Brazil's first democratic presidential election in twenty-nine years. It was won by Fernando Collor de Mello, a wealthy forty-year-old who advocated a free-market policy and a crackdown on corruption. I was rather in favour of him, particularly after I discovered that in 1975, when he married Lilibeth Monteiro de Carvalho, a seventeen-year-old heiress to one of Brazil's largest private fortunes, the reception for 3,000 people was held at the Copacabana Palace Hotel in what one society columnist described as 'the last great wedding of the era'.

On his first day in office, the new president launched the Collor Plan, a brutally austere set of measures designed to deal with inflation, which by then was running at over 1,000 per cent a year (it actually peaked at 5,000 per cent a few years later). Among other draconian measures was the enforced conversion of bank deposits into non-cashable government bonds – which seemed to me very close to institutionalized theft. At the same time Collor increased the printing of money, a contradictory measure that could only end in disaster – as of course it did. Two years later, Collor, the anti-corruption president, was himself impeached on charges of corruptionand had to resign.

That was the background against which we took over Brazil's

grandest hotel, and set about tackling our own problems, which, given the state of the hotel, were pretty daunting. The first challenge was to hire a new general manager who could assume the enormous task of refurbishing the hotel. I found our man at the far end of Copacabana Beach at the Rio Palace Hotel, which at that stage, thanks to his management, enjoyed the best reputation of any hotel in the city. Philip Carruthers, despite his quintessentially English name, was Brazilian by birth and had grown up in the hotel industry where he was highly regarded. I offered him the job and he moved in to begin work early in 1990. He was immediately asked by the Brazilian press what his plans were for the hotel, and he replied that no expense would be spared to modernize and improve it.

'The hotel is considered to be part of the country's heritage, so the façade won't be touched,' he said. 'But the inside will be completely updated, so we can make the place successful again.'

It quickly became apparent that we had seriously underestimated the amount of work required, or the time it would take to put it right in 1990s Brazil. The hotel hadn't been touched in decades and the whole building required major work, which we decided to do in stages over several years. We first closed the annex, or Tower Wing, and restored it, then moved on to the main building. Looking back on my annual reports, I realize now how slowly it all came together:

In April 1992 I reported that the hotel was 'still under renovation and cannot achieve its full potential for another year or two'.

In 1994 it was 'still in the midst of major reconstruction', and would not make a contribution to profits for another two years.

The following year I was able to report that it had reopened but there was still 'much work to be done' before it was fully operational.

The renovation of the 225 rooms was finally finished in October 1996, six years after we bought it, and took longer and cost more than the original hotel. Everything had to be redone, from the pool to the gardens, the plumbing, wiring and air-conditioning systems, the roofs and of course the soundproofing. The classic façade was carefully restored and delicately lit at night, making it one of the landmarks of the Rio skyline. Still sensitive after my battle with Arrigo Cipriani, I persuaded Carruthers we should create a new restaurant, which we would call the Hotel Cipriani Restaurant and which would feature the same menu as its Venetian sister. Philip was able to convince a chef from the hotel in Venice, Francesco Carli, to come to Rio and launch it, and it was an immediate hit. Francesco married a Brazilian girl and eventually became the executive chef of the hotel and a Brazilian TV personality.

One day in London I saw a large Canaletto of a Venetian scene on sale at Christie's, which I thought would be perfect for the restaurant in Rio. Unfortunately it sold for £15 million, which is more than I bought the whole hotel for, but I was able to obtain a colour transparency, from which a copy of the picture was painted in St. Petersburg at a cost of $50,000. It now graces the Cipriani restaurant in Rio, adding a little bit of Venice to the scene.

All this time, the political and economic health of Brazil was looking up, as I had always believed it would. The Brazilian Army, which had once fought urban guerrilla groups on the streets of Rio, now engaged the criminal gangs, which had been getting the upper hand. Television pictures went around the world showing jeep convoys of soldiers carrying light weapons in downtown Rio, alarming American and European tourists. But the Brazilians welcomed the crackdown on crime, and a flood of bookings filled the Rio hotels.

'All the hotels will be full over New Year's,' Carruthers predicted in December 1994. 'If this army exercise works out, I think we are going to get more Brazilians for the summer and for Carnival.'

He was right: a fireworks display and a concert by Rod Stewart drew more than three million people to Copacabana Beach over the New Year. Alas, Rod got himself banned from the hotel for playing football in his room and trashing the place. I thought it could have been a great deal worse and that Carruthers had maybe been a bit harsh on him.

As the Brazilian economy came under control and the currency stabilized, the tourists came back in droves, and I took great pride in the renaissance we had performed at the hotel. Philip restarted the traditional Carnival Ball, which had always been held in the hotel ballroom on the Saturday night of the Carnival weekend in February. He made it into a spectacular event, bringing in set designers from the Broadway stage, engaging great entertainers and turning the whole hotel into a fairy-tale palace. Shirley and I went there for Carnival weekend, which is an incredible experience. The highlight is the Samba school parades, which are held on four nights, starting about 9 p.m. and continuing beyond sunrise. Each Samba school has between 4,000 and 8,000 members, and they choose their own theme, write their own new tune and then pass through the parade ground in ninety minutes, with a half-hour break between parades. Guests watch from private boxes, and in our hotel box dinner was served between the breaks. The parades are judged and the winners repeat their parade a week later in the Sambadrome where the prizes are awarded. The new tunes are broadcast from every street corner and café throughout the week, as each school vies to win the prize for the best one. Between the Copacabana Palace's all-night Carnival Ball and the all-night parades, the weekend is exhausting but tremendous fun.

Dona Mariazinha Guinle, who had sold me the hotel, died in April 1993 leaving Octavio's nephew Jorginho as the last of the generation of Guinles who had built the hotel. Although he was already in his late seventies when we arrived on the scene, we kept him on as a sort of public relations person, and he did seem to know everyone. I had heard many stories of him as a legendary playboy and lover of beautiful women, but it was only after he died, aged eighty-eight, in 2004 – in his favourite suite at the Copacabana Palace Hotel – that I realized just what an extraordinary character he was. The *New York Times* and other international newspapers all gave him lengthy obituaries, depicting him as 'the last of the millionaire playboys whose free-spending ways and romantic exploits made them global celebrities from the 1930s onward'.

Although he stood only 5 feet 5 inches in his high-heeled shoes, when his friend Nelson Rockefeller persuaded him to join him in Hollywood before World War II his great wealth and charm made him one of the great lovers of his era, friend or rival to playboys

such as Porfirio Rubirosa, Howard Hughes, Aly Khan and Aristotle
Onassis. His great friend was Errol Flynn, with whom he once shared
a house, and his name was romantically linked to some of the biggest
stars of the day. Asked by one of the society magazines how he did it,
he replied: 'You dance cheek to cheek, or body to body. You tell her
she is beautiful. Sometimes she is game, sometimes not.' On the 'game'
side, he claimed, were Marilyn Monroe, whom he first bedded when
she was twenty, Jayne Mansfield, who 'liked to do it anywhere', Anita
Ekberg ('when I saw her for the first time I almost flipped'), Veronica
Lake and Hedy Lamarr. He was even said to have tried it on with
the future Queen of Denmark on the eve of her coronation (apparently she wasn't 'game'). According to one obit I read, he went round
to Marilyn Monroe's house one night bearing a beautiful diamond
necklace only to be told she had just committed suicide, so he continued his journey on to the apartment of Jayne Mansfield and gave the
necklace to her. He was also a massive spendthrift, squandering much
of his family's fortune on his romantic pursuits. 'The secret to living
well is to die without a cent in your pocket,' he said in an interview in
2002. 'But I seem to have miscalculated.'

Philip Carruthers ensured he died in great comfort in the hotel,
dining on chicken stroganoff, raspberry sherbet and tea for what
turned out to be his final meal. 'He died as he lived, in grand style and
with his eyes shining,' our hotel spokeswoman Claudia Fialho was
quoted as saying. 'Coming here was his last wish.' So ended the last
Guinle link with the Copacabana.

One of my vivid memories of the hotel is one evening, as we were
having a pre-dinner cocktail, spotting a familiar figure sitting on his
own in a corner of the bar of the Cipriani restaurant. It was Kenneth
Clarke, then British Chancellor of the Exchequer and the second
most powerful man in John Major's government. When I invited him
to join us, he explained he was waiting to catch the overnight British
Airways flight to London, had been to Brasilia to explain Britain's
privatization policy to the Brazilian government, and had taken the
day off to go bird-watching, which was his passion. We asked him if he
had ever tried a caipirinha, the national drink of Brazil (a concoction

of limes, alcohol distilled from sugar cane called cachaça and a bit of powdered sugar on top, served in a glass full of ice-cubes), and he said 'no', so the barman brought him one. He liked it so much that he ordered a second. You need good tolerance to drink two, but Ken is a big chap and asked for a third. I think he slept well on the flight to London. Peter Heap, the British ambassador and a great supporter of the hotel, was a bit miffed that we had been so generous with the caipirinhas. The caipirinha is now fashionable in trendy bars throughout the world, despite the difficulty of pronouncing or spelling the name.

I think we have done pretty well in restoring the edifice, atmosphere and international reputation of the Copacabana Palace, but I have two regrets. I once tried to persuade Andrew Lloyd Webber to create a musical from the film *Flying Down to Rio*, which I proposed to put on in the theatre of the hotel. Andrew was interested and looked into the possibilities but eventually one of his people concluded the theatre was too small for such an expensive production. The theatre remains closed, but I still think such a musical would be successful although the cost of refurbishing and enlarging it would be expensive.

My other regret is a more serious one. The hotel is a national monument, and we have to have lengthy negotiations with the fine arts people whenever we want to make the smallest change. But I felt we could do something imaginative with the old casino rooms at the back of the property, which had been unused ever since the Catholic Church managed to get gambling banned in Brazil after the war. I thought there was a great opportunity to create a modern, high-rise building, and who better to do it than Oscar Niemeyer, the architect of all the signature buildings in Brasilia? Niemeyer was already in his late nineties by then (he is still alive, aged 104), but every morning went into his studio overlooking Copacabana Beach, where his parents had a summer cottage when he was a boy, and he would watch the fishermen haul in their catch. He had worked with Le Corbusier, who greatly admired him, as did Frank Lloyd Wright and Mies van der Rohe, the giants of the twentieth century. He was – and is – highly controversial, and many people hate his work, such as the U.N. building in New York (which he designed along with Le Corbusier) or the Brasilia Cathedral, but I thought some of his designs, including the Niterói Contemporary Art Museum, a building that juts out from the sheer rock face with a view of the whole city of Rio de Janeiro, were brilliant. More recently he built a temporary pavilion for the Serpentine Gallery in Hyde Park in London, which became a big hit among young British architects ('a postcard of Brazil in the middle of Hyde Park,' a fellow architect called it).

Niemeyer was keen to take on the job and did some sketches. I liked them but my colleagues were not so keen and in any case the authorities thought they were too modern and out of tune with the art deco front of the hotel. Perhaps they were, but they would have given the rear of the hotel a new dimension. We eventually converted the casino rooms into large ballrooms for functions, and they have been a great success. So who am I to complain?

I was awarded the Order of the Southern Cross by the Brazilian government in 2002. In 2011 the Copacabana Palace was the most profitable property of Orient-Express Hotels that year.

CHAPTER FOURTEEN

A Streetcar Named Desire

After the successful acquisition of the Copacabana Palace, I felt it was time to take stock of the company. In 1990 Sea Containers was twenty-five years old and in that time we had floated the company, created a worldwide marine leasing business, launched our train, developed from scratch a worldwide hotel group, achieved record profits and seen off a hostile takeover bid. Annual dividends had grown from 60 cents a share to $1.40 and profits that year hit $343 million, the result of the asset sales, which we gave back to shareholders in the form of cash. Sea Containers still owned 42 per cent of Orient-Express Hotels (I held another 15 per cent), which made $14 million that year.

But the hostile bid, the break-up of the company which followed and the speed at which we had expanded had exhausted me and the team, and it was time for a re-think. We were now a very different company from what we had been just two years before: many of the container and shipping interests, which had been the original engines of growth, had gone, and the company had been downsized from assets of $1.8 billion to $1.1 billion at the end of 1990. The good news was that debt, which had traditionally been high, as you would expect in a leasing company, had halved and our equity per common share increased from $22 to $34 that year.

We now had a very different spread of assets, and we had to reconsider our structure and our long-term goals. Although we'd had a rough time, we had come out on the right side of our takeover battle, and in retrospect the timing could not have been better. We had sold assets, but on the whole we had managed to keep the more profitable ones. Part of the container fleet had gone, but it was ageing and would have required costly repair and maintenance, and we were able to start replacing it with the purchase of 22,000 new units within a year (at a cost of $120 million). The main part of the Sealink ferry business across the English Channel had also been sold, but with the Channel Tunnel due to open in 1993 (it actually opened a year later) I wasn't too unhappy about that. In any case that year we announced we would start new high-speed ferry services from Dover to Calais and Folkestone to Boulogne, using a revolutionary catamaran-type vessel called a SeaCat, which could carry both passengers and cars across the Channel in less than an hour. The vessel, the *Hoverspeed Great Britain*, achieved an average speed of 36.96 knots on its record-breaking run across the Atlantic, winning the Blue Riband, and we had high hopes for it, which alas were never realized.

We had shed all sorts of other assets we would not miss: the low-margin container chassis fleet in the U.S. and the tank container forwarding business, which had never achieved its potential. There were other businesses I was genuinely sorry to see go, including the Irish Sea ferries (we had kept the valuable Isle of Man routes). But we immediately made plans for getting back into these areas with SeaCats, which we worked on through that year and the next. Thus, as we entered our second quarter-century, we were, as I explained to shareholders, 'a company in transition'. We were also back on the acquisition trail.

The target this time was the Windsor Court Hotel, the best and most expensive hotel in New Orleans (or the whole of Louisiana for that matter). Like most of the ports in the world, I knew New Orleans fairly well, in this case thanks to my long-time shipping associate, Jim Amoss, chairman of the Lykes Bros Steamship Company, who liked to show his visitors the sights of this most un-American of American cities. I always felt an emotional tie to New Orleans because in the eighteenth and nineteenth centuries generations of Sherwoods sent their tobacco down the Ohio and Mississippi rivers to the port, from where it was shipped to Europe. But its economy has historically been based on cotton – even today the region produces the finest cotton and is the world's largest exporter. The Robert Penn Warren book and film *All the King's Men* and Tennessee Williams' *A Streetcar Named Desire* from my Yale days were reminders of Louisiana life.

Jim gave me the low-down on the background to the hotel, which had been opened in 1984 by a local property developer and civic activist, Jim Coleman, whose family had also built the New Orleans Hilton and several other downtown hotels. The Windsor Court, which was designed on the theme of the House of Windsor and was full of British paintings and sculpture, had run well over budget, and when recession struck, Coleman had to restructure his property holdings. The hotel passed into the ownership of Equitable Life whose chairman, Dick Spangler (married to Bob Riggs' sister, Meredith), asked me whether I was interested in buying it.

I found it an impressive place, airy and modern, with large suites and elegant restaurants and bar areas. Coleman had done a good job, and looking around at the lavish finish and décor, I could see how he had come to run over budget. It was ideally situated in the heart of the business district and just a short walk from the historic French Quarter and the Mississippi. New Orleans has always had a slightly sleazy reputation, but at the same time the French Quarter has been well maintained and the nearby Garden District (reached by taking the *Streetcar Named Desire* trolley) is full of beautiful antebellum houses, the finest of which is owned by our friends Sarah and Prescott Dunbar, who we were to see a lot of in the years that followed.

Once I had looked it over, we agreed a price and Orient-Express took over ownership on 1 October 1991. From the beginning it was a good business. As with the Copacabana Palace, we soon found it had its peak seasons, notably the enormously popular JazzFest in the spring, which attracts tens of thousands of visitors, as do the Carnival celebrations in February (although it isn't a patch on the Carnival in Rio). There are also low seasons of course, notably the hot summers when no one in his right mind wants to visit New Orleans.

For some years we did very well out of it, with operating profits running at $12–14 million, making it one of the most profitable hotels in the company. But then in 2005 Hurricane Katrina came along and changed all that. It trashed New Orleans, flooding the city when the levees collapsed. The city lost all electricity, fresh water and sewerage. The hotel itself avoided flooding, but nothing worked until our innovative regional manager, Dean Andrews, brought in a huge generator, fresh water supplies and portable toilets to keep the place functioning. Dean also had to cope with armed gangs of looters trying to break into the hotel to steal cars, and he got no help from the local police who had disappeared from the scene in the general chaos. Fortunately Dean was friendly with Joseph Riley, the mayor of Charleston, South Carolina, where we owned Charleston Place, and Riley sent over a platoon of Charleston police to protect the Windsor Court.

But the crisis was far from over. A building at the back of the hotel caught fire, and with no water pressure and no fire department to fight it, Dean had to stand back and let it burn itself out, hoping it wasn't going to collapse onto the hotel. The heat was so intense that windows in the hotel began to blister and burst, but fortunately the burning building eventually collapsed upon itself, sending showers of debris across the street which were quickly dealt with. It was a stressful time for staff: the general manager, Tony McHale, whose family was in the hotel during the crisis, asked to leave New Orleans to regain a more stable life and a few months later went to Charlottesville, Virginia, to manage our Keswick Hall property.

It took days before services were eventually restored, and as the waters slowly subsided the hotel housed relief workers, government employees, journalists, insurance adjusters, and even President Bush, who spent a night there – everyone other than ordinary tourists. The building was fundamentally undamaged, but the flying debris broke some of the guest room windows and the rooms immediately became waterlogged, requiring complete redecoration.

We were insured for physical loss of course and also for loss of earnings for the first year after Katrina. At the end of the year the insurance ran out and now we had a major problem. New Orleans did not recover, tourism dried up, and the hotel plunged into losses, tearing a big hole in the group's overall profitability. We had a loan of $50 million from the Singapore bank OCBC secured on the hotel and, as the losses continued, we were in danger of breaching our banking covenant. Unfortunately, this all happened right in the middle of the 2008–9 banking crisis. The banks were panicking and OCBC informed us it wanted its money back. Basically it called in its loan, giving us a year to repay it or refinance it from another source.

This posed a tough decision for the Orient-Express board: did we take $50 million from our working capital, which was already tight, or dispose of the property at a price that would allow us to pay off the bank? I argued that we should find another source of finance for the hotel, which I believed would come back within a few years, but my colleagues reckoned that the banks were in no mood to lend, particularly on real estate in a city like New Orleans. They may have been right. Not many hotels in the U.S. were sold in 2009, but a local group in New Orleans came up with an offer and we accepted it.

Unfortunately we sold right at the bottom of the market, as later events were to prove. I was not at all happy with the decision, but in the end I had to vote with the board. We could have survived the disaster of the hurricane if there hadn't been a banking trial at the same time. But in the end we were faced with one trial too many.

CHAPTER FIFTEEN

SOUTH PACIFIC

We were still in our transition stage in 1991 when the first Gulf War arrived, bringing recession and leaner times for the hotel industry worldwide. Americans temporarily stopped travelling, people spent less and overall we had to batten down the hatches and wait for better times. In Britain interest rates rose sharply and the economy stalled, causing property values to collapse and making me very thankful we had sold Sea Containers House at what turned out to be the top of the market. Sea Containers remained highly profitable but 1991 was a poor year for Orient-Express Hotels and 1992 was worse still, with an overvalued lira and Italy's political problems hurting the Hotel Cipriani and the other Italian hotels, only partly compensated for by healthy trading in Cape Town and New Orleans (Rio was still in the midst of its major reconstruction).

But in 1993 the Italians devalued the lira, good times returned to the world economy, and we were back on track. The Cipriani recovered quickly, the Windsor Court forged ahead and South Africa was approaching its historic election, which I knew would bring boom times for our hotel there.

We were just emerging from this period when the 'greenmailers' struck. 'Greenmail' was a phenomenon of Wall Street in the 1980s and early 1990s, employed by corporate raiders such as Ivan Boesky or Michael Milken to make an easy buck by on occasion targeting companies which happened, for one reason or another, to be vulnerable at that particular moment. The term 'greenmail' actually meant exactly that: 'green' as in greenback and 'mail' as in blackmail. Basically what happened was a raider, say Carl Icahn or T. Boone Pickens, bought a stake in a target company, demanded a place on the board, put forward a series of demands and, with a mixture of threats, legal actions and shareholder resolutions, caused so much disruption that the target company eventually gave in and bought them off – which was often what they wanted in the first place.

In our case the greenmailer bought a shareholding in Orient-Express Hotels on the open market and then said they were going to sue Sea Containers for conflict of interest. They knew what they were doing, and struck at the weakest moment when Orient-Express Hotels was going through its bad patch and Sea Containers, in order to protect its 42 per cent shareholding and keep the momentum going, had extended a line of credit to it. So we bought out the greenmailer.

To be frank, although we had gone to great trouble to ensure there was no conflict of interest, the situation was confusing, and even people inside the company didn't understand it. In its history so far, Orient-Express Hotels (or the Sea Containers leisure division as it originally was) had gone from being 100 per cent owned when we started it in 1976, to zero per cent when we decoupled the shares in 1984, and to 42 per cent in 1987. In June 1994 we decided to make it 100 per cent again (just for the record, it has been through further iterations since and in 2005 came back to zero per cent).

We now had an investment of $214 million in the leisure industry, with nine hotels, management contracts for two others, the Venice Simplon-Orient-Express and a 25 per cent shareholding in the Eastern & Oriental Express train, which is discussed in the next chapter. But it was barely profitable – it made $1.4 million in 1993, which was actually a $5 million improvement on the previous year. And it needed urgent attention.

More importantly it needed its own full-time chief executive, and after some thought I convinced the board to appoint Simon Sherwood, my stepson, who I concluded was the best man for the job. I was aware this would raise some eyebrows and inevitably draw down criticism on me (and him), but the truth was there were very few people who were better qualified for the role, or could do it better. Simon was thirty-four years old at the time, a Cambridge and Harvard Business School graduate who had learned his trade at the Boston Consulting Group, and for the past few years had been working by my side as vice-president of Sea Containers in charge of strategy, which was his forte. He was keen to run a business for a change – in effect practising what he preached – and I thought he was ready for it. The task I set him was to dispose of the unprofitable leisure investments, impose strict financial disciplines across the organization and achieve a return of 10 per cent in 1995, and more after that. Simon created a new management structure, appointing regional managers to look after Europe, North America and 'Rest of the World', each with overall responsibility for the hotels in their regions, which they were required to visit on a regular basis, and to find and develop new investment opportunities. This practice was to serve the company well. In 1994, Simon's first year in the job, the operating profit of the consolidated leisure division was $14 million; when he stepped down as chief executive in 2007, much to the board's regret (particularly mine), operating profits were $155 million.

While all of this was going on we were still trying to grow the business, although sometimes it was two steps forward and one step back. We were offered the management contract of the Fancourt golf resort in George, on the south coast of South Africa, but after taking over the property the company providing the development finance got into all sorts of financial problems and Fancourt had to be sold. The new owners announced they would manage it themselves.

But we did better in Sydney, where in February 1993 we took over the management contract of a new five-star hotel being built in the 'Rocks' district by the Nara Corporation of Japan. It was not yet finished and didn't have a name, so I suggested we call it 'Observatory' for the fairly obvious reason that the hotel was positioned immediately under the Sydney Observatory. It had an excellent location, within easy walking distance of Reserve Bank Square, the centre of the financial district, yet close to the two great symbols of the Sydney landscape, the Opera House and Sydney Harbour Bridge. We hired

Patrick Griffin to manage the hotel, and encouraged him to act as if it was his own personal property, and to do all the things an owner would do, which he did with great success until he retired in 2011.

In addition to the Observatory, the Nara Corporation, a family-owned construction company based in Yokohama, had invested in two other hotels. One of them, Lilianfels, in Katoomba in the Blue Mountains, was a two-hour drive from Sydney. The third was the Bora Bora Lagoon Resort in French Polynesia in the South Pacific, an hour's flight from Tahiti. We took over the management of all three, a relationship which continued until Nara, which had borrowed heavily when the Japanese banks were offering loans at almost zero interest rates, got caught in the collapse of the Japanese property market in the late 1990s. When Mr. Nara offered to sell us all three hotels on very favourable terms we took them over.

The two Australian hotels turned out to be good investments, but Bora Bora, which is a very beautiful island with classic coral reefs and white sands, had problems. Initially there was little competition on the island, but the French government, in its desire to encourage tourism in French Polynesia, provided all sorts of soft loans and other incentives to anyone prepared to build hotels there. The result was that many of the big companies did so, and Four Seasons built a five-star resort, as did Sheraton and various others. Our Lagoon Resort was a nice property but the new hotels were even better and offered more facilities, and we found it more and more difficult to compete.

But there was an even bigger problem. The French Polynesian government controlled the inter-island airline and refused to allow planes to land in Bora Bora after dark, even though there was a modern runway with lights and all the rest of the kit originally put in by the Americans in the war. The international flights all arrived after midnight and landed in Papeete, the capital, and to make their connecting flights to Bora Bora, passengers had to wait around for many hours.

Americans and Japanese loved the beaches and kept coming, but there were not enough prepared to make the inconvenient and lengthy trip to get there. The hotel never did well, particularly after a couple

The *ss. United States* in whose hold I loaded containers with Swiss cargo, bound for New York from Le Havre. The valuable contents arrived in New York almost as fast as by air. © Getty Images Ltd.

My boss in France at United States Lines, Michael Edwards (*left*) with Pauli Grindrod, whose husband Murray served on the Sea Containers board for many years; and (*right*) Philip Schlee, one of the original partners in Sea Containers, with Shirley.

Maury Pinto, my classmate from Yale, whose family was one of my early backers. (*Right*) In 1968 we had a number of containers specially painted for lease to the Rolling Stones for their round-the-world tour.

An 18-year-old Shirley Briggs just before she went up to St. Anne's College, Oxford, to read botany.

The Sherwood and Briggs families celebrate our wedding on 31 December 1977. My parents are seated front and left, and Shirley's are either side. To Shirley's left are Charles and Simon Sherwood.

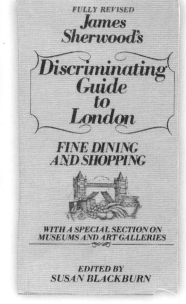

FULLY REVISED
James Sherwood's

Discriminating Guide to London

FINE DINING AND SHOPPING

WITH A SPECIAL SECTION ON MUSEUMS AND ART GALLERIES

EDITED BY
SUSAN BLACKBURN

(*Above*) My interest in fine wines resulted in my being elected to *La Confrérie des Chevaliers du Tastevin*; I was later promoted to *Commandeur*. (*Centre*) My good ship *Barinia* on which I explored much of the Mediterranean. And (*right*) my *Discriminating Guide to London*, first published in 1975, was a runaway success but made me unpopular with some of the best-known restaurants which we panned.

My first hotel acquisition, the Hotel Cipriani in Venice, on the island of Giudecca across from San Giorgio Maggiore with its sixteenth-century church by Andrea Palladio. (*Below*) The famous Hotel Cipriani swimming pool, built by Giuseppe Cipriani in metres rather than feet.

The three Guinness sisters, from left, Lady
Patricia Boyd, Princess Brigid von Preussen
and Lady Honor Channon.

Giuseppe Cipriani (*right*) with Enzo Cecconi,
then manager of the Hotel Cipriani and later
restaurateur in London and Paris.

Dr. Natale Rusconi, who ran the Hotel Cipriani for thirty years; and (*right*) with our most critical guest,
Michael Winner.

Elizabeth Taylor and Sugar with Rusconi at the Hotel Cipriani where she mislaid the 33-carat Krupp Diamond in the ladies' washroom. The ring was sold in 2011 for $8.8m. Inset image © Getty Images Ltd.

Julia Child teaches aspiring chefs at the Hotel Cipriani. Her book, *Mastering the Art of French Cooking*, was generally credited with introducing the American public to French cuisine.

Heads of State at the Hotel Cipriani: Ronald Reagan works on his speech in the bar; Jimmy Carter after a swim in the pool; Prime Minister Margaret Thatcher attended the G7 Summit in Venice in June 1980 and sent the staff a very nice 'thank you' note afterwards; and (*right*) Mikhail and Raisa Gorbachev sign the hotel's Golden Book.

(*Above*) Harry's Bar in London: the walls are covered with original Peter Arno cartoons featured in the *New Yorker* magazine. © Fritz von Schulenberg.

(*Left*) Debonair Mark Birley escorts his former wife, Lady Annabel Goldsmith, to a party. Mark named Annabel's nightclub in London after her.
© Getty Images Ltd.

Portofino Harbour, not far from Genoa in northern Italy. The boutique hotel Splendido Mare is in the centre of the village on the waterfront.

The Villa San Michele in Fiesole overlooks Florence. Its façade derives from a Michelangelo drawing.

The Hotel Splendido sits on the hill above Portofino village.

The Observatory Hotel in Sydney, Australia, is located under the Sydney Observatory, a short walk from Circular Quay and the Sydney Opera House.

Hotel Caruso in Ravello on the Amalfi coast.

The *m.v. Orient-Express* transits the Corinth Canal with just inches to spare. Franco Delle Piane, my long-time associate in Italy, assisted in the acquisition of a number of the Italian hotels and the start-up of the cruise ship service from Venice to Turkey, via the canal.

Sea Containers House at Blackfriars Bridge on the south bank of the Thames in London. We completed this landmark fourteen-storey head office for both Sea Containers and Orient-Express Hotels in 1985. From my office I could see all the way from Big Ben to St. Paul's.

The Mount Nelson in Cape Town was built to accommodate first-class passengers escaping the northern winter. The *ss. Scot* did the run from England in fifteen days in the 1890s, a record not beaten until World War II.

The Mount Nelson Hotel, which opened in 1899, nestles under Table Mountain in Cape Town. We bought it in the dark days of apartheid, taking the view that the South African political system would change for the better. (*Left*) The ceremonial street entrance, built for the Prince of Wales's visit in 1925.

A luxurious tent in one of Orient-Express Safaris' Botswana camps.

The Copacabana Palace on Rio de Janeiro's Copacabana Beach with the Corcovado Christ statue behind. (*Below*) The entire Sherwood family sang the old millennium out and the new one in on 31 December 1999 at the Copacabana Palace.

Philip Carruthers, who has managed the hotel since we bought it in 1989.

The Eastern & Oriental Express crosses the Bridge on the River Kwai in Thailand. The railway into Burma was called the 'Death Railway' and never became operational because of Allied bombing.

Philip Anschutz and his daughter Sarah watch from the train's observation car.

The inaugural journey of the Eastern & Oriental Express, graced by their Royal Highnesses, Prince and Princess Michael of Kent.

Happy-snappers Shirley and Lord Snowdon compare photographers' notes.

Prime Minister Mohamad Mahathir (*centre*). To his right is Francis Yeoh whose YTL Corporation was our partner in the train.

SeaCat Great Britain wins the Hales Trophy – Blue Riband for the fastest crossing of the North Atlantic by a passenger vessel in 1991. The *ss. United States* was the previous holder.

(*Left*) I receive the trophy, held by many great ships of the past, including the *Queen Mary* and *Queen Elizabeth*.

One of the Lake Windermere cruise vessels owned by the Windermere Iron Steamboat Company, which we bought as part of the Sealink privatization in 1984.

of hurricanes came through and caused a lot of damage. As with the Windsor Court in New Orleans we were insured, but we had started to lose money when the new competition came along, and we eventually put it up for sale.

There were better places to spend our money. It was time to go back to trains.

CHAPTER SIXTEEN

From Singapore to Bangkok

The launch of the Venice Simplon-Orient-Express and the publicity surrounding it made us the acknowledged world leaders in the operation of de luxe trains. To be truthful, there was not a huge amount of competition for the role but insofar as it went, we were it. The few brave souls who did operate luxury trains in various parts of the world often sought our advice and help, and we received a number of proposals for joint ventures, none of which suited us. In the early days it was a bit like the blind leading the blind, but as we gained experience, often the hard way, we graduated to being the one-eyed king.

A couple of years into the operation we considered ourselves the professionals who knew how to do it. But how to make the most of our skills? Almost by accident, in that train station in Monte Carlo on that fateful day in 1977, I had strayed onto an interesting and profitable business and the issue now was how to grow it – or, as they would say now, 'leverage the model'? I was keenly aware that it was always going to be difficult for a one-off tourist train, like a one-off hotel, to operate profitably because its sales and marketing expenses would be too high. But if we had a number of trains, we could market them all together and therefore have one central management. We had identified a number of other tourist trains around the world and I believed that, when they came to a certain point in their cycle, they would come to us and ask us to take them over. In the meantime, we had to do it ourselves.

Among the various lessons we had learned early on from operating the Venice Simplon-Orient-Express is that repeat business is small. Hotels have a loyal client base and are therefore less impacted by recession – for instance I have South African friends, the Ovenstones, who have stayed at the Cipriani year-in, year-out, in the same room, for donkey's years. Many visitors stay for a week at a time, sometimes more. Not so the train, where it was usually a one-off 'journey of a lifetime', maybe a honeymoon, an anniversary or a big celebration of some kind – and passengers spent only one night on the train. Few people travelled both ways, so it wasn't even a return business. That meant the trains were much more sensitive to a recession or even temporary slow-down in tourism caused by bombs or acts of terrorism in Europe (of which there were many in the 1980s and 1990s). Our cost base was largely fixed, but our revenues were volatile – not the best of business models.

We countered this by getting the trains to work harder. The British Pullmans were only needed two days a week for the service to Venice, so we used them as much as possible on the other days, running excursions out of London to places such as Leeds Castle in Kent, Lord Montagu's car museum in Beaulieu or sometimes even to Scotland. We took parties to race meetings, on trips around historic spots, such as Stratford or Chatsworth, and in December we were booked solid with Christmas parties. On the continent we started a service from Venice to Paris with the Venice Simplon-Orient-Express including stops in Vienna, Prague, Krakow and Dresden, and generally ran the train wherever there was a market. But we only had one train on the continent and it was mostly busy on the route Calais–Paris–Venice, which was by far the most profitable.

We had all sorts of imaginative ideas of how we might expand: we occasionally ran the Venice Simplon-Orient-Express all the way to Istanbul, recapturing the original flavour of the pre-war train. We looked at trains in Scotland, the Rockies and Vietnam. We explored the possibility of taking over the Blue Train in South Africa which ran between Pretoria and Cape Town, but that fell through (it was relaunched by President Mandela in 1997, on that now-famous trip with Naomi Campbell aboard). The Wagons-Lits company owned a train of vintage Orient-Express day-cars, and we had some negotiations about us operating them but they wanted to do it themselves. We looked at some magnificent old rolling stock from the Italian royal train, but it had no commercial potential. We were offered old wooden carriages in Antofagasta, where there was a famous railway to La Paz in Bolivia, and we thought about doing a deal with the operators of the Palace on Wheels, an old train made up of maharajas' coaches, which operated from Delhi to Jaipur.

Influenced by Bill McAlpine, we even considered steam. There were a number of tourist trains pulled by a steam engine but these were run more by preservationist societies than by commercial concerns – steam engines are expensive beasts, both to maintain and operate, and often have to be accompanied by a diesel. Steam was, to coin a phrase, a non-runner.

For a while I had high hopes of a train in the Rockies, running from Denver down into the Arizona desert in Utah and Nevada. My friend Phil Anschutz (ranked by *Forbes* magazine as the thirty-fourth richest man in America and now the proud owner of the O2 dome in London), who has substantial interests in American railways, lent me his private train for Shirley and I to explore the track which he controlled between Denver and Salt Lake City. The route we envisioned was to start at Denver, then across the Rockies to Salt Lake City and on to Las Vegas, with a stop at Bryce Canyon National Park in Utah on the way. After that the route would cross into California and stop at Barstow, then back on the Santa Fe line to the south rim of the Grand Canyon and across the desert, which is very beautiful, to end in Phoenix. We did the trip by car from Salt Lake City but it was the end of the season and we had to dine on whatever was available in the local towns. Shirley rebelled when we got to Phoenix, saying she would never eat another McDonald's or Kentucky Fried Chicken again.

We were ultimately defeated by the operating costs, which would have been astronomical. The American railway companies are essentially freight operators and don't want passenger trains on their tracks – they reckoned our train, designed for sightseeing in the desert and mountains, would have slowed them down, which was probably true.

Phil agreed we could use his Denver & Rio Grande tracks to Salt Lake City, but the trip after that involved tracks owned by two other railway companies and we would have had to use Amtrak engines, so the total cost would have been prohibitive.

Asia on the other hand, where I was determined to put down roots, looked much more promising, and I dreamed up the idea of operating an Orient-Express train running between Hong Kong and Shanghai. This was a venture we could not do on our own, so I flew to Hong Kong and enlisted the support of Timothy Fok, a member of the influential Fok family in Hong Kong. He was introduced to me by his brother-in-law, John van Praag, who was based in San Francisco where he looked after the Asian interests of Dillon Read, the boutique New York investment bank. John spoke Mandarin and his Chinese wife Pat was a well-known photographer of Chinese subjects. One of my shipping friends, C. H. Tung, who later became the first chief executive and president of the Executive Council of Hong Kong when the British handed back the territory to China in 1997, also offered to use his influence with the Chinese government.

Hong Kong was the gateway for increasing numbers of tourists visiting China and we all agreed that a luxury train could be a big winner. But we would need the approval and support of the Chinese National Railways and no one underestimated the complexities involved in getting that. Tim and John arranged for me to meet the railway officials in Beijing and Guangzhou (Canton), and after days of discussions followed by long ceremonial dinners, I put forward our proposals for a Hong Kong–Shanghai route.

I have never found it easy to do business in China, and never got far with any of my plans. On my first trip in the early 1980s, I went to Shanghai but found no decent hotels there and we stayed at the former French ambassador's residence. Michael Sandberg (now Lord Sandberg), who was then chairman of the Hongkong & Shanghai Banking Corporation (and, even more importantly, also chairman of the Hong Kong Jockey Club where the real decisions were taken in the days of British rule), counselled me to bring my own alcohol if we wanted a drink. I ignored his advice, but fortunately the French ambassador had left behind a wine cellar when he moved out. I asked the wine waiter to produce a few sample bottles, and he brought up five, which he indicated were $5, 'same price for each'. One of the bottles was a '71 Château Latour, and the rest were plonk. The next night, among the plonk, was a Château Lafite and a Mouton Rothschild – and the price was always $5. I enjoyed the wine, but made no progress with my business proposition.

On this occasion I was hoping for better luck but the railway officials, who initially seemed responsive to our proposal, soon began picking holes in it. The biggest problem, they indicated, was that the main line was single-tracked at one point, and although they were building more tracks, they would have to give up four freight trains to take our tourist train, making the costs astronomic. I've never been absolutely certain if this was for real or just a Chinese way of saying they were not interested. We had to drop the project.

But there were other countries to look at. I read an article by a travel writer who had made the trip from Singapore to Bangkok using local trains through some incredibly beautiful and relatively unknown country, and he made it sound like a lot of fun. I thought we might do something along that route. Both cities had major international airports and more than their share of splendid hotels – some of which, such as Raffles in Singapore or the Oriental in Bangkok, I would like to have owned – and both were big tourist destinations. A luxury train running directly between them seemed an exciting prospect.

The Sea Containers' regional manager, Chresten Bjerrum, reckoned the authorities in Malaysia and Thailand would be much more responsive to the idea of a through train than the Chinese had been, and suggested we immediately explore the possibility with them. At that stage there were no through trains along the peninsula, and passengers had to change trains at Butterworth, near Penang, making it a tedious and lengthy journey on rickety old cars. When Singapore and Malaysia split, Malaysia retained possession of the track into the main Singapore rail station so we would only have to deal with two rail companies, KTM in Malaysia and SRT in Thailand, which made it a little bit less complex.

Our first step was to get the Malaysians onside, which meant gaining the support of the Prime Minister, the formidable Dr. Mohamad Mahathir, who was largely responsible for engineering Malaysia's own version of an economic miracle in the 1980s and 1990s. Mahathir's controversial record on curbing civil rights had been strongly criticized in Britain and the U.S., and he was not renowned as a friend of the West. I sought the advice of Adrian Zecha, the famous Dutch Indonesian-born entrepreneur who had been a partner of Bob Burns and Georg Rafael in Regent Hotels International, one of Asia's first luxury hotel groups. Adrian later sold his Regent stake and developed the Amanresorts group, a chain of small, highly individual luxury hotels in beautiful locations, starting in Bali with his flagship Amandari in 1988. When I first got to know him and his wife Bebe, they were living in Hong Kong and we became good friends. Adrian served on the Orient-Express Hotels board during the first period of public ownership.

Adrian didn't know Mahathir well but he put me in touch with Francis Yeoh, chief executive of the YTL Corporation in Kuala Lumpur, who he said was close to Mahathir – which indeed proved to be the case. YTL is one of the biggest and most powerful companies in Malaysia, with a wide range of industrial activities, and Francis, son of the founder, wielded considerable influence in the country. He offered to talk to Mahathir, who turned out to be a train buff and became the most important advocate of our project. Without him we would never have got it off the ground.

By early 1989 the pieces of the project were falling into place. We needed local partners and we found them in the shape of YTL and another Malaysian company, Landmarks Berhad, a major rubber and palm oil producer, and Italthai Industrial, a leading Bangkok-based trading conglomerate. We set up a new company to run the tourist train in which the two Malaysian companies held 50 per cent between them. Orient-Express Hotels ended up with 25 per cent and, just as important, the management contract.

While the political wheels were in motion, I was in motion too, exploring the actual route and trying to form an impression of the visual experience our passengers would have. The railway authorities allocated Shirley and me two private railcars, one of them an observation car, and we were hitched onto a series of local trains to take us over the entire route pulled by a variety of different engines. We travelled for the most part on single track, stopping often to let other trains pass, but that didn't matter as we wound through some of the most beautiful country we had ever seen, with verdant tropical hills and immaculate wayside stations where children rushed to greet the passing train and graceful women in sarongs delicately hid their faces behind bright parasols. We found it utterly enchanting, less dramatic than the route through the Alps but just as interesting. We insisted on making the trip in daylight, as by now we had realized how irate passengers became when they whistled through the best sights in the dark (we were not going to make that mistake again).

On the Kuala Lumpur–Penang stretch the train passed near the Cameron Highlands, the old British hill station where the former American intelligence officer Jim Thompson mysteriously disappeared in 1967. He went for a walk after lunch on Easter Sunday and never came back, giving rise to all kinds of conspiracy theories and hypotheses, ranging from suicide, to abduction by the Chinese, being spirited away by the aborigines or even a Spielberg-style close encounter with a UFO. The speculation rages to this day but an author friend, Bill Warren, who knew Thompson well and has investigated most of the theories, has concluded that he probably got lost in the jungle. This is a pretty dull theory, and not good for tourism, so I discarded it.

We found Penang, with its British colonial architecture, delightful, and stopped for a Singapore Sling (gin, Cherry Heering, Benedictine and fresh pineapple juice, preferably made from Sarawak pineapples) at the Eastern & Oriental Hotel, which opened in 1885 and was part of the chain of luxury hotels founded by the Starkie brothers, who also owned Raffles in Singapore. Maybe it was the effect of the drink, but it was there we had the idea of calling our train the Eastern & Oriental Express.

We continued on past the enormous limestone karst cliffs on the Thai coast, similar to those featured in the James Bond film *The Man with the Golden Gun*, but the highlight for me was the bridge on the River Kwai, scene of the classic Alec Guinness and William Holden film. The story in the film is not strictly accurate: there is certainly a bridge there and British prisoners of war did work on it, but it has stone foundations and steel spans. The bridge depicted in the film was wooden, just north of the permanent bridge and was intended to carry supplies for the railway gangs. The Allies bombed the stone and steel bridge, destroying one of the spans. The railway never became operational, but an estimated 106,000 people lost their lives building it, hence the name: the Death Railway. It is a beautiful, tranquil spot and it is hard to imagine, until you visit the cemeteries and the Death Railway Museum downriver, what took place there.

I always find Thailand's stance during the war rather baffling. The country was officially neutral yet the Japanese were building a railway in the country using forced labour, including Thai citizens and prisoners of war. The Japanese had inadequate lines of supply into adjoining Burma, and the British Army under General Slim eventually defeated them at Colima, and then steadily moved south, building airfields closer and closer to the Death Railway until finally they could reach and put it out of action before it became operational. The Japanese intended their railway to extend to Rangoon, but the line now stops at the Burmese border, although there is talk of reinstating it to Rangoon (now called Yangon) in one direction, and Cambodia and Vietnam and on up to Kunming in China in the other. That would open up some exciting new routes for our Eastern & Oriental Express train.

The trip took us four days because we had to make so many stops and travelled leisurely and only in daylight. When we eventually arrived in Bangkok we were met by Adisorn Charanachitta, the director of our Thai partner Italthai, a part-owner of the iconic Oriental Hotel. Adisorn proved extremely helpful in the battle to get permission from the Thai government to run the train all the way. The Thai government proved unexpectedly unhelpful until Francis Yeoh enlisted the support of Prime Minister Mahathir, who agreed to intervene on our behalf. Mahathir said later that he had to hold a number of meetings with his Thai counterpart, and almost threatened to break off diplomatic relations before he gave in and signed the order (without a kickback).

The final piece of the jigsaw was the most important – the train. There was nothing suitable in Southeast Asia where luxury trains had never operated, but we found what we wanted in New Zealand where the railway company had withdrawn its two de luxe sleeper trains, the Silver Star and the Silver Fern, which had operated between Auckland and Wellington. The train was launched as a prestige project in 1972, but the railways wrestled with an increasingly intractable labour force and in 1979, after only seven years, they withdrew their premier train service in the vain hope of getting the unions to see sense. The New Zealand railways had no expectation of ever using the train sets again, so we bought both of them at a very reasonable price, with the intention of converting them into one, with three dining cars, a bar car and fourteen sleeping cars. The company was anxious to get them out of the country before the unions noticed or the government changed.

The trains had been sitting in the sidings for a dozen years and needed a lot of work, although nothing compared to what we'd had to do to the Wagons-Lits cars in Europe. Malaysian Railways rented us a large shed next to Singapore Station where we built our own railway workshop and set to work. The train would be operating in a tropical climate, so good air-conditioning was a priority and the existing system had to be beefed up. Passengers would spend two nights on the train, so every cabin had to have its own bathroom complete with shower. The insides of the cars were stripped bare and we brought over Gérard Gallet, who had done such a splendid job on the Venice Simplon-Orient-Express train, to create new luxurious interiors based roughly around the theme of the train in *Shanghai Express*, the 1932 film starring Marlene Dietrich. Gallet is a consummate interior designer and did a great job, even choosing the china and glassware for the dining cars.

The project had so far taken three years, but at last all the pieces were in place, and we scheduled a ceremony in Kuala Lumpur to mark the successful signing of the contracts with the governments and rail companies. We invited Dr. Mahathir to the ceremony and he accepted along with many other dignitaries from Bangkok, Singapore and Malaysia. I was engaged in negotiations for various hotels in India at the time and decided to fly to India in the Sea Containers company plane, hold my meetings and carry on to Kuala Lumpur in good time for the signing. It turned out to be a nightmare trip.

Over the years I had made three interesting but unsuccessful trips to India, exploring opportunities for hotel acquisitions or management contracts, and this was my fourth. We had been invited to visit Udaipur by Arvind Singh of the Mewar family, owners of the famous Lake Palace Hotel on the lake of Udaipur, as well as the Jag Mandir Island Palace where the young Shah Jahan, who later built the Taj Mahal, was given refuge after he had rebelled against his father who he succeeded as Mughal emperor four years later in 1627. The City Palace on the lake shore, which has 1,000 rooms, is also part of the Mewar holdings, as is a small boutique hotel, the Shiv Niwas Palace, where we were staying.

We flew to Bombay where we were required to deposit a bond for the value of the plane before we were allowed to proceed on to Udaipur. We arrived over the airport where it was raining but the pilots could not raise the tower and circled a couple of times before finally putting the plane down. They then walked to the tower, which was fully manned, and asked why their radio calls were not answered. The manager replied: 'Because it is raining.' 'What has that got to do with it?' the captain asked. 'Because when it rains the water drips on the radio, and it won't work,' was the reply.

Arvind Singh was an excellent host and a great Anglophile. A brass band played for us at teatime, and we cruised on the lake that evening in a large barge propelled by oarsmen in national costume (used in the James Bond film *Octopussy*). Between the rowers on the lower deck were charcoal braziers where our meal was cooked and brought up to the guests on the raised stern, dish by dish. We stopped at the Jag Mandir Island, which was bathed in floodlight, and returned late to the Shiv Niwas.

The next day we settled down to business. The Lake Palace Hotel was managed by the Taj Hotel Group, controlled by the powerful

Tata family, but the management contract had expired and I hoped Orient-Express Hotels could get a new contract to manage it as well as the Shiv Niwas. Taj argued that the language in the contract, which was unclear, meant it remained in force indefinitely, and Singh, who wanted to end the arrangement, had taken them to court – a slow and complex process in India. Singh also thought that houseboats along the lake's edge would be successful, and we looked at that too. We negotiated a deal and signed a letter of intent. I thought the trip had been a success and set off for the airport, anxious to be well on time for the ceremony in Kuala Lumpur the next day. Some weeks later, when I was back in London, I received a registered letter from an Indian law firm informing me that Arvind Singh was not the Maharana of Udaipur. His elder brother was. On the death of his father, Bhagwata Singh Mewar, Arvind became the official head of the family, but his brother still retained the title Maharana Mahendra Singh Mewar, and no contract could be entered into without his consent – which he was not going to give. It was a blow to me and an even bigger blow to poor Arvind who was the custodian of the Mewar dynasty. The hotel to this day is called the Taj Lake Palace Hotel.

I didn't know this of course as I flew back from Udaipur to Bombay, clutching my precious letter of intent which I believed was my very first successful deal in India. I was already formulating the press release in my mind, working out who I could get to manage the hotels and how we might best promote them. At Bombay it all went dramatically wrong. First of all, the customs couldn't locate the aircraft bond, and we sat on the runway for several hours fretting about the flight to Kuala Lumpur and the ceremony the next day. Then, when we finally lined up for take-off, the tower called us back because the customs people had forgotten to check the alcohol seals on the plane to verify nothing had been touched while we were in India. We finally took off many hours late, and when we reached Malaysia we were told the runway at Kuala Lumpur Airport was closed for the night for repairs. We diverted to Penang and grabbed two hours' sleep in a hotel there before continuing on to Kuala Lumpur in the morning, landing just an hour before the signing. The tropical heat of Kuala Lumpur is not conducive to rushing around in a panic, and we arrived looking the worse for wear (or at least I did) just as the ceremony was about to begin. We managed to greet the guests, including Dr. Mahathir, and get through the ceremony before collapsing in our room at the local Aman hotel.

We were back several months later for the inaugural trip of the Eastern & Oriental Express which set off from Singapore on 19 September 1993, with Prince and Princess Michael of Kent as royal guests. Mahathir boarded at Kuala Lumpur with a large entourage including bodyguards. I was worried about him rubbing up against Prince Michael as his rhetoric by this time had become very anti-British, and I had been warned that he could pull the plug on our project at the drop of a hat. But on this occasion he behaved immaculately, handling Prince Michael, a fellow train buff, with consummate courtesy.

As the train pulled out I breathed a huge sigh of relief because, for the past year, the political tensions between Malaysia and Britain had been mounting to the point where they could have exploded at any moment and killed our project stone dead. For months British newspapers had been investigating the Conservative government's odd decision to donate £234 million of British overseas aid, normally destined for the poorest countries in the world, to build the Pergau Dam in Malaysia. The allegations were that this aid was linked – illegally under the government's own rules – to a £1.3 billion contract Malaysia had awarded to British companies for Tornado fighters and other weapons. Questions were asked in the British Parliament and eventually the Public Accounts Committee, appointed by Parliament to watch over how government money is spent, decided to start a formal inquiry.

Mahathir eventually became so angry about the allegations being made by the British press involving bribery and corruption in his government that he imposed a sweeping trade ban on all British firms which, thank goodness, didn't include us. We kept our heads as low as possible and waited for the storm to blow over – which it eventually did.

For my part, my dealings with Mahathir were always fair and above board. He never asked me for anything and it never occurred to me to offer him anything either – or any other official for that matter. I would never have got the train off the ground without Mahathir's help and support, and I'm grateful to him for that. I think he genuinely saw it as a high-profile project which would not only bring in tourists to Malaysia but would enhance the perception of the country – which the British press, he believed, was intent on denigrating.

As far as I'm concerned, at the end of the day both Orient-Express Hotels and Malaysia (and Thailand of course) were winners. And I think there is more to be done: in addition to its core route of Singapore–Bangkok, the train now does excursions from Bangkok to Chiang Mai and even to Vientiane in Laos. Once the line is restored into Cambodia, the train will run to Phnom Penh, the capital, and no doubt many passengers will take the opportunity to visit the ruins of Angkor, where Orient-Express Hotels has a delightful hotel nearby in Siem Reap. It's a magical part of the world.

CHAPTER SEVENTEEN

THE ROAD TO MANDALAY

Burma (now called Myanmar) is a strange, complex, potentially rich, and in my view at least, much misunderstood country. In 1948, when the British lowered the Union Jack for the last time, it was the second-wealthiest nation in Southeast Asia, and the world's largest rice exporter. It was one of the first countries to find oil, producing its first barrel in 1853, and possesses large quantities of natural gas. In the early 1950s it still produced 75 per cent of the world's teak, a much prized material, and with a highly literate population it seemed set fair on a path to economic prosperity comparable to that enjoyed by its neighbours Malaysia, Thailand and of course, Singapore, the most successful of the tiger economies.

Today, after decades of isolation and stagnation, it is one of the poorest countries in Asia and in 1995, as I arrived in Rangoon (now Yangon, but as everybody there still calls it Rangoon, I will too) and Mandalay with a view to extending leisure interests in the region, I found the contrast between Burma and the Malaysia of Dr. Mahathir bewildering.

How had it happened this way? And who was this Aung San Suu Kyi everyone talked about so much? The second is more easily answered than the first. Like everyone else, I had of course read about Aung San Suu Kyi and knew that her pro-democracy stance and victory in one of the country's very rare general elections had resulted in her spending the last dozen years under house arrest. I remembered her being awarded the Nobel Peace Prize, although of course she could not receive it in person, and her gentle, intelligent face with its haunted eyes was very familiar from the newspapers and TV channels. But that was about the sum of my knowledge as I started on my quest.

My experiences in getting the Eastern & Oriental Express train off the ground in Malaysia, Singapore and Thailand had persuaded me there was a great deal of tourism potential to be unlocked in Southeast Asia, and Myanmar was the least known and least-developed country in the region. In the late 1980s I had taken a gamble on the South African political situation coming right, and it had paid handsome dividends. Although Brazil was proceeding slowly, I had little doubt it would get there too (which it most certainly has). It was clear that democracy and economic development in Myanmar might take longer – everything does there – but it would happen, and I was keen to get in before it did. And if I was going to do business in Myanmar, I needed to know a bit more about it.

To say that Myanmar got a bad press in the West would be the understatement of the century. The military regime had shut itself off from the world, and the world in turn had turned its back on the junta, imposing sanctions and boycotts and heaping censures, U.N. resolutions and condemnations on its head. But as I got to know a little more, I found the politics were not as clear-cut as commentators, most of whom had never been there, liked to make out. I'm not suggesting for a moment its reputation was undeserved: the truth is that while most of Britain's colonial empire, including India and Pakistan, adopted some form of democracy, Burma evolved into a military dictatorship within a few years of gaining independence and a military junta has ruled over a disastrous and troubled economy ever since. I would simply, and maybe naively, suggest that the issues are more complex than Western critics like to make out, as indeed they were in South Africa in the apartheid years, in Brazil and in other countries which have been demonized.

The story of Aung San Suu Kyi, the cause of so much of the obloquy over the years, also needs to be put in context. Her father, General Aung San, was a revolutionary firebrand, founder of the Burmese Communist Party and leader of the resistance to British colonial rule who fought alongside the Japanese for most of the war. As a student at Rangoon University just before World War II, he led a series of strikes against British rule, and received military training in Japan in the early 1940s. He returned to Burma a few weeks after Pearl Harbor to support the Japanese invasion, and when Rangoon fell in March 1942 the Japanese appointed him war minister of a new Burma puppet state. The Japanese Emperor personally decorated him with the Order of the Rising Sun, but as the tide of war turned and General Aung San realized Japan had no intention of granting his country real independence, he made contact with the British. Just weeks before Lieutenant-General Slim's armies retook Rangoon, he led a revolt against his former allies. Churchill branded him a 'traitor rebel leader', but Attlee, who succeeded Churchill in 1945, treated him as the future Prime Minister and negotiated an agreement in London guaranteeing Burma's independence.

In 1947, when General Aung San met with his shadow cabinet to prepare for a full takeover from the British six months later, an armed gang of paramilitaries broke in and killed all of them. The former Prime Minister U Saw, who was his main political opponent, was tried by the British and hanged for the assassination, but a number of British middle-ranking officers were also implicated and several of them imprisoned.

Although General Aung San is a national hero today, with statues and pictures of him all over the place, he was no saint. The British accused him of persecuting the Karen people, mostly hill tribesmen living near the Thai border, and actually tried to bring him to trial for the murder of a village headman in 1942. Lord Mountbatten ruled that this was not a wise thing to do in the politically charged atmosphere of the time and the charges were dropped.

The British left behind a deeply divided country, with warring factions, religions and provinces. General Aung San might have held them together but the new government, hastily cobbled together after the assassination of the shadow cabinet, failed miserably and in 1962 the military took control under the leadership of an eccentric man called Ne Win. He proved to be a bumbler and a hopeless administrator, so while its neighbouring countries were starting to ride their economic tigers, the poor Burmese collapsed into abject poverty. Eventually Ne Win was overthrown by his own military colleagues, who called elections in 1989. And that's where Aung San Suu Kyi enters the picture.

Aung San Suu Kyi was only two when her father was assassinated, and she grew up as the privileged daughter of the great hero (her mother became an ambassador), got a degree in Oxford and later a Ph.D. from the University of London. She married an Oxford don, Michael Aris, a gentle Tibetan scholar by whom she had two children. In 1988 she went back to Myanmar to look after her sick mother, with no intention of becoming involved in politics. But shortly after she arrived Ne Win was deposed, mass demonstrations in favour of democracy were brutally put down, a new military junta took power and Aung San Suu Kyi, greatly influenced by the Gandhi doctrine of non-violence, became one of the founders of the National League for Democracy.

In 1990 the pro-democracy parties won the elections, and riots broke out in Rangoon and state capitals, which the military stepped in to repress. Aung San Suu Kyi was never allowed to assume power on the argument that the nation needed strong government to prevent it collapsing into anarchy, and only the military could provide it. She was invited to leave the country but refused and had been under house arrest for six years when I first arrived.

Until the military coup in 1962, Burma was open to the world. For decades its elite spoke good English, which was the official language (the junta banned it for a while but then relented) and even today you find people in Rangoon and Mandalay who speak English better than many native Brits do. During our negotiations with the ministers, I got to know one of them, David Abel, and persuaded him to tell me his side of the story. He was in charge of inward investment, such as it was: Myanmar got some foreign investment from China, which was always keen to strengthen its economic ties with its neighbour to the south, as well as from India and Thailand, but the U.S., Canada and the European Union had all imposed investment and trade sanctions.

Abel was a highly educated civilian who had been drafted into the government. This was not untypical – over the years I was to meet several ministers who were educated in British or American universities, and were basically civilians like Abel.

Abel's thesis was that from its inception as an independent country, Burma was deeply flawed and divided, and struggled with its different ethnic groups in the various provinces, with which the central government has been in almost continuous armed conflict. There are eighteen provinces, each with its own ethnic mix and culture, and the actual Burmese make up just one of them, although it's the dominant one in terms of language and culture. He pointed out that the decision by the military government to change the name of the country to Myanmar was a gesture aimed at uniting the country and countering the perception that the Burmese race dominated everything. Abel contended that the regime had little choice but to take tough action against its opponents, and the only way to keep control was through the army. Without it, he argued, the country was ungovernable and democracy would just not work, although it might sometime in the future. I was to hear that many times over the next fifteen years.

Back in 1995, as I explored the possibility of investing in tourism in Myanmar, I took the view, over-optimistically, that sense and economics would prevail and the country would emerge, either peacefully or through an 'Arab Spring' type process, as a member of the international community of nations before too long. I confess at the time I was more interested in the business opportunities than the politics, although, as always, they were closely intertwined. I looked at the railways built by the British a century before, but they were in a sorry state – they had never been upgraded or even maintained and they were useless for the purpose of running a tourist train. I didn't spend long on them, as I had already decided to do what the old colonial traders had always done in this hot and humid country: take to the water.

Burma has plenty of it, particularly the Irrawaddy River which is 1,400 miles long, and has provided the main artery of transportation through the trackless tropical jungle for hundreds of years. The British used it as their route upcountry, hence the rousing Kipling song:

On the Road to Mandalay,
Where the flying fishes play

The 'road' was of course the river, which the British, with their long maritime tradition, made good use of. Kipling never did travel the Road to Mandalay, and only ever spent three days in Burma when he stayed in Rangoon and was, he wrote in his diaries, 'struck – very struck', with the beauty of the Burmese girls. He was on a three-month cruise on board the *ss. Madura* from Calcutta to San Francisco, and stopped briefly on the way.

Orient-Express Hotels' project began in 1994 when Chresten Bjerrum came back from one of his regular trips to Myanmar, where Sea Containers did business with the Burma Five Star Line, the national flag carrier. He reported on the country's chronic lack of hotel infrastructure and suggested there might be an opportunity for Orient-Express Hotels to do something there. But there were issues, not least the fact that no bank in the world would lend on real estate in Myanmar with its military regime and shaky economy. In any case it was impossible at the time to acquire properties without the special consent of the government, and we were unlikely to get it. But Chresten, who is a resourceful fellow, had a better idea: we should buy a cruise ship, fit it out as a luxury hotel and moor it in Rangoon on the banks of the Irrawaddy. This could be more easily financed as, unlike real estate, a ship could be sailed away if things turned sour and it would have a value on the international market, which the banks were prepared to recognize.

We were full of the joys of Asia at the time and I immediately embraced the idea. We identified a ship we thought would be perfect for the purpose, a beautiful old liner called the *Princesse Marguerite*, which had run between Seattle and Vancouver Island before being retired. She was about to be sold for scrap, so we bought her for next-to-nothing and towed her to Singapore. But then it turned out that the cost of fitting-out was going to be very high and we didn't think the ship would be worth what we would need to invest in it. We were also not very happy with the berth we were allotted by the authorities in Rangoon – it was right next to a ferry, and was noisy and over-crowded, with thousands of people crossing the river. To be fair, the riverfront was pretty full and there were no decent berths available, so it wasn't a question of the authorities being unhelpful. They did their best but, although the berth we were offered was not far from the government-owned Strand Hotel, built by the Starkie brothers as the grandest hotel in Burma in its day (but by then terribly run-down), we didn't think it was a five-star location.

We abandoned that one and decided instead to go upriver to Mandalay, the second biggest city in Myanmar, and operate a cruise ship rather than a floating hotel. The Irrawaddy seemed to me the ideal place for a river-borne Orient-Express-style experience. It may not be one of the great rivers of the world – it ranks fifty-fifth in length, a third the length of the Nile, the Amazon, the Yangtse or even the Mississippi – but it offers a river travel experience which in my view is just as interesting as the Nile. Life on the riverbanks and on the water is much as it was centuries ago: oxen pull water-carts to the river's edge for filling; clothes are washed and laid out on stones to dry; small boats are oared across the river with supplies or bulk cargoes; large numbers of riverboats and self-propelled barges lumber up and down, with some going aground in low water on the soft silt bottom, awaiting rescue by the many small tugboats which ply the busy waters. It's a fascinating, unchanging kaleidoscope of an ancient world and a long-gone unhurried way of life, and I could sit and watch it for days (in fact I have done so).

Chresten led the negotiations, and on 27 January 1995 we signed a contract with Union of Myanmar Economic Holdings Ltd. to operate a cruise ship on the 90-mile stretch of river between Mandalay and Pagan (now called Bagan), the capital of the ancient kingdoms of Burma from the eleventh to the thirteenth centuries when Burmese culture was at its height.

I chartered an old riverboat to explore the route personally, as I always liked to do before committing to buying anything. Supplies for the trip had to come from Singapore, and Eastern & Oriental Express sent a chef and waiters with food and drink, but they had intended to buy wine in Rangoon, only to discover none was available. When we boarded the plane in Singapore to fly to Myanmar, we were each given three bottles of excellent French wine to carry aboard in our hand luggage, and this saved us from the terrible fate of a dry trip. This was our first voyage along the river and we were bowled over by the sheer beauty and visual impact of it. I could see it was going to prove a popular destination once we started marketing it.

The Irrawaddy is a temperamental and mercurial river, changing moods with the seasons: it floods in August and September when the monsoon rains come down from the Himalayas and has very low water in the dry months of January and February. At its low point the channel at Mandalay is only 2.5 metres deep, so our ship would have to have a maximum draft of 2.1 metres, and even then it would often ground on the soft silt bottom before floating off. We found a Rhine cruise vessel which was ideal for our purposes, but she needed extensive refitting, and when we got a quotation from one of the German shipyards it was prohibitively expensive. Someone mentioned that the Harland & Wolff shipyard in Belfast, where the *Titanic* was built, had closed down and its expert craftsmen were out of work. So we rented a berth on the Elbe River and flew in fitters from Belfast who slept aboard in the guest cabins – and did a great job at a fraction of the cost.

To get her to the Irrawaddy we sailed her downriver to the mouth of the Elbe where a semi-submersible ship obligingly sank below the surface allowed our ship to float on top. It then blew its ballast tanks and the *Road to Mandalay* rose magically out of the water. A few weeks later the process was reversed in the mouth of the Irrawaddy and she made her way up the river to her new berth in Mandalay, quite a change from the Rhine. The former master of the *m.v. Orient-Express* cruise ship, Brian Hills, was called out of retirement to skipper the *Road to Mandalay* and he remained on board for a couple of years while training up his Burmese replacements. He commented with relief that the Irrawaddy was a darned sight wider than the Corinth Canal that I had made him navigate.

The *Road to Mandalay* commenced operations in September 1995 and, as with the launch of the two trains, we invited a shipload of friends and press to make the trip with us. We included Michael Winner who on this occasion gave us a splendid review in his *Sunday Times* column. You never knew with Michael. There was a last-minute panic when one of our guests, the historian Sir Alistair Horne, decided to go and meet Aung San Suu Kyi and was questioned by the police. He was on an innocent mission to deliver some personal effects from her husband in Oxford, but we were concerned that the government would find out that he had written controversial books about General Pinochet in Chile and the Algerian war (he has also written a definitive book on Napoleon, but Napoleon wasn't big in Myanmar, even among the generals). Fortunately they didn't put two and two together and we got him safely back on board before we sailed.

It takes the better part of two days to steam down to Pagan from Mandalay and, as navigation is not permitted at night because there are no navigational aids, the ship anchors at sunset. The old British charts of the river proved completely useless because the river constantly changes course with the floods and when we tried to match the GPS readings with the charts they were miles apart. Even while the ship was clearly in a deep channel in the middle of the river, the charts often indicated she was on dry land – that's how much the course of the river, like the course of life in Burma, had changed since the British left.

Pagan, as we thought it would, turned out to be a big hit with our passengers. It's an amazing place, one of the richest archaeological sites in the world. It was from here that the ancient Burmese kings ruled over the Irrawaddy basin for 250 years and built 10,000 temples, 4,000 of which remain. It was also the centre from which the Burmese language and culture, now the cause of so much tension, spread across the empire. Pagan is best seen at sunset or, better still, at dawn when the temples, stretching to the horizon, rise out of the mist like Oxford spires. It was sacked by the Mongols in 1275 and an earthquake in

1975 knocked down another 1,000 temples. But there are plenty left. Personally, I find Pagan more interesting than the better-known Angkor in Cambodia because of the varied temples, while in Angkor the structures are all very similar. Pagan is a great centre for the manufacture of beautiful lacquer-ware, and we encourage passengers to watch it being made.

Not far north of Mandalay is the enormous stupa of Mingun which in the distant past had what was reckoned to be the largest bell in the world. Unfortunately, the king of the day ran out of money so the stupa was never completed, but the vast foundations and bell are still there. When the water is exceptionally low at Mandalay we hire a local boat to take the passengers up to Mingun, but if the river is deep enough the *Road to Mandalay* itself is able to tie up at the shore. When the river is in flood the ship can go almost to the Chinese border to a town called Bhamo, but in winter's low water it cannot operate north of Mandalay. The government allowed us to use satellite telephone and TV links, which meant we were always able to stay in touch with the outside world, even at times when they had cut off such links from the capital.

As the venture prospered, inevitably other groups tried to copy us. The exclusivity clause in our contract to operate the *Road to Mandalay*, the only proper cruise ship on the river, protected us from direct competition, but several operators bought ancient riverboats and converted them to carry perhaps a dozen passengers in pretty rough conditions. We had created a market and had to guard it jealously.

In all the years we have operated in Myanmar, we have never experienced the slightest difficulty with the government. Over that time the tourist infrastructure and economy have slowly but steadily improved, and we find today that we have to put up with fewer inconveniences than we did in the early days, such as paying for fuel in cash because of the lack of a working international banking system. It is still difficult to source all the ship's needs locally, so refrigerated containers of food, drink and supplies have to be sent up by ship from Singapore, arranged by the Eastern & Oriental Express office based there. The government has become much more aware of the value of tourism, and of the importance of Pagan in particular, and has cleaned it up wonderfully – the last time we were there, there wasn't a bit of plastic or scrap of rubbish to be seen, which was not necessarily so in the early days. One day we passed a gang of 'volunteer' labourers working on the moat around Mandalay and stopped for a chat. The workers explained that every week they devoted unpaid time to work on projects such as this to improve tourism. Civil liberties groups in Britain and elsewhere deplored the use of forced labour in Myanmar, but these labourers all seemed to be content. We never saw any slums in the Mandalay/Pagan region, and when we visited the Pagan general hospital we were rather impressed by the facilities – although when the doctor in charge told us that snakebite was one of his worst killers, we trod more carefully around the temples.

Over the years I have had lengthy discussions and debates with ministers, often centred around the transition to full democracy and the opening up of Myanmar to the world, which I have always desperately wanted to happen. I met several times with Khin Nyunt, the former head of intelligence, after he became Prime Minister in 2003, and he told me he would like to move quickly to a democracy but other members of the junta thought it was premature. On one occasion he said, only half joking, that he was personally very anxious to transition to a civilian government so he could sleep in his own bed at home, rather than bunk down in the military compound where we held our talks. He was replaced in 2004 after just a year in power.

In May 2008 we had a natural disaster to cope with when Cyclone Nargis, one of the strongest tropical storms ever recorded, made landfall in the mouth of the Irrawaddy River. Winds gusting up to 150 m.p.h. caused catastrophic destruction and an estimated 140,000 casualties, making Japan's 2011 tsunami look like a minor event (about 21,000 killed). Most of the delta was flooded, and many of its 4 million population were left homeless. In the weeks that followed the government was criticized for the slowness of its response and its reluctance to accept large-scale international foreign aid. President George Bush said that an angry world should condemn the way Burma's military rulers were handling the aftermath, and awarded

Aung San Suu Kyi a Congressional Gold Medal. A few days later the regime gave in and accepted India's offer of aid, but it was all a bit late and by that stage disease was spreading among the shelters and ruins in which the homeless sought refuge.

The *Road to Mandalay* was in a shipyard in Rangoon when the storm hit and one side was stove in, requiring extensive repair. Thankfully, she did not sink, and was back in service a year later. But the cyclone, and the subsequent publicity surrounding the government's reaction to it, hit tourism hard: only 47,161 people arrived from Europe in 2009, mainly from France and Germany, and Myanmar that year was the least visited country by British people in all of Asia, with the sole exception of North Korea. In 2010 it began to pick up again and things now are more or less back to normal.

So our ride so far in Myanmar has been a bumpy but at times an exhilarating one, and I'm glad we have been able to stick with it. Cyclone Nargis was followed by significant political changes which go some way at least towards meeting the demands of the West. The difficulty of persuading the provinces, particularly the Shan State, to sign up to a new constitution had always posed a major obstacle on the road to democracy. However, in 2008 the new constitution was finally adopted by national referendum, opening the way for democratic elections, which were duly held in 2010. The constitution still provides for 25 per cent of the seats in the new Parliament to be held by the military, and before the elections a number of military figures stepped down and put themselves forward for election. As no effective opposition parties had yet formed, they were elected – which means a majority in the Parliament is pro-military.

However, this was at least a first step towards democratic and civilian rule, and the American ambassador in Rangoon assured me that the next and successive elections will be more representative of the wishes of the population. We shall see. Aung San Suu Kyi was released from house arrest on 13 November 2010, three days after the elections, and in December 2011 the U.S. Secretary of State, Hillary Clinton, was allowed to visit her in the famously ramshackle lakeside villa where she spent most of her fifteen years in detention. 'The fact that the meeting was able to take place at all is a measure of how much has changed in Burma since Ms. Suu Kyi's release from house arrest just over a year ago,' commented *The Times*.

For all the controversy that still surrounds Myanmar and its regime, I retain my love of the country and my optimism about the future. Tourism, as it has done in many parts of the world, may yet prove the catalyst for change in this fascinating country with all its para-doxes, contradictions and complexities. I accept it's been a longer haul than I envisaged when we started out with such hopes in 1994. But we'll get there.

CHAPTER EIGHTEEN

CHARLESTON PLACE

Some deals can take a long time to gestate, and conception can start in the most unlikely of places with the most unexpected people. In the case of one of the best buys Orient-Express ever made, Charleston Place Hotel, it took thirteen years and began one winter in the ski resort of Gstaad in Switzerland, at the birthday party of Sir Jocelyn Stevens, a handsome Old Etonian charmer whose varied career took him from proprietor of the society magazine *Queen* to president of the Royal Society of Arts and English Heritage via managing director of the *London Evening Standard* and *Daily Express*. To mark his fiftieth birthday in 1982, Jocelyn's partner, Dame Vivien Duffield, gave one of the most memorable parties any of the guests can recall. Vivien is one of the most generous hostesses of her generation, and flew in 130 of Jocelyn's 'closest friends', including Shirley and me, and threw a glittering ball at which every table was decorated with a tree of diamonds, sapphires and emeralds.

Among the guests was Alfred Taubman and his wife Judy, a former Miss Israel, whom I had never met before but instantly took to. Born in Michigan to Polish Jewish parents, Taubman was to the shopping mall what Malcolm McLean was to containerization – that is, he basically invented the concept. As a retailer he was a genius, and had pioneered the idea of siting lavish shopping centres, with prestige 'anchor' stores such as Nieman Marcus, in upmarket suburban areas. His attention to detail was legendary, down to the fountains and the flooring, which had to be expensive, preferably Italian, tiles. 'Carpet is the worst thing you can have,' he once said, 'because it creates friction.' Shoppers, he reckoned, travelled faster on terrazzo – and therefore spent more.

When I first met him, Taubman was still little known to the general public, but at fifty-nine was already one of the richest men in America. He had created a property empire with twenty-five major shopping centres across the U.S., 100 movie theatres, 800 fast-food outlets and a fortune which *Forbes* magazine estimated at $525 million – which really was a fortune in 1982.

We were both staying at the Palace Hotel in Gstaad and we chatted and skied together, although as I recall, even though it was February (the big dinner was actually on St. Valentine's Day), it wasn't very good skiing weather. It was the kind of event where you bond with your fellow guests and we formed a friendship which lasted for years. We had two particular attributes in common: we were both Americans and we were both large men.

Saturday night's dinner was fancy dress (circus style), and the beard of one of the guests caught fire, burning his face badly. The floor of the hall was covered with straw and the windows were tiny. Al and I realized around the same time that if the conflagration spread, we were never going to get out. I think someone must have thrown a glass of champagne over Burning Beard, because we got through the weekend alive, probably with a raging hangover. Vivien gives great parties, and this was one of her best.

A year later Taubman shocked the British establishment by making a takeover bid for one of its most prestigious companies: Sotheby Parke Bernet, the 239-year-old tradition-laden art auction house, which had got itself into deep trouble through bad management and overexpansion during the heady 1970s when the auction business was booming. Sotheby's was losing money and its shaky finances and declining reputation were persuading collectors to take their artworks elsewhere – particularly to its archrival Christie's.

In other circumstances Sotheby's might have fiercely resisted Taubman simply because of his background, but in this case they welcomed him with open arms, seeing him as a white knight who would save them from the clutches of two other wealthy Americans, Marshall Cogan and Stephen Swid, who had mounted a hostile takeover bid (we shall encounter Cogan again in the next chapter). Taubman was actually a big art collector with a genuine love and feel for fine paintings, and assured the Sotheby's board his intentions were honourable and he had no plan to rape the company. Cogan and Swid were also big collectors of art, were almost as rich as Taubman, and already owned 29.9 per cent of Sotheby's stock. When the board resisted them, largely on the grounds they weren't 'our kind of people', they went hostile, causing the aristocratic head of Sotheby's, Graham Llewellyn, to threaten to 'blow my brains out' if their bid succeeded. The Sotheby's staff of experts in London warned they would quit en masse. Taubman obligingly stepped into the breach, offered $100 million for the business, got the board's support and sent Cogan and Swid packing. He was pretty pleased with his purchase: 'This is like coming over here and buying the throne,' he declared.

Over the years that followed he did a great job with the auction house, restoring confidence among its clientele and redesigning the New York headquarters, where he added luxury boxes for clients' privacy and even escalators. He took the company public in 1988, by which stage it was back to its rightful place as the leading auction house in the world. But he made the fatal (almost literally) mistake of hiring Dede Brooks, a preppy, long-legged, short-skirted blonde who soon became the darling of American millionaires as she handled high-profile auctions including the sale of the Duchess of Windsor's and Jackie Kennedy Onassis' personal jewellery. Brooks made the business highly profitable, but she wasn't too fussy about how she did it.

I often went to Sotheby's in both London and New York, and ran into Taubman there or saw him socially from time to time. But it was years later before I broached the subject of the Charleston hotel which he owned – and which I wanted Orient-Express Hotels to manage.

Sea Containers had its North American administration offices in Charleston, South Carolina, so I was a frequent visitor there and always stayed at Charleston Place, which was the only decent hotel within the historic district. Charleston is a charming colonial town on the Atlantic coast, where the Americans suffered their biggest defeat in the War of Independence. It seceded from the Union in the Civil War and fought on the side of the Confederates. Fort Sumter, whose siege and surrender marked the start of the Civil War, is nearby and is a big tourist attraction. Although Charleston was also besieged and shelled by Union forces, it survived remarkably undamaged and the centre, which is a conservation area where the main means of getting round is horse-drawn transport, has been beautifully restored. Charleston Place Hotel was right in the heart of it, and it was clear the conservationists would make sure no new hotel would ever be built in the historic district, so there could never be a competitor – the dream of all hotel owners. I thought often of how it could be so easily upgraded into a five-star hotel which, like the Splendido in Portofino, would have the market to itself.

It never occurred to me that Taubman might sell the hotel, but I did think that we could do a much better job of managing it than Omni Hotels, its current manager. I ran into him at a reception somewhere and proposed this to him. He suggested I visit him in his office in Bloomfield, Illinois to discuss the matter. It turned out to be a remarkably opportune moment. By this time Taubman was one of the most high-profile businessmen in America and in the decade since we first met he had followed up his Sotheby's purchase with the acquisition of California's Irvine Bank, the A&W restaurant franchise, a professional football team and a couple of department store chains. But he had backed the $3 billion buy-out of Macy's, which had filed for bankruptcy a year earlier, and he was now forced to sell off assets. When we met in Bloomfield, an upmarket suburb of Detroit, he said he wasn't really interested in my offer to manage the hotel, which he dismissed out of hand. He said he wanted to get out of the hotel business altogether. 'Why don't you buy it from us?' he asked. I almost fell off my chair.

We agreed a price of $80 million, which was the highest figure we had yet paid for a hotel, and I now had to find it. Fortunately 1995 was a banner year for Sea Containers, with a net income of $92 million on revenue of nearly $500 million. The Copacabana Palace in Rio was still largely closed for renovation so it was a drag on earnings, but the rest of the leisure business was going strong, and we were ready for another acquisition. The only fly in the ointment was that Taubman had put in place a complicated tax structure with the result that we could only get to 100 per cent ownership over a period of years.

We took over Charleston Place in October 1995, a month after the launch of the *Road to Mandalay*, and it contributed to profits from the start, developing over the years into one of our most valuable properties. Under the management of Paul Stracey, the son of the executive vice-president of Sea Containers, Michael Stracey, we successfully upgraded it to five-star standard. It is the largest hotel in the Orient-Express Hotels portfolio with 440 rooms, eighty of them suites.

The hotel presented us with an unusual conundrum in that it is back-to-front. The Mount Nelson in Cape Town had the same problem, solved long before our time by the creation of a great avenue of palms, planted for the Prince of Wales's visit in 1925, which sweeps up to the new frontage. The same story is told of the Taj Mahal Palace Hotel in Bombay, which is also said to have been built back-to-front when the local builders inadvertently reversed the plans, which had been sent out from England. The original front roadway in Charleston was too small for the volume of traffic, so the rear door of the hotel had to become the main entrance. To make it look more prepossessing we built a large *porte-cochere*, and got the sculptor John Mills to create a huge fountain with four bronze Charleston dray-horses which dominated the new arrival area. We reserved the original entrance for horse-drawn carriages which provide tours of the beautiful ante-bellum houses.

I went back a long way with John Mills who I met soon after I arrived in Britain in the 1960s. We were introduced by Donald Turner, Shirley's great friend, who lived in Hertfordshire, just north of London. Donald's great ambition in life was to be an artist, and he was friendly with Henry Moore and with Mills, who also lived in Hertfordshire. I later got Mills to make a sculpture of St. George for the Windsor Court in New Orleans.

I continued to meet Taubman from time to time, but just two years after he sold us the hotel he was arrested and charged by the U.S. federal authorities with leading a price-fixing scheme with his rivals Christie's which, it was claimed, had swindled auction house customers out of more than $100 million. For the next five years he was in and out of Manhattan courts fighting an investigation into the rigging of commission fees by the two auction houses which, to protect what was left of their reputations, finally agreed to settle class actions with 100,000 customers for $512 million between them. Taubman had to pay $156 million personally, plus another $30 million to settle a stockholder's suit.

But that didn't end it. In return for conditional amnesty from criminal prosecution, Christie's handed over key documents to the U.S. government investigators which incriminated Taubman. Then the glamorous Dede Brooks pleaded guilty to price-fixing in return for leniency in her sentence and testified against Taubman, saying she was simply carrying out the orders of her boss. The Old Etonian chairman of Christie's, Sir Anthony Tennant, was indicted along with Taubman, but refused to travel to the U.S. from his home in England and was never extradited. Christie's, seen by many as the real culprits, was a British company and operated under its more lenient competition laws, whereas Sotheby's was subject to the full rigour of U.S. anti-trust legislation.

That left Taubman to carry the can alone, and in April 2002 a Manhattan federal judge, rebuking him for not showing remorse, sentenced him to a year and a day in prison and fined him $7.5 million, despite pleas from Henry Kissinger, the former President Gerald Ford and even Queen Noor of Jordan, all friends of his. I felt like joining them, and would have done if I thought it would have had any effect. 'The law does not countenance a robbery,' the judge pronounced. 'Price-fixing is a crime whether it's committed in the grocery store or the halls of a great auction house.' Taubman, who was seventy-five by then and in poor health, served ten months, emerged in 2003, and got on with his life. In April 2011, he gave $46 million to the University of Michigan for stem-cell research and is reckoned to have donated more than $650 million to charity in his lifetime.

As for Dede Brooks, she was sentenced to six months home detention in her $5 million Manhattan apartment, where she was reported to be doing volunteer work for troubled girls in public schools. It was an extraordinary tale, which my great friend, the novelist (Lord) Jeffrey Archer would sympathize. He was convicted of perjury on the basis of very thin evidence and not given the right to appeal. There were political overtones to it as well. At least he wrote some very engaging books about his experiences when he was in prison.

Charleston Place has more than earned its keep over the years and is one of the cornerstones of the Orient-Express portfolio today. It may not be as glamorous as the Hotel Cipriani or the Splendido, but it's perfect for its market, which is a rich and growing one. I shall always be grateful for that weekend in Gstaad where it all started.

CHAPTER NINETEEN

'21' CLUB

On 15 September 1995, the same week we launched our riverboat on the Irrawaddy and a few days before I agreed the purchase of the Charleston Place Hotel, a story appeared in the *New York Times* under the heading: 'London Group Buys '21' Club'. The first paragraph said it all:

> The '21' Club, a Prohibition-era speakeasy that became one of New York's most popular dining and drinking places, was sold yesterday to an international hotel and restaurant corporation based in London. The new owner is James B. Sherwood, president of Sea Containers and chairman of Orient-Express Hotels.

If I'd bought the Statue of Liberty I doubt I could have made a bigger stir. Reports over the next few days referred to '21' as 'legendary', a '1950s icon', one of the 'premier drinking establishments in a city with more than 30,000 of them', and even 'one of Manhattan's most beloved and enduring restaurants'. Everyone knew about '21' Club, even if they had never been there, and everyone had a view on it. There was a lot of comment on my statement that I planned 'no changes in the staff, menu and price structure', although I did add we would expand the interior space in the old brownstones where it was housed. I had earmarked some of the offices and storage space on the upper floor as potential banqueting rooms, and also thought we might find room to create some dining space in the wine cellar, which held 10,000 bottles.

I knew I had to tread warily when it came to change at this august institution where 'change' was a word not to be used lightly. Many of the patrons had been dining there two or three times a week for decades and liked it the way it was. The owner, Marshall Cogan, the same New York industrialist who had made the hostile bid for Sotheby's in 1983 and been topped by Alfred Taubman, had made some changes which the regulars didn't like, and the business had been immediately affected.

I was familiar – although not overly – with '21' Club from my student days at Yale in the 1950s, and had been there from time to time when I was in New York. It wasn't a club at all but a fancy restaurant with a club-like atmosphere which generations of 'Yalies' frequented. It got its name from its location on West 52nd Street, which was known for its jazz clubs such as Eddie Condon's, which I would sometimes visit then. Some of my richer fellow-students, like many Ivy Leaguers, often went to '21' to eat but in my case it was too expensive. One regular said at the time: 'I can eat in just about any restaurant in New York for what it costs for the tip in the men's room in '21'.'

The success of Harry's Bar in London, probably the nearest equivalent to the '21' Club, had long convinced me that a top restaurant in Manhattan would be a very good addition to the Orient-Express portfolio. There were regular stories and rumours over the years that '21' was for sale, and at one stage the owner of the Tavern on the Green, Warner LeRoy, was quoted as saying he was approached by a real estate agent to buy it, but 'the price quoted to me was so far out – around $40 million – that it wasn't even realistic', he said.

Over the years, I made several approaches, some oblique, some direct, to Cogan about buying '21', but was always told it was not for sale. Then in 1995, out of the blue, I got a call from an investment banker in New York who had once represented a group of shareholders in Sea Containers. He told me he was acting for Marshall Cogan, who was now prepared to sell '21' and he thought we would be the ideal owners.

Cogan, like Taubman, was experiencing some reverses in his main businesses because of the high levels of his borrowing. At one stage he was a big player on Wall Street, the principal shareholder of the Knoll furniture group, Foamex, which made polyurethane panels, and United Auto group, which operated car dealerships across America. When he bought '21' in 1985 he declared: 'There are three great institutions in corporate America: General Motors, Coca-Cola and '21'. And I own one of them.' He also made a bid for the Boston Red Sox, on the grounds that it, like '21', was 'entertainment'. But by the mid-1990s he had overborrowed, was caught unprepared by a downturn in the auto industry and, although no one knew it at the time, his main holding company, Trace International, was already on the long slippery slope towards bankruptcy. A few years later he sold his large house in Southampton on Long Island for $10.5 million, and most of his large art collection. By 1999, four years after he put '21' Club up for sale, Trace International filed for bankruptcy with assets of $135 million and liabilities of $280 million.

But none of us knew that back in 1995 when I got my first look at the books and began trying to put a value on the restaurant. The figures were not encouraging and showed that, although the '21' was still profitable, the earnings record was poor. I thought we could make something of it, and after some reflection and discussion with my board and advisers, I made an offer of $23 million, which was less than the asking price but still a bit of a stretch considering the profits history. It was also a bit of a stretch for Sea Containers and Orient-Express Hotels, as we were now committed to paying $80 million for the Charleston Place Hotel, and were spending heavily on other ventures. But we all agreed we should acquire this prestige asset, which we could develop and make more profitable, and I flew to New York expecting to negotiate directly with Cogan.

When I arrived at his office high up in the Citicorp Building, I found myself meeting not with Cogan but with his deputy, who basically told me I was wasting my time because Cogan had received a higher offer. I was not even asked to improve my bid, which I had no intention of doing in any case. I decided the game was over and went off for lunch, but not without agreeing to their request to pop back afterwards – why, I had no idea.

I had a good lunch as a guest at the Harvard Club and duly returned
to Cogan's vast conference room which I remember had a huge Leger
on one wall, while another wall was entirely a window, through which
much of Manhattan was visible, from river to river, bisected by the spire
of the Chrysler Building. I sat for a while gazing at this until the door
burst open, Cogan came in, walked straight over to me, shook my hand
and said: 'Done!' It was one of the more bizarre negotiations I've had.

When people wrote about the 'glamorous past' of the '21' Club,
which they often did, they always referred to it having started life
as a 'speakeasy', which indeed was how it opened on 31 December
1929, the very last day of the 1920s. The term 'speakeasy', common in
the 1920s and 1930s, simply referred to an establishment where liquor
was freely available during the days of Prohibition, introduced by
President Hoover in January 1920. Some speakeasies were operated
by organized criminals such as 'Legs' Diamond or Lucky Luciano,
but most of them were simply underground establishments where
ordinary folk could still have a drink. Prohibition was considered a
'Washington, D.C. law' and not a law of New York State or the City
of New York, and far from having the effect the temperance societies
sought to achieve, the opposite happened. 'People merely threw back
their heads and laughed, gave the Big Bad Act a big Bronx cheer,
and set out to prove that legislated morality basically stinks,' wrote
Marilyn Kaytor in her celebrated history of '21' Club published in 1975.
Prohibition closed New York's great wining and dining bars in the big
hotels, but for every bar that closed, two new ones sprang up. It has
been estimated that during the thirteen years of Prohibition, some
80 per cent of the American adult population learned to 'break the
law and love it'; by 1922 there were 32,000 speakeasies in New York
alone, double the number of legal drinking places that had existed
before Prohibition. 'Booze', the new term used to describe alcohol of
any kind, was also available from the local fruit store, pharmacy and
even the shoeshine parlour. The speakeasies were often raided by the
police and agents of the Bureau of Prohibition (the so-called 'Feds')
but because there were so many of them and the local cops were easily
bribable, they continued to flourish.

'21' was the creation of Jack Kriendler, a Jewish immigrant from Austria, and his cousin Charlie Berns. In 1920 they started serving contraband liquor from a nondescript former tea room in Greenwich Village, which they called the Red Head. It soon became popular with students, artists, musicians and newspapermen who came for the atmosphere as much as the drink. Kriendler's younger brother Pete, who continued to work for us after we bought '21', described it as a 'jivey, jazzy place, good clean fun – everyone dancing the Charleston and playing practical jokes'. The illicit liquor was stored in flasks which were hidden in coat pockets in the cloakroom and sold to customers, who drank it out of tea-cups, for a dollar an ounce.

As their business flourished the cousins moved to better premises, first to Washington Place, then a sleazy, run-down area of New York where they created a bright and stylish new speakeasy called the Fronton. The bar consisted of wooden planks balanced on two wooden sawhorses, under which was the main drain. On top of it were four pitchers, containing Scotch, rye, gin and bourbon which could be tipped down the drain in the event of a raid while Jack and Charlie 'scooted out the back through the coal cellar door onto Sixth Avenue', as Charlie later related. The club was put on the map by the regular presence of the Mayor of New York, Jimmy Walker, who frequently turned up dressed in his hallmark top hat, striped trousers, frock coat and gardenia in his button-hole, with a retinue of politicians and their ladies. Not surprisingly, the Fronton was never raided, one of the few that weren't. Walker was later immortalized by Bob Hope in the film *Beau James*.

They moved twice more, each time to bigger and better premises, before settling in 21 West 52nd Street, which they bought just after the Great Crash in 1929 for $130,000. They decided to call it Jack & Charlie's '21'. Their dream had always been to create a speakeasy which would combine the elegance of a Parisian café with the old City of London-style taverns associated with Samuel Johnson, where Wall Street bankers could mix with men of letters and read newspapers, chat and take their wives or girlfriends to an excellent dinner with great food and wine. There was no place like it in New York, and soon it was attracting clientele such as Howard Hughes, Jean Paul Getty and Gary Cooper, although the cousins remained very fussy about who was allowed in, with the door securely guarded by a peep-hole receptionist who only opened up for callers he knew. If it was the Feds, he could press a button to warn the barmen inside who would scoop up the bottles from the shelves and hide them in the cellars. The club didn't really get going until after eleven in the evening, and by midnight chauffeured Pierce-Arrows, Packards, Cadillacs and Brewsters would be vying for kerb space outside. Jack himself preferred to travel by horse in full flamboyant cowboy attire, stopping at fancy apartments on Park and Fifth Avenue to deliver liquor to his favourite customers. It all helped make '21' Club the most talked- and written-about watering hole in town.

It had never been raided by the Feds until Walter Winchell, a popular newspaper columnist who had never been allowed inside the club, wrote a piece in 1930 in the *Daily Mirror* headed 'A Place Never Raided, Jack & Charlie's at 21 West Fifty Second Street'. It was, of course, a red rag to a bull and shortly afterwards the Feds arrived, personally directed by Frederick Lohman, assistant secretary of the U.S. Treasury in charge of administration of the Prohibition Act. Jack and Charlie were arrested and charged with conspiracy to import and traffic in liquor and spirits, copious quantities of which were found on the premises. The trial was a *cause célèbre*, making '21' even more famous. The Feds made a number of legal mistakes and after a great deal of posturing Jack and Charlie pleaded guilty to possession of alcohol and got off with fines of $50 each. They were later pardoned.

But they had learned their lesson. Once they were free of prosecution, Jack and Charlie secretly bought the townhouse next door and had its basement converted into a liquor storage room. They hired a builder from Florida to create an elaborate swinging wall between the basements of number 21 and number 19, which was so cleverly designed that it would remain concealed even to the most diligent of searchers. The wall weighs more than two tons and today is opened to allow guests into the wine cellar where parties are held. It opens by inserting a small wire through one of the many holes in the bricks, releasing the lynchpin, but if you didn't know where to find the hole you could be there for ever.

The last Prohibition raid of '21' took place in June 1932. Jack just had enough time before the Feds broke down the door to signal to the barmen to rack all the bottles and glasses on the bar shelves. Customers, who were told to sit tight and remain calm, watched dumb-struck as the shelves tipped back towards the wall and everything vanished, leaving just bare shelves. Although the place reeked of alcohol, a ten-man team of Feds could find no evidence of liquor anywhere – a smell, as someone pointed out, cannot be used as evidence in court. They could even smell the liquor in the cellars and brought in experts to examine the walls inch by inch, but they never found the secret door. They finally gave up after twelve hours and returned to their cars, only to find that the New York police, tipped off by Jack, had given them parking tickets.

Prohibition was finally repealed in 1933, the same year I was born. Some of the fun went out of the '21' and Jack and Charlie almost went bankrupt, kept going largely by the loyalty of the 'Yalies' who remained faithful through thick and thin. When Jack died in 1947, aged only forty-nine, he left an estate valued at $1 million, a thriving club – and $180,000 in cash in a safety deposit box.

We were fortunate that when we took over '21', Pete Kriendler and Jerry Burns, younger brothers of the founders, were prepared to be consultants. I was determined to retain as much of the tradition and atmosphere of the original club as possible, and these two had been largely responsible for transforming '21' from a speakeasy into one of Manhattan's most beloved and enduring restaurants. For decades, Pete, the more outgoing of the two, was its public face and ambassador, and I can well remember him making the rounds, stopping by tables to greet customers he knew well (which was most of them) and asking after their wives and families, all of which I encouraged him to go on doing, much as I had Giuseppe Cipriani do in Venice. He died, aged ninety-six, in 2001. I also persuaded the suave restaurant manager, Bruce Snyder, who had been around for years and knew every regular customer by name as well as their seating preferences, to stay on until his eventual retirement a few years later.

I thought I knew a lot about '21' before I arrived, but I soon learned a lot more as the stories and legends tumbled out, either from Kriendler, or from customers: of how Marc Chagall was allowed the privilege of dining for free without a tie as long as he left behind a little sketch on the menu; Joan Miró insisted on paying for himself but also inscribed the menus; Salvador Dali used to tout for commissions for paintings in '21', charging outrageous prices; Ernest Hemingway assaulted a young lady on the stairs; and Prince Rainier courted Grace Kelly at one of the corner tables. There are hundreds of stories like that, and over the years there is hardly a leading film star, Wall Street banker, industrialist or billionaire who hasn't dined in '21'. Fords, Rockefellers, Du Ponts, Vanderbilts, Sulzbergers and Forbes were all regulars, as was the Shah of Iran. I can recall seeing Aristotle Onassis (pre-Jackie O) at a corner table, and later Jackie O herself liked to dine in the club's upstairs dining room while her sister Lee was down-stairs in the bar. The club liked to boast that every U.S. President since the war dined there. It's a tradition I tried to maintain but George W. Bush, who liked to be in bed early and didn't drink, eluded me, the first President the club has missed out on. I hope Barack Obama will return to the tradition.

People often ask me about the cast-iron jockeys which adorn the balcony above the entrance and have become one of the best-known emblems of the club. They were painted in the racing colours of some of the richer patrons of the club, who were also horse-owners, who presented them as a mark of appreciation. They date back to the 1930s and there are thirty-three of them outside and another two inside. They traditionally get rotated so as not to show favouritism to any one owner.

The ground floor of '21' is famous for its bar-room where hundreds of model airplanes, football helmets, baseballs, toy trucks, oil derricks, a croquet mallet, cowbells and even a crocodile hang from the ceiling or line the walls. This eclectic collection began when the chairman of BOAC brought in a model plane, which annoyed the heads of Pan Am, American and United so much they insisted on hanging up models of their planes too. Each of the items in the bar has a story to it involving one of the regulars who donated them. When we engaged Massimo Vignelli, the famous graphics designer, to create a new menu style, he included pictures of the hanging toys in the bar-room on the backs of the menu cards.

The huge mahogany bar was also one of the legendary features of '21' and I was hesitant about touching it. People talked about it with awe, and it certainly had quite a history, but we found it was actually little-used and after much thought we cut back its size in order to get in more tables, which were badly needed. Warren Platner, one of Eero Saarinen's partners who helped with the redesign, changed the lighting so it remained subdued but was still strong enough to read the menu – I find restaurants where the light is too dim to make out the menu very annoying.

We promoted Bryan McGuire, who was the chief financial officer of '21', to take over as general manager, and from the start he did an excellent job, keeping a tight control of operations and getting things done efficiently and without fuss.

One of the bigger problems we had to deal with from the outset was the quality of the food. '21' had been renowned for its cuisine in the old days, but by the mid-1990s it had lost its reputation and regulars, who wanted traditional food, were complaining about the 'creative' menu our chef was producing. I sought the advice and help of Natale Rusconi at the Hotel Cipriani in Venice and he persuaded his friend Julia Child, the well-known chef and TV personality who gave a week-long course in the Hotel Cipriani every autumn, to come and advise us. Julia's cookbook, *Mastering the Art of French Cooking*, was generally credited with introducing the American public to French cuisine and her arrival at the club created quite a stir. Julia, who died in 2004, was a very tall woman with a commanding presence, and the first thing she did was to ask a *sous chef* to prepare a dish. When he'd finished, she picked up the pan and dumped it into the bin, saying 'Let's try this again, this time using my method.' That caught everyone's attention.

I found her a delight to work with and under her guidance the quality of the food immediately improved. But diners were still complaining it was overly 'creative', which I agreed with, so I asked Bryan to produce a computer-generated list of the dishes actually ordered by guests at both luncheon and dinner. As I expected, they favoured the more traditional dishes, so gradually the 'creative' stuff became less prominent on the menu. I asked the kitchen to start preparing 'pommes soufflés', a speciality at the La Cabaña restaurant in Buenos Aires, and one of my favourites, which they did. In 1997 we bought the name and artifacts of La Cabaña with the idea of developing a new steakhouse brand.

The second floor front used to be a more formal dining room, quieter than the bar-room, and attracted a lot of the more elderly customers who perhaps were a bit hard of hearing. The room eventually became so much in demand for parties that it could no longer be used as an *à la carte* restaurant, so I proposed that a back room on that floor be converted into a small formal dining room called 'Upstairs'. Warren Platner designed the new room with murals of four iconic views of New York set in 1929.

We also changed the décor in some of the smaller banqueting rooms. Ladies tended to choose the banqueting rooms for meals, and they didn't much care for the Winchester Room, which displayed a collection of firearms. Shirley suggested that we convert it into an Orchid Room and one of her botanical artists, Francesca Anderson, produced large black and white drawings of orchids, which now grace the walls, along with a live orchid display. Bookings of this room increased immediately.

Everything we did was done for a reason, and only after considerable thought and debate. Above all, I was intent on retaining the club atmosphere and traditional feel of the place. Peter Lawson-Johnston, chairman emeritus of the Guggenheim Foundation and grandson of Solomon Guggenheim, likes to relate the story of how one day he entertained his aunt, Peggy Guggenheim, at '21' and afterwards she said how much she had enjoyed the meal and asked how one went about joining 'the club'. Of course, '21' is not a private club but it is often mistaken for one, and few people just walk in off the street looking for a table. It looks far too imposing for that.

When we signed the original sale and purchase agreement with

Marshall Cogan, we believed the building had no air rights, which was irritating as we wanted to increase the space but assumed we were prevented from doing so. I was also intent on adding a hotel in New York to the portfolio, preferably attached to '21' Club, and over the years explored all sorts of ways of doing it. A couple of years after we bought the club, I met a New York property lawyer who was involved in the sale. He enquired how the investment had turned out, and I told him it was fine, but we were being held back from expansion because the air rights had been ceded to the Paley Centre for Media next door. 'Nonsense,' he said. 'The only air rights ceded were those above a fire escape for the museum!' We had been labouring under a delusion all this time.

We discovered we could build a forty-storey building on the site, but this news was to lead us down an unfortunate path. As I shall describe in more detail in Chapter 30, we decided to buy the old Donnell Library building behind '21' Club, facing on to 53rd Street, with a view to building a hotel using '21's air rights, while expanding the banqueting facilities in the process. It took several years to pull off, and we had just signed the agreement committing us to buying the library when Lehman Brothers collapsed and the financial crisis of 2008 rolled over us, making it impossible to finance a hotel project in Manhattan. By that stage the cost of the project was beginning to get out of hand and the return on investment looked poor. I was keen on finding a partner to complete it, creating a joint venture and contributing '21' Club as our share of the equity, with Orient-Express Hotels retaining the management of both the restaurant and hotel. But we had already committed $30 million, and with recession threatening the tourist industry across the globe, the board felt this was too risky. We sold the agreement in 2011 to Starwood Capital and Tribeca Associates who are expected to build a hotel on the site.

I was told later that Marshall Cogan actually did have a higher offer for '21' when we were negotiating the purchase in 1995. It purportedly came from Steve Wynn, the Las Vegas entrepreneur and, if true, we were lucky to be able to acquire '21' as his resources were infinitely greater than ours. Steve called me one day to arrange a booking at the

Hotel Cipriani for his mother, and I met him on a couple of occasions afterwards when I tried to interest him in a 'Hotel Cipriani
West' in Las Vegas which would incorporate a '21' Club restaurant.
Steve's Mirage Resorts company was taken over while we were in the
middle of these discussions. He then purchased the old Desert Inn,
which had a golf course right on the 'Strip'. His plan was to build a
new casino complex, simply called Wynn, and to sell plots on the golf
course for other hotels. We could have been one of them.

Because Wynn's new development was so far in the future, we got
in touch instead with Sheldon Adelson, owner of the Las Vegas Sands
Corporation, who was building a gigantic casino-hotel on the Strip
with a Venice theme, to be called The Venetian. Adelson thinks big
– his Venetian and Palazzo complex covers 18.5 million square feet,
three times the size of the Pentagon, and includes the largest hotel in
the world. During the planning stages for his project he and his wife
visited Venice and stayed at the Hotel Cipriani, and Rusconi helped
them with research on Venetian structures which could be copied and
incorporated into The Venetian.

Adelson planned to build a giant multi-storey car park, and I
had the idea of building a replica of the Hotel Cipriani on the roof,
which would have great views, not over the lagoon and San Giorgio
Maggiore, but of the Nevada desert. It would have had no gaming
because I felt that many wealthy visitors to Las Vegas wanted something more discreet than having to walk through hundreds of yards
of slot machines before reaching the elevators to the guest rooms.
An elevated walkway would connect the hotel with the main body
of The Venetian. I believed guests would pay $1,000 per night for
a room with this privacy. Adelson vacillated about the idea, keen
at the beginning, then saying that it might be more profitable to
build more banqueting space on the location I had in mind. He
then became preoccupied with his gigantic casino-hotel ventures
in Macau, where he spent $2.4 billion on a 3,000-room resort, and in
Singapore, and Hotel Cipriani West was stillborn. *Forbes* magazine
estimated Adelson's wealth at $40 billion, making him the third richest
American after Bill Gates and Warren Buffett, but he too got

caught in the 2008 financial crisis and his shares fell 90 per cent. He seemed totally unperturbed: 'So I lost $25 billion,' he said. 'I started out with zero.'

Wynn and Adelson were complete contrasts. Wynn was sophisticated and elegant, while I found Adelson a much more rambunctious character. I enjoyed our trips to Las Vegas and the opportunity to see the leisure business there from an insider's perspective, and would like to have made one of those deals work. And have built a hotel in New York. But you can't win them all.

However, the acquisition of '21' Club has proved a winner. It has performed well since our purchase in November 1995, although like everything else it went through a few shaky years. It has had to contend with ferocious competition, from Brian and Keith McNally, Graydon Carter and so many others who have created newer and trendier restaurants, many of which have come and gone without trace. The whole New York restaurant scene has altered out of all recognition even in the years since we took over '21' and very few of the top ten restaurants in 1995 would be on the list today. '21' is still up there with the best of them, not necessarily for food, although it's pretty good (tastes change all the time and food critics are fickle people), but certainly in overall ambience and character. It has lived through financial and political crises, and a different kind of crisis with 9/11, but it has emerged from it all with an enhanced reputation, better food, improved facilities and with its regulars as loyal as ever. It has proved to be well worth what we paid for it. And it has been fun as well.

CHAPTER TWENTY

HAVE SOME MADEIRA, M'DEAR

They always say that it's best to be the third owner of a hotel because only then can one achieve really good profits. In July 1996 we became the third owner of Reid's Palace Hotel in Madeira, which I can only describe as a splendid anachronism. It opened in November 1891, making it the same vintage as the Mount Nelson in Cape Town and the Grand Hotel Europe in St. Petersburg, which we were to acquire a few years later. It was a great era for vintage hotels.

Reid's was built by William Reid, a Scot who arrived in Madeira in 1836 with only £5 in his pocket and made a fortune in the Madeira wine trade, which was then at the height of its popularity before the dreaded *phylloxera* spread from the French vineyards and almost wiped it out. Today Madeira is used mostly to make sauces ('*Sauce Madère*').

The hotel, like the Mount Nelson, owes its existence to the big shipping lines, particularly the Union-Castle Line which operated a weekly mail-boat from Southampton to South Africa with stops in Lisbon and Madeira. Passengers found this steep-sided volcanic island, with its balmy climate and pleasant scenery, a very acceptable place to escape the European winter without having to go all the way to Cape Town. It was also recommended by doctors as an ideal destination for people suffering from TB, laryngitis or one of the many other bronchial ailments that so affected their patients living in smog-laden northern cities (particularly London). The medical journal *The Lancet* advocated it as a 'stepping stone for consumptive patients', adding 'there is no warm country in the world where the irritating influence of wind and dust is so completely absent as Madeira'.

It also had the major advantage of being easy to get to, and guests could take one of the weekly mail-ships out, spend a few weeks on the Portuguese-owned island, and pick up a mail-boat on its way home. For squeamish passengers who wanted to avoid the often unpleasant crossing of the Bay of Biscay, there was an alternative route: by train to Lisbon where the mail-boat stopped en route to Madeira. By the end of the century Madeira had become so popular that whole families, accompanied by servants, grooms and nannies, were making the trip, staying for the entire winter season.

William Reid was also a consumptive when, on the family doctor's orders, he left his father's farm in Scotland to seek a healthier climate. He was only fourteen and must have been an amazingly adventurous young lad as he managed to find his way to London, got himself a job as a cabin boy, sailed to Lisbon and then on to Funchal, still clutching the £5 he had started off with. This was a time when nearly all shipping bound for South Africa, India, the Far East and South America called at Madeira, so he may have been heading further east, only to find himself in what must have seemed like paradise, Funchal. He got a job in a German bakery but soon spotted that the growth industry on the island was the Madeira wine trade, then at its zenith.

Madeira is a fortified wine, not dissimilar to port, dating back to the days of the great Portuguese explorers who discovered that the heat and movement on long sea voyages transformed the flavour and alcoholic strength of the wine. The sweeter, stronger wine that emerged after months at sea had the major advantage of remaining drinkable long after it had been opened. It became very popular in the New World and played an important role in the American Revolution, when the seizure by the Royal Navy of the sloop *Liberty*, with twenty-five pipes (3,150 gallons) of best Madeira aboard, caused riots in Boston in 1776. Thomas Jefferson used it to celebrate the Declaration of Independence. When young William Reid ventured into the trade, Madeira was widely drunk in English

drawing rooms, both as an *aperitif* and a *digestif*, particularly by the
ladies who didn't care for the heavier sherries and ports which were
the alternatives.

William's health must have recovered fast in the Atlantic sunshine
because by age twenty-five in 1847 we have him setting up his own
wine-exporting company, which flourished. He probably had about
thirty good years before the *phylloxera* epidemic arrived in Madeira,
probably via Portugal. The less serious *oidium* (powdery mildew) had
hit Madeira first in 1851, causing a sharp fall in production, but probably drove prices up to the benefit of merchants such as William.
The industry soon bounced back before *phylloxera* struck, and by 1880
the Portuguese wine industry was almost completely devastated and
Madeira followed a few years later. Foolishly, the government refused
to allow replanting with New World rootstock until 1883, by which
stage demand for Madeira had given way to an alternative, probably
sherry. It never recovered.

How did our William fare in this time? He had probably seen it
coming, because he had begun diversifying into the hotel business
twenty years earlier, starting off with the renting of *quintas*, large
houses with their own grounds which, before the days of hotels in
Madeira, were much in demand by visiting Europeans. He bought
the Quinta das Fontas in Funchal and changed the name to the Royal
Edinburgh Hotel after Alfred, Duke of Edinburgh, Queen Victoria's
second son (who called William, with whom he became friendly over
his many visits to Madeira, 'Auld Reekie'). Then he added two more
quintas and a string of boarding houses, before he was ready for the
venture which would make him a household name in the hotel industry: a grand hotel.

For the site of his hotel William Reid chose a promontory 150 feet
above the Atlantic, looking out across the broad sweep of Funchal
Harbour and the steep green hills of Madeira (which means 'wood'
in Portuguese. Funchal means 'fennel' which João Gonçalves Zarco,
who discovered Madeira in 1418, noted grew in profusion there). For
his architect he chose George Somers Clarke, who had designed
Shepheard's Hotel in Cairo, and work began in 1887. Madeiran

workers must have toiled up the hill carrying thousands of basketfuls of rich soil to create Reid's ten acres of gardens, which are a haven for semi-tropical plants. The gardens are very special with all sorts of exotic plants which only Shirley fully understands: I remember one night being awakened by the noise of voices in the garden at 2 a.m. to discover that flower buffs had gathered to observe the spectacular display of a night-flowering cactus, apparently a rare event best seen at Reid's. The jade plant, which has the colour of the most expensive jade stone, is another rare plant which grows profusely there.

William, alas, never lived to see his dream completed. He died aged sixty-six, shortly before the hotel opened, but at least he'd lived a lot longer than he would if he had stayed in Scotland with his eleven siblings. His sons took over and expanded the business into other hotels on the island, but then decided to have a go in areas they knew nothing about – banking and financial services – and they lost everything. They sold the hotel in 1925 to an English company which went into voluntary liquidation in 1937 where it was rescued by the injection of £35,000 by the Blandy family, who were long-established (1811) Madeira wine merchants.

I later got to know Richard Blandy, the head of the family business, and found him a bright and resourceful man. His family history was in many ways similar to that of the Reid's in that the business was founded by a former British quartermaster who was stationed with the British garrison on Madeira during the Napoleonic wars. He returned a few years later and established a wine-exporting business, just as William did thirty years later, which thrived until *phylloxera* killed the wine trade. William diversified into hotels but the Blandys became prominent in coaling and victualling ships in the busy harbour of Funchal. They also had interests in banking, real estate, travel, the local daily newspaper and a wide range of other businesses.

Reid's was another diversification for the family, and they invested in improvements and upgrading. It was in their reign that it really established itself as an institution, mainly for British guests who included Lloyd George, Edward VIII, Winston Churchill and George Bernard Shaw. When Richard took over the business he decided there were more fruitful places to invest in than what he called a 'trophy asset' with a low return. And so Reid's came on the market for the first time in nearly sixty years – which is where I entered the scene.

One day in 1996 I got a call from Michael Miles, an old friend from the Far East who was chairman of the Schroders merchant bank in the City of London. I had first met Michael when he was the shipping manager for the Swire Group in Hong Kong, which represented Sea Containers in its early days, and he had gone onwards and upwards through the Swire organization, eventually running Cathay Pacific Airways, which the Swire brothers controlled, before going into banking. Michael told me that Richard Blandy was a friend of his and wanted to sell Reid's Hotel 'quietly'. Since Reid's was an icon, almost a symbol of Madeira in the public eye, Blandy wanted to ensure it went to people who would maintain standards and invest in the property. The idea of a privately negotiated sale appealed to me because when there is an auction process brokers often 'shop' your offer despite promising they will not do so. I lost quite a few deals over the years that way.

I was immediately interested of course, easily reached agreement with Richard Blandy and his brother Michael, and took over Reid's in July 1996. It was a gem, ideal for the Orient-Express Hotels' portfolio, but it needed investment and we had only recently taken on Charleston Place and '21' Club, just finished the Copacabana Palace and were still spending heavily on other properties. Our cap-ex budget was tight. Fortunately, Portugal was still a relatively new member of the European Union (it joined in 1986) and was the recipient of large amounts of taxpayers' money, which the officials in Brussels were happy to shovel into the poorer members. We did what everyone else in Portugal was doing and helped ourselves to some of this largesse, and we put it to good use, extensively improving the property.

Reid's today is still a step back into the world of the late nineteenth and early twentieth centuries, although its black-tie dress code in the main dining room has been relaxed.

The ornate grand dining room, comparable to that of the Ritz in London, is largely unchanged, as are the main parts of the hotel. But we did modernize some key features: there is now a children's play-ground, and large plasma-screen TVs in the bedrooms. When Reid's opened there were no elevators and all guests had to debark from the seaside boat landing. Today one takes five different elevators between the seaside and the top floor of the main building.

Overall, however, I insisted that we kept the atmosphere as it was when Winston Churchill wintered frequently in Reid's, sometimes flying in by Clipper, those majestic flying boats which I still associate with the now defunct Pan Am. Churchill's first stay, in January 1950, was cut short when the Labour Prime Minister Clement Attlee called a snap election and he had to rush back to fight it (Labour scraped home with a tiny majority of five seats and had to go to the country a year later, when Churchill got back in). He loved to paint in the village of Câmara de Lobos, where a plaque records his visits. The hotel had just reopened after wartime closure and other locals sent some of their best furniture to adorn his suite, such was the reverence in which Churchill was held. One local even lent him his Rolls-Royce. Shirley and I always stay in the Churchill Suite, which has been beautifully restored by Graham Viney. It is a thrill to think the great man occupied the same rooms in those years.

Lord Peter Carrington, the former British Foreign Secretary, is a good friend who lives not far from us in Oxfordshire, and first visited Reid's when he was Secretary General of NATO. Despite my oft-repeated assurances that black tie is no longer required, he refuses to go back because he says he doesn't like to dress up for dinner when he's on holiday. But I notice that some guests, mostly Germans for some reason, do like to put on black tie in the evening in the grand dining room, and it's a nice tradition which I hope continues. The hotel has a highly popular Cipriani restaurant on the grounds where informality is the keynote.

Not all is perfect of course: as we had discovered through our brief involvement with the Quinta do Lago in the Algarve, Portugal is not the easiest country in which to operate a hotel. The Socialist govern-ment which replaced the old Salazar regime in 1974 introduced a series of industrial relations measures aimed at protecting the workforce,

which it felt had suffered under the previous regime. But it went much
further than any other European country, making Portugal one of the
most difficult countries in the world in which to run a business – and
highly uncompetitive, particularly now with the high value of the euro.
Let me provide an example of this: one of the head gardeners at Reid's
was seldom to be seen as he would be ill, and would return to work
for just a few days before the mysterious illness would start all over
again – and again, for years. We couldn't replace him, even though his
job was an important one and he wasn't doing it, but we had to pay
someone else to do his job. There were many other examples which
drove the general managers wild with frustration.

Keeping good general managers was a real problem, partly because
of the constant struggle with staff, but also because they quickly
felt isolated from the mainstream of life on such a remote island.
Nonetheless, we did keep standards high as requested by Richard
Blandy, who sadly died of cancer in 2001, and the hotel makes a good
contribution to group profits.

I was in the process of completing the Madeira deal in 1996 when an
old friend from Geneva, Nicholas Krivosheia, called me. He was a
management consultant and said he had taken on the task of buying
a company based in Carcassonne, France, called Chippie, which was
engaged in clothes design and manufacturing for younger women.
The design and studios were in Carcassonne, but the clothes were all
manufactured in Morocco. The owner was a M. Jean-Michel Signoles,
who owned a loss-making hotel in Carcassonne called Hôtel de la
Cité which he wanted to dispose of quickly, but he wanted to do so
in a way that would not bring any political criticism. He also owned
a lot of property around the hotel, which he intended to sell off piece
by piece.

When I asked what exactly was being offered, Krivosheia told me
that Signoles would give us the hotel for nothing and the option of
buying the nearby buildings at fair market value – which of course
we exercised, acquiring all the adjoining properties as the only way to
expand the hotel. Carcassonne is in south-west France, not far from

the major city of Toulouse. It is the original model for Disney World, but it is for real and not a fantasy. It has fifty-three watchtowers, which surround the city walls, two of which are actually in the hotel. The Trencavel family acquired the city in 1067 and it became a stronghold of the Occitan Cathars during the Albigensian Crusades in the thirteenth century. It is a UNESCO World Heritage Site.

Cité means fortified hilltop and it is a warren of narrow pedestrian streets. In season in daytime there are so many visitors that car traffic is impossible. Hotel guests have to leave their cars below the ramparts and are taken up to the hotel in golf carts via a secret passage behind the hotel. Their cars are moved to the hotel garage at night when the city empties of visitors.

This part of France is associated with the Holy Grail, the cup used by Jesus at the Last Supper and said to possess miraculous powers. It was thought that the Grail was brought to the Carcassonne area by the Crusaders and has been guarded by a society of successors ever since. Hitler was so taken in by the Grail story that he funded excavations in the region during the war.

The hotel had an operating loss of 1.6 million French francs in 1996 (about $500,000) so the question was whether an investment and improved management could turn it around. I fear I was more impressed with the Walt Disney connection and the Holy Grail than the profits, and in retrospect the investment was a mistake. We brought in an excellent manager, Jacques Hamburger, and improved the room stock but the best he could achieve was an operating profit of $1 million. It was losing money in the year we sold it, 2011, although Hamburger had retired a couple of years earlier.

It was probably a good lesson because operating hotels in France is an enormous challenge. France introduced the infamous 35-hour week in February 2000. Extra hours had to be paid at overtime rates and there was an annual limit of 180 overtime hours per person. The whole idea was to force hotels and restaurants to hire more staff but instead hotels and restaurants rationalized their service periods. It was not uncommon to be told that guests would be allowed in a restaurant at noon but there would be no service beyond 2.30 p.m. It is also extremely difficult to terminate employment in France, with large awards made by the labour courts. With labour costs being the primary cost of hotels and restaurants this has meant that tariffs have had to be increased enormously. Thank goodness Italy hasn't fallen into the French trap.

So in 1996 we made a relatively poor investment in France, and a great one in Portugal. Maybe it's for this reason that when I arrive in Madeira I find myself humming that old Flanders and Swann ditty:

> *Have some Madeira, m'Dear!*
> *It's so very much nicer than beer.*
> *I don't care for sherry and cannot drink stout*
> *And port is a wine I can well do without.*
> *It's simply a case of 'chacun à son goût'.*
> *Have some Madeira, m'Dear!*

I sometimes do – but I prefer French wine with my dinner. Or better still, a bottle of Capannelle 50&50.

CHAPTER TWENTY-ONE

TSUNAMIS AND HURRICANES

The wind had shifted from the north-east to the south-west that afternoon, a most unusual occurrence on the west side of the Caribbean island of St. Martin. The white sandy beach, normally sheltered by the bluff to the north, was no longer in the lee of the trade wind but in the teeth of it. Yet the sea was calm enough as I set out for my usual afternoon swim in the warm waters that lap the shore. There was no hint of warning, no sinister stirring of air or ruffling of the water as I walked down to the sea's edge and waded in. I was up to my knees when it struck: a 15-foot tsunami-like wall of water which picked me up bodily, carried me across the beach and smashed me onto the sand. I was knocked unconscious and then tossed helplessly about in the foam of the ferocious backwash, which forced me under again.

Shirley, who had been slightly behind me, had seen the wave coming and instinctively moved back up the beach, but was caught as the wave swept back again, and only with great difficulty managed to get her head above water to grab a breath of air. She found me lying on the beach where members of the hotel staff were desperately trying to revive me. She said I was deadly blue, the colour of dirty jeans, and for a moment she thought I was already a goner. I nearly was. They got as much water out of my lungs as they could, but I couldn't breathe properly and I realized there was something seriously wrong with my chest. Someone clamped an oxygen mask on my face and somehow they got me up to the hotel veranda and then to the tiny clinic, which did duty as the only hospital on the island of St. Martin. There was oxygen there but not much else, and at that moment I was in desperate need of emergency medical treatment.

The hotel located a small jet on the island but it required two pilots to fly it and the second one had to be scooped out of a local bar. There was some debate as to whether we should go straight to Miami, which was over 1,200 miles away, or Martinique, which was less than 300, but I was too groggy to contribute much. Shirley couldn't take much part in the conversation either, as she had sand in her ears, had lost her hearing aid and couldn't hear a thing. But, looking at my colour and watching my laboured breathing, she wasn't sure I would survive the three-hour flight to Miami. She decided on Martinique.

The hospital in Martinique proved to be ghastly, which was surprising as French healthcare has a deservedly high reputation. But at least there were qualified doctors with modern equipment who could assess the damage and regulate the flow of oxygen. I had a broken collarbone, which they could do nothing about, and several broken ribs, which were in danger of puncturing the lungs. They were mostly worried about the water in my lungs, which they said could all too easily lead to infections, and indicated they could not look after me properly in their overcrowded intensive care unit. Shirley, although she hid it from me, was still deeply concerned about my chances of survival, and summoned Simon Sherwood, who flew immediately to Martinique and set about organizing a plane to get me out of there. We could have flown to the U.S., but by now I was anxious to get back to London where I was more familiar with the medical facilities and specialists. We eventually took off on the long flight with a paramedic aboard, stopping to refuel in New York where a physician could clear me for the London hop. I don't remember any of it.

I was taken by ambulance to the London Clinic where I spent the next eleven days in intensive care, setting some sort of record for that ward. Even after I was allowed home it took me a long time to recover and, as I shall relate later, I had some lasting problems as a result of my involuntary immersion on the golden sands of St. Martin – where I have swum again on a number of occasions, but only when the wind was in the right direction.

I was on the beach in St. Martin that day in 1997 because I was paying one of my regular visits to La Samanna, the beautiful luxury hotel we had added to the Orient-Express Hotels portfolio eight years before in 1996. I had first heard of La Samanna early in 1995 when the New York real estate brokers Eastdil Realty contacted us to ask if we would be interested in a luxury resort and spa on the French side of the island. The Dutch and French divided St. Martin between them back in 1648 and although there have been various iterations since – inevitably the British owned it for a while – it still stays divided. La Samanna was on French sovereign soil.

The hotel had been built by a remarkable man called James Frankel, who named it after his three daughters, Samantha, Anouk and Natalie. When it opened in 1974 it was the only hotel retreat of its kind in the French West Indies, and had enjoyed nearly 100 per cent occupancy in the winter months until Frankel became ill and died in 1989. The girls – one of whom, Natalie, still worked in the hotel – tried to carry on, but Frankel's estate got hit for inheritance tax in both France and the U.S., and they were eventually forced to sell.

I was intrigued by the proposition, but my unfortunate experience with the Windermere Island Club in the Bahamas back in 1984 made me cautious about rushing into anything in the Caribbean. I had learned three basic lessons from Windermere which I was determined not to un-learn: first, a successful beach resort must have guaranteed warm sunshine all year round; second, access must be convenient; and third, labour must be cooperative and reasonable in cost. Without those in place I was not going to get involved.

La Samanna scored two out of three. The weather, give or take the odd hurricane (and rogue wave), was superb. For such a small island it had a whacking great airport, capable of handling 747s, and there were direct flights daily from Paris and three times a week from Amsterdam, making it very accessible for European tourists. The North American market was even better served, with daily flights from New York, Miami and other cities.

But – and there's always a 'but' – the labour situation, while not as bad as on Eleuthera, did not look promising. Two unions competed for membership among the workforce and they had forced the only other major hotel on the French side of the island to close its doors a few years before.

The more I looked at it, however, the more prepared I was to take the risk and ignore my third principle on the labour issue. La Samanna had the considerable advantage over other parts of the Caribbean of being located in a department of France, which assured good infrastructure, political stability and the rule of law. It also meant that European citizens did not require work permits, a big issue across the Caribbean, and we could import French food and wine without paying duty.

I also found that Frankel had done a great job when he built the hotel, which for him was the fulfilment of a lifelong dream, more a labour of love than a commercial project, although he had made it highly profitable. He had found a wonderful site on a bluff on the south-west side of the island, sheltered from the trade winds which blow constantly for months on end. It faces west, so gets the most fantastic romantic sunsets and overlooks a perfect sandy beach. I was told the beach, the scene of my near-drowning experience, completely disappeared in 1960 when Hurricane Donna struck, but was back in place in time for the peak Christmas season. There had been no hurricane since, I was told – I should have known better.

In my research on the place, I came across a November 1993 article in *New York Magazine* which told me almost all I needed to know about La Samanna:

> With its Augean-inspired architecture and pricey French cuisine, it was a novelty in the islands when it opened back in 1974. The rich and famous flocked to it. Richard Nixon came. Jacqueline Onassis came. So did Jane Fonda, Diana Ross, David Bowie and Robert de Niro.

But then Frankel became sick and that all changed.

> Furnishings faded. Service faltered. The food grew pedestrian. A few celebrities remained faithful, but most started drifting elsewhere.

New York Magazine added witheringly, in a remark which could have described the Copacabana, the Cipriani, Reid's or any one of a dozen hotels I had bought, that La Samanna now looked out of date, 'a faded beauty to be admired for her longevity but – when you get right down to it – unable to compete with younger, more *à la page* challengers'.

It was a familiar picture, but exactly the type of property I specialized in: great hotels in great locations that had become run-down and could therefore be bought at a good price and restored. After their father's death, the girls gave the management contract to Rosewood Hotels, the Dallas-based group founded by Caroline Rose Hunt, daughter of H. L. Hunt, once the richest man in the world. She was also the sister of the two Hunt brothers who lost their shirts when they tried to corner the market in silver – but that's another story. I have met Caroline Hunt on several occasions, and at one stage we talked about combining Rosewood and Orient-Express Hotels. I thought it would be a great match, but she was a billionaire already in her own right and there was never really a will on her part to do it. Rosewood was bought by Hong Kong interests in 2011.

We agreed a price of $20 million and everything was proceeding nicely for completion in November 1995, in time for the 1995–6 peak season, when Hurricane Luis struck. As hurricanes went, Luis was a biggie, best remembered (by those it didn't affect) as the cause of the gigantic wave which famously struck the QE2, almost causing her to founder. It created havoc and catastrophe across Antigua, Barbuda, Anguilla and devastated St. Martin, which was right in its path. La Samanna escaped the worst of it but had to be closed for the winter season, and that altered all our projections, so we put the deal on hold for a year. The hotel was insured, and the insurance money was well spent through the winter months. When I went to see it after it reopened in April 1996 it looked sparkling. We had an even more sparkling ceremony on 26 October 1996 when we took control.

We appointed Bernard de Villele as manager, and under his guidance the hotel soon regained its place as the premium resort in the French West Indies. But nature hadn't finished with us yet. The gap between Hurricane Donna and Hurricane Luis was thirty-five years, and it seemed reasonable to assume St. Martin would be hurricane-free for a couple of decades. But that's not the way hurricanes think. In 1999, three years after we took over the hotel, Hurricane Lenny came along, hitting the unfortunate St. Croix first and almost battering it to death before making St. Martin its second landfall. Fortunately Lenny had already begun to weaken as it approached St. Martin, and came ashore as only a Category 3 hurricane (Luis was a 4), but it still did us serious damage. It hit La Samanna on 18 November, just as we were coming up to our peak season, obliterating the gardens and giving the buildings a good hammering.

The hotel was not fully protected with storm shutters so when flying debris broke a window, the room was quickly filled with water and had to be laboriously dried out and redecorated. We missed out on most of the winter high-season, but the worst part was that our insurance costs were greatly increased. Having served on the board of an insurance company for many years, I can safely say that under-writers never miss an opportunity to raise rates whenever there is a claim. They always forget about all those years when there were no claims and they pocketed 100 per cent of the premiums. We later installed proper storm shutters throughout the buildings and, needless to say, there hasn't been a hurricane since. And we're still paying those high insurance premiums.

The labour situation in St. Martin proved to be every bit as bad as I feared, and I was concerned that it would cause the island to lose ground to nearby St. Barts and Anguilla who did not have anything like the same problems. Once, as I was preparing to fly to St. Martin, I saw TV news footage of what appeared to be a full-scale battle on the frontier between the Dutch and French sides of the island, which was blocked by burning cars (there is only a single road) and rioters. When I called the manager to enquire whether I would be able to reach the hotel from the airport, which is on the Dutch side, he replied confidently: 'There will be no problem – you are arriving after 6 p.m.' When I asked the significance of this, he explained: 'The leader of the rioters is our *maître d'* and he must be on duty by 6 p.m. or he will risk losing his job.' Relations reached their nadir when the manager was locked in his office by the staff for twenty-four hours but after that things began to improve.

Over the years we have owned La Samanna we have been extending the property and developing some of the surplus land that surrounds it. The whole estate comprised about fifty acres in all, mostly on the French side of the island, but some on the Dutch side where the planning restrictions were not so tough. In 2005 we decided to take advantage of the booming demand for second homes in the Caribbean and designed an apartment complex with a marina and shopping facilities on our Dutch land. We pre-sold 100 out of the 180 apartments planned, with buyers required to put down staged deposits in cash. Unfortunately the work proceeded slowly and they were not finished until 2009, just in time for the collapse of the U.S. property market. Caribbean property values were even more badly affected, and buyers started to default on payments on the assumption that house prices had fallen by more than their deposits – which was not necessarily the case. Fortunately we completed enough sales to pay off the bank debt, so sales of the remaining units will go to the company's cash reserves. There is still a lot of potential for further development when the market improves.

On the French side of the property we built eight villas for sale on the basis that the owners would put them in the hotel's rental pool for letting when they were not in residence. These units also got caught in the property market collapse and have been treated as additional hotel room inventory rather than being sold.

Our other Caribbean beach property, Maroma, on the Yucatan coast of Mexico, was acquired on 14 March 2002. I had been on the hunt for Mexican properties for some time, particularly on the Caribbean side, on the rather subjective analysis that I found the Mexicans friendly, there were no trade unions, wages were low and so were construction costs. I therefore reasoned that if we could charge Caribbean island prices and pay Mexican costs we should be able to operate at a healthy margin, which is how it turned out.

I had been going to Mexico since my naval training days in San Diego in 1955, when we would nip over the border to spend the evening

in Tijuana, and have always enjoyed it. In the Navy we used to refer
to the food, such as refried beans and bready tortilla, and the loosen-
ing effect it had on people, as 'Montezuma's Revenge', but Mexican
cuisine now includes some of the most delicious dishes I've tasted
anywhere. Over the years I had built up a wide range of Mexican
connections, who I thought might be useful in our quest for decent
properties. One of them was Patricia Romandia Jacchia, who lived
in Rome and was married to Senator Enrico Jacchia, a distinguished
Venetian who wrote a column for the *Herald Tribune* on international
military affairs. Patricia, a Mexican, introduced us to Emilio Azcárraga,
the flamboyant owner of the Televisa media group in Mexico City,
which produces many of the programs for Spanish-language television around the world. Emilio used to arrive in Venice in the summers
with two identical yachts, one for him and his German wife Paula
and their French chef, and the other for their guests. Enrique's great
friend was Dr. Javier Barbosa de la Tour who owned an enormous
estate in San Miguel de Allende where we bought a hotel, which I
will describe later. It was often through these roundabout trails of
connections and relationships that the best proposals for new hotels
tumbled out.

The proposal that we buy Maroma came from Dean Andrews,
our regional manager for North America based in New York who,
at my request, had been scouting around for some time. Dean, who
loved Mexico almost as much as I did, had come into my life after we
bought Charleston Place when he was working for the Omni Hotels
group. He was the man responsible for putting it on the map. After
the handover I asked him to join us, and he set up his regional office
in Manhattan in the Sea Containers' offices.

After looking at various properties in Mexico, Dean was put in
touch with a local architect in the Cancun area, José Luis Moreno,
who had acquired a beach site on the coast about an hour's drive
south of Cancun. Moreno had built a delightfully creative resort but
he lacked the capital to complete it to the standard required for the
international market and was looking for investors. 'Maroma' means
'capsize' and José Luis chose the name because of the number of boats

that capsized on the outer reef of the bay, but it could just as well have applied to his finances at the time.

Dean took Shirley and me down to see it, and we instantly fell in love. It had everything: a beach with sand so fine it was almost like talcum powder, spectacular coral reef just offshore, verdant jungle behind, spa and nice restaurant, all of it right in the heart of some of the best Mayan ruins. The ancient city of Tulum, one of the best preserved of coastal Mayan sites, is nearby and Chichen Itza, probably the most visited of all the Mayan ruins, is two hours' drive away.

I went through my tick-list, starting with accessibility, and found that Cancun Airport had 125 international flights a day, including non-stop service to London; immigration and customs clearance was among the quickest in the world; and the Mexican government had built a four-lane express highway along the Yucatan coast, well back from the beaches but near enough to make Maroma easy to get to. As for the weather, it was superb, warm all year round. And there were no labour problems. Where La Samanna had ticked two of the boxes, Maroma ticked all of them.

There were, as there always are, issues but nothing that couldn't be dealt with and which would be reflected in the price we offered. The infrastructure was in a dreadful state, and we would have to completely replumb and rewire as well as build an entire new kitchen. José Luis had little experience in hotel construction, but he was a truly original and innovative man, and Maroma contained flashes of his genius, such as the clever way he incorporated Mexican artifacts into the rooms and public spaces. The entrance from the main road, about a mile away, was nearly invisible and had no signs, so guests would be convinced they were entering a private enclave. The property is spread across a wide beachfront, and Moreno had built and sold a few houses facing the beach which the hotel rented out when the owners were not in residence.

On 14 March 2002, we announced we had bought a 75 per cent stake for $7.5 million, leaving Moreno with the other 25 per cent. We also said we had agreed to invest $2 million that year on upgrades and finishing off rooms then under construction to take the number from fifty-seven to sixty-five. In all we invested $5 million in the property, expanding the hotel with additional beachside suites, a second pool, a spa and a new restaurant. We were able to buy Moreno's remaining 25 per cent stake a few years later. The success of Maroma helped make this part of the Yucatan coast increasingly popular, and it is now called 'Riviera Maya'. Mandarin Oriental and Rosewood have built hotels not far away, but Maroma in my opinion is still the outstanding property. José Luis Moreno was one of the first people to spot it.

José Luis was very keen on ancient Mayan spa treatments and persuaded me to try a sort of oven on the beach where guests were 'steamed'. He explained this was a traditional Mayan *temazcal*, or 'spiritual sweat lodge', but I confess the spirit never moved me. I later asked Tony Blair, who had taken a family holiday in Maroma when he was still Prime Minister, how he had enjoyed his Mayan steam bath on the beach and he made a face and replied, 'Not at all.' Clearly the spirit hadn't moved him either.

In the statement we put out announcing the Maroma deal I got a bit carried away and remarked: 'Mexico is a land of margaritas, mariachis and Mayans, a delightful recipe for holiday-makers.' I appreciate a good margarita, which is best tasted in Mexico, made with genuine Mexican tequila, is not always easy to come by. Tequila comes from the remarkably versatile agave plant, which grows painfully slowly in desert conditions – hence its nickname, the 'century plant'. The Aztecs used it for making paper, needles, thread, food (from the roots) – and, most importantly as far as I'm concerned, alcohol. The right to use the word 'tequila' is officially restricted to agaves grown in Mexico, in much the same way that champagne is supposed only to come from the Champagne area of France. But demand has long outstripped supply, so the distillers ship in alcohol made from agaves in Central America, the United States and elsewhere, often using Sea Containers' tank containers, and blend it with the home product. To be frank the subterfuge doesn't matter that much, because it tastes just fine whether the agave is grown in Mexico or somewhere else. Either way, it makes great margaritas.

CHAPTER TWENTY-TWO

HIGH IN THE ANDES

Sea Containers reached a tipping point at the end of 1998. By that stage the company had been in existence for thirty-three years, during which time it had been primarily a marine container-leasing business which had diversified into luxury rail transport, ferry and port operations, hotels, restaurants and river cruises. But now the roles had reversed, and the child had outgrown the parent: two-thirds of the group's profits came from hotels and passenger transport. The mid-1990s had been a period of rapid growth, with a string of new properties acquired and older ones, such as the Copacabana Palace, coming on stream. One of our busiest years yet was in 1998: we opened the 120-room Westcliff Hotel in Johannesburg, acquired ownership of the 141-room Quinta do Lago Hotel in Portugal, inaugurated the sixteen-room Splendido Mare on the waterfront of Portofino village and purchased the Lapa Palace Hotel in Lisbon. It was a good financial year too: the leisure division, 100 per cent owned by Sea Containers at that stage, had an operating profit of $49.5 million, well up on the previous year. We were also able to say that the market value of our hotels was substantially greater than what we had paid for them. All of this activity, however, was just the prelude to what came next, which was to be probably the most successful investment in the company's history: our venture into Peru.

It began early in 1999 with a call from the Peruvian ambassador to London, Eduardo Ponce-Vivanco, to the PR director of Orient-Express Hotels, Nadia Stancioff, saying that he had been asked by his government in Lima to draw up a list of potential investors for tourism projects in Peru. Would Orient-Express be interested? Of course we would, although I confess I had not given much thought to Peru as a prospect for a five-star hotel up to that point. The reputation of the Shining Path guerrilla movement, although it had effectively been destroyed when its leader, Abimael Guzmán, was captured in 1992, lived on. My perception, obviously out of date, was that it was a rather dangerous place for tourists, particularly if you were an American. I was distantly aware of the success of Alberto Fujimori, the President, in pulling the country back from the brink of anarchy, but I didn't recall it figuring prominently on the top 10 destination lists of the travel magazines that year. I had the impression that most of the tourists were either intrepid back-packers or even more intrepid archaeologists, neither of which was exactly our market.

I met with the ambassador and he filled me in on the recent history, lauding his President who he said had saved Peru from financial collapse: the standard of living was now rising rapidly, new roads and airports were being built, foreign investment was encouraged and the government had identified tourism as an industry it wanted to develop. I explained that we were only interested in upscale tourism, and took him through my philosophy, the kind of hotels and railways we owned, and how we liked to operate. He was very civil and at the end of our agreeable conversation promised to see what investment possibilities existed on his next trip to Peru.

He was as good as his word, and a few months later called to suggest I contact two Peruvian gentlemen, Rafael Lopez and Lorenzo de Sousa, who owned a company called Peruval in Peru. They had acquired a long lease from the Catholic Church on an old Spanish monastery in Cusco in the Andes and transformed it into a five-star hotel. They had also bought a lease from the government on a small hotel near the ruins of the old Incan city of Machu Picchu, by far the best known of all Peru's tourist sites. Peruval had spent heavily on converting the monastery, and Lopez and de Sousa were now seeking a 50 per cent partner so that they could repay borrowings and take out some cash.

It sounded just up our street, and a few months later I set out for Peru to look at the properties, meet Lopez and de Sousa, and generally get the feel of the place. Could Peru ever be the next hot tourist destination? I didn't know, but I was intent on finding out before everyone else did.

I flew to Lima, the capital, which is on the coast, and then on to the city of Cusco, which I found breathtaking – in more ways than one. Having skied all my life, altitude didn't bother me much, but at more than two miles high (Cusco is actually 3,400 metres, or 11,200 feet above sea level) the air was pretty thin. My first impression was that the Incans knew what they were doing when they built their capital on this spectacular spot. It sits on the continental divide, the Andean ridge, with waters flowing to the east on one side via the Urubamba River down through Machu Picchu to the Amazon; on the west side, the water cascades down precipitous gorges and into the Pacific Ocean. Above and around us soared the magnificent peaks of the high Andes, with great banks of cloud rolling through the verdant valleys. The town itself was a marvel, a beautifully restored Spanish colonial city set against the vast Inca fortress of Saqsaywaman (known as 'Sexy Woman') on the hillside above. As I walked around the famous Plaza de Armas, or the 'Square of the Warriors', and gazed in wonder at the basilica and the Church of La Compañía, I decided we had to be here. I don't think I'd ever seen a more awe-inspiring place.

This was my first exposure to Inca culture, or what was left of it: massive cut-stone walls and terraces, the stones so precisely sculpted and fitted without mortar that you can't get a playing card between them. Cusco must have been a very imposing city, the capital of a vast and fabulously wealthy empire, until Francisco Pizzaro and his conquistadores (there were only 168 of them) arrived in the city in 1534 and virtually wiped out the Incas, destroying every building, temple and palace. The Spanish used the remaining walls as the base for their own city, building monasteries, convents and the imposing cathedral – religion came first in those days – on top of the huge stone blocks. As the Incas had done, the Spanish made Cusco their capital, the centre from where the priests set forth to bring Christianity to the Andean world, which they did with fanatical zeal and even greater savagery. Inca culture was systematically destroyed, and tons of beautiful gold and silver ornaments, vessels and jewellery looted and sent back in shiploads to Charles I of Spain, where it was just melted down. Incas were literally worked to death in the gold and silver mines and smallpox, imported from Colombia, did the rest, killing probably two-thirds of the population.

My hosts put me up at the Hotel Monasterio in Cusco, which exceeded my best expectations. If I had been hoping for something special in the way of an architectural treasure, then this was it. Like so many of the Spanish buildings, it was built on Inca foundations, and had been, as the name suggested, a seventeenth-century monastery within which was a richly decorated chapel with ornate gold orna-ments, painted ceilings and carved wooden panelling – and even a pulpit and organ. The chapel was a tourist attraction by itself. The bedrooms, 123 of them, were built around four cloisters and although I thought at first it was all a bit solemn, after a few of the local pisco sours, the national drink of Peru, it rapidly grew on me and I warmed to its elegance and comfort – a perfect five-star addition to the Orient-Express Hotels portfolio.

The next day we descended by train through the dramatic Sacred Valley of the Incas, the heartland of the old empire, to Machu Picchu, a drop of over 3,000 feet in 75 miles. The Machu Picchu Ruinas Hotel, when we got there, was definitely not five-star, three at best, and had only thirty-two rooms, all of them in need of renovation – but all of them booked solid. It obviously had great value as it was the only hotel in the national park next to the legendary ruins, and even in its dilapidated state commanded premium rates. Guests travelled from all over the world to stay there so that they could access the ruins at any hour, and participate in mystical experiences by candlelight, or watch the dawn light up the great walls and stone sculptures of the ancient city.

Personally I have never had the slightest interest in watching the dawn light up anything, but I couldn't help falling under the spell of Machu Picchu, often referred to as the 'Lost City of the Incas'.

Astonishingly, the Spanish never found it, and as they obliterated every other city and vestige of Inca civilization, it is the only intact Inca cultural site in existence. Although it was known to the local Incas, it remained hidden to the outside world for nearly 400 years until the American historian Hiram Bingham 'discovered' it in 1911. About half of it has now been restored, and they're still working on it.

Back in Lima, Lopez and de Sousa arranged for me to see President Fujimori, which I was keen to do before committing finally to the investment – although secretly I had already made up my mind. I was taken into the imposing presidential palace through strict security and finally into the presence of the man himself. As his name implied, he was of Japanese extraction, although several Peruvian newspapers had been running stories alleging that he was actually born in Japan and his Peruvian birth certificate was forged. As in the U.S., the Peruvian Constitution requires its presidents to be born in the country, and Fujimori had already been President for eight years, which he was accused of serving illegally (he survived another two years before being impeached for corruption and civil rights abuses). I liked his sincerity and humility and, despite his later disgrace and jail sentence, he deserves the credit for putting Peru politically and economically on the sound foundation it enjoys today. When he was elected in 1990, there were real fears Peru would be taken over by the well-armed and trained terrorist movements who controlled large parts of the country. But against all the odds he defeated the terrorists, stopped hyperinflation, settled a centuries-old dispute with Ecuador and – something he never gets credit for – slashed the production of coca, used for manufacturing cocaine.

He had studied in the U.S., and I found him very articulate and persuasive as he laid out a clear vision for addressing Peru's economic needs. With the state-owned Peruvian railways in mind, I probed his attitude on privatization of state assets, and he indicated the process was already under way. He knew of my connection with railways in Europe and Asia and encouraged me to consider investing in the railways in Peru when the time was ripe.

He was elaborately courteous and gave us a tour of the historic rooms of the palace, where he lived in a house at the rear with his daughter Keiko who acted as his first lady. He was not accompanied by the usual retinue of flunkies, and at the end of the tour he walked us to our car, we shook hands and he closed the door for us. Of course, we knew nothing of the various scandals which were brewing at this time and which exploded two years later when his long-serving head of security, Vladimiro Montesinos, was forced to flee the country after secret videos were televised showing him bribing an elected congressman to switch to the Fujimori side. The ensuing allegations, involving money-laundering, arms trafficking and just about every form of corruption and coercion you can think of, led to the resignation of Fujimori – but not, thank goodness, before he had initiated the rail privatization process which was so important to us. He is still in jail, but remains popular in Peru – his daughter Keiko ran for President in June 2011 and was only narrowly beaten by Ollanta Humala.

Long before that, however, we had established our base in Peru, on which I was determined to build. In March 1999 we agreed to buy a 50 per cent stake in the two Peruval hotels for $10 million, plus a loan of another $5 million to the joint venture to improve the properties. The joint venture also acquired the Nazarenas Convent adjoining the Monasterio, and a 7.5-acre site on the valley floor next to the river at Machu Picchu on which I planned to build hotel rooms to supplement the Ruinas Hotel, which was fully booked the year round.

The more I visited Peru, the more fascinating I found it and wanted to know more. It has a culture which the archaeologists now argue may be as old as Egypt's. Our friend John Hemming, who wrote *Conquest of the Incas,* the definitive study of the Spanish invasion of Peru, taught me a great deal about the extraordinary Inca empire which extended throughout the Andes all the way from present-day Colombia down to Chile, a distance of 3,500 miles – longer even than that of the Roman empire. The Incas never developed a system of writing, but used a sophisticated method of knots on string, which have unfortunately rotted so there is remarkably little record left. They laid down a vast network of roads along the Andes, 20,000 miles of them, yet never used the wheel. They were gifted engineers,

architects and stonemasons, as one can see from the elaborate agricultural terraces they constructed on the steep hillsides.

The Inca empire, the best documented of Peruvian civilizations,
lasted less than 300 years and was in the midst of a savage civil war
when Pizarro arrived, which partly explains why he succeeded so
easily in overthrowing it. John has become even more interested in
what went on before the Incas, whose empire was just the culmina-
tion of a long line of Andean civilizations which new archaeological
discoveries keep putting back further and further into the past. Even
in the time I have been involved with Peru, evidence has emerged
of civilizations dating from 4,700 years ago, the oldest identified in
the New World. In 2005 excavations on the desert coast uncovered
ruins that include 70-foot-high pyramids contemporary with those of
Egypt or the ziggurats of Mesopotamia. The city of Caral, in the Supe
Valley north of Lima, covers 165 acres and probably stood at the centre
of a large civilization with buildings which have been carbon-dated to
2,727 BC.

At Lake Titicaca, the highest navigable waterway in the world
at 12,725 feet, archaeologists are still excavating the remains of
Tiahuanaco, the site of a technologically advanced culture, which may
be among the oldest in the world. Although it is at an altitude of 13,500
feet, 800 feet above Titicaca, and twelve miles away from the lake,
archaeologists are agreed it was once a flourishing port on the lake's
southern edge. Early explorers attributed the buildings at Tiahuanaco
to the Incas, but it has now been established they were ruins even
in Inca times, and Tiahuanaco culture probably began in the region
at about 1600 BC and flourished until at least AD 1200. The lake has
shrunk a great deal since then, and goes on shrinking although no
river flows out of it.

In 1999 our partners Lopez and de Sousa informed us of the
looming privatization of the railways, and we decided to make a bid
together with another group, which had gold mines up the mountain
behind Lima. I had no interest in the line which led to the mines, but
was particularly keen to acquire the Machu Picchu railway and the
network in the south of the country, mirroring what we had achieved

with the Venice Simplon-Orient-Express where the train was linked
to the Cipriani. Although they are not very extensive and are mostly
single track, the railways in Peru, which ascend as high as 15,000 feet,
are an essential part of the country's infrastructure. For instance, the
only way to get to Machu Picchu other than by hiking along the Inca
Trail (which takes four days on foot and is recommended only for the
fittest) is by rail, and the mining industry is dependent on the railways
for its supplies and for transporting its copper concentrates down to
the coast for export. PeruRail's tracks also run from Cusco along the
spine of the Andes to the city of Puno on Lake Titicaca, and on down
to Arequipa, Peru's second largest city, and then to the sea.

By now I had considerable experience in the privatization of railways, having acquired from British Rail the franchise to operate the
main line on the east coast of Britain, and of course we had owned and
operated the Venice Simplon-Orient-Express since 1982. The railway
privatization process in Britain had been a lesson in how not to do
it, and the railway system in Britain today still reflects the muddled
thinking and botched process put in place by the Major government
in 1993. Railways were almost the last asset to be privatized in Britain,
and there was a huge debate about how to do it, with proposals ranging from British Rail's own view that it should be privatized as a
single entity to the Treasury argument that there should be seven,
later twenty-five, passenger railway franchises. The Treasury prevailed
and the railways were privatized piecemeal, leaving the biggest cost
components, the track, signalling and main stations, in a company
called Network Rail, which is basically under government control.
The result was an enormously expensive track regime and a bunch of
franchises micro-managed by the Department of Transport. It was
the worst of all worlds.

They did it better in Peru. Bids were invited for the entire railway
system on the basis of the percentage of revenue, which the operator
would pay over to the government. For the first few years the payment
could be used in part to upgrade the track to U.S. railway standards.

In our case the bidding process was complicated by the fact we
were bidding with a partner, and we had to agree between us how the

revenue would be split to arrive at a single 'blended' percentage rate to be paid to the government. The gold mine part of the concession was much less valuable than the bulk of the railway which we wanted to acquire. After a great deal of debate, we decided to bid 30 per cent of revenue for the whole system. The bids were due to be opened at noon in Lima on a Monday. I was in Buenos Aires the night before when I got a call from Simon Sherwood, who was leading the bid process for Orient-Express Hotels, to say he felt 30 per cent was too low and we should increase our bid to one-third of revenue, or 33.33 per cent. Lopez and de Sousa suggested we go a little higher, to 33.375 per cent, and as they were the people on the ground, I readily consented. On the Monday morning it turned out there were only two bidders, and when the bids were opened it was revealed that the other party had offered 33.33 per cent. Our offer of 33.375 per cent won the day by the narrow margin of a third of a per cent. There was considerable speculation afterwards that our Peruvian partners had somehow learned in advance what the other side was offering, but if they did, they never told us.

Buying the railways of course was just the first stage. Now we had to manage them. The system was antiquated and nothing had been invested in it for years. It was also vastly over-manned, with probably the highest number of people per mile of track in the world. Today it has many fewer employees and operates many more trains. I brought in a seasoned American railwayman, Glen Michaels, to head up PeruRail, which was the name I had given to the railways, and Romy Guidino, who worked for the Sea Containers agency in Lima, took over freight operations. Full credit must go to Michaels for transforming the Peruvian railways from a loss-making transport system into a highly profitable one.

When Orient-Express Hotels acquired some luxury passenger cars from a bankrupt railway operator in Malaysia, we sent them to Peru where they were refurbished and then made into a train set (or 'rake' in rail terminology). We called it the Hiram Bingham, and put it on the tracks between Cusco and Machu Picchu, offering meals, guides, bus service and entrance to the ruins as part of the luxury package

ORIENT-EXPRESS: A PERSONAL JOURNEY

deal. For reasons I found inexplicable, tourists preferred to rise at the ungodly hour of 4 a.m., take the first (6 a.m.) Vistadome train to Machu Picchu, see the ruins along with thousands of others, have a pretty average lunch and return exhausted to Cusco in the afternoon. The Hiram Bingham train, I determined, would do it the decent way: guests would depart on our gleaming blue-and-gold carriages, with a civilized send-off of pisco sours and music, at the leisurely hour of 10 a.m., have a relaxed luncheon on board, visit the ruins in the after-noon when all the early visitors had left, then enjoy dinner and a nice bottle of wine on the train back to Cusco. The Hiram Bingham has been a great success.

Hiram Bingham, on whom the film character Indiana Jones is supposed to be based, was not an unqualified hero in Peruvian eyes. He was a Yale professor who made his first visit to Peru in 1908, visited some of the old ruins and became fascinated by pre-Columbian civili-zations. In 1911 he came back and was led to the jungle-covered site by some of the local farmers who had always known the city was there. He became a celebrity overnight when he made the existence of the forgotten city known to the world, in much the same way Johann Ludwig Burckhardt did when he revealed the existence of Petra, 'the rose-red city half as old as time', in 1812.

Bingham's expedition had been arranged by written contract between Yale and the Peruvian government, which allowed him to remove artifacts and send them to the Peabody Museum at Yale for study, but they had to be returned if requested. In 1912 and 1915 Bingham made further expeditions, backed by the National Geographic Society and by Yale, and each time he carted away crates filled with archaeological finds, some 5,000 in all.

The Peabody refused to give them back and in the 1990s this esca-lated into a serious diplomatic row, not dissimilar to the battle which has raged for years over Greece's demands that the British Museum give back the Elgin Marbles. The Peabody received a lot of favourable publicity for organizing an exhibition of some of the more interesting artifacts, which toured America. I saw it as a good advertisement for tourism to Peru, but not everyone in Peru agreed with me.

The row over the Peabody collection surfaced at a meeting I had with President Alejandro Toledo (who led the opposition against Fujimori and became President in 2001) to discuss trains and further expansion. I was keen to develop a project in the Colca Canyon, the deepest canyon in the world. Toledo was hours late for the appointment, and when he finally appeared I found myself mesmerized by the bits of sparkle scattered through his dishevelled hair. One of his aides explained later that the President had attended a party the night before and hadn't had time to wash his hair. After we had discussed the railways, Toledo lectured me on how foreign mining interests were bloodsuckers taking away Peru's resources and providing nothing in return. I got nowhere with my Colca Canyon plans.

But this was not the end of it. Toledo's wife Eliane, a French-born anthropologist and economist, discovered I was a Yale graduate and waded into me on the iniquities of the Peabody, demanding that I use my influence to have the Bingham artifacts returned to Peru where they belonged. I had already been approached by the Peruvian ambassador in Washington asking for my financial support for a lawsuit they were bringing against Yale, and I had delicately side-stepped that one. The Peabody was actually willing to cooperate but they wanted a guarantee that the artifacts would be properly housed and protected, and proposed a compromise arrangement whereby they would be rotated between Yale and Peru. In 2011, worn down by the controversy, the Peabody finally gave in and agreed to return all the objects unconditionally. By then I was on the International Council of the university.

My most exciting trip to Peru was in February 2001 when Shirley and I invited friends from around the world to see Peru and the operations now controlled by Orient-Express Hotels. By this time we had acquired a third hotel, the Miraflores Park Hotel, set in beautiful gardens on the Pacific shore in Lima, which neatly complemented the hotels in the Andes. Although it was a personal invitation, we hoped that our friends would spread the word about the attractions of the country and the Orient-Express Hotels properties – which is indeed what happened. We had originally planned for 100 guests,

expecting many of the invitations to be declined, but such was the
enthusiasm for Peru that 150 accepted. Several of the guests, such as
Philip and Nancy Anschutz from Denver and Julio Mario and Bea
Santo Domingo from Colombia, arrived in their personal planes, and
others flew in to Lima by scheduled flights from every corner of the
globe. The only guest who didn't turn up was Prue Leith, the chef,
writer and restaurateur, who went missing. We eventually tracked her
down to a hospital in New York where she had had a taxi accident on
her way through.

Shirley and I flew to Lima a few days before the event and were
joined by Princess Michael, with whom we have done a lot of travelling.
We both knew slightly Pérez de Cuéllar, the former Secretary-General
of the United Nations, who is Peruvian and had been invited to serve
temporarily as Prime Minister after Fujimori stepped down following
the scandal.

Pérez de Cuéllar invited us to visit his offices in Government Palace,
originally built by Francisco Pizarro but substantially remodelled in
the 1930s by Peru's dictators in the style of grandiose French Baroque.
Pérez de Cuéllar then took us to his club for lunch where we told
him of our plans to visit Colca Canyon the next day. I wanted to
inspect the small Hotel Parador del Colca, which we were thinking of
buying, enlarging and adding to our portfolio of Peruvian properties.
The canyon, twice as deep as the Grand Canyon although not so steep,
is the home of the Condor, which has the largest wingspan of any
land-bird in the world and floats in the updrafts between the canyon
walls. It's a remote place in southern Peru, and our trip involved flying
to Arequipa and then driving over a 15,000-foot mountain pass on a
rough largely unpaved road – by no means an easy trip, but worth it
just to see the Condor.

Pérez de Cuéllar was horrified by this plan and insisted that instead
of driving over the pass we take the presidential helicopter from
Arequipa airport direct to Colca, and, unwisely, we accepted. The
next day our small party set out: Princess Michael and her British
bodyguard, a doctor (who rather foolishly wore only a short-sleeved
shirt), Simon Sherwood, Paul White, then a regional manager of

Orient-Express Hotels, Roger Collins, our construction vice-president, Shirley and I. We took a private plane to Arequipa where we were met by a huge Russian helicopter. Russian helicopters, developed for the war in Afghanistan in the 1980s, at the time had the highest altitude-rated performance in the world and were the only machines which could operate in the high Andes. This surprised me as I had always thought the American-built ones were top of the range, but they were built for much lower altitudes.

The plan was to fly over the Andes, which should take less than an hour, view the canyon and join the author and historian John Julius Norwich and his wife Mollie, who had preceded us into the canyon, for dinner at the Parador where we all planned to spend the night. I would inspect the hotel the next day.

We had a hiccup at the outset when it was discovered that the Russian helicopter, mighty though it was, could not carry all of us and our luggage. So the luggage (containing our warm clothes) was sent on by road while we took to the air, all of us fairly lightly clad. The flight started well enough and we had a spectacular view of the valleys and streams as we flew in bright sunlight through the mountains and over the pass, and finally turned towards the canyon. That's where it all went wrong. Without any warning we hit a wall of freezing rain and fog, visibility went down to nothing and the pilots, as helicopter pilots are required to do in these circumstances, slowly descended. The visibility was so poor that they couldn't go forward or even back toward the mountain pass. They put the helicopter down gingerly on the flattest bit of land they could see, a ledge which was still at a steep angle, and there we settled pretty precariously. We were at 16,000 feet stuck in fog, which showed no signs of lifting, and it was getting cold.

We then sat there waiting for the weather to clear, but it grew even thicker as the afternoon wore on. We used the satellite phone to contact the Parador, who alerted the police and they started to assemble a group of four-wheel drive vehicles to rescue us, but we were high in the mountains with no road within miles, and there was no way they were going to reach us before nightfall.

After four hours we were getting very cold indeed. I had a woollen

bathrobe in my hand luggage, so I gave it to the doctor who was half
my size and it wrapped around him twice. Shirley lent me her spare
shawl, which gave me some warmth but I was still shivering. Paul
White, a diabetic, was verging on diabetic shock, but the doctor was
able to locate some half-eaten sandwiches, which revived him a bit.

Finally, at about 4 p.m. the mist lifted enough for the pilots to see
the terrain a few hundred yards in front and below, and they started
up the helicopter, intending to move us to a lower altitude. At 16,000
feet the helicopter could manage only five passengers at a time, so
Shirley and I, Princess Michael and her bodyguard and one other
went in the first group. We descended about 2,000 feet to a flattish
spot where there was a building, which turned out to be a locked-up
schoolhouse. Princess Michael's guard quickly broke the lock while
the helicopter returned to bring the other five to join us. It was still
bitterly cold but we found some smelly old rugs in a corner of the
schoolhouse, and wrapped them around ourselves. Simon Sherwood
had the bright idea of making a fire using fuel from the helicopter, but
this nearly asphyxiated us and we hastily put it out.

The rescue party had our exact position programed into their satellite navigation systems, and at around 10 p.m. we started to see flashes
of light down in the valley. Four Land Rovers set out but one was lost
crossing a stream, and the remaining three finally appeared through
the mist to save us. Our rescuers had the foresight to bring several
bottles of Johnnie Walker with them, which was gratefully received,
and we reached the Parador around midnight, much to the relief of
the Norwiches (and us).

The next day Princess Michael, who had been a tower of strength
during our forced landing, went about her duties and opened a new
market in the nearby village of Yanque. Then we set out on the drive
back to Arequipa, and no one complained about the condition of the
road over the pass.

Our regional manager in Peru, Filip Boyen and his wife Joanna,
along with Glen Michaels of PeruRail, organized a splendid visit for
the party, which included the inaugural trip of our new passenger
train from Cusco to Puno on Lake Titicaca. The trip was scheduled

to take eight hours but we were late starting and it wound up taking twelve. The crew had been working all night to get the train ready, and had failed to secure fully the glass partitions in the bar car. Leopold de Rothschild, Vivien Duffield, Christopher Bailey and I played bridge most of the day and by evening the consumption of pisco sours had reached such a level that when the glass panels began to pop out no one seemed to notice.

Our plan for the next day was to mobilize our 150 guests and take them aboard the *ss. Ollanta*, a marvellous old 260-foot steam-driven vessel which we had acquired along with the railways (we weren't even aware she was part of the package as she was laid up at the time). She was originally built on the Humber in England as a 'knock-down' ship, loosely assembled using only nuts and bolts, then taken apart and the thousands of components, all carefully numbered, shipped to Peru in kit form. The parts arrived at the port of Matarani and were then taken by rail up to Puno, on the lake where the ship was riveted together. She was launched in 1930, the biggest vessel that has ever sailed on the lake where nothing rusts because of the lack of oxygen in the air. She is quite a sight steaming at full speed on the blue still waters against the Andean peaks: her turbines give off huge clouds of steam and smoke, making her look, to all intents and purposes, like the *ss. San Pablo* in the film *Sand Pebbles*, steaming up the Yangtse in the 1920s.

It was dark by the time we reached Lake Titicaca and checked into the Hotel Libertador after a long day. I had been asleep for a couple of hours when the phone beside the bed woke me. It was Christopher Garnet, chief executive of GNER, our rail company in Britain, who tersely but calmly told me there had been a horrendous accident in North Yorkshire between one of our high-speed passenger trains and an oncoming coal-train. At least ten people had been killed, including both train drivers, and more than eighty injured, many of them seriously. It was a freak accident, which we could have done nothing to foresee, yet was to have significant consequences for our U.K. train business.

What happened was this: one of our trains, GNER InterCity 225, left Newcastle at 4.45 on the morning of 28 February 2001 and travelled south at its cruising speed of 120 m.p.h. towards King's Cross Station in London. At around six, as the train was approaching Selby, a man called Gary Neil Hart, driving a Land Rover Defender towing a car on a trailer, fell asleep at the wheel on the M62 motorway. He veered off the road, ran down an embankment, went through a fence and landed across the southbound railway track, right in the path of our speeding train. Because of the trailer, the driver couldn't reverse off the track, so he pulled out his cell-phone and, instead of dialling the emergency 999 line, he called his girlfriend. The emergency services could have quickly arranged for the signals to be switched to red, but instead precious minutes passed in useless conversation with the girlfriend.

He finally got through to the emergency services at 6.13 a.m. and was actually talking to the operator when InterCity 225, travelling at full speed, smashed into the front of the Land Rover, went straight through it, derailed, but somehow managed to remain upright. By one of those freak sequences of events, the points on the nearby sidings deflected it into the path of an oncoming freight train, which happened to be running twenty minutes early. Accident inspectors later calculated the InterCity was still travelling at 88 m.p.h. and the freight train was doing 54 m.p.h., a combined speed of 142 m.p.h., when they hit head-on near the village of Great Heck. Both locomotives were overturned as were nine of the InterCity's coaches, which came to rest on the embankment. The drivers died instantly.

It was a pretty unpleasant message to get at five in the morning 12,750 feet up in the Andes. I debated returning immediately to Britain but getting from Lake Titicaca to London was going to take the better part of three days, so there was little I could do to assist. I spent the rest of the day on the phone talking to Christopher and the team who, although shocked by the accident, handled it very well, probably better than I could have done. Christopher was on radio and TV through most of the coming days and made an excellent spokesman.

By late afternoon, our now sombre party was aboard a chartered wide-body jet on the way back to Lima, where our guest Christopher Bailey, one of the world's great funny men, relieved the gloom with a witty speech at the farewell dinner at the Miraflores Park Hotel. He and his wife Sarah then joined Shirley and me on a trip to Easter Island and the South Seas in search of hotels.

A month later I was back in England for the memorial service for the victims of the Selby train crash, which took place at York Minster. Prince Charles joined 2,000 people including relatives of the ten people killed, as well as some of the survivors and members of the emergency services who had helped with the rescue. Charles behaved very impressively, holding private meetings with relatives of the dead, then with the injured and finally with the emergency service personnel. The Archbishop of York, Dr. David Hope, delivered a moving eulogy, describing the crash as an event which touched the lives of many people both at home and abroad. He later revealed he had almost travelled on that train on that fateful morning, but changed his mind at the last moment.

The Deputy Prime Minister John Prescott also attended and told me afterwards that the government felt no blame attached to GNER for the accident. He believed our franchise would be renewed because of the excellent job we had done operating the service, which stretched from King's Cross Station to Inverness. But this was the second fatal accident on the east coast main line since privatization: just five months before, an InterCity train heading north at 115 m.p.h. on the same line went over a fractured rail and came off the track at Hatfield. On that occasion, four people died and over seventy were injured. Two major crashes coming so close together raised serious questions about the safety of the tracks, and led to the partial renationalization of Railtrack, the company responsible for the track.

King's Cross was the focus of terrorist bombings on 7 July 2005 which ultimately destroyed the GNER franchise when a then-hostile government insisted on GNER bearing the revenue loss arising from the bombings. Sea Containers was not financially strong enough to bear it, and was forced to surrender the franchise to another operator, National Express, which encountered a similar problem in the recession of 2008–9.

But we've made up for it with our railways and hotels in Peru. We eventually bought the Hotel Parador del Colca, where we had nearly come to grief with Princess Michael, and changed the name to Las Casitas del Colca. The country has had its up and downs, but there are many historical sites still to be opened up and I think Peru is still in its infancy as far as tourism is concerned.

As for Gary Hart, the man who caused the Selby crash, he escaped the collision unhurt, was tried on ten counts of causing death by dangerous driving, found guilty and sentenced to five years' imprisonment. He served half his sentence.

CHAPTER TWENTY-THREE

———

DAYS OF WINE AND ROSES

I first became a wine enthusiast when I went to France in 1960 and started visiting the châteaux in Bordeaux. Michael Edwards, the sophisticated Englishman who was my boss at United States Lines, was something of an expert (at least he knew a darned sight more than I did) and began taking me to the great vineyards where he seemed to know everyone and was always a welcome visitor. We carried large amounts of Bordeaux wine on the United States Lines cargo ships in those days, and maintained stocks of fine vintages in Le Havre for the passenger ships, so we were good customers. The châteaux owners were more than happy to educate me, and I quickly learned to tell a good wine from an average one, even if I couldn't identify the year just by the taste as they seemed to be able to do. Wine became something of a passion for me, and I always asked for my annual bonuses to be paid in wine at the company's cost price. It has been one of my great interests ever since.

When I grew up in Kentucky no one drank wine. The standard drink was bourbon and it never occurred to anyone to drink anything else, unless it was Budweiser beer made in nearby St. Louis. Half of Kentucky and large tracts of the southern states in those days were 'dry' – some still are – but fortunately Fayette County, where the city of Lexington is located, was 'wet'. Bourbon was actually a local drink: it came from Bourbon County, which was one county over from Fayette, so it would have been seen as disloyal to drink anything as snobby as Scotch. I always remember my father, who wasn't a big drinker, enjoying his glass of bourbon on the rocks when he came home from his office. Limestone water contributes to the taste of bourbon and builds the bones of race-horses. Fayette and Bourbon counties are in the heart of the Bluegrass country and it is the limestone which gives the green grass a slight tinge of blue.

I have often noticed around the world how certain drinks can taste great in their homeland, but not so great somewhere else, and it may be that bourbon tastes better in the South, in the same way as Scotch, drinkable anywhere, tastes best in Scotland, as I discovered when I arrived in Britain in my twenties. Pisco sours are wonderful in Peru but try one in the '21' Club and you won't order another. Margaritas taste best in Mexico and the arid American south-west, and of course vodka is best tasted in Russia.

Kentuckians often drank their bourbon in the form of the mint julep, made from mint sprigs, bourbon, powdered sugar and water, and always served in an ice-cold silver cup. Friends give each other julep cups for birthdays and special occasions, and I must have a couple of dozen inherited from my parents or given to us as gifts. Alas, the mint julep has not spread much beyond Kentucky and some of the other southern states, where it is still very popular.

At Yale and in the Navy wine barely featured in my life, but after I arrived in France I rarely drank anything else, a habit I have been happy to maintain for the last fifty years. In those early days my exposure was largely to the wines of Bordeaux, and one of my great regrets is that it was only some years later that I discovered the joys of Burgundy wines, which were shipped through Marseilles, the nearest port to the vineyards in the Saône-Rhône valley. United States Lines didn't operate in the Med, and the Burgundy business went to American Export Lines, Admiral Dutch Will's company, while United States Lines carried Bordeaux wines to the U.S. direct from the port at Bordeaux.

As I travelled around the world building up Sea Containers I made a habit of studying the wine menus in the hotels and restaurants I visited, and began building myself a modest collection of wines I liked. When Susan Blackburn and I wrote *James Sherwood's Discriminating Guide* in the 1970s, my interest was as much in the wine London's restaurants were serving as in the food, and each review also included a comment on the wine list, often uncomplimentary.

After I got into the hotel business I took a more professional interest in wines, and made up for my lack of exposure to Burgundy wines when I was elected to *La Confrérie des Chevaliers du Tastevin*, a club whose aim is 'to hold in high regard and encourage the use of the products of Burgundy, particularly her great wines and her regional cuisine'. You have to be a serious wine connoisseur to be elected, and I felt very honoured when I was chosen. About ten times a year they give an elaborate black-tie dinner in the twelfth-century Château du Clos de Vougeot in the Côte-d'Or, between Dijon and Beaune, and I go when I can. These dinners are great fun, with members encouraged to talk about the history and character of each wine in the interests of promoting 'viticultural and gastronomic education'. Eight Burgundy wines are tasted over dinner, one for each course, and coffee is served about two in the morning. There are usually about 600 guests, all of them wine enthusiasts, and towards the end of the meal the new *Chevaliers* are inducted into the order. Everyone is pretty sloshed by then, and you go up on the stage, get kissed on both cheeks by the *Grand Maître* (all the titles are in French) and presented with a silver *tastevin* (pronounced *tatt-a-van*) on an orange and yellow ribbon. We once took our friends Max and Joy Ulfane, and I was rather surprised to be put at the front of the great banqueting hall. Without warning I was singled out, brought up on stage, kissed several times, and promoted from ordinary *Chevalier* to *Commandeur*, a significant promotion in the ranks of the order. Max loves his wines and has a wonderful cellar at Fighine, his *castello* in Tuscany, so he was mightily impressed. He got his own back when the Italian government made him a *Commendatore* for his contribution to conservation in restoring Fighine. Joy was also made a *Commendatore*.

White Burgundy, which is made from the Chardonnay grape, has long been one of my favourites and is generally recognized by the experts as the finest white wine in the world. Red Burgundies lagged behind the Bordeaux reds for a long time. However, fashions change and I have watched with interest how taste has moved to the lighter Pinot Noir wines and away from the fuller-bodied Cabernet Sauvignons of the Médoc region in Bordeaux. Red Burgundy, which has steadily improved over the years as the winemakers have upped their game, is made from the Pinot Noir grape and is not normally barrel-aged, as Bordeaux is. This means it can be released on to the market sooner than the Bordeaux wines, a significant cost advantage.

However, Bordeaux retains its reputation, deservedly, for producing the finest red wines in the world. The five first growth wines, or *Premier Cru Classé*, are all from the Bordeaux region, four of them Cabernet Sauvignons and one a Merlot (Château Cheval Blanc). Four come from the Médoc and the fifth, Château Haut-Brion, from Graves, better known for its sweet white Sauternes and Barsac.

I was very partial to the wines of the Haut-Brion vineyard, and it has odd links to America which I have always found fascinating: Thomas Jefferson, when he was living in France, was greatly impressed by Haut-Brion wine and on a visit in 1787 he bought six cases and shipped them home to Virginia, thus making Haut-Brion the first recorded first-growth wine to be imported into the United States. Haut-Brion's owner, Joseph de Fumel, was guillotined in the French Revolution and in 1801 the vineyard was bought by the legendary – some would say infamous – Prince de Talleyrand, then Napoleon's foreign minister. The American banker Charles Dillon, a great wine-lover, purchased Haut-Brion in 1935 and it has been in the Dillon family ever since. It is said Dillon would have bought Cheval Blanc too, but it was a rainy day and he decided not to venture too far from Bordeaux. His son Douglas, who inherited the property, was the U.S. ambassador to France and served as Treasury Secretary in the Kennedy and Johnson administrations. He left the Château to his daughter, Joan Dillon, now the Duchess of Mouchy, and mother, from her first marriage, of Prince Robert of Luxembourg. Joan was a great friend of Michael Edwards', and I met her on several occasions at Michael's house in the Luberon district of France.

I recall once, in 1988, we were about to visit Médoc with some friends and were invited to lunch at Château Haut-Brion, which I was hugely looking forward to. But I had to stay in London to deal with an ugly industrial dispute developing at Sealink Ferries. The National Union of Seamen, led by my old antagonist Sam McCluskie, was trying to drag Sealink into a strike, which threatened to close all passenger ferries operating between England and the continent. They had already effectively closed down the operations of our rivals, P&O Ferries, which, in anticipation of the competition from the Channel Tunnel, had announced plans to trim its over-large labour force by 500 people and tackle the 'Spanish practices' prevalent among the union- ized seamen. The P&O chairman, Jeffrey (now Lord) Sterling, who had built the company into one of the great shipping and property companies of its day, was determined to defeat the union and in order to step up the pressure McCluskie threatened to seal off the Channel completely. That meant picketing our ships too, even though we had no dispute with him.

British industrial historians regard the seamen's strike of 1988 as one of the three seminal strikes of the Thatcher era which effectively destroyed union power: the miners' strike in 1983–4, Rupert Murdoch's Battle of Wapping in 1986 and the P&O strike of 1988. We were never the main player in the Channel dispute but we were on the edges of it and our ferry services were disrupted, although not for long.

Very reluctantly I made my apologies to our friends in Bordeaux and met McCluskie at the dreary offices of the conciliation service ACAS in London. We spent all day in tedious negotiation, getting nowhere. At about eight o'clock I called Shirley in France and she recounted, in elaborate detail, the splendid luncheon she and our friends had enjoyed in the sunshine at Haut-Brion, whereas in London we had dined on greasy fish and chips wrapped in newspapers which McCluskie had generously sent in to us. The next day I took the first plane to Bordeaux and for the rest of the week more than made up for it.

We were staying with our great friends, Eva and Anthony Barton, who own the 'super second' growth vineyards of Château Leoville Barton and Château Langoa-Barton (and were on our trip to Peru). Long before I knew the Bartons, I discovered Langoa-Barton in the Savoy Restaurant in London. My *Discriminating Guide* records a bottle of 'excellent' 1964 costing £4.85.

From the comfort of their Château, I kept in touch with the battle with McCluskie who refused to give in. We took the union to court for secondary picketing, which Mrs. Thatcher had made illegal, and won. The courts ordered the union's assets to be sequestrated, its offices seized and its funds frozen so that it couldn't even pay its officials – including Sam, who soon ordered his Sealink members back to work. P&O held out for another year and eventually won a resounding victory over the unions. It had cost P&O over £40 million, which we could not have afforded, but Jeffrey felt it had been worth it.

Over the years I had often thought of buying my own vineyard, and in the mid-1990s decided to take this a stage further. Initially, my chosen region was the Médoc, and the Bartons were keen to help. They took us to meet the famous Alexis Lichine, the Russian-born wine writer (author of the seminal book *Wines of France* and many others) who entertained us at his Château Prieuré-Lichine vineyard. Lichine was a fascinating man (he died of liver cancer the following year), who had actually worked as the export manager for Château Haut-Brion after the war, in which he served with distinction in the American forces, before moving to the village of Margaux and creating his own shipping company, Lichine & Cie. He was a brilliant marketer of wines, the man who really opened up the U.S. market for Bordeaux wines, and was the first winemaker to set up tasting rooms for the general public.

Thanks to another friend, Michael Pearson, son of Lord Cowdray, whose family controlled the Pearson Group, we were well received by the management of Château Latour, which the group owned at the time. It also owned the *Financial Times*, Lazards, *The Economist* and Madame Tussauds, an eclectic bunch of assets if ever there was one. Our London banker friend Leopold de Rothschild gave us introductions to his French cousins who owned two of the five first growth vineyards, Château Laffite and Château Mouton Rothschild.

On the face of it, the 1990s seemed a good time to buy a Bordeaux vineyard; fine wine prices, reflecting the surge in demand from the new rich all over the world, had soared in the past few years, and I could see them going on upwards. There was no way to increase production

Charles, Simon and Shirley accompany
me from the Hotel Cipriani to
the Venice Town Hall where I was
made the thirteenth honorary citizen
of the city since Italy's independence.
My immediate predecessors were
Ambassador Ashley Clarke and
Peggy Guggenheim.

m.v. Road to Mandalay cruises at Saigang near Mandalay after (*below*) being transported from the River Rhine in Germany to Myanmar on a semi-submersible ship; she was floated off at the mouth of the Irrawaddy River.

The plain of Pagan (or Bagan as it is now known) in the evening sun with the Irrawaddy River beyond.

(*Left*) Adrian Zecha, founder of the Aman Resorts group, and Lady Carla Powell (*right*) on a *Road to Mandalay* outing. (*Bottom*) Anthony and Eva Barton from St. Julien in the Médoc wine region of France on the same trip. They gave me sound advice when I became a wine producer.

The Governor's Residence in Yangon (*top left*), formerly the residence of the Shan State governor. (*Right*) Villas at Napasai in Koh Samui, Thailand. (*Left*) Ubud Hanging Gardens in Bali. (*Below*) The Westcliff in Johannesburg which overlooks a forest of jacaranda trees.

Le Manoir aux Quat' Saisons in Oxfordshire with its founder and celebrity chef Raymond Blanc (*below*).

The Royal Scotsman tourist train winds its way through the mountains and lochs of Scotland.

La Residencia in Deià, Mallorca. The poet Robert Graves lived in the village for many years.

(*Top*) Reid's Palace Hotel in Madeira, with spectacular gardens and views over Funchal.

(*Centre*) Charleston Place in Charleston, South Carolina. Carriage trips through the historic city are popular with guests.

(*Bottom*) La Samanna in St. Martin, French West Indies. The finest French food and wine arrive on the daily non-stop flight from Paris.

Machu Picchu, Peru, the country's best-known tourist attraction. (*Inset*) Hiram Bingham, the Yale professor who rediscovered the abandoned ruins.

(*Left*) The Hiram Bingham luxury train of PeruRail which operates between Cusco and Machu Picchu. (*Right*) The Miraflores Park Hotel in Lima overlooking the spectacular Pacific coast.

(*Left*) Hotel Monasterio in Cusco, formerly a Spanish monastery built on Inca ruins; and (*right*) Machu Picchu Sanctuary Lodge, the only hotel at the ruins.

(*From left*) Ken Burroughs and Erica Jong (author of *Fear of Flying*), Ivan Fallon, Joy and Max Ulfane and Elizabeth Rees-Jones (Mrs. Fallon) aboard the Hiram Bingham train.

Sir Timothy Clifford (*left*), former director of the National Galleries of Scotland, and Leopold de Rothschild of banking fame.

Galen and Hilary Weston explore the ruins of 'Sexy Woman' near Cusco.

Ambassador Mario and Julia Gibson Barbosa without whose help we could not have acquired the hotels in Brazil.

Prime Minister Pérez de Cuéllar of Peru insisted we fly from Arequipa to the Colca Canyon in his helicopter but we were forced down on a mountainside at 16,000 feet.

President Alberto Fujimori of Peru who encouraged our investments in his country.
© Getty Images Ltd.

The doctor wore my bathrobe to keep warm while Princess Michael of Kent and I made the best of it in light anoraks. (*Right*) The hotelier Georg Rafael, who has served as director and vice-chairman of Orient-Express Hotels and who suggested the company's name; and (*far right*) Christopher and Sarah Bailey with whom I sailed throughout East Africa on the lookout for hotel opportunities.

La Cabaña in Buenos Aires, a steakhouse which failed in the 2008-9 recession. The concept still survives but with another owner in another location in Buenos Aires. (*Top right*) Thomas Gibson, the Anglo-Argentine art dealer who assisted our art purchases and Argentine investment.

Sir David Davies (*left*) and (*right, left to right*), Viscount John Julius Norwich, Lady Susan and Sir Timothy Sainsbury.

A luxury barge of 'Afloat in France' cruises along the Burgundy Canal in France.

The Bar Room at '21' Club in New York City. The restaurant, a former speakeasy, was opened in 1931 by Jack Kriendler and Charlie Berns (*below left and right*) and remains an important landmark to this day.

ST. PETERSBURG.
GRAND HOTEL D'EUROPE,
Perspective Newski et Rue Michel. Most Central Position.

Leading Hotel of the Capital, with all Modern Comforts. Single Bedrooms from 3 roubles, and with Private Bath from 7 roubles upwards. Elegant Restaurant. Largest Roof Garden in Europe. All languages spoken. **Under Swiss Management.** *Telegraphic Address : "EUROPOTEL, PETERSBURG."*

J. WOLFLISBERG-GIGER, General Manager.

The Grand Hotel d'Europe in St. Petersburg in Russia in the nineteenth century. It occupies an entire city block on the Nevsky Prospekt.

The main entrance. The hotel was used as a hospital during the siege of Leningrad (1941–4) when over 800,000 people died.

(*Above*) The historic main dining room with skylights and murals.

(*Left*) Harry Fitzgibbons who entertained his friends for his sixtieth birthday in St. Petersburg and Dame Vivien Duffield, the philanthropist daughter of Sir Charles Clore. At one of her parties in Gstaad, Switzerland, I met Alfred Taubman which led to the Charleston Place acquisition.

Hotel das Cataratas at Iguassu Falls in Brazil, the most impressive waterfalls in the world.

Casa de Sierra Nevada in San Miguel de Allende, Mexico.

César Ritz and his wife; and (*bottom right*) Las Casitas del Colca in the Colca Canyon of Peru, home of the condor.

The Hotel Ritz in Madrid, next to the Prado Museum.

(*Above*) The Shirley Sherwood Gallery of Botanical Art at Kew Gardens, London. (*Centre*) The wines produced by Capannelle in Tuscany's Chianti Classico district. (*Bottom*) The main house of Capannelle at twilight. The garden sits on top of the winery.

The Grand Hotel Timeo in Taormina, Sicily with the ancient Greek amphitheatre behind. Actors reach the stage through the back door of the hotel.

The board of Orient-Express Hotels Ltd. in 2000 when the company made its initial public offering. (*From the left*) James Hurlock, John Campbell, me, Danny O'Sullivan, Simon Sherwood and Bob Lovejoy.

The company's management in 2004. (*From the left*) Paul White, regional manager southern hemisphere, and later chief financial officer and then CEO; James Struthers, chief financial officer; David Williams, vice-president sales and marketing; Dean Andrews, regional manager North America; Nicholas Varian, vice-president trains and cruises; Roger Collins, vice-president, design and technical services; Ned Hetherington, company secretary and general counsel. (*Seated from left*) Adrian Constant, regional manager Europe and Pippa Isbell, director of public relations and communications.

at any of the estates, which were mostly quite small, usually between twenty and forty hectares of planted vines. Demand on the other hand was infinite.

The top vineyards were out of my range, and were not available anyway, so I began looking at some of the lesser-known ones with a view to acquiring one, not for Orient-Express Hotels, but for myself. The first one to interest me was Château Gruaud-Larose, then owned by the Cordier family who wanted to sell. It was one of only fifteen *Deuxièmes Cru* (second growth) vineyards, and had 80 hectares of vines, but when I looked at the accounts, as best I could tell it generated a return of about 3 per cent – provided there was a reasonable harvest. The asking price seemed too high and I turned it down.

What I had not anticipated was the ability of the new owners, Compagnie de Suez, to raise prices dramatically and make it highly profitable. It would have been a good investment.

However, in retrospect, I'm not unhappy about it. The Médoc region may have had some wonderful châteaux, vineyards and quaint old towns, but there was not much in the way of social or cultural life. The Bartons, who had come over from Ireland in the nineteenth century, told us the other estate-owners were not that friendly to newcomers. Anthony and Eva, by contrast, loved to entertain at their beautiful château, and when they were there they had a constant flow of visitors: wine writers, buyers and even private customers. They were most generous hosts and were good friends of Princess Margaret and Lord Snowdon, who invited them back to royal events in Britain. Shirley and I found Princess Margaret rather tedious (as did Tony Snowdon). Shirley once refused to invite her to a party and the *Daily Mail* reported it the next day.

We gradually went off the Médoc as the location for our vineyard, and turned to Italy, a country I always felt was lucky for us and I thought might hold more promise for a wine business. I asked Franco Delle Piane, my long-time associate and regional manager of Sea Containers, to start looking for a property in Tuscany, which is well-known for its red wines, notably Chianti and Brunello di Montalcino. The Chianti Classico district is north of Siena, and the principal grape variety is the Sangiovese, which produces a distinctive taste when it is grown in the Chianti Classico area. To qualify as a Chianti and display the black rooster emblem on the bottle-neck, a wine must have a minimum of 80 per cent locally grown Sangiovese grapes.

I looked at a number of vineyards but they all seemed to be priced on the basis of their cubic volume of buildings rather than on the vineyards and I had no interest in buildings other than for a winery. And the wineries on those estates were ancient and not conducive to producing fine wines. Many of the vats were made of cement rather than stainless steel, there were no temperature control systems and blending was a haphazard process. Not surprisingly, their wine was often of poor quality.

Early in 1997, Franco called and said that he had found the ideal property. It was near the village of Gaiole, right in the heart of the Chianti Classico region, about 25 kilometres north of Siena and 50 km south of Florence. It was called Capannelle, and the owner, Rafaelle Rossetti, was something of a legend in the region. He had quit his job, twenty years before, as a businessman in Rome (he worked in laminated plastics of all things) and bought a derelict sixteenth-century Tuscan farmhouse which he restored, replanted the vines and installed a state-of-the-art winery.

Rossetti was a brilliant marketer and launched his first vintage in 1975 with a campaign which really got him noticed: he sent out special edition bottles with 18-carat gold and .925 silver labels made by a Florentine artisan. They quickly became collectors' items and were said to have been bought by the likes of Frank Sinatra and Donald Trump. It all helped put Capannelle on the map, and his excellent wines did the rest.

We went to see it and instantly felt this was what we had been looking for all this time. The house, which was built on top of the old winery, had open fireplaces, a large terrace overlooking the village and spectacular views across the rolling Tuscan countryside. The winery was in great shape, the vines were immaculate and we particularly appreciated the proximity to two of our favourite cities, Siena and Florence – where we had the Villa San Michele Hotel. Our great friends from Hong Kong, (Sir) Win and Rosemary Bischoff, lived nearby. Win had started his banking career with Schroders, where he became chairman, took over as temporary chairman of Citigroup in the 2008–9 financial crisis, then moved to become chairman of the beleaguered Lloyds Banking Group. He's a glutton for punishment.

Rossetti had been a remarkably innovative and creative owner, full of energy and new ideas. In addition to his Chardonnay and Chianti Classico Riserva labels, he developed a new blended variety he simply called 50&50. As he told the story, he was having dinner with the owners of the Avignonesi vineyard in Montepulciano at the Enoteca Pinchiorri restaurant in Florence and, at the end of a pleasant evening of drinking each other's wines, the two owners wondered what it would be like if they mixed a bottle of Capannelle's Sangiovese with a bottle of Avignonesi Merlot. They were so pleased with the result that Rossetti decided to market it, cleverly registering the 50&50 trademark around the world.

My calculations showed that a Tuscan wine estate was likely to achieve at least a 10 per cent return on investment compared with the 3 per cent I had identified in the Médoc. The growing season was longer and more dependable than in the Médoc where Atlantic storms can hit just before harvest, while the autumns are very mild in Tuscany. Furthermore, I now knew enough to realize that, although the Bordeaux reds would always be grander and more highly rated than Tuscan wines, the lighter Sangiovese wines were increasing their market share, just as the Pinot Noirs from Burgundy were doing.

In August 1997 I agreed a price with Rossetti and became the proud owner of a vineyard, a long-held ambition fulfilled. I kept the autumn harvest of 1997 as part of the deal and this vintage turned out to be, according to one of the wine magazines, the 'vintage of the century', and sells for astronomic prices today (unfortunately I have only a few bottles left). I persuaded Rossetti to stay on as a consultant, but the poor man was a chain smoker and eventually died of emphysema.

Capannelle was small, with an annual production of only 40,000 bottles, so the first thing I had to do was to step up production, which meant enlarging the winery. That required planning permission, but we quickly obtained it, as well as the addition of guest rooms to the house and the construction of a large infinity-pool. Shirley designed new gardens, and now the property is able to host guests, including many customers. The rating of our wines has steadily increased and the *Wine Spectator Magazine* and Robert Parker's *Wine Advocate* have given our 50&50 a 95, while our other reds, the Chianti Classico Riserva and Solare, are 92 or better.

About half the Capannelle wine is sold in Italy, but interestingly there has always been strong demand in Switzerland, Austria and Germany, while Japan, Russia and China have also emerged as important markets. We'd like to sell more in the important U.S. market, but it has such antiquated laws regulating distribution, taxes and labelling that profit margins suffer. Capannelle's production is now up to 80,000 bottles per year, and we also make organically grown olive oil and a wonderful grappa. We are well-advanced on our plans to increase production to 100,000 bottles a year.

Is it profitable? The answer is I don't know yet, because every year I have invested in the development of the estate, and my theory of a 10 per cent return has yet to be tested. But I have had great fun building up what many connoisseurs regard as one of the best vineyards in the Chianti Classico region, which, long past my time, will give generations of wine-lovers some of the pleasure it has given me. Two young men now run the estate: Simone Monciatti, who trained in oenology at the University of Siena, and Manuele Verdelli, who is the commercial manager, and they do a great job.

Around the time of my Capannelle purchase I decided that Orient-Express Hotels should enter the wine-trading business by buying every year a significant quantity of top Bordeaux wines, keeping it in store in Bordeaux and then selling when the price was right – or using it in the company's restaurants where the margin is good. I employed Sacha Lichine, son of Alexis, to advise us and he suggested the brands to buy. First- and second-growth Bordeaux were almost impossible to come by as they had already been committed *en primeur* (sold in advance of a wine's release) to regular clientele. Sacha was able to shake loose some small allocations and Anthony Barton generously sold us some of his second-growth wines. We had several million dollars of wine stored in Bordeaux when the 2008 financial crisis hit the hotel industry. It proved a godsend: in order to help our cash position we sold the entire inventory at a substantial profit.

And that was the end of my brief wine-trading career. I prefer making it.

CHAPTER TWENTY-FOUR

THE GHOST OF THOMAS JEFFERSON

Thomas Jefferson, author of the American Declaration of Independence, third President of the United States, diplomat, historian and philosopher, seems to crop up in these memoirs rather a lot – as tobacco farmer in the time of my Sherwood forbears, as imbiber of Madeira and as connoisseur of Château Haut-Brion *Premier Cru* Bordeaux wine. He appeared again – or at least his ghost did – in May 1999 when we bought Keswick Hall, within sight of the great man's home, Monticello. He designed the house himself (he was a skilled architect along with his many other accomplishments) when he was only twenty-six and lived there until he died fifty years later. Monticello is the only historic house in America on the U.N. World Heritage List, a distinction it shares with the Great Wall of China and the Pyramids of Egypt.

Sometimes when I look across at Monticello from Keswick Hall I imagine the great man sitting in his study amidst all the pictures, statues, architectural drawings and scientific instruments he sent home from France, surrounded by the books which became the nucleus for the American Library of Congress – and enjoying a bottle of Haut-Brion. Maybe he even has a glass of his favourite Madeira as a *digestif* as he pens his ringing Inaugural Address:

Sometimes it is said that man cannot be trusted with the government of himself. Can he, then, be trusted with the government of others? Or have we found angels in the forms of kings to govern him? Let history answer this question.

I think history probably has – and the answer is 'No'.

Jefferson once described the area around Charlottesville as 'the Eden of the United States', and that's where Keswick Hall is, looking as if it has been transplanted from the hills of Tuscany to the glades of Virginia. It's a beautiful spot, nestled up against the Blue Ridge Mountains. Richmond, the capital of the Confederate States during the American Civil War, is only an hour's drive away, and the whole area attracts thousands of tourists who come to see the battle sites. It always amazes me when I visit Richmond, how close Washington, D.C. is – and yet the Confederate Army was there for most of the war, camped on Mr. Lincoln's doorstep.

We acquired Keswick Hall as part of a package with another historic hotel, the second one of even more significance to me personally: the Inn at Perry Cabin, which, as I have already mentioned, stands on the site in Maryland where young Francis Sherwood came ashore in 1645 and started farming tobacco. We bought both properties from a rather strange Englishman called Sir Bernard Ashley, who had been married to the brilliant fabric designer, Laura Ashley.

Shirley and I had known the Ashleys slightly, Laura better than Bernard, and, like everybody else in the 1970s and 1980s, used Laura's distinctive floral printed fabrics in our homes (and in Shirley's case, the odd dress and scarf). She was a very talented and original lady whose designs were all the rage in Britain in the 1970s and became even more fashionable in the U.S. when Katharine Ross wore a dress made from Laura Ashley material in *Butch Cassidy and the Sundance Kid*. We were very saddened when Laura died in 1985 of a brain haemorrhage, which occurred after she tragically fell down the stairs of her daughter's country house on her sixtieth birthday.

Bernard took over the running of the company, very unsuccessfully. He expanded recklessly, particularly in the U.S. where he lost his shirt and within a few years was in every kind of trouble, battling financial crises, changes in management and catastrophic drops in share values. In 1990, when he announced the company had gone from a £20 million profit to a loss of £4.7 million, the City institutions had had enough and forced him to step down; the company was finally rescued by a Malaysian group.

Ashley remarried and began to look for new areas to expand in, which is when he alighted on the Inn at Perry Cabin, just a six-room hotel when he bought it in 1989. Over the next two years he expanded it to forty-one rooms and added Keswick Hall, which he bought in 1990 and spent heavily on restoring (it was built in 1912 as a private home), decorating the forty-eight rooms with antique furnishings. He spent over $20 million on a golf course and country club designed by Arnold Palmer. He then opened a chain of country house hotels called Ashley Inns in the U.S., which ran into heavy losses, and ploughed another £3 million into a country house hotel, Llangoed Hall, in South Wales, near one of his homes.

In 1999, Sir Bernard decided he was done with hotels, and approached me with the suggestion that we buy Keswick Hall, the Inn at Perry Cabin and the hotel in Wales. We declined the one in Wales but quickly agreed a deal on the other two. They made useful additions to our American portfolio which by that stage consisted of the Windsor Court Hotel in New Orleans, Charleston Place in South Carolina and of course '21' Club, our landmark restaurant in New York.

Although Bernard had invested heavily on Keswick Hall, we had to spend a great deal more to bring it up to Orient-Express Hotels' standards. We built a beautiful new pool overlooking the golf course, and a restaurant with floor-to-ceiling windows which we called Fossett's, after Thomas Jefferson's cook, Edith Fossett, who was one of his 200 slaves. Jefferson trained Edith to cook 'in the French style' and took her to the White House when he became President, prompting gossip that some of her ten children were sired by him. There is no evidence for it, but there is a great deal of evidence that Jefferson did indeed father children by another of his slaves, Sally Hemings. DNA analysis seems to prove it but when I put this to the historian Daniel Jordan, who headed up the Thomas Jefferson Foundation for many years, he immediately replied: 'Jefferson had a brother, you know!' At least a dozen books and hundreds of articles and studies have been devoted to the subject of Thomas Jefferson's black and white descendants, and opinion still remains divided as to whether he did it or didn't.

The Inn at Perry Cabin was built by a naval veteran after the war of 1812, and is named after Commodore Oliver Hazard Perry, who famously proclaimed: 'We have met the British and they are ours.' Orient-Express Hotels completed a $17 million improvement plan in 2003, bringing the room count up to 80. My first visit there caused me to begin the research into my Sherwood ancestors who lived and farmed in the area for 150 years before moving to Kentucky.

While we were busy shadowing Thomas Jefferson in Virginia, we were also developing our rail interests, this time in Australia. We had already taken over the management of the Observatory Hotel in Sydney and Lilianfels in Katoomba (but did not yet own them) in February of 1993 and a few years later, when Queensland Rail, or QR, asked us to operate a new luxury train they were building, it seemed like a good idea. QR basically hauls enormous quantities of coal and iron ore from the big open-cast mines to the east coast seaports from where it is shipped off to feed the voracious Chinese industrial machine. It carries passengers as well but, in common with the big U.S. railway companies, QR finds human cargo a nuisance and loses money on it. Overall QR is a very profitable enterprise, but it is subject to all sorts of political interference and pressure from the government of Queensland, where it is a vital part of the infrastructure. The export of raw materials to China, India and Japan has helped make the east coast of Australia one of the richest and fastest growing areas of the Western world (it has also got a wonderful climate and some excellent beaches).

In 1998 the QR management decided it needed to rationalize its overly large workforce and announced it was closing its railway workshops in Townsville, putting a couple of thousand people out of work. The unions exploded and the political backlash was such that it threatened to bring the state government down. QR had to do some lateral thinking to ameliorate the job losses.

Vincent O'Rourke, the chief executive of QR, came up with the idea of using the workshop to build a luxury tourist train to be called, rather grandly, the Great South Pacific Express. This would have the benefit of reducing the numbers of redundancies, at least until after the election, but left another problem: QR had no expertise at all in operating luxury tourist trains. O'Rourke was wise enough to realize he was going to need expert help on this one – and that's when QR contacted Nick Varian, the vice-president for trains and cruises at Orient-Express Hotels.

Australia is a huge territory with not a lot to see, but we identified some pretty stretches of track near Cairns, the jumping off stop for the Great Barrier Reef, the biggest coral reef system in the world and a major tourist attraction. The deal was that QR would use its skilled craftsmen to build the train – which ended up costing them A$35 million (almost the same in U.S. dollars) – and own the carriages, and we would operate it for a management fee.

It was not, I freely admit, our finest moment. From the start we had problems, some logistical but others inflicted on us by the bureaucracy and inflexibility of the railway company. The carriages, made to our specification and design, were fine but QR insisted on coating the windows with a dark film to reduce heat build-up. The result made even the most spectacular of landscapes – and most of it was pretty dull to begin with – look grey and sad, not what you expect on a once-in-a-lifetime trip which is what luxury train trips tend to be.

Then there was a problem with the suspension, which was designed for heavy freight wagons, and was awful. The QR track was basically built to carry freight, which doesn't mind a rough ride, but our passengers did. The only way passengers could sleep on the train was by stopping in a siding overnight, which made the trip too long.

But we didn't get where we were without perseverance. The Great South Pacific Express service was inaugurated on 23 April 1999 – and lost money from the start. We tried everything, including running excursions to the Blue Mountains, Hunter Valley and even Canberra (where there's not a lot to see). QR insisted on operating it occasionally on the Brisbane–Sydney route, which was even more boring than the Brisbane–Cairns route we were already running on. Then along came 9/11 and Japanese tourists, among our more enthusiastic ones, stopped coming. The operation limped along for another couple of years before QR threw in the towel. It had cost them $12 million on top of the money spent building the carriages. We made sure we collected our management fee so at least we didn't lose money, but it hadn't been comfortable.

The carriages were mothballed and put into storage at the Ipswich workshops, and I had completely forgotten about them until one day, some years later, QR called to ask if we'd like to buy them 'at a very special price'. When we asked why they were selling, we got the answer: 'Because the new Queensland premier is talking about running the train again.' They wanted to get rid of it to avoid yet more losses.

We had no immediate use for the carriages, but I was toying with the idea of operating a train between Hồ Chí Minh City (formerly Saigon) and Kunming in China via Hanoi and we bought them at a fraction of their original cost. They are still in their Queensland shed, awaiting an exciting venture sometime in the future.

I still felt that Australia had great potential and believed we could create a continent-wide hotel business. My philosophy for developing hotels has always been to own a key property in a country, such as the Cipriani in Italy or the Mount Nelson in South Africa, and add on to it to create a meaningful regional presence. Nick Seewer did this from his Cape Town base, building The Westcliff in Johannesburg and adding lodges in neighbouring Botswana, Philip Carruthers did it in Brazil and Filip Boyen, who later became the group's chief operating officer in London, did it in Peru.

I wanted to do the same in Australia, but there were obstacles. We found that only affluent overseas visitors would pay international rates for five-star hotels, and the Australians themselves were quite satisfied with the four-star brands such as Marriott and Sheraton where room rates were substantially lower. We looked at several five-star properties, and identified the Beaufort in Brisbane and Hayman Island near the Barrier Reef. We got close on the Hayman Island Resort but the owner, Ansett Airlines, also wanted to include its airport on a neighbouring island as part of the deal, and we backed off.

But we could still do it in Italy where by the late 1990s we had five properties: the Hotel Cipriani and Palazzo Vendramin in Venice, the two Splendidos in Portofino and the Villa San Michele in the Fiesole suburb of Florence. I had looked at various properties in Rome where I could never quite pull anything off, but the Amalfi Coast, south of Naples, offered better possibilities. This is a marvellous part of Italy, a spectacular coastline stretching roughly from the island of Capri to the city of Salerno, where the mountains drop away dramatically into the sea. The Via dei Limoni, a two-lane road with hairpin bends, snakes along the cliffs, and is as scary as it is breathtaking.

The village of Positano, which unfortunately has now been overdeveloped, is about halfway along this stretch of coast, and is known for its two top hotels, Le Sirenuse (fifty-nine rooms) and San Pietro (fifty-two rooms). Shirley and I stayed occasionally at these hotels, which are both family-owned, both of them wonderful establishments. Carlo Cinque personally built the San Pietro, which is a brilliant feat of engineering, literally suspending himself on a rope on a sheer 300-foot cliff above the Mediterranean and carving the terraces with a chisel out of the rock face. He left it to his niece Virginia Cinque who now runs it with her children. Planning laws were more relaxed in the 1950s, and we were told Carlo didn't have the proper approvals, but in Italy it is common practice to build without proper consent and then take advantage of periodic *condonos*, or pardons with a modest fine, which then nicely legalize everything retrospectively. Le Sirenuse is owned by the Sersale family, also managed by the new generation, and which, like the San Pietro, has been maintained at a very high standard.

Virginia Cinque commented to me that there was a great shortage of five-star hotel capacity on the Amalfi Coast and said San Pietro ran at near 100 per cent occupancy during the season. Both hotels opened at Easter and closed at the end of October, and were very popular with the large population of Italian-Americans who have roots in the south of Italy. With no more than 111 five-star rooms on offer in the high season along the coast, it was obvious to me that there was room for another five-star hotel.

Neither of these owners ever charged us a penny for staying in their hotels. They felt we were all part of an Italian 'family' of owners of top luxury properties and, while Orient-Express Hotels was a public company, they considered that I was actually the owner, or at least the proprietor, and should be treated as family. I felt greatly honoured to be part of this exclusive club. I would have liked to have bought either one of their hotels, but they were not for sale, so I went on looking.

Lucien and Moira Tessier, from whom we had acquired the Villa San Michele back in 1981, now lived very close to the San Pietro, immediately above Franco Zeffirelli's home, Tre Ville (Three Villas), which was beautifully decorated in the Neapolitan style. They knew the area well and introduced us to the families and hoteliers in the area who might be interested in selling us a property.

One of the possibilities was the Tre Ville itself, where every summer Zeffirelli entertained film stars such as Elizabeth Taylor and Richard Burton (he directed them in the classic film of Shakespeare's *The Taming of the Shrew*), Peter O'Toole and many others, including Gregory Peck, and invitations to Tre Ville were deeply coveted by the great and the good. But Zeffirelli was now in his mid-seventies, spent less and less time in Positano and preferred to live in his house in Rome. He couldn't cope with the steps, was no longer travelling as much, and the U.S. film industry had rather turned its back on films set in Europe. He decided to sell, remarking that 'I cannot enjoy it any more, and so it is right that other people should be able to'. I thought it could make a spectacular hotel, although it had problems: Zeffirelli had built rooms on the strictly preserved shoreline and, even for him – Franco was an Italian senator at the time – no *condono* could be obtained under Italian law. The entrance was also awkward with an uncomfortably long flight of steps from the road down to the property. We thought we could probably sink an elevator shaft from the road, but there were too many difficulties so we reluctantly abandoned the project and continued our search.

Franco Delle Piane, who had lived in Naples for many years, scouted around for us and eventually found an old hotel in Ravello for sale. Ravello is a village about 1,500 feet above the sea, not far from the town of Amalfi, and just far enough above the Amalfi Drive to avoid the despoliation that Positano has suffered. The John Huston film *Beat the Devil*, starring Humphrey Bogart, Jennifer Jones, Gina

Lollobrigida and Robert Morley, was shot in Ravello, and Gore Vidal had his home there for many years. The hotel was called the Caruso Hotel & Belvedere and was still owned by the Caruso family (no relation of the opera singer, alas).

Italy is really two countries, the rich north and the poor south, jammed together in an uneasy alliance by Garibaldi in 1870 and nestling uncomfortably under the same flag ever since. Unfortunately in many respects it is still two countries, with the *mafia* and *camorra* still very much in evidence in the south, and I should have heeded the advice I was given by those who knew the region well and followed the old Roman principle *caveat emptor*, or 'buyer beware'.

We bought the Caruso in September 1999 with planning permission for improvements attached, which we regarded as a great bonus because we reasoned (in our innocence) that we would not have long to wait before being able to crack on with them. The mayor of Ravello was very supportive as he could see the hotel attracting wealthy visitors to the town, more spending in the shops and jobs for locals in the hotel. Like most places in southern Italy, there was high unemployment in Ravello and a development such as ours would have a significant impact.

Little did we know that ahead of us lay six long years of legal battles, court cases, appeals and much ill-will before we finally opened the hotel in June 2005. Shortly after construction started on the renovation and additional rooms, we were 'denounced' to the planning authorities by unnamed parties, who claimed that the planning application made by the previous owner was false. We appeared before the local magistrate, who was much more interested in listening to the case made by the anonymous denouncer(s), sided against us and ordered the premises to be sealed while an investigation was made. This investigation took ages and was deeply flawed, but it gave the magistrate the excuse to order further court action, which turned into five separate hearings spread over several years. The judge gave every indication after the first four hearings that he would throw out the case against us but – surprise, surprise – at the fifth hearing a new judge appeared (said to be from the same village as the magistrate) who ruled against us. We then appealed to a higher court where the case against us was thrown out, but the clerk of the first court refused to take off the seals, and we had to go to a tribunal of judges in Rome to obtain an order before they were finally removed.

But even then our denouncer(s) did not give up. The Fine Arts Commission (Belli Arti) wrote to us requesting various changes to be made to the approved drawings for 'artistic reasons'. We made the changes – at some cost – and then the magistrate appeared yet again and sealed the rooms where the alterations had been made on the grounds that the Belli Arti had no authority to request such changes. We then had to go back and restore the original construction. In the case of our two best suites the seals were not removed until the spring of 2011, twelve years after we bought the hotel.

The six-year delay and the costs of the legal proceedings made the Hotel Caruso the most expensive hotel we had ever bought on a cost-per-room basis. But it was beautiful when we finally finished it. We employed Federico Forquet, the well-known Italian interior designer who came originally from Naples, to create the interiors in Neapolitan style, which he did brilliantly. He also designed the garden with some advice from Shirley (he had earlier designed the superb Italian gardens for our friends the Ulfanes at their *castello* in Tuscany), and Maurizio Saccani, our vice-president in charge of Italian hotels, oversaw the creation of an eye-level pool at the end of the Belvedere which seems to merge with the sky and the blue of the Tyrrhenian Sea.

The denouncers, it turned out, were rival hotel owners in Ravello, one in particular, who shamelessly took advantage of the creaky Italian legal system for their own purposes. I'm afraid it is not unusual in southern Italy, and the only surprise is that anything gets built at all. We have friends who can tell even more hair-raising stories, which Simon Sherwood calls 'barriers to entry': by making it almost impossible to develop properties, an artificial shortage is created which then permits high profitability for the existing hoteliers and insiders.

Every summer Ravello hosts the Wagner Music Festival, named after the great composer who visited the town in 1880 (and wrote at least part of *Parsifal* there), which has developed into a two-month-long arts event attracting great numbers of tourists. When the audiences outgrew the capacity of the outdoor amphitheatre, which could not be used in bad weather, a new one was commissioned from Oscar Niemeyer, our old friend from the Copacabana Palace. It is pure Niemeyer, a spectacular modern concrete curved structure, which hangs out over the cliff face, with baleful eyes and a slit of a mouth. After ten years of controversy, it was opened in 2010 when Niemeyer celebrated his 103rd birthday. Many locals think it is far too *avant garde* and out of keeping with the more traditional structures along the coast, but opera-lovers, including me, like it, if only on the grounds one doesn't get wet. It has been built into a terrace below the Caruso so one can walk down from the hotel, but you need to be a mountain goat to return on foot.

Ravello and the surrounding area are particularly noted for their lemons and the increasingly popular after-dinner drink limoncello. Unfortunately limoncello is not a protected name so bars all over Italy make their own although their lemons are not as good. I always buy a bottle or two of limoncello when we visit Ravello, although to be honest I much prefer Capannelle grappa as an Italian *digestif*.

We have a boat which can run guests to Capri for the day and the great Roman and Greek sites of Pompeii, Paestum and Herculaneum are only an hour or so away by car. But for me a visit to the world's most famous pizzeria, Di Matteo in Naples, is a must. No other pizza tastes quite like it.

CHAPTER TWENTY-FIVE

SINGING THE NEW MILLENNIUM IN...

New Year's Eve is always a big occasion in Brazil, but on 31 December 1999 it was something special. The entire Sherwood family, including all the grandchildren, was there to sing the old millennium out and the new one in at the Copacabana Palace Hotel, which put on a ball in its famous Golden Room, excelling anything we had ever been to. I can think of no better place to greet the new age, with all it might have in store for us and for the world, or company with which to share this magical evening.

The evening started out unnervingly low-key. Copacabana Beach was almost deserted when we looked out as we went to our table at nine in the evening. But at 11.45 p.m., when we came back out onto the terrace, the scene was transformed with 3 million people dressed in white occupying every foot of the three-mile long beach. Down by the shore we could see people putting candles on tiny floats and gently pushing them out to sea, a tradition passed down from the African slaves brought over by the Portuguese in the eighteenth century. Barges of fireworks were moored offshore and at midnight we had an hour-long display of vast proportions, the most impressive I've ever seen – and I've seen many. It started to drizzle about two in the morning, but this in no way deterred the revellers who danced the night through. The next morning when we arose (rather late) the beach was empty and spotless. We were told that there had been no crime reported in the entire city of Rio that night, nor were there any deaths until after the start of the New Year. It was almost a religious experience. We were also pleased that the clocks and computers still worked after all the Y2K speculation that they would fail.

The dawn of a new year was a time for taking stock and doing some planning, if not for the next millennium, at least for the next decade – although, as Robbie Burns liked to say, 'the best laid plans of mice and men…' But at least we would start the decade in good order. I sat down to work out some figures: Sea Containers, owners of 100 per cent of Orient-Express Hotels, had increased profits by 12.5 per cent in 1999. It had been a tough year for marine container leasing, still the engine-room of the whole group, but it remained highly profitable. That had been complemented by other parts of our well-diversified business. We had a large ferry operation, with new routes just opened, such as Scotland to Northern Ireland, and extra capacity on our New York fast-ferry commuter service which couldn't keep up with demand. But it was the leisure business that had taken over the running. It had emerged as the biggest contributor to profits and was beginning to overshadow everything else. The old Sea Containers was becoming unbalanced, with the subsidiary driving the parent.

I made a list of all the properties Orient-Express now owned: there were thirty-seven of them, spread across fifteen countries, and the Hotel Caruso in Ravello, south of Naples, was under construction. Sea Containers' investment in the leisure industry now stood at $726 million and our return on that, before interest, taxes and depreciation, was $84 million, or about 11.5 per cent.

Then I made a separate list of all the projects we were currently working on: forty new suites at La Samanna in St. Martin; an annexe planned for the Windsor Court; refurbishment of the old casino rooms of the Copacabana Palace; the acquisition of the old granary in Venice for conversion into a banqueting facility for the Hotel Cipriani; a health spa at Reid's in Madeira; the new Upstairs Room at '21' Club; doubling the number of rooms in the Inn at Perry Cabin (from forty to eighty-one) and improving Keswick Hall. We were also in the early stages of creating the new Palladio Suite at the Cipriani, which in the high season Natale Rusconi reckoned we could charge $6,000 a night for (and he was right).

But there was so much still to do: I wanted to do more in Peru, and our British Pullman train had been so oversubscribed we had bought and were restoring another one, the Northern Belle. Mandalay was getting a new airport, which would help our cruise ship on the Irrawaddy, and I wanted to see what we could add to give us critical mass in that region. I was also looking at properties in Australia, the U.S., the Caribbean and Mexico. Beyond that was the rest of Asia, and Russia. The list stretched on until I had to ask the waiter to bring me some more paper.

Looking at the figures of our main rivals at the upper end of the market, I now calculated that Orient-Express Hotels' operating profits were greater than those of Four Seasons and 50 per cent more than Mandarin Oriental. That made us a very serious player in the luxury hotels sector, and the industry recognized it. We were often the first stop for bankers and brokers when iconic hotels were being offered for sale, and it also meant we could keep our prices and occupancies up when others were cutting theirs.

The big disappointment was the performance of the Sea Containers share price, which did not reflect the strength of the company. Analysts were telling me the markets were increasingly looking for what they called 'pure play' companies, which they could more easily understand and compare against others in the same industry. The day of the conglomerate, or even well-diversified company, was gone. What I had always considered a strength had become a weakness, and we were low fashion, yesterday's story.

What to do about it? I had been pondering this question on and off for months, and now I could put it off no longer. The year 2000 was to be the year when Sea Containers, the mother company, cast its fully grown child adrift into the world to fend for itself. We would float Orient-Express on the stock market as a separate company with its own board and its own management.

And that's what we did. In August 2000 Sea Containers sold 37 per cent of Orient-Express Hotels Class A shares in an initial public offering, or IPO, which was well received by the markets. At a share price of $26.25 the company had a market value of $747 million soon after the issue. Sea Containers' 62.5 per cent stake was worth $466 million, which bizarrely was more than the market value of Sea Containers itself. All the Sea Containers' interests in container leasing, property, ferries, the GNER train franchise in the U.K. and the rest were accorded a negative value. But markets are markets and the only thing you can do in circumstances like that is to put your head down and get on with your business.

When Nara Corporation of Japan offered us ownership of the two Australian hotels we already managed, the Observatory in Sydney and Lilianfels in the Blue Mountains, we bought them for $40 million, largely financed by a bank loan.

Then we made a brief foray into Argentina where in 2000 we bought a residential property in Buenos Aires' fashionable Alvear district, where I planned to recreate the country's most famous steakhouse, La Cabaña. We had bought all the artifacts of the old La Cabaña after it shut down a few years earlier, with the intention of creating a steakhouse brand which could be rolled out to our hotels in various parts of the world. Shirley and I flew to Buenos Aires from Cape Town, a flight of only seven hours thirty minutes, and stayed, as we always do, with the art dealer Thomas Gibson, who owns a wonderful *estancia* in the Pampas about 200 kilometres to the south. I enlisted Thomas to help get our restaurant off the ground, which I envisioned along the lines of '21' Club, with an *à la carte* restaurant on the ground floor and banqueting in the rooms above. Thomas was great and we eventually opened the new La Cabaña in October of 2003. It was a flop. We made a number of misjudgements, the main factor being that Argentina was going through tough times and there was no local market for a restaurant like ours. We were also in the wrong area: the Buenos Aires waterfront was developing as a trendy restaurant location with lots of outdoor dining, but we were located in a more staid part of the city. We also had problems with managers who sought to go *off-piste* and create a restaurant different from the American steakhouse image I was after. One manager thought the restaurant should be Italian, another thought it should be French.

The result was we never made a profit, and sold it in 2009 to a delightful Argentine lawyer, Senora Karina Barreiro, who has done a lot better with it than we did. She sold the house, rented a waterfront location, moved all the old fittings and artifacts, added more covers – half of them on an outdoor terrace – and cut out the banqueting rooms. She has retained our menu and staff and I wish her every success – not, I think, that she needs it.

The events of September 11th 2001 caught us as off-guard as everyone else, but out of evil comes some good and the 'good' in this case was Richard Branson of Virgin fame. Branson is a charming rogue, full of innovative ideas, many of them outrageous, some of them inspired, but overall he is a brilliant entrepreneur. When we first met him at a party given by David Frost, now probably more famous for the *Frost/Nixon* play and film than for his thousands of TV interviews, Branson dropped to his knees and kissed Shirley's hand. No one had ever done that before – or since. He told us he greatly admired what we had done in relaunching the Orient-Express train, and wondered if there was there a project we could do together. There wasn't at the time, but there soon would be.

As it happened, two of our senior executives, David Benson, the senior vice-president in charge of Sea Containers' ferry businesses, and Paul Clark, his deputy, had worked for Branson and stayed in touch with their old colleagues. One day Paul Clark called to say he'd heard from his Virgin contacts that the group's cash flow had been badly affected by 9/11 and Branson had decided to sell Virgin's hotel assets. His intelligence was right and shortly afterwards they were on offer.

With my lifelong passion for good food and restaurants, the property that most interested me was Le Manoir aux Quat' Saisons, the two-star Michelin restaurant in the village of Great Milton in Oxfordshire, created by the great chef Raymond Blanc as his personal dream in 1984. Le Manoir, as it is simply called, is one of the best-known and highly regarded restaurants in England. It is within driving distance of our country home, Hinton Manor, and I had been going there from the beginning.

Everyone assumed Raymond owned all of Le Manoir, but when he originally took it over, he only held 50 per cent of the shares. He had the idea of enlarging it, but when costs ran well over budget he had a cash crisis. Richard Branson came to the rescue and injected cash. Now Branson's shares were for sale as well as Raymond's remaining shares.

So we bought them, adding a third world-renowned restaurant to Harry's Bar in London and '21' Club in New York (I would like to have been able to add La Cabaña to that list). I insisted on keeping our ownership low-key, because Le Manoir is so closely associated with the very high-profile Raymond and I didn't want to disturb the general perception of him as Chef/Patron. It would have been bad for business – and it is also a mark of respect for the man.

Raymond is an extraordinary, ebullient Frenchman from the Franche-Comté region of France (he was born in Besancon), who was taught to cook by his mother, a star in her own kitchen. He is a brilliant and imaginative chef, always seeking to improve his menu and, in an age when TV chefs have acquired astonishing celebrity status with often foul-mouthed or downright vulgar (at least in my view) programs, he has retained his standards and the respect of his fellow chefs. He is also very amusing in person and on TV, where I think many viewers must struggle to understand him. He has lived in England for thirty-seven years yet still speaks English, as one inter-viewer remarked, with an accent 'as thick as crème anglaise'. He is much given to great Gallic flourishes, and phrases like 'food is for life, for joy, for saying I looo-ove you'. He is also a very serious profes-sional who has put his stamp all over Le Manoir, be it the gardens, the food or the hotel. He also created his own school of cooking which has had an enormous influence on food in Britain today. Le Manoir has become a culinary university and twenty-seven chefs who have worked for Raymond have gone on to win Michelin stars. He is a natural teacher.

Given my lofty status as a *Commandeur* of *La Confrérie des Chevaliers du Tastevin* I felt obliged to offer my contribution to the success of Le Manoir's restaurant, so I suggested that we offer high quality wines by the glass. I'm pleased to say that when Raymond implemented this wine sales soared. I think he was as gratified as I was.

The Manoir has thirty-two rooms, mostly suites which Raymond has decorated individually using themes from different countries he has visited, with the talented interior decorator Emily Todhunter assisting him as needed. But it needs to be further enlarged and getting permission against entrenched local opposition in the area has been a challenge. Raymond has been working on it for years, and at one stage invited the local vicar to dinner in an attempt to enlist his support for a planning application. When the neighbours heard about it, they were so incensed the vicar was drummed out of the parish.

The other property we bought off Branson was La Residencia in Deià, Mallorca, which had been developed by the German architect Axel Ball (who married Branson's first wife). Deià holds a special place in my heart. When I came to Europe in 1959 after my stretch in the Navy, I didn't know many people but I had a great friend who lived in Deià, and I spent several holidays there, staying in the local inn. The personality and presence of the writer and poet, Robert Graves, dominated village life and attracted artists, poets and actors from all over the world – Alec Guinness, Peter Ustinov and many others were familiar faces to the villagers. One of the best-known visitors was Ava Gardner, who bewitched Graves, and he dedicated a poem, *Not to Sleep*, to her. It described the happy and excited state her visits aroused in him:

> *Not to sleep all the night long, for pure joy,*
> *Counting no sheep and careless of chimes...*

He also wrote a short story tribute to her for the *New Yorker* titled 'A Toast to Ava Gardner'. In her autobiography, written many years later, she responded: 'And I have to admit that I also loved him.' Their relationship, however, was totally platonic.

I got to know a number of artists in Deià, particularly the American Bill Waldron and his wife Jackie who were great hosts. Bill, one of the most charming, open and inspirational men I've ever met, had been a successful artist in Paris until he took a vacation in Mallorca in 1953 and stayed. He made beautiful sculptures out of materials as simple as driftwood, and it was said in the village that no piece of wood, stone or metal was safe in his presence. But his real passion was archaeology, in which he was entirely self-taught – he came from humble beginnings in New Jersey. I can remember him talking enthusiastically and knowledgeably about Mallorca's Bronze Age culture, remnants of which had been excavated some years before.

In the early 1960s he became a full-time archaeologist and made a series of outstanding discoveries in the rock-shelters in the northern, mountainous part of the island. Over the years he identified and excavated dozens of other important sites, including the (now) famous Muleta cave, which was a natural animal trap and preserved remains of extinct native animals on the island, including a dwarf antelope, along with human remains. His finds revolutionized the accepted theories of the prehistory of the island, and made him an international figure. Although he had only a high school education, he found himself in demand as a lecturer, and after one of them he was approached by a professor from Oxford who invited him to teach there. I have always thought it was highly commendable of Oxford to accept a scientist without any higher education qualifications – although he lived long enough, and studied hard enough, to acquire professional status. And he never gave up his art.

When I first went to see La Residencia, our new acquisition, it brought back memories of my lazy days and nights in Deià when we would sit and talk in the cafés over drinks, eat dinner at midnight – an excellent meal with local wine cost $1.00 in 1960 – then tour the music bars and go to bed near sunrise. We would sleep until noon and then take the trail from the hilltop village down to the secluded swimming cove below, where we would meet the girls and consume grilled chicken or seafood for lunch on the beach. I recall the climb back to the village in the late afternoon being demanding (La Residencia has now put in a road).

The Spanish planners have protected this part of the coast remarkably well from new construction and it's almost as pretty as I remember it. The hotel turned out to be a twin manor house, set among the orange groves on the edge of Deià, almost directly over what had been our private cove. The Branson publicity machine had cleverly cata-pulted it into the top league. Children were not permitted and guests were required to stay for a minimum of a week – even then there was a waiting list.

As always, I wanted to create more suites, increase the number of rooms, and upgrade the bathrooms, and we eventually got permis-sion on the basis that they were strictly of Mallorcan traditional design. Then a landslide, caused by heavy rain, carried away part of the construction works and when we restarted, our friend Andrew Lloyd Webber, who had moved with his wife Madeleine from their holiday home in Cap Ferrat to the hill above Deià, complained about the noise and the appearance of the roof line. He was quite right about the roof line, which we changed, and we did our best to keep down the noise when they were in residence. Shirley designed the garden and a new entrance to the hotel, which worked very well.

Shirley and I had a strange, spooky experience in Deià. A friend from Manila days rented a grand house near the town, which had once been the property of Archduke Ludwig of Austria, second cousin of the Emperor Franz Joseph. Ludwig settled in Majorca in the middle of the nineteenth century, and bought up some wild areas around Deià to preserve them. His main home near Deià is now a museum but he converted an old ruined manor house into a Moorish-style palace for one of his mistresses (he is said to have sired many children in Mallorca), which is now owned by the actors Michael Douglas and Catherine Zeta-Jones. The house appeared in the film of a Vladimir Nabokov novel, *Laughter in the Dark*, where the wheelchair victim falls down steps after his wife and chauffeur have deserted him, the gate to the steps locks and he can't get out. We asked our friend how he was able to afford such a grand house, and he said it was because everyone who had lived there had experienced an unexpected death, the locals said there was a curse on it and no one else would touch it, so he got it cheaply. When we visited him the next year, he told us that he had returned from a winter break to find his gardener floating face-down in the cistern. The following year, we found our friend had moved out and a wealthy society beauty, Barbara Baekeland, heiress to the Bakelite plastic fortune, had moved in (by chance, when I gave up my old flat in Isle Saint Louis in Paris, she rented it – at double the rent I was paying). Some months later I read the lurid headline in the *Daily Mail*: 'How a society beauty was finally murdered by her gay son she tried to "cure" of homosexuality.' It was Barbara, who had been stabbed with a kitchen knife by her drug-crazed son. I hope for Mr. and Mrs. Douglas' sake the 'curse' stops there.

CHAPTER TWENTY-SIX

———

PUTTIN' ON THE RITZ

I had my eye on the Hotel Ritz in Madrid for many years. It had a splendid location on the Paseo del Prado in Madrid's famous 'Golden Triangle', with the Prado Museum on one side, the memorial to the Spanish Civil War on another, and the Thyssen Museum just opposite. The Ritz was the third iconic hotel created by the great Swiss-born hotelier César Ritz, who was known as 'king of hoteliers, and hotelier to kings'. His stylish hotels in Paris and London inspired the word 'ritzy', and Irving Berlin to write the song, made timeless by Fred Astaire:

> *Come, let's mix, where Rockefellers walk with sticks*
> *Or 'umber-ellas' in their mitts, puttin' on the Ritz.*

Ritz's equally great partner was the legendary French chef Auguste Escoffier and the pair established their names and reputation in the 1890s when they ran the Savoy Hotel in London, before being sacked when large quantities of wine went missing. César returned to Paris, opened the Ritz in the Place Vendôme and a few years later, partly to get back at the D'Oyly Carte family who owned the Savoy, he returned to open the London Ritz on Piccadilly, attracting back many of his royal and aristocratic former customers. Not to be outdone, the young Spanish monarch King Alfonso XIII wanted his own Ritz in Madrid to match Paris and London. César duly obliged, and the Madrid Ritz opened in 1910. Its luxury amazed and delighted the rich and famous who soon flocked to it from all over Europe: there were four to five bathrooms in each section of the hotel, and a telephone on every floor next to the lifts. No one had ever heard of such luxuries before.

Despite the high prices charged by the Ritz in Paris, bought by Mohamed Al Fayed in 1979 after César's son Charles died, I have always stayed there. The first office of Sea Containers in 1965 was in the Place Vendôme, a few short steps away, and I often dined in the famous L'Espadon restaurant or met people for a drink in the Hemingway Bar. In those days, as I've already described, my old classmate from Yale, Maury Pinto, lent me space in the offices of the private family bank Pinto & Cie. in the Place Vendôme, before we moved the operation to London. Morris, Maury's cousin, eventually moved to New York and Maury and another cousin, Joe, based themselves in Madrid from 1996, giving me a good reason to visit that city often, where I naturally stayed at the Madrid Ritz, just down the street from the Pinto offices.

The hotel was partly owned by Spain's royal family, which had returned to Spain after Franco died in 1975, and, needless to say, all visiting royalty stayed there (as they continue to do, even though the family no longer owns shares). The main dining room was an exceedingly elegant space facing the Paseo del Prado, on a par with the beautiful dining room of the Ritz in London which faces Green Park.

The Madrid Ritz was eventually acquired by the British hotel group Trusthouse Forte, which also owned the George V and Plaza Athénée in Paris and the Café Royal in London, as well as all sorts of downmarket Little Chef, Travelodge and Happy Eater motorway restaurants and motels. It was founded by one of the great catering entrepreneurs of the day, (Lord) Charles Forte, an Italian immigrant who set up his first milk-bar in London's Regent Street in 1935, and by the time he passed on the reins to his son Rocco it was a great sprawling asset-rich empire which was a perennial takeover target for predators.

In 1996, Granada, a British media and catering company, made a hostile £3.9 billion takeover bid which had the Fortes on the ropes.

Having been through my own hostile bid in 1989–90, I had every sympathy for Rocco, whom I have always liked, and invited him to lunch. I recommended that, in return for agreeing to abandon its bid, he should offer Granada his downmarket assets while he kept the good stuff. He disagreed, saying he wanted to fight on and had the support of his shareholders, the largest of which was the Pearson publishing group. When Granada increased its offer Pearson's board wobbled, and the game was lost.

Rocco, however, had put up a good defence and had made Granada pay too much and overstretch itself. Over the next few years it was forced to sell assets, and the Ritz in Madrid came on the market early in 2003. Orient-Express Hotels now had La Residencia in Mallorca, which was settling in well, and another Spanish property made sense. Landmark hotels like this maybe come up for sale once in a generation and if you miss out, it is unlikely you'll get another chance.

Even before the Ritz in Madrid came on the market, I had a try for the Ritz in Paris. I had been outbid for the Plaza Athénée by the Sultan of Brunei, so with great audacity I contacted Mohamed Al Fayed, who owned the Paris Ritz as well as the Harrods store in Knightsbridge, Fulham Football Club and various other assets. I had first met Mohamed in the 1960s when he was involved in expanding and managing the Port of Dubai (Port Rashid), and we had met from time to time over the years since. He was involved in one of the most bitter corporate battles of all time over ownership of Harrods with Tiny Rowland, a buccaneering tycoon whom the British Prime Minister Edward Heath immortalized by labelling his company Lonrho as 'an unacceptable face of capitalism'. Lonrho owned 29.9 per cent of Harrods holding company House of Fraser, but 'parked' its shares with Al Fayed in an attempt to sidestep a Monopolies Commission decision to prevent him gaining control. Al Fayed claimed he had bought the stake fairly and squarely and, with the support of the House of Fraser board, who hated Rowland, bought the rest. Rowland waged a war against him for the next ten years until the two men, by now ageing (Rowland died a few years later), eventually shook hands in the Harrods food hall under a large shark, which Mohamed had mischievously called 'Tiny'.

I took Simon Sherwood along for my meeting with Mohamed, an ebullient and forceful man with a wicked sense of humour, and suggested that he might like to sell the Paris Ritz to us. He roared with laughter, and said he'd be delighted to – but the price would be $1 billion. It was his way of saying no, and with the benefit of hindsight, I'm not certain he would have sold it even for that ridiculous price: the last pictures of Princess Diana and Mohamed's son Dodi taken alive were of them emerging through the swing doors of the Ritz to get into the car that would take them to their deaths on that fateful evening in 1997.

To take the sting out of his refusal, Al Fayed gave us some Turnbull & Asser ties (he also owned T&A) and frozen bags of what he claimed were stags' testicles from his estate in Scotland, which he said would improve our sex life. Mohamed is a great tease and very likeable – as long as you don't cross him. In 2010 he unexpectedly sold Harrods to the Qatar royal family for £1.5 billion, probably about ten times what he had paid for it in 1984 when you take into account the assets sold over the years.

My view was – and still is – that an important hotel is needed on Paris's Left Bank, the fun part of the city. The Israeli hotelier Alfred Akirov has renovated the classic Hôtel Lutetia on Saint-German-des-Prés, but there is still an opportunity for a really great hotel, perhaps in one of the big state-owned buildings, which occasionally come up for sale.

Having failed to land the Ritz in Paris, I was doubly determined to succeed with its sister in Madrid. But the price was rich, well over $100 million, more than we'd ever paid for a property before, and we had committed ourselves to a series of developments in Peru, Asia, the Caribbean and elsewhere. The answer, I decided, was to bring in a local partner for a 50 per cent stake while we retailed the management contract. We were introduced to Omega Capital, a major Spanish investment company controlled by the powerful Koplowitz family, entered into a joint venture, and we took possession of the Ritz on 25 April 2003. The price was a heady $135 million, and in our announcement we said we also agreed to invest a further €25 million in improvements.

It soon became apparent that Alicia Koplowitz, Seventh Marquisa de Bellavista and Spain's richest woman, would be an active partner. She is a formidable entrepreneur who had turned an already large fortune, which she and her sister inherited from their father, into an estate valued by *Forbes* magazine at $5.2 billion with investments in property and hotels in Spain, the U.S., Hong Kong and elsewhere. She has exquisite taste, visible in her own homes where she has a serious collection of art and antiques, including a number of Goyas, and is not a lady to be trifled with.

Alicia took a keen interest in her new investment and wanted to give the hotel a major makeover with a much more contemporary feel. We were all agreed that the 167 rooms in the Ritz should be refurbished, and that some of the public spaces needed upgrading, but we were worried about the cost. I was also uneasy about altering the ambience of this iconic hotel, particularly when friends such as the Duke and Duchess of Segorbe from Seville argued vehemently that the Ritz decoration should not be changed. The Duke's foundation owns twenty-seven great palaces in Spain, including the Pilatus in Seville, and he has a great feel for historic buildings, so when he speaks, you listen. We had problems with the fine arts authorities and with the city, who advised us that improvements made by the Fortes had never been given formal approval, which we had to apply for retrospectively. After that there was a question as to whether the hotel should be closed for two years for top-to-bottom renovation, or implement a rolling program to cover one wing at a time – which is what I wanted to do.

We were still discussing what improvements to make, when to make them and how to finance it all, when the sub-prime mortgage crisis hit Spain in 2008 and made it all academic. Spanish property values crashed, the banks, which had previously boasted the strongest balance sheets in the world, were suddenly in trouble, and the Ritz, like many other five-star properties, saw its earnings decline as Spanish businesses cut their spending back hard. Everything was put on hold. By 2011 unemployment in Spain was running at 20 per cent, and the country trembled on the brink of default.

In a way some good may come out of it, because the hotel, which is profitable, has essentially remained as it was. Under the excellent management of the Swiss hotelier Anton Kung it delivers an experience which would have pleased César Ritz. There are some things I would still want to do: the Fortes closed off the main dining room, and moved indoor dining to the former library which I think was a mistake. If the decisions were mine I would reopen the beautiful old dining room, and upgrade the hotel little by little as I did successfully at other properties starting with the Hotel Cipriani.

Spain of course was not the only issue on my mind during this time. I was still trying to get a decent beachhead in the Asian hotel market, which had always been a conundrum for me. Sea Containers had done brilliantly in the Far East, recognizing early on that all Asian exports would be containerized and a great deal of money was going to be made out of the process. We were also quick to move to having our containers made in China and other Asian countries because it made sense to put them into service at high export demand points. Because of the time I had spent in the Far East in the Navy, I felt I was a bit of a veteran and knew a bit more than the next person how to conduct business there.

Actually, it didn't help. We could not buy a hotel in Japan because the Japanese felt they would lose face if they sold to a 'gaijin' (white man), and in retrospect I'm glad of it – it has not been a great hotel market. In Hong Kong, land prices were outrageous in the 1990s, although I wish now I had had the courage to face up to them and buy, because they just went on up – and up. I remember turning down an offer from the Blue Funnel line to buy Holt's Wharf in Kowloon for $10 million, which would have been the bargain of the century. It was bought by a Chinese group, which built a spectacular hotel with views across to Victoria on Hong Kong Island, and leased it to Regent Hotels where it became their flagship. When the lease finally expired it became the Intercontinental. I did put a toe into the Hong Kong property market in the 1980s when I bought a house on the Peak and built five townhouses in the large garden, all of which were eventually sold at a huge profit. The development was called 'Sherwood's Bluff' and still carries that name.

Adrian Zecha, whose Aman Resorts group was making major waves in Asia with its hallmark small hotels in beautiful locations, gave me his view that it was pointless to try to buy existing hotels in Asia because the owners would only sell to their friends. Adrian, an Indonesian of Dutch descent, knows Asia as well as anyone and his recommendation was to go for new builds, which is what he did and what I had studiously avoided.

I did make one forlorn attempt to acquire the Starkie-built Raffles Hotel in Singapore in partnership with an old shipping friend, Sir Kerry St. Johnston, one of the pioneers of the containerization revolution in the 1960s. Kerry by that stage was chairman of a Singapore-based bank called PICA, and he thought it would be fun to have a go at the legendary old hotel, which was then owned jointly by two big Singapore banks, OCBC and the Development Bank of Singapore. It was seedy and needed a major rebuild, but still had an international reputation and was ideal for my purposes. We got some way down the road before OCBC decided to develop the site itself.

The success of the Eastern & Oriental Express and the *Road to Mandalay* ship on the Irrawaddy persuaded me to have another crack at the Asian hotel market around 2002. Chresten Bjerrum had lots of ideas for further developments in Myanmar, and on one of our trips up-country to visit the ship, we got back to Rangoon with most of the day free before catching our evening flight. Chresten suggested we have lunch at the Pansea Hotel, which didn't sound very upmarket to me, but I was astonished to find myself in a handsome ex-colonial governor's residence with beautiful gardens and a wrap-around reflecting pool. The management and chefs were French and we dined on tables set out on an immaculate lawn. The owners had built a number of rooms in three-storey groups around the residence and, in the absence of the general manager, we persuaded the obliging food and beverage manager to show us around. I thought the rooms were smallish by Orient-Express Hotels standards but were stylishly decorated with good bathrooms and air-conditioning.

The hotel was owned by the Pansea Group, which I'd never heard of before that day. It had been created by two Frenchmen, Robert

Molinari in Bangkok and Stanley Rollin in Paris. As soon as I got to Singapore I asked Adrian Zecha what he knew about them, and Adrian told me he had bought the original Pansea Hotel in Phuket to enlarge his Amanpuri resort there, and knew the owners well. He had heard they were having difficulty in arranging bank finance for Southeast Asian investments, and were looking for an investor prepared to put $8 million into the company.

As soon as I got back to Europe, I got in touch with Rollin in Paris and over lunch he confirmed that he and Molinari were looking for an investor. Pansea had five properties in their portfolio, he explained: one in Bali on the beach, one in Siem Reap in Cambodia (where Angkor Wat is located), one in the old capital of Laos, Luang Prabang on the Mekong River, and one in Koh Samui, an island in the Gulf of Siam in Thailand, plus of course the one in Rangoon. A sixth hotel was under construction in the Ubud Gorge in Bali, and there were plans for still more.

We agreed to take things forward and Molinari took Chresten to inspect the properties. He reported back enthusiastically, saying they had all been developed with remarkable style and, critically, were market leaders in each location. Over the next few weeks we structured a deal whereby we would put in our investment by way of a convertible $8 million loan and enter into a five-year arrangement with a put/call option, which enabled the owners to exit part of all of their investment at multiples of operating profits. The owners could develop additional properties in the region, and after five years Orient-Express Hotels would have the right to buy 100 per cent of their holding company, Hosia, in Hong Kong.

When we announced the deal in February 2004, I confess I allowed myself a brief moment of self-congratulation. I had been trying for years to break into the Asian market and ironically we had found the key, not through Asians, but through Europeans. At last we now had a decent base from which we could expand. We agreed that the names of the hotels in each location would be changed to something more evocative than 'Pansea': the Rangoon hotel was renamed The Governor's Residence, the Siem Reap hotel became La Résidence d'Angkor, Bali became Jimbaran Puri and Ubud Hanging Gardens, Luang Prabang remained Phou Vao and Koh Samui became Napasai.

I was particularly interested in the properties in Bali, an island Adrian Zecha had introduced us to, and which he always said was a 'must' for hotel companies – and for visitors to Southeast Asia. He and his brothers have a beautiful home there where Shirley and I have stayed. It looks a bit like a Mayan ziggurat with steps up to the library overlooking long reflecting pools. Adrian eventually bought his spectacular resort hotel Amandari (meaning 'peaceful spirits') on the Ubud Gorge, and built a beach resort and a golf club hotel in other parts of the island.

Rollin and Molinari had seen the potential of Bali and built two properties, one of them at Ubud Gorge, which we found a delightful place when we visited it. Ubud is the cultural centre of Bali, with hundreds of small arts and crafts shops, galleries, museums, artists' studios and the Pasar Seni market which offers every kind of sarong, clothing and very pretty jewellery and woodcarvings which are made in the local villages. The gorge carries the rains down from the volcanic slopes, irrigating the rice paddies, and also providing white-water rafting for the adventurous – not to be recommended when it rains. The hillside is so steep that we had to install a funicular to move the guests up and down to their rooms and the public spaces. Interestingly, few Americans visit Bali because it is so far away, although it's a favourite destination for Australians, which explains why almost half the people killed and injured in the terrorist bombs in 2005 were Australian.

My vision was to upgrade the properties to five-star (by local standards) as soon as we could. Pansea had marketed the hotels largely to the French tour operators so we had to broaden the client base and raise rates in the process. We set up our own in-house destination agents to sell our hotels at full rate, plus ground services at cost, to selected high-end travel agents like Geoffrey and Jori Kent's Abercrombie & Kent. I had expected that more clients would make their bookings direct by internet, using the company's website, but interestingly they scan the website but still prefer to book through travel agents whom they trust.

We were able to acquire more land next to the beach resort in Bali, doubled the size of the hotel, and also enlarged the hotel in Siem Reap. One of the pleasant surprises was the Phou Vao property in Laos, which was the only hotel I had not been able to inspect prior to our acquisition because flights were cancelled due to heavy ash clouds (caused by farmers burning stubble). Shirley and I finally got there in early 2010 and were delighted with the hotel, which is head-and-shoulders above the competition, including Aman's recently opened property.

Within a few years of the acquisition of Pansea, the original owners had both gone. Molinari, who had been the driving force behind expansion, developed health problems and was forced to slow down, while Rollin, who had originally been a senior executive of the French Accor Group, had a number of investments in France he wanted to look after. They were also keen on developing a property in Havana, which I remembered as a beautiful colonial city from my visit when I was a midshipman in 1954 but had no desire to invest in. Hotels in Cuba have to be 50 per cent state-owned, and if they are properties which were originally nationalized by Castro, the U.S. government has the power to refuse entry to anyone who invests in them.

As time went by and we invested in improvements and more rooms, Molinari and Rollin could see that the profits target required to trigger the maximum pay-out on their sale was not going to be met, and in July 2006 they suggested we buy them out early, which we did. We parted company on good terms and I was always impressed by their vision in starting the group and building such fine properties in such good locations. I was also grateful to them for opening our way to hotels in the region.

We never cracked the Chinese market, but then no one has. A few years ago, we were asked to consider the acquisition of an important property in Beijing in partnership with a Hong Kong company. I was invited to go there, but it was mid-winter and the air pollution in Chinese cities at that time of year is so great that I demurred because of my lung problem. A team was sent out from London and when they met the official responsible they were asked: 'Why are you here?' China, he made clear, had no interest in inward investment, and was trying to find a home outside China for the $1 trillion it already held. All new hotels in China are effectively owned by Chinese companies, and the brands attached to the hotel are just franchises or management contracts. Overbuilding and seasonality are other problems. Occupancies in Shanghai and Beijing have been less than 50 per cent, which is too low for a Western owner.

CHAPTER TWENTY-SEVEN

My Uncle the Admiral

Santa Barbara has been a feature of my life since just after the war when the Sherwood family, all three of us, moved to California. I was thirteen at the time and we lived in Berkeley, but my father's sister, my Aunt Henrietta, came to live in Montecito, a very pretty area just to the east of Santa Barbara. Henrietta had only recently arrived back from London with her new husband, my Uncle William, who my parents talked about in hushed tones. He was that highly revered personage in post-war America: a genuine war hero.

Uncle William was my hero as well, and came to have a considerable influence on my life. He was actually Vice-Admiral William A. Glassford, a tall imposing man (although in later life I realized he was actually rather jovial) particularly when he was in full uniform with all his gold braid and epaulettes. He was born in 1886, so he must have been about sixty when he first came into our lives. Everyone, especially me, treated him with great respect, and when he later encouraged me to join the Naval Reserve Officer Training Corps at Yale as a midshipman, I did so (and it was one of the best things I ever did).

Uncle William had quite a record in the U.S. Navy, which he joined as a teenager, commanding a destroyer in World War I and moving steadily up the seniority structure to become a Rear Admiral in the 1930s. In 1941, as war threatened in the Far East, he was in China, in command of the Yangtze River Patrol, a squadron-sized unit of fast gunboats which patrolled the Yangtze as far inland as Chungking, 1,300 miles from the sea (as featured in the film *Sand Pebbles*). Its original job was to protect U.S. citizens, commerce and property from pirates and warlords, but by Uncle William's day it was there to protect them from Mao Tse-Tung's Communists who controlled the north bank of the river. He was one of the first to warn of the threat of the Japanese fleet, which early in 1941 he described as 'well fitted out and organized'.

On 2 December 1941, with hostilities imminent, Rear Admiral Glassford deactivated the historic Yangtze Patrol (it would never be activated again) and was steaming with his little flotilla towards Manila when the Japanese fleet struck Pearl Harbor. He was immediately given the command of Task Force Five, the fighting unit of the American Asiatic Fleet, and hoisted his flag aboard the legendary cruiser *U.S.S. Houston*. The Japanese forces advanced with frightening speed through Southeast Asia and by mid-January Admiral Takahashi's Central Invasion Force was heading towards the Balikpapan oil-fields in Borneo. Admiral Glassford's task force, then located at Koepang Bay on the island of Timor, was directed to intercept and destroy the Japanese troop transports. He set off with eleven ships, but one of his two light-cruisers, the *U.S.S. Boise*, ran aground on an uncharted reef and had to retire, shepherded by a destroyer escort. His only other cruiser, *Marblehead*, with my uncle aboard, developed engine trouble and had to slow to 15 knots, also with an escort. But four old 'four-stacker' destroyers, led by a very brave man called Commander Paul Talbot, increased speed to 27 knots, somehow evaded the Japanese destroyer screen and got in among the convoy of twelve transport ships and three patrol boats where they created havoc, sinking four ships and damaging several others. The attack didn't save Balikpapan, but it was a major morale booster for the whole U.S. nation in those early days of the war when the Japanese seemed to be invincible.

A few weeks later Uncle William took part in the Battle of the Java Sea, one of the biggest naval battles of the war, after which he was appointed Commander of the U.S. Naval forces in the southwest Pacific. In March 1942 his former flagship, the *Houston*, was immortalized in the annals of U.S. naval history when she steamed to her death in a desperate attack on a large Japanese fleet group which she had strayed upon unexpectedly in Sunda Strait, between Java and Sumatra. The Navy assumed that everyone aboard was killed, but in fact a third of her crew survived in captivity.

When President Roosevelt, angered by the series of military and naval defeats, demanded a list of the most able officers in the Navy, my uncle's name was on it (amazingly William Halsey, the most successful admiral of the war, was way down the list) and Roosevelt from then on took a particular interest in him. He was airlifted back to the U.S. and appointed Commandant of Naval District Six, a military and administrative command ashore where he was in charge of beefing up production of shipping, notably Liberty ships desperately needed to transport food and supplies to the fleet in the Far East as well as across the Atlantic to the beleaguered British. He was based in Charleston, where of course years later I bought the Charleston Place Hotel. Roosevelt personally promoted him to Vice Admiral in 1943 (he was one of only two singled out that day, the other being Rear Admiral Raymond Spruance, hero of the Battle of Midway, the turning point in the Japanese war). He was then posted to French West Africa, which Allied forces now controlled, as the President's personal representative with the rank of Minister.

In London, where he headed up a mission of U.S., British and Russian senior staff planning for the demobilization of the German navy, he met my aunt, Henrietta Sherwood, who was working for the OSS, an intelligence precursor of the CIA. My father used to joke that in his sister's case OSS stood for 'Oh So Social', and it was certainly true that she liked parties. My uncle was married when they met, and after the war there was a messy divorce case, which my parents never talked about, before he married Henrietta.

My uncle's last job in the Navy was Commander of the Eighth Fleet, after which, for a few years, he was a representative of the Radio Corporation of America, which paid him to 'promote good will' in Europe. Back home in Santa Barbara Henrietta continued to entertain in some style after William retired. Santa Barbara is nearly 300 miles down the coast from Berkeley, but we often visited and later when I was in the Navy I was a regular guest. When the *APA-212*, on which

I was serving at the time, returned to Long Beach for a refit in 1956, I had plenty of time to kill and often went to their elegant Spanish colonial home in Montecito, where my aunt and uncle were very generous hosts. There were always people there, and Aunt Henrietta in particular loved to give glittering dinner parties. Once, when I was staying for a few days, Admiral Louis Mountbatten, uncle of Prince Philip and cousin of the Queen, was also an overnight guest and they held a dinner for him. Mountbatten had been the Supreme Allied Commander of Southeast Asian forces which recaptured Burma in 1945, and the last Viceroy of India. He oozed privilege and charm, but I was a young lieutenant and seated 'below the salt' at dinner, so I was not able to engage in any memorable conversation.

Admiral Glassford died in 1958, aged seventy-two, when I was in the Far East. It was a great blow as I was very fond of him.

From those early visits I remained very taken with Santa Barbara and what seemed to me the most wonderful climate in the world – a view I have never altered. Over the years I kept an eye open for a hotel in the area, and although I was offered plenty in California, they never seemed right. Los Angeles gets very hot in summer, and resort areas like Palm Springs to the east and San Diego to the south become unbearable. Santa Barbara, just eighty miles north of LA, enjoys a much cooler summer climate and 'Angelinos' are more than happy to drive there for a weekend. It is ninety minutes away from Hollywood and has a year-round season, all of which made it a perfect site for an Orient-Express Hotels luxury hotel. Five-star hotels in the Santa Barbara area enjoyed 75 per cent occupancy rates and the going room-rate was $400 a night. The problem was that luxury hotels were not readily available. I had once tried to buy the Biltmore Hotel on the beach in Santa Barbara, but I was put off by residual oil in the water from offshore production platforms. But I kept on trying.

Then in 2004 I got a call from the San Francisco branch of Bank of America asking if we would be interested in El Encanto Hotel and Garden Villas in Santa Barbara. I knew it slightly, located in the hills above the beautifully restored Spanish Mission from where it commands a spectacular view of the Pacific coast. It looked promising.

It was owned by Eric Friden, whose family had made their fortune out of Friden mechanical calculating machines, which were installed in just about every shop in America. They had the reputation of being the 'Cadillac of adding machines', and had the advantage over other calculators in that they produced a tape for the customer. When someone asks my age I tell them I am so old that when I started out in business we used carbon paper to make copies. Friden calculators fall into the same category.

We went to Santa Barbara to inspect the property and meet Friden, who, in the course of the conversation, talked about his passion for playing polo, which surprised me as he was on the portly side and didn't look very agile. I was no great polo expert, but I had been to charity matches at the Bathursts' polo ground not far from our country home in England, where it struck me that you had to be supremely fit if you were to survive a tumble of the kind Prince Charles seemed to have with great regularity. I shuddered at the thought of Mr. Friden falling off.

I liked El Encanto (which means 'the enchanted') immediately. It was built in two styles of early Santa Barbara architecture, which the locals called 'California Craftsman' and 'Spanish Colonial', and was perfectly set into the Santa Barbara hills on a ten-acre estate with a garden of tropical plants. The clubhouse had no guest rooms, just the restaurants, bar and small meeting rooms with a pool at the garden level. The accommodation was in cottages spread throughout the grounds. There were clearly problems with the property: there was no decent banqueting room for weddings and events, and the cottages were very run-down. Nonetheless, the bones of a splendid hotel were there.

The main competition in the area came from Ty Warner, the American toy manufacturer who made his fortune out of 'Beanie Babies', and was estimated in 2005 to have a net worth of $4.4 billion (down from $6 billion the year before). Warner made large investments in hotels, including the Four Seasons in New York, and had two hotels in Santa Barbara, the Four Seasons and the San Ysidro Ranch in Montecito, for which he was reported to have paid a huge amount per room. Shirley and I once stayed at the San Ysidro and found it isolated and rather small, although the rooms were elegantly appointed. I was convinced that a revamped El Encanto would run circles around it.

Simon Sherwood and Dean Andrews were equally keen and it was left to me to negotiate the deal. We inspected the property and I had lunch with Friden, agreeing to meet the following morning for a final session. But when I later checked with the hotel manager what time we were to meet, I was told that 'Mr. Friden has gone to Palm Springs and will not be back'. I called Friden's office and only got voicemail. How bizarre! We had a flight to Tahiti booked for the next afternoon, so off we went, still without a word from Mr. Friden. I was disappointed but philosophical – over my career I had learned never to count a deal as done until it is formally signed and the keys (metaphorically) handed over. This looked like another lost deal, and I wondered if Ty Warner might have nipped in with a higher offer, giving him dominance of the area. That kind of thing had happened to me before.

I never fully got to the bottom of Mr. Friden's vanishing act, but a few weeks later I was startled to hear that he had been thrown from the saddle of his polo pony, which had stumbled during a weekend practice match at the Santa Barbara Polo Club. He died of a brain stem injury two days later.

I sent his son my condolences, and added that if he ever wanted to sell El Encanto he should not hesitate to contact me. This is indeed what happened. Estate taxes in the U.S. at that time were so high (in excess of 50 per cent) that unless property passed tax-free to a spouse, the beneficiary had a mountain to climb to meet the tax bill. The same thing had occurred with the Frankels in the case of La Samanna, which we bought from the children, and now the Fridens were in the same position.

When we completed the purchase of El Encanto, our forty-eighth property, in November 2004, we had a serious portfolio of luxury hotels and restaurants in North America, all run by Dean Andrews: Charleston Place in South Carolina, '21' Club in New York, Keswick Hall & Club in Virginia, the Windsor Court in New Orleans, the Inn at Perry Cabin in Maryland, La Samanna in St. Martin and Maroma in the Yucatan. It made a formidable company just on its own.

We paid $26 million for El Encanto and immediately set about redesigning it. We closed the hotel for the low season, pulled down the clubhouse, and began rebuilding it – the planning authorities insisted we use the same footprint – with proper banqueting and spa space at ground floor level. We wanted to put an eye-level swimming pool in the garden to replace the rather dated existing pool, but were told it was not permitted because public pools had to have concrete walkways all the way around so that drowning swimmers could be more easily rescued. We showed them pictures of eye-level pools in private residences all over California, but they refused to budge.

All this added to the cost. We had budgeted $50 million to increase the number of rooms from eighty-eight to ninety-seven, add a spa and banqueting space, and generally upgrade the hotel to five-star luxury, but it was soon apparent we were going to overrun. We could see why Ty Warner had been forced to pay such a huge amount for his San Ysidro Ranch. When the recession of 2008–9 hit we had to suspend work, but bank finance was gradually becoming available in 2011 and hopefully the property will be completed in 2013.

One of our other purchases in 2004 was a 50 per cent stake in 'Afloat in France', which, like El Encanto, came about because of an earlier experience. The travel agent Geoffrey Kent had been telling me for some time how profitable the French canal cruising business was, and as we had made a success of the *Road to Mandalay* he thought we should invest in it. Abercrombie & Kent had chartered several canal barges and he was very pleased with them. We were approached by a minority investor in a company called French Country Waterways who wanted to exit, and we inspected his barges and took a sample trip. We found cruising down a French canal a dreamy experience, with the barge gliding through ancient villages, past superb châteaux through a Monet landscape. Plane trees, originally planted close together to stabilize the banks, provided a cool, shaded green tunnel.

We liked the idea – but pulled out of the deal when we found the majority shareholder, whom we never met, didn't want to sell.

A few years later another canal business came on the market, but when we went to look at it we found the barges were mediocre and not up to Orient-Express Hotels' standards. The owner, seeking to impress us, arranged a luncheon aboard a glamorous barge owned by a Canadian couple, Joe Souccar and Maureen Maguire. The barge was the flagship of Souccar's company, 'Afloat in France' – which described it perfectly. The Souccars operated five barges like this one, which could accommodate between six and twelve people and several even had their own swimming pools. Looking around at this fabulous barge, I suddenly had the thought that maybe we could buy out the Canadians instead of the poor-quality barges we had just been looking at. Over lunch we chatted with the Souccars and discovered they spent some time every summer in Gaiole in Chianti, the home of my Capannelle wine estate. I said we were always in Capannelle in the last week of August, and we invited them to come over for dinner.

Joe Souccar was reaching a certain age, and my impression was that he felt 'Afloat in France' was becoming too demanding, so when we met in Capannelle, I asked him if he might be interested in letting us invest in the company, giving him an option to sell his remaining shareholding later on at a pre-determined price. I said we would like to buy an initial 50 per cent, but management would remain in his hands and we would market it through our worldwide sales operation.

Although the barges were unprofitable at the time of the deal because of a slump in American tourists, we invested $3 million in a 50 per cent stake with an option to buy the rest within five years at seven times profits. We bought the second half in April 2007, two years before the option expired, for a further $2.7 million, by which stage the business was doing very well.

The barges are rented by the week to a single party, with everything provided, from being met in Paris (rail or plane) to food, drink, and excursions to castles, open air markets and all the rest. A van and driver is assigned to each barge and it ferries guests wherever they want to go, picks up provisions and performs all the small tasks such an operation requires. We even provide bicycles on which to ride along the towpaths or into the towns.

In 2011 we charge about $50,000 to hire a barge for a week and demand exceeds supply, so my hope is that the company converts more barges and expands the business. It is a perfect addition to Orient-Express Hotels' trains and cruise division.

So was our final acquisition of 2004, the Royal Scotsman tourist train. It wasn't a big deal, but it was a nice one, a natural extension of our train business. It brought the number of railway tourist trains we were operating to six: the Venice Simplon-Orient-Express in Europe, the British Pullman and Northern Belle in the U.K., the Eastern & Oriental Express in Southeast Asia and the Hiram Bingham in Peru. On 15 November 2004, we announced we had bought a 50 per cent stake in the Royal Scotsman for $2.75 million, the balance to be paid on an earn-out multiple of future profits.

The Royal Scotsman was the brainchild of Fergus Hobbs, whose sister is our close friend, Lady Romilly McAlpine. Shirley and I had travelled with the Hobbses on the train some years earlier and had been greatly impressed by it. Scotland has its own very special charm, and the train operates very much like 'Afloat in France', with a minibus following it around, taking the passengers on day excursions to famous castles, Scotch whisky distilleries, salmon smokehouses and lunches with famous locals and chiefs of clans. Every night the train pulls into a remote siding so guests sleep undisturbed in the fresh (sometimes very fresh) Scottish air. The standards of food and service on board are superb, and every compartment has its own private bathroom.

When we bought it, it was running with nine Edwardian-style coaches, including staff car, kitchen car, restaurant car and lounge car. Much of the demand came from the U.S. where persons of Scottish ancestry are anxious to visit the homeland of their forefathers.

It was the third deal we had done that year on an earn-out basis: Pansea Hotels was the first, with an earn-out based on eight times operating profits; 'Afloat in France' was done on seven times; and the Royal Scotsman on 5.5 times, reflecting the more seasonal and vulnerable quality of its earnings. Earn-outs had become more commonly used in the leisure industry, and protected both parties.

I enjoyed travelling to Scotland by rail, and did so on a number of occasions to visit friends. Tyninghame House, West Lothian, had been divided into three parts and we knew the inhabitants of all three: Asa Briggs, probably the most respected historian on Victorian England, and his wife Susan lived in one part; Tim and Jane Clifford lived in another; Alistair and Judy Grant in the third.

All were fascinating people, and we loved them. Susan Briggs was a classmate of Shirley's in St. Anne's College, Oxford, and Asa had been (among many other things) Provost of Worcester College, Oxford for twenty-five years, during which time he changed the whole perspective from which historians viewed the Victorian era. Harold Wilson gave him a peerage in 1976, which was well deserved.

(Sir) Tim Clifford, an art historian, was the very eloquent Director of the National Galleries of Scotland who did a great deal to increase both attendances and revenues in his twenty-year tenure. He and Jane were with us in Peru and I asked him one evening to rise and tell us something about the ornate Spanish chapel in the Hotel Monasterio where our party of 150 was having dinner. Tim, who had no warning (and not much knowledge of that particular period either), rose without the slightest hesitation and for twenty minutes talked about seventeenth-century Spanish art and how it was represented in the scenes around us. Shirley and I often attended the Edinburgh Festival late in August until Tim had to retire upon reaching the compulsory government retirement age.

We were invited to visit them at Tyninghame, and our friends asked if I could get one of the high-speed Edinburgh–London trains to stop at Dunbar, just a few miles away, to pick up east-of-Edinburgh passengers. I reckoned as chairman of the Great North Eastern Railways, operators of the trains, I could exercise my prerogative (sparingly) to get trains to stop to suit my wishes. The management hated it – but I only did it very rarely. After a trial period there wasn't enough demand so the stop was withdrawn.

The other occasion was when we were invited by the Duke and Duchess of Northumberland to spend the night at their famous Alnwick Castle (where the Harry Potter films were made). The young couple had only recently taken the castle over; she wanted to develop a big garden and sought Shirley's advice. I arranged for the London high-speed train to stop at the little 'halt' near the castle where the butler was waiting with the shooting brake. Much to my amazement a number of other passengers got off, and I was worried that they had made a mistake. However, the stop had been put on the departure board at Newcastle station and some people must have been destined for Alnwick on a later local train. I didn't feel so guilty about that one.

The Royal Scotsman is a very special travel product. I expect it will be enlarged by having more sleeping cars and another restaurant car, which can be added when needed to meet demand.

CHAPTER TWENTY-EIGHT

FROM RUSSIA WITH LOVE

Sometimes when I enter the Grand Hotel Europe from the Nevsky Prospekt in St. Petersburg I think of the people who have done exactly the same before me: Turgenev, Tchaikovsky, Dostoyevsky, Debussy, Shostakovich, Stravinsky and maybe even Tolstoy (although he is not recorded in the visitors' book). When it opened in 1875 the Grand Hotel Europe was immediately hailed as one the great hotels of Europe, an elegant addition to Peter the Great's spectacular palaces and buildings which surrounded it. Peter laid out Nevsky Prospekt as the main street in his new city and the start of the road to Novgorod and Moscow, and today it is a busy, bustling thoroughfare with modern shops interspersed with churches, museums and palaces. The Grand Hotel Europe occupies an entire block of it, all to itself. I know of no other hotel, other than maybe the Ritz in Madrid, which is better located in the heart of a great historic city. In February 2005 it became the forty-eighth five-star property in the portfolio of Orient-Express Hotels, which now spanned twenty-two countries.

St. Petersburg is a truly astonishing city. Founded by Peter the Great in 1703 as the 'Venice of the North', it has changed its name twice in recent memory: from Petrograd to Leningrad and then back to the original St. Petersburg. Its fortunes have changed along with the name: when Napoleon marched into Russia in 1812, it was the capital of one of history's largest empires. The Germans almost obliterated it in a 900-day siege, which cost 800,000 lives, 200,000 of them in the winter of 1943, one of the coldest on record. Three revolutions started there: the rebellion of 1905 which won major concessions from the Tsar; the revolution of February 1917 which caused Nicholas II to abdicate; and the storming of the Winter Palace in November 1917 when Lenin's Red Guards swept past the Grand Hotel Europe on their way into the history books.

Stalin hated the city and it became a backwater, but Vladimir Putin, its favourite son, brought it back to life, causing it to throb around its now famous White Nights Festival when the days are endless and so is the entertainment. The Grand Hotel Europe has been in the centre of it all for well over a century, hosting tsars, tsarinas and even the 'Mad Monk' himself, Grigori Rasputin, the debauched mystic who helped bring the Romanov dynasty down. More contemporary visitors have been President Clinton, Jacques Chirac – and even Elton John.

I arrived rather more prosaically in 2005, on the hunt, as ever, for an iconic hotel, preferably a bit the worse for wear (the hotel – not me!), and preferably without too much neighbouring competition. I had been to St. Petersburg before, of course, but on Sea Containers' business, the last time a few years earlier when I had been approached by a Los Angeles-based investor, Daniel Schein, who wanted me to invest in a container terminal. At that stage, the banks were still licking their wounds after Russia defaulted on its sovereign debt in 1997, and didn't want anything to do with it, and nor did I after I learned of the mafia-type activity in the St. Petersburg docks. I declined Schein's invitation.

I went again a year later, this time on a much more enjoyable occasion, when our good friends in London, Harry and Ruth Fitzgibbons, decided to celebrate Harry's sixtieth birthday there. They took rooms for all of the guests at the Grand Hotel Europe, which was then managed by Kempinski, and it was the first time I had stayed there. At that stage I saw no prospect of buying it, but just by walking around I could see the potential if we could ever get our hands on it. Harry, who speaks Russian, knew St. Petersburg well and laid on a fascinating program of visits to the palaces and other places of interest, as well as lunches and dinners in grand surroundings. Museums, concert halls, palaces, the River Neva and the canals are all within easy walking distance.

Harry Fitzgibbons is a most interesting and amusing man, given to making speeches at the drop of a hat with a slight stutter, offering a poem which he has made up for the occasion and which is usually very funny. Like me, he is an American, and is very proud of the fact that he served as an officer in the U.S. Special Forces (also known as the 'green berets', the American equivalent of the SAS), studied law at Harvard, worked for the State Department and eventually, having married the tall, leggy and beautiful Ruth, came to live in London where he was a pioneer of the venture capital industry. When the Soviet Union collapsed in 1990, Harry was the first over the Wall, and set up a venture capital fund in St. Petersburg to invest in early-stage technology-based Russian companies. In 2000 he sponsored the Mariinsky, then still called the Kirov, opera and ballet season at London's Royal Opera House, to which he invited Shirley and me. His local partner in St. Petersburg was an ex-KGB agent who took us around some of the bars and pubs, where we were glad of the vodka, which, true to my principle, tastes best in Russia. Staff would snap to attention when he entered – Harry was a good man to introduce you to life in St. Petersburg.

In 2004 I was again approached by Schein, on this occasion acting on behalf of five Russian investors who owned the Grand Hotel Europe which, he divulged, had been on the market for a few months. None of the big players was interested, he explained, because it was impossible to arrange finance. We wheeled into action and Simon Sherwood and Adrian Constant, our European regional manager, were on the next plane. They reported back that by their calculation it was making $17 million in operating profits, and if we could purchase it for $100 million, which they had been told we could, it would be a seriously good buy. The market price for hotels in this period was ten times earnings before interest, tax and depreciation, but we would be paying only seven, six if we could get the profits up as we thought we could (and did).

The hotel had a tangled ownership history. When the new Russian state privatized many of its assets in the 1990s, a Swedish group acquired it and refurbished it, but their taste left something to be desired, and they had cut corners. They also ran into trouble with the city over allegedly unpaid taxes. The city took over the hotel in lieu of payment, and then sold it to a bank, which in turn sold it to a Cypriot-based company – which meant nothing of course, because many Russian companies are registered in Cyprus for tax reasons.

The owners wanted to unlock their investment so they could invest in residential premises and office buildings, which were in short supply all over Russia and rents and prices were rocketing. Simon and Adrian were convinced we should acquire the property and, after I'd been to see it myself, I concurred. We agreed to buy the hotel for a price of $95 million, a big bite for us, although operating profits of Orient-Express Hotels were $79 million in 2004, up a gratifying 14 per cent over the previous year. Even so, given the reluctance of the banks to lend money on Russian properties, we were still going to have problems financing it.

Then someone had a bright idea. The International Finance Corporation, a cousin of the World Bank and IMF, whose mission is to provide 'soft' loans for projects in developing countries, had extended to us a line of credit for investment in Southern Africa and South America, and we had never used it fully. The IFC was pressuring us to invest the money, so we asked them if the IFC funds could be used in Russia rather than the original designated countries. They agreed and, with a syndicate of other banks, provided us with $57 million towards the purchase price. The company raised $122 million in an equity offering in March 2005, part of which was used to complete the Grand Hotel Europe purchase and fund the upgrade.

No transaction in Russia goes without a hitch and this one unnerved even me. We all gathered at the offices of the lawyers in Zurich where there was the usual mountain of documents to be argued about, redrafted and finally signed. The lawyers sat around a table in a conference room waiting for confirmation that the funds, which we had asked to be transferred, had arrived. The hours went by and it was well past midnight when word came through that the bank had sent the funds – but to the wrong party. By then all the banks were closed and it was too late to correct the mistake. They were promised for the next morning, but the Russians went ballistic, convinced that this was some kind of trick. They called in security guards who stood outside the lawyers' office for the entire night, only relaxing when they were satisfied the money was actually in the bank. An interesting dimension of working in an ex-Communist state like Russia is the degree of suspicion and paranoia which exists, almost as part of a genetic culture. For the Russians the humiliation of the collapse of Communism and the 1997 sovereign debt default runs deep. I detected a fierce desire to sweep aside the seventy-five years of Communism as if it had never been, and return to the Russia of Tolstoy and Tchaikovsky. The decision to change the name of the city from Leningrad to St. Petersburg epitomized this, as did the development of the city in the years I have been going there.

The hotel has 301 rooms, seven restaurants and a staff of nearly 1,000. The security staff alone numbered sixty and our due diligence revealed that one of the men was running a call-girl ring and also controlled the hotel cars. We had to make a special payment to him to disband the call girls and let us take over the car operation. He kept his side of the bargain and we have never had the slightest difficulty since. I facetiously asked the general manager how many 'bugs' had been installed in the rooms by the KGB and he said he didn't know of any, but they had 150 CCTV cameras 'mostly to control the staff'.

Once we had acquired the Grand Hotel Europe we set ourselves a major program of renovation, which we planned to spread over three winters when St. Petersburg is very quiet. Just as there is no night at mid-summer, there is no real daylight in mid-winter and temperatures of minus 12°c are normal, minus 20°c not unusual. In the winter of 1942–3 temperatures dropped below minus 30°c, which actually saved the city – Soviet troops broke the siege lines to create a narrow corridor across the frozen Lake Ladoga along which reinforcements, food and munitions could reach the starving population. Tourists tend to avoid St. Petersburg in the depth of winter, when fur hats and gloves are obligatory and only the brave walk any distance in the streets.

We brought in our favourite Parisian interior designer, Michel

Jouannet, to take charge and he did a beautiful job on the luxurious suites, giving each one its own theme, with strong historical undertones yet decidedly modern. We named each of them after a well-known figure that had some connection with the hotel: Pavarotti (who stayed there), Dostoyevsky and Stravinsky. Jouannet themed the latter after *The Rite of Spring*, and even added an antique chess set, which he said was inspired by the chess game in the film *Coco Chanel & Igor Stravinsky*, the story of the rumoured affair between the two in Paris in 1920, the year Chanel No. 5 was invented.

We were outbid for a folio of 100 beautiful coloured engravings of Russian historical subjects which came up for auction in Sotheby's, but Thomas Gibson, our highly experienced dealer friend, located another set in private hands and we bought them. Jouannet had the engravings copied and today there are four in almost every guestroom in the hotel. Long corridors were broken into sections to create a cosier, less institutional feel.

St. Petersburg owes a lot of its recent economic success to its formidable lady governor, Valentina Matviyenko, whose candidacy was personally – and controversially – supported by Putin when she decided to run for election in 2003. Two years later Putin passed a law giving him the right to dismiss all the regional governors and propose new ones who would not have to be elected, and not surprisingly he proposed Valentina Matviyenko, known by her political opponents as 'Putin's Pet'. She has proved both honest and extremely able and has improved the city enormously during her period in office. Rather amusingly we discovered that Putin had previously been responsible for the city's property department, and many of the hotel's papers contained his signature. I was keen to meet him, but it would have meant travelling to Moscow, not one of my favourite cities. Although we considered having a presence in Moscow, I must confess to dragging my feet because I hate the idea of owning a hotel in a city that I would not want to visit myself.

But I did think we should expand our Russian interests by developing a hotel at Pushkin, a village about 30 kilometres from St. Petersburg where the tsars had their summer palaces. The Catherine Palace is the highlight of Pushkin, a vast structure which the Germans completely and intentionally destroyed before they retreated in 1944 and which the Soviets painstakingly restored. Pushkin attracts large numbers of visitors, making it ripe territory for a luxury hotel. Oddly enough it was Stalin, an admirer of Alexander Pushkin (author of *Boris Godunov* and *Eugene Onegin*, on which the operas by Mussorgsky and Tchaikovsky were based), who changed the name of the town from Tsarskoe Selo to Pushkin in 1937. Sacha Abercorn (Duchess of Abercorn) is a direct descendant of Pushkin and she and her husband James, friends of ours from Windermere Island days, urged us on to create a hotel there.

Thomas Noll, whom we appointed as manager of Grand Hotel Europe, was given the task of locating suitable Pushkin properties, and a few months later called to suggest we fly to St. Petersburg to meet the man responsible for the Catherine Palace who might have something for us. Simon Sherwood by this time had taken a great interest in all things Russian and was learning the language, mostly, as far as I could see, by watching Russian films on DVD. We invited the Pushkin official to join us for Sunday night dinner in the grand dining room of the hotel, where we soon discovered he didn't speak a word of English. Noll plied him with excellent clarets and Simon astonished us by conducting the entire discussion in what sounded like very good Russian.

We got down to business at around midnight, and I told our guest (courtesy of Simon) that we would be visiting Pushkin the next day to look for a suitable hotel site. By this stage our guest had made considerable inroads into the hotel's cellar of fine red wines, which he seemed particularly partial to, and after complimenting Simon on his excellent Russian (admittedly this was what Simon *thought* he said, and we were in no position to contradict), he became very conspiratorial. 'I have a very special site for you,' he said, 'which you don't know about and it will be my pleasure to show it to you.'

When we arrived at Catherine Palace the following morning it was Monday and it was closed to the public, but we were met at the entrance by a huge sleigh and given a tour of the grounds in the snow. We finished at the front door to the Palace where we were greeted by a trumpet blast and uniformed footmen and taken to the famous Amber Room in which our host had thoughtfully set out an indecent number of decanters of red wine. After an hour of drinking we were finally taken through the park to some old abandoned buildings, which he explained had been the stables of the tsars and had somehow escaped the destructive intentions of the Germans. They were actually the property of the local university, which didn't have the funds to convert them, and were available if we wanted them for a hotel.

I was keen on the project, which would be managed out of the Grand Hotel Europe with the two hotels marketed as a package – which is what we do in locations like Portofino, Cusco and Venice (and now Taormina). But unexpected problems were looming, one of which was the sudden passing of our gracious host, so the project was never pursued.

Orient-Express Hotels ended 2004 with a profit of $108 million, up 37 per cent on the previous year. But darker times loomed, and 2005 was destined to bring some nasty surprises.

CHAPTER TWENTY-NINE

BEST OF TIMES, WORST OF TIMES

As Claudius says, 'When sorrows come, they come not single spies but in battalions.' They started coming at me at the end of 2005 when a series of blows, all individually out of my control, struck me with the power of Hurricane Katrina hitting New Orleans. It started, unlikely enough, in the Moroccan city of Marrakesh where I began to develop a dry cough, which initially I attributed to the dusty conditions. I had never fully recovered from being bashed onto the beach at St. Martin eight years earlier, although I had returned to work and continued to travel the world as busily as ever. What I didn't realize was that a rib I'd broken that day had never fully healed, and was about to come back to haunt me.

There were some projects in Morocco which I was being encouraged to look at, and Shirley and I made a tour of sites in Tangiers, Fez, Casablanca and Marrakesh. We even considered running a Royal Scotsman-type tourist train between these cities, but I soon dismissed it as a non-runner – much of Morocco is pretty featureless desert. The Moroccan state ferry company, Comanav, was being readied for privatization, and I had a passing look at that with my Sea Containers hat on. We loved Fez and I thought the Palais Jamaï Hotel, located right in the heart of the city overlooking the medina, was stunning. It was owned by a wealthy local family who were prepared to sell. Unfortunately it was managed by Accor, and try as I would, I could not get them to sell the management contract (it is now part of their Sofitel chain), so we gave that one up.

In Casablanca, the Royal Mansour Hotel was for sale but, despite the Humphrey Bogart movie, Casablanca is essentially a commercial centre with very little tourism. In Marrakesh the local government offered us a twenty-two-acre hospital site at the foot of the gardens of the famous Mamounia Hotel, said to have been one of Churchill's favourites. I would love to have acquired the Mamounia itself but it was owned by the royal family and was not for sale. The hospital was to be torn down, and we were being offered the opportunity to build a hotel in its place. Simon Sherwood was very sceptical about the project because he felt, quite correctly, that Marrakesh was being overbuilt and the city was desperately hot in the summer when guests would more likely drift to the seaside resorts. We were presented with a contract which could not be transferred, even in part, and committed us to a very large capital investment. The hospital site began to look more like a hospital pass, and we demurred.

Initially I tried to ignore the cough and carried on to the port of Nador, in the north-east of the country, to look at a possible fast ferry service to Spain. Then I travelled to the Hotel Caruso in Ravello, Italy, which had finally opened, and where we were holding a board meeting. The cough still persisted and Shirley called in the hotel doctor, who prescribed antibiotics, but our suite was just above a smoking chimney and I thought maybe it was giving me an attack of asthma. Unwisely I persevered and after the board meetings, where there were a lot of difficult issues to discuss, I moved on to Geneva for an important meeting with 'Gigi' Aponte, the owner of Mediterranean Shipping Company, the second largest container ship operator in the world (and now Italy's largest cruise ship operator as well). Sea Containers had a joint venture with him to operate fast ferries between Ancona and Pescara, on the east coast of Italy, and Split in Croatia. Gigi took one look at me and called in his doctor who strongly advised me to return home immediately for medical treatment.

In London I was diagnosed with pneumonia and spent a few days at the London Clinic recovering. I went home but I still had a nasty cough and one night, in the midst of a particularly bad coughing spasm, I felt a rib crack in my chest. The bone drove into my lung and I was rushed to the Brompton Hospital (very near to my London home) where they quickly identified that I had internal bleeding. The surgeon, after looking at the X-rays and tests, said he would have to operate immediately to stop the bleeding. The Brompton is a National Health hospital, the first one I had ever been treated in, and I was greatly impressed by the quality of the doctors and medical care, although the standard of cleanliness was not so great, and Shirley threatened to take pictures of the mess in my room and send them to the press unless it was properly cleaned.

I guess the operation was a success, in the sense it stopped the bleeding, but it was a major one and it slowed me down a lot. It took some time to recover and I lost about a litre of lung capacity. I was seventy-two at this time, and although I felt there was much to be done, it was clear, even to me, that I was going to have to slow down and could no longer serve as president of Sea Containers and chairman of Orient-Express Hotels at a time when both companies were at critical stages in their development. Sea Containers was going through a particularly demanding time and, although I believed it was sound, it needed a full-time focused president.

Orient-Express was in good shape with profits that year of $60 million, and we were now investing around $100 million a year in renovations and upgrading the new hotels we had taken on. Simon Sherwood was doing a very good job of running it and I thought, once I had recovered, I could carry on as chairman working closely with him. At the end of 2005 Sea Containers sold its remaining 25 per cent of Orient-Express Hotels, raising more than $300 million in cash. Reluctantly, I decided to give up my first baby, Sea Containers, the company I had founded all those years back in 1965 and which I had seen grow from just an idea into a multi-billion-dollar global operation, one of the biggest marine container leasing companies in the world. I tendered my resignation and sold my shares in the company.

My focus now switched entirely to Orient-Express Hotels, which was still housed in Sea Containers House on the Thames. As my health improved, I was beginning to look forward to working along-side Simon and resuming my old routine of trying to visit all our properties individually at least once every two years, and finding interesting new acquisitions, but with a much reduced other involvement.

In February 2006 we announced the purchase of another Mexican property, the Casa de Sierra Nevada in San Miguel de Allende, about 160 miles north of Mexico City. It is a beautiful hotel, housed in a collection of old Spanish colonial buildings with courtyards, fountains, cool cloisters, frescoes and even the old archbishop's house which dates from 1580, all at 6,400 feet above sea level. The historic town of San Miguel, with its cobbled streets and lush parks, was once the richest in the silver-rich 'New Spain', and was also the centre of revolutionary activity in the struggle for Mexican independence in the last century. We paid $8.4 million for our 75 per cent stake and agreed to spend another $5 million on twenty new suites, a spa, new pool and other improvements.

The acquisition was particularly significant for me in that it became the fiftieth property in Orient-Express Hotels' unique portfolio, which now ranged across twenty-five countries. We had come a long way since that day in 1976 when I bought the Cipriani, more or less on a whim. If I hadn't bought it, we would never have developed the Venice Simplon-Orient-Express train, and if we hadn't done the train there would never have been an Orient-Express Hotels group. One thing had led to another and here we were, almost exactly thirty years later, with one of the most highly regarded luxury hotel collections in the world.

The fruits of our earlier investments were now paying off: the Copacabana Palace completed the $4 million refurbishing of the old casino rooms and they opened as the most elegant venue for social and corporate events in Brazil. We were cracking on with the Cupecoy residential development in St. Martin, and in St. Petersburg our improvements were already getting through to the bottom line – by the end of 2006, 180 of the 301 rooms were refurbished and profitability had grown by $1.4 million to $18.8 million, further reducing the already low multiple we had paid for the hotel. Right through 2006 we announced very good quarterly results and ended the year with revenues just short of $500 million and operating profits of $138 million, up 28 per cent over the prior year.

But in August 2006 the roof fell in. Simon Sherwood, whom I had come to rely on even more after my illness, indicated his intention to step down within a year. All the board, particularly me, tried to get him to change his mind, but to no avail. His wife was seriously unwell and that was a major influence on his decision. At one point we thought we had convinced him to stay, but he set as a condition that the company be taken private and was voted down. Of course, in retrospect he was right, but none of us saw the 2008 sub-prime mortgage crisis coming and I voted against his proposal. I had seen Simon as my successor, and had groomed him for the top job for a number of years. He had responded superbly, and I was genuinely very proud of many of his initiatives and innovations, as well as his diligence and professionalism. He had built a core team of managers who liked and respected him, and my intention had been to phase myself out over the next few years, while still retaining an involvement, and hand him the reins. Simon finally resigned in February 2007, giving six months' notice.

For several years he had borne the burden of the day-to-day management, while I saw my role increasingly as finding new properties, inspecting the existing ones and providing both continuity and the odd flash of inspiration for further growth. But my illness had so incapacitated me that I couldn't even do that. I tried to resume my regular travel cycle, but this was proving too demanding, not only for me but for Shirley who was diagnosed with severe *lupus erythematosus*, an unpleasant auto-immune skin disease exacerbated by sunlight, heat and dust. Barbara Amiel Black, wife of Lord Conrad Black, who was a friend when he owned the *Daily Telegraph* newspaper, has a similar problem and Shirley and she communicated about the latest treatments. Shirley had travelled everywhere with me for years, and knew all the hotels, the managers and staff as well as I did. She knew the gardens a great deal better – she had been responsible for developing a number of them and her usual routine when we arrived at a hotel was to tour the garden with the head gardener when I was going around the rooms and kitchens. But she was finding it hard going and it was clear that neither of us could continue the pace. Whether Simon stayed or went I was going to have to reduce my involvement. By then

I had served as chairman of Orient-Express Hotels and its predecessors for thirty-one years, and that was enough. I agreed with the board I would be giving up my executive role.

All of this meant a change at the top of both Sea Containers and Orient-Express Hotels, in one year. The Enron scandal had resulted in the Sarbanes-Oxley legislation which, along with changes in the New York Stock Exchange rules, created an enormous bureaucracy for U.S.-listed companies, which we conformed to. In the past, rather than use elaborate nomination and remuneration committees, I had always recommended people for the board on the basis of the balance of skills and expertise available, and the contribution each individual could make, but this was no longer considered good corporate practice. In 2006 the board of Orient-Express Hotels was well balanced: Bob Lovejoy was an investment banker and securities expert, who had come up trumps during the hostile takeover bid for Sea Containers; Jim Hurlock was the retired managing partner of the White & Case law firm and an old friend from my Paris days; John Campbell, chairman of the Bank of Bermuda, was our former counsel in Bermuda, originally appointed because Bermuda required a local resident to be on the board of international companies registered there; Prue Leith, the author, TV personality and culinary expert, was there for her perspective on the restaurant industry, and to give us a female view in an otherwise all-male board; Georg Rafael was one of the best-known hoteliers in the world, and latterly founder of his own Rafael Hotels; Simon was president and chief executive.

When the company had to find a new chief executive officer to replace Simon, the new rules required us to have a governance committee composed of independent directors, on which neither Simon nor I could participate. And it was this committee that set out to conduct the search for a new CEO.

In December 2006 it was announced that I would be retiring as chairman at the next annual shareholders meeting, to be held in Hamilton, Bermuda on 15 June 2007, providing plenty of time – or so I thought – for an orderly succession. I would become 'Founder and Director', Jim Hurlock would take over as the new chairman.

Although Simon Sherwood had agreed to stay on until August 2007, the company was now operating in a virtual vacuum and takeover rumours were beginning to swirl around it. Stories were appearing in the press about potential bidders prepared to pay $3 billion and more, and the company was in danger of becoming seriously destabilized. The committee at the last minute proposed that Paul White, the chief financial officer, take on the CEO role. Simon had originally hired Paul when he was only twenty-seven, and I regarded him as a safe pair of hands and voted for him on the basis that he would continue to operate the company in much the same way that Simon and I had.

When Simon departed on 10 August 2007, the company had never looked stronger, and there was no lack of parties interested in investing in it. Speculation in the press and in the markets was intense and every week seemed to produce a new name. Von Essen Hotels, the British luxury hotel operator, was touted as a possible buyer (it went into administration in 2011); and I woke one weekend to see a headline in the *Sunday Times* which read 'Marland and the Reubens to join forces in $3 billion bid for Orient-Express' – I had not then met either Lord Marland, the former Tory Party Treasurer, or the Reuben brothers, and had no idea where this particular bit of speculation came from.

By September 2007, we were receiving genuine expressions of interest. The Dubai Investment Group wanted to invest and the share price moved up to an all-time peak of $65.36, capitalizing the company at nearly $3 billion. Another serious potential bidder was the Tata Group, the largest Indian conglomerate and owner of Taj Hotels (it now also owns Jaguar and Land Rover as well large chunks of the world's steel industry). It announced it had paid $211.3 million for a 10 per cent stake, which it said was 'a reflection of its deep commitment to the possibility of an association with Orient-Express Hotels'. Its vice-chairman, Krishna Kumar, had already been to see me to test the waters and now publicly announced that he had held 'cursory discussions over an alliance' and was committed to working in a 'friendly and supportive manner' with Orient-Express Hotels.

I was no longer serving in an executive role, but because of the structure we had put in place to protect us from the kind of hostile bid Sea Containers had received in 1989, interested parties seemed to feel they should have me on their side. My view was that Orient-Express Hotels had a better future on its own than it did as a subsidiary of one of the other groups whose culture would be very alien to ours. Tata wanted to 'ally' the business with their Taj Hotels group, and the Dubai people wanted to absorb it into their Jumeirah Hotels. Both Taj and Jumeirah were very successful in their home markets of India and the Middle East, and felt an association with us would accelerate their development in other markets. In retrospect we should have joined forces with one of them, but we were unable to see the 2008 crisis approaching, so we declined their invitations.

One reason for our hesitation was that I had discovered early on that independent top luxury hotels always achieved higher occupancies and room rates than branded properties such as those operated by Taj and Jumeirah. Indeed, Orient-Express Hotels had consistently outperformed Four Seasons Hotels before the 2008 crisis, because ownership and management is more profitable in a strong market than management on its own, and Four Seasons had become merely a management company. Of course, in a recession managing a hotel can be more profitable than owning it, as many owners discovered after 2008. However, I am still convinced that ownership-plus-management is the most profitable route, long-term. Neither Taj nor the Dubai people made an offer after the 'Do Not Disturb' sign had been put on the door.

CHAPTER THIRTY

Iguassu Falls – and the 2008 Banking Crisis

Thank goodness, in the midst of all these labyrinthine corporate machinations, there was some constructive work to be done, and as the months passed I was well enough to do it. The success of the Copacabana Palace Hotel had increased my appetite for further acquisitions in Brazil, and I was particularly taken with the Hotel das Cataratas at Iguassu Falls, where the film *The Mission* was shot. They are the most spectacular falls in the world, outstripping Niagara or even Victoria Falls. The Iguassu River becomes the Parana River separating Argentina and Brazil, and eventually it reaches the sea as the River Plate.

The Hotel das Cataratas, built in the 1930s in Portuguese colonial style, is only a short walk from the edge of the falls and is the only hotel in the national park on the Brazilian side. I had been stalking it for some years, but it was owned by the Parks Commission and leased to Varig Airlines, which was bust and hadn't spent anything on it for years. My idea was to buy the remainder of the lease from Varig, which needed the money or, failing that, to get the Parks Commission to take the lease away from them and issue a new one. Our credentials in having made the Copacabana Palace the finest hotel in South America would help us a lot, I was assured.

My old friend Mario Gibson Barbosa, the former Brazilian ambassador in London and the man who had opened the way to the Copacabana Palace, accompanied me to meet the Varig senior

management, but they would not budge, arguing it was the corner-
stone of their hotel division, such as it was. It took some time, but with
the support of another Brazilian friend, Marcus Pratini de Moraes,
who served on the Copacabana Palace Hotel board when he wasn't
in the government (he served as Minister of Agriculture from 1999 to
2002), and that of the Parana Provincial Governor, Roberto Requião,
we finally got the Parks Commission to agree to a tender process for
a new lease.

In June 2006, still not feeling fully well, I flew out with Roger
Collins to Brazil for the formal viewing of the property attended by
all the potential bidders. The Parks Commission had intelligently
required the successful bidder to create a bicycle path from the main
gate of the park, ten kilometres distant, to the hotel and falls immediately beyond, and to bury the power cables which were on poles along
the road. I was glad I had made the effort – all the other attendees
were low-budget operators, and I was the only senior executive there.
I have always found that personal attendance at events like this has
the effect of 'cooling' the competition, and I think they realized I had
not come all this way for nothing and would be determined to win the
auction – which we did.

On 25 September 2007 we entered into a twenty-year lease of the
property and announced a $20 million refurbishment program (which
was completed in 2010). The whole process had taken several years
and the announcement came three months after I had stepped down
as chairman.

Despite all of this, Orient-Express Hotels had a great 2007 under
Simon Sherwood's leadership, with revenues up by 21 per cent to $578
million and operating profits 13 per cent higher at $154 million. As 2008
opened, the share price was riding high at $58.56 and the market value
of the company was $2.6 billion, with bidders still sniffing around.
Given the fact that our debts were about $800 million and allowing
for the usual bid premium, a bidder would in effect have to pay nearly
$4 billion for Orient-Express Hotels (debt free) – and there were
several parties out there who thought it well worth it. Little did we
know we would be unlikely to see those heights again anytime soon.

The sub-prime situation in the U.S. was rumbling through the year, but nothing prepared any of us for the catastrophe of the autumn of 2008 when Hank Paulson unwisely allowed Lehman Brothers to go bankrupt, ushering in the worst financial crisis since the year I was born. In my opinion, history will record Paulson's decision as one of the most monumental blunders of the era.

The effect on Orient-Express Hotels was immediate. The company still made a good operating profit in 2008 of $125 million, but it progressively declined during the year and the final quarter was a wipe-out. The share price just went down, down and still down, touching $3.80 at one point, valuing the company at just over $200 million. It was a massive erosion in the wealth of shareholders and managers – including me. The board met urgently to decide on a course of action, which included asset sales, cutting staff numbers, a freeze on capital expenditure and a reduction in operating costs, provided service standards were not compromised. In the first three months of 2009 revenues were 22 per cent down on the same quarter of 2008. In all my years in the business I had never seen anything like it – and nor had anyone else in the industry. I still feel an enormous anger against those who had allowed it to happen.

Concerns were looming in the shape of some of our debts falling due for repayment, a regular event in the cycle of every company. What would normally happen is that we would replace these maturing instruments with new ones, i.e. 'roll them over'. This time it was different. The banks, in deep trouble themselves, were now looking for money back and were only prepared to make new loans on harsher terms. The sharp fall in the cash flow from our hotels had reduced our key ratios of interest cover and net debt-to-operating profit, and the banks told us they wanted their loan exposure reduced by about 25 per cent as a condition of roll-over. Where were these funds to come from?

One source of course would have to be asset sales. I had always bought in times of recession and sold in good times and here we were doing it the other way around. That having been said, Paul White was able to sell the Lapa Palace in Lisbon for $42 million, a profit of nearly $5 million; Lilianfels in Katoomba went for $19 million, my little venture in Buenos Aires, the La Cabaña restaurant, fetched $2.7 million and the Hôtel de la Cité in Carcassonne later went for a respectable price. Much to my regret we sold our largest property, the Windsor Court in New Orleans, for $44 million, half what it was worth in a normal market. New Orleans had still not recovered from Hurricane Katrina and the hotel was haemorrhaging cash. It was heartbreaking to see these choice assets being sold into a buyers' market after we had laboured so long and so hard to acquire and develop them. The Windsor Court in particular will one day be a big money-spinner, and I regret losing it more than any of the others.

It did have the effect, however, of calming the banks who could see that even in the worst market for fifty years there were still buyers out there for choice hotel properties, and if the company ever had to sell its flagships, such as the Copacabana Beach, the Grand Hotel Europe or even – heaven forbid – the Hotel Cipriani, there would be a ready market at prices well above what they had in their calculations.

The remainder of the cash needed to roll-over the loans had to come either from the sale of a strategic stake in the company, or a placing of more shares in the market at low prices. I favoured the 'strategic partner' route and began to sound out various people. An old German friend of mine, Dieter Bock, who had formerly owned the Kempinski Hotel group and who still owned five important hotels in Germany, proposed that he and a group of friends would acquire a one-third interest in Orient-Express Hotels at $10 per share for $500 million, extend a $500 million line of credit at a reasonable interest rate, and put two of his own directors on the board.

The board ruled that one out, and I was asked not to seek any other strategic shareholder solutions. This left only the option of raising cash through sales of more shares into the market, which I was far from happy about. However, Deutsche Bank felt this would be possible and indeed we eventually raised $441 million through selling tranches of shares at between $5 and $10 per share, but in the process we diluted shareholder equity from 42 million shares to 102 million. The company was again financially sound and still independent, but the cost had been heavy.

I finally came off the board altogether in June 2011, just two months before my seventy-eighth birthday, and became 'Founder and Chairman Emeritus', agreeing to provide advice and to undertake special assignments for the company as requested. Shortly afterwards, in July 2011, Paul White resigned 'for personal reasons'. Three new directors were appointed to the board: Mitchell C. Hochberg, former president and chief operating officer of the Ian Schrager Company, joined in 2009; Harsha Agadi, a restaurant business entrepreneur of Indian origin, who was chairman and CEO of U.S.-based Friendly Ice Cream Corporation, joined in June 2011; and Philip R. Mengel, who for five years ran English Welsh & Scottish Railway Ltd., the primary rail freight operator in Britain, was recruited in June 2011. Bob Lovejoy temporarily assumed the role of CEO pending recruitment of a new one.

There is still more to be done, but there are bright and able younger people across the group who have learned the importance of quality and service in running a luxury hotel company, and the tradition developed by me and Simon Sherwood carries on.

CHAPTER THIRTY-ONE

BIG CITIES AND SICILY

The opening of the Shirley Sherwood Gallery of Botanical Art in April 2008 came as a welcome relief from the rigours of the past couple of years. It was a happy evening, with friends, botanists and artists joining us in the beautiful new purpose-built gallery in the Royal Botanic Gardens, Kew, for a ceremony widely welcomed for the fact that it opened up to public gaze the treasure trove of botanical art which had lain hidden in drawers and boxes in the library at Kew, in south-west London, for generations. More importantly from Shirley's point of view – and therefore from mine – there was now a home for her magnificent collection of contemporary botanical art, one of the biggest and most important in private ownership. Sir David Attenborough, the famous naturalist, made a brilliant speech and said some very generous things about Shirley, who responded just as graciously, and the gallery was formally opened. It's comforting to think that a hundred years from now people will still be coming to this gallery to look at these paintings.

I was particularly pleased because it was recognition for the effort that Shirley had put in over so many years in building up the collection. I had a hand in it too, quite literally, in the sense that I often had to carry the pictures on to planes or travel with them in taxis and hotel cars. If I had sometimes complained, I now took it all back; I was very proud of her and what she had achieved over this time. After we married in 1977 Shirley gamely tried to continue her scientific work at Smith, Kline & French in Hertfordshire as a part-time consultant, and she even managed to complete her D.Phil. before we tied the knot. But she eventually gave up her position as we were travelling all the time.

In any case Shirley's first love was always botany, in which she got her degree from Oxford in 1955, the same year I graduated from Yale. But it was then (and probably now) almost impossible to make a living out of botany, and that led her into drug research and her D.Phil. in the subject. When she left Smith, Kline she decided to explore the field of botanical art, and once, when we were in Brazil, Mario Gibson Barbosa introduced her to the Margaret Mee Foundation, of which he was chairman. Margaret Mee was an intrepid British botanical painter who travelled the Amazon in the mid-twentieth century and painted many of the specimens from the rainforest. Some of the species she painted, sketched on location in pencil and later finished in gouache, had never been recorded before and are only known scientifically because of her detailed botanical drawings. It took her twenty-four years and fifteen solo trips to record it all properly, and she was one of the first environmentalists to raise the alarm on the impact of mining and deforestation on the plants in the Amazon Basin. She was a great hero of Shirley's, who bought a number of her original paintings.

That was the beginning of the Shirley Sherwood Collection. She met other Brazilian botanical artists and bought some of their work as well, and gradually, as we travelled in other countries, she made contact with local botanical artists, buying selectively and with increasing confidence and knowledge.

Botanical art traditionally flourished in England and Japan in the eighteenth and nineteenth centuries, but had long since spread to Australia, South Africa, the U.S. and Brazil, where Shirley found a number of excellent artists. She developed a habit of visiting the local botanical gardens, such as Kirstenbosch in Cape Town, one of the most interesting in the world for the variety of unique indigenous plants there, or the Jardim Botânico in Rio, and seeking out promising local artists. Brian Huntley, the director of Kirstenbosch, and his wife Merle introduced her to the endless varieties of flora in the Cape and we spent a lot of time with them over the years.

Shirley has written half a dozen books about botanical art, often published in connection with major exhibitions, which have included works from her collection. I found one, *The Art of Plant Evolution* (Kew Press), on the development of plant life over 600 million years, particularly interesting. It starts with seaweeds and finishes with sophisticated flowering plants like roses. Among the little bits of useful knowledge I gained was that mushrooms are not plants at all, but are part of the animal kingdom. Not a lot of people know that, as Michael Caine might say.

As the years passed, her collection of paintings grew until it numbered in the hundreds (now close to 1,000), and the question arose as to where to house it. I converted a building on our Oxfordshire estate so it could be used for safe, dry and controlled temperature storage, and also incorporated study facilities, but the artworks were not very visible there – and a collection needs to be seen. She was happy to lend them out of course, and as news of her collection spread, museums and galleries from around the world began asking her if they could borrow her works for exhibitions. That required a great deal of administrative effort, as well as expense, and something more permanent was needed to do full justice to her collection.

Over this time we got to know and admire greatly the director of Kew Gardens, Sir Peter Crane, and Shirley often discussed with him his dream of creating Kew's own permanent gallery of botanical art. There was plenty of room there: Kew is a big place, 121 hectares of beautiful gardens on the banks of the Thames, with a staff of 700 and 2 million visitors a year. It has the largest collection of living plants in the world, more than 30,000 of them, and its library has more than 750,000 volumes. It had also built up an enormous collection of prints, drawings and paintings dating back to 1700, which virtually no one ever looked at. Many of them were horticultural illustrations made on scientific expeditions in the eighteenth and nineteenth centuries, and had originally been kept for scientific rather than artistic reasons. Some were beautiful as well as illustrative, and often (too often) depicted species of flowering plants which are already extinct or threatened with extinction. Peter reckoned there were something like 200,000 individual works in the Kew collection of illustrations.

Kew is government-owned and is always short of funds, so a new gallery would have to be privately financed. As the premier botanical garden in the world, I thought it a fitting location for Shirley's collection to be displayed, and Peter convinced our family and the Kew Foundation, a private institution, to sponsor a gallery devoted exclusively to botanical art, the first in the world. The actual building, which is located halfway between Victoria and Lion Gates, is a large cube within a cube, with a dramatic bust of Shirley in the foyer, and it embraces the latest environmental protection features. It has six large exhibition rooms, and a glass façade which offers unencumbered views of the gardens at their best, as well as the next-door Marianne North Gallery, a Victorian building dedicated to the nineteenth-century botanical artist Marianne North. Shirley curates a major show in her gallery each year which includes works from her collection, often alongside others from Kew's own archives, as well as works borrowed from collectors, artists and museums around the world. In the brief time since its opening, the Shirley Sherwood Gallery has become the focal point for botanical art worldwide, with an average of 2,000 visitors a week. Shirley was awarded an OBE from the Queen in the New Year's Honours List in 2012 for services to botanical art.

Welcome though the distraction was, I still had a lot of unfinished business in the hotel industry. There were still significant gaps in the Orient-Express Hotels portfolio, which I would dearly love to have filled but, given the financial situation, that may be for someone else who follows me. Acquiring hotels in New York, Paris, Rome and London had always eluded me, as had Hong Kong and Tokyo. Most of the big hotel groups in these cities are what we call 'cookie cutter' brands, where the assets are owned by property companies and the brand owners, such as Hilton, Intercontinental, Hyatt, Marriott or Sheraton, are simply hired managers. The reason is that property prices in these cities are very high, and often hotels cannot support the huge carrying cost of the investment. They are property plays for real estate companies, and are often part of a larger development involving shops, apartments and offices.

That hadn't stopped me trying. I tried to rebuild Frank Lloyd Wright's Imperial Hotel in Tokyo, but this was in the 1990s when property values in downtown Tokyo were insane – it was said that Tokyo's value at one point exceeded that of all the real estate assets in the entire U.S. In Hong Kong I made an offer for the lower level of the Ocean Terminal in Kowloon, owned by the Hongkong and Kowloon Wharf and Godown Company. It had splendid views across the harbour but the Wharf Company, then controlled by Jardine Matheson, was taken over by Y. K. Pao's World-Wide Shipping Group which was not at all interested. I then had the idea of building a hotel above the Peak Tram Station on Hong Kong Island, and tried to get my friend, Michael Kadoorie, who controls the Peninsula Hotels group, to sell it to us. I proposed that the tram would stop at the level below for ordinary travellers, then rise to the lobby level of the hotel, where the views, looking out across the harbour to the Chinese mainland, would be to die for. But to my great disappointment, although probably not to that of his shareholders, Michael developed the Peak station into a mass market restaurant complex instead.

In theory it was easier to acquire properties in London, Paris, Rome and New York than in Asia but they were still pretty expensive, particularly as great hotels became trophy assets for buyers with very deep pockets. I lost the Plaza Athénée in Paris to the Sultan of Brunei, and Mohamed Al Fayed wouldn't sell me the Paris Ritz. In London I tried to buy the Savoy Hotels Group when Sir Hugh Wontner and the D'Oyly Carte family still controlled it, but Charles Forte relentlessly pursued it and its sister hotels, the Connaught, Berkeley and Claridge's. We were sidelined in the battle, which ran for years. The Fortes never got it, and the group was finally sold to the Blackstone private equity group, on whose European advisory board I served. I had to step down because of the conflict of interest. Blackstone eventually sold it to a group including the Irish property developer Derek Quinlan for £1 billion, but Quinlan flipped the Savoy on to Prince Al-Waleed bin Talal for £250 million within a year, while keeping the other three hotels. Al-Waleed, one of the richest men in the world, closed it for three years and spent another £250 million restoring it, making it probably the most expensive hotel in history. I'm afraid we were never in that league.

Then there was New York, where I once came close to acquiring the venerable Carlyle Hotel at 76th and Madison Avenue, which is where Shirley and I always stay when we are in the city. It is the only hotel I know in New York which still employs elevator operators. The building is a co-op, similar in some respects to the Pierre Hotel but with the difference that the hotel controls its own part of the building and the apartment owners control theirs, while at the Pierre the apartment owners own the entire building. The legendary New York property magnate and hotelier, Peter Sharpe, bought the Carlyle in 1967 and developed it into the most exclusive hotel in the city, which many say it still is. It used to boast that U.S. presidents always stayed there, and certainly Truman, Kennedy and Johnson did, and President Sarkozy of France still does, as do other heads of state and notables. Sharpe died in 1992 and a decade later his executors sold the property. As I have already described, we agreed a price but our offer was 'shopped'. Wolff Maritz of Los Angeles, a partnership between Lou Wolff and Philip Maritz, paid more than $130 million but we were not allowed to match it. They had also bought 50 per cent of the Rosewood Group, Caroline Hunt's company.

I was pretty annoyed to lose this property at the time but as it turned out the deal was signed just before 9/11, and it took a long time for it to recover to its old level of profitability. Despite our battle, Philip 'Flip' Maritz was, and is, a good friend – he lives in Vail, Colorado and we meet there every year when I take the family skiing.

After I bought '21' Club I explored all sorts of ways of adding on a hotel which would be physically connected to it, taking advantage of both the location and the '21' Club's reputation and clientele. Eventually we settled on the old Donnell Library building on West 53rd Street, directly behind '21'. The existing library, which opened in 1955, was probably best known for the fact it housed the original Winnie-the-Pooh dolls behind bullet-proof glass in the Children's Reading Room, but otherwise it was a conventional library lending out hard-copy books for which demand was declining. It had become very shabby and the New York Public Library system, which owned it, was prepared to consider proposals for sale on the condition that a digital library was built into the basement and ground floor.

An old friend, Sam Butler, formerly managing partner of the Cravath, Swaine & Moore law firm, had been chairman of the New York Public Library system and he helped us initiate discussions. Bob Lovejoy also had good contacts with Sam and several members of the library's board, so we all met to discuss a deal, which involved razing the building to the ground, putting up an eleven-floor structure, and creating a new Donnell electronic library at ground level and on two basement levels, with its own separate entrance.

I worked on this project for several years to bring it to fruition and it very nearly came off. It was proceeding nicely when Simon Sherwood stepped down and I became a non-executive director, so we played no part in the final negotiations. But when I finally read the agreement, which was binding on the company, I found it lacking. It committed Orient-Express Hotels to buying the old library for $59 million in cash and building a new library, with no exit strategy if things went wrong – as they quickly did. It was now a much more ambitious project than I had envisaged. Paul White had changed the specification and wanted to buy air rights from the building next door in order to build a much larger hotel of more than forty floors, while my idea had been something much more modest. We calculated his design was going to cost $400 million to complete, and finance was not available for such a large undertaking. Then came the Lehman Brothers crash and no finance was available at all for any new hotels in Manhattan. The board decided to get out and in March 2011 Starwood Capital and the property group Tribeca Associates eventually bought the contract with the New York Public Library.

In Rome I had been offered the palace of the Volpi family at the Piazza Quattro Fontane, quite close to the Quirinale Palace (where the President of Italy resides). Giovanni Volpi lives in Venice and the Rome property was unoccupied, except for his mother who was infirm and lived in a small part of the palace with her nurses. The contents had been sold and when we inspected it we found some windows had been blown open by the wind, so leaves swirled around the ballroom floor. Giovanni was asking about $25 million, which seemed high at the time but would be a snip today. He eventually sold it to the Italian government for this price. The cost of conversion would have been enormous and, given our experiences in Ravello and elsewhere in Italy, permission to convert might have been difficult to obtain, so I weakened at the knees, much to my regret later on.

Carmen Wirth owned the Hassler Hotel, the most famous hotel in Rome, which would have made a perfect addition to the Orient-Express Hotels portfolio. Carmen was a frequent visitor to the Hotel Cipriani, and at one stage we discussed the possibility of Orient-Express Hotels taking a stake in her business. The Hassler was highly profitable, but she also owned some properties in Umbria, which had absorbed a lot of cash and were losing money. We were only interested if the Hassler was part of the deal but unfortunately she had leased the Rome hotel to her son Roberto, and he did not want a partner. Her other son, Peter, owned the Casa de Sierra Nevada in San Miguel de Allende, Mexico, which we eventually acquired. On Carmen's death the two sons inherited the Hassler, but Roberto bought out Peter's share so there was no chance for us to invest in it.

So, no cigar for Hong Kong, Paris, London, New York or Rome, although full marks for trying – and who knows what will happen in the future? Many deals, as this book has shown, take years, even decades, to consummate and the courtship in some cases is still ongoing. Circumstances change, people die and companies go bust. When Orient-Express Hotels is again in a position to commit the capital required I'm certain that exciting acquisitions will be made in at least some of these cities.

In the meantime I got some consolation, and a great deal of satisfaction, from the one acquisition we made in 2010, my last for the company. I bought my very first hotel, the Hotel Cipriani, in Italy in 1976 and it is appropriate that the final one, some thirty-four years later, should also have been in Italy – or at least Sicily. For many years I had my eye on the Grand Hotel Timeo in Taormina on the east coast of Sicily, not far from Catania, which has an excellent airport. The

Timeo has a spectacular location high on a rocky outcrop overlooking the Bay of Naxos, directly across the valley from Mount Etna, which is capped with snow for half the year. Every so often Etna provides the Timeo's guests with a perfect view of the most spectacular of nature's fireworks as it erupts, which it does at obligingly frequent intervals. The only five-star hotel competitor in the town is the San Domenico, an old monastery where the rooms are ex-monk's cells and very tiny. It features in the 1960 Antonioni film *L'Avventura*, and has always had the reputation of being the outstanding property in Taormina. The Timeo, now that we've refurbished it, puts it to shame.

The ancient Greeks who ruled Sicily 2,500 years ago knew what they were doing when they chose the site for their theatre on to which the Grand Hotel Timeo literally backs, and so did old Don Francesco La Floresta when he built his house, which he called Timeo, there in the 1850s and began renting out rooms to passing travellers. The hotel in its recognizable form dates from 1896, which makes it a contemporary of the Mount Nelson and Reid's, all three of them built in places which were easily accessible by sea. Taormina has always been a magnet for writers, artists and poets and the local guidebooks are full of references to the good and the great who fell under its spell: the poet and philosopher Goethe, friend and mentor of Beethoven, wrote of the town's 'inexpressible beauty', Alexandre Dumas says he went into 'raptures at the sight of Taormina', while Guy de Maupassant wrote that it was 'created on Earth to seduce the eyes, mind and fantasy'. There's a lot more like that.

All classic hotels have their fair share of celebrities in their guest books, but the Timeo's is more glittering than most: Salvador Dali, Klee and Klimt stayed there; from the world of music came Brahms, Bernstein and the mighty Wagner. There have been so many famous actors, politicians and royals that you wonder how they all managed to get a room. Most hotels suffer from the problem of guests who stay a couple of days then pass on, but the Timeo has suffered from the opposite: D. H. Lawrence checked in in 1920 and checked out again two years later. Truman Capote also stayed for two years, and Jean Cocteau, the actor Jean Marais, André Gide and Tennessee Williams (among many others) all extended their stays from days to months. Even the German Kaiser, Wilhelm II, came back three times, taking the entire hotel for a month in 1906. His uncle, King Edward VII, and his cousin, King George V, were also frequent visitors.

When I first became seriously interested in it the hotel was owned by a construction company in Catania, and when they declared bankruptcy we registered a formal interest in buying it. Under Italian law the trustees in bankruptcy are required to hold an auction of the assets, and we awaited a response to our query – and waited and waited. The trustees had appointed the Franza family, who operated the main ferry service across the Straits of Messina, to manage the hotel on a short-term contract, and our lawyer in Rome, Carmelo Alessio, kept pressing the trustees to start the auction, but without result. Then we were told that new trustees had been appointed and the hotel had been sold to the Franzas without going through the auction process. The Franzas apparently had been able to get permission from the Rome authorities to do this. Our lawyer reckoned this was irregular and recommended that we sue the agency which had given the permit. This seemed to be a monumental waste of time and money, but we did file a complaint and at least the Franzas knew that we were still keen to acquire the hotel.

The Franzas also acquired another hotel, Villa Sant' Andrea, on the beach below the town. It was formerly the home of an English family and had been converted to a beach hotel after the war. A cable-car links Taormina village to the beach, stopping next to the Sant' Andrea. I had come across the Franzas before: their ferry company was enormously profitable because their only competitor was the Italian State Railways which operated slow train ferries across the Straits. During my Sea Containers days I had considered operating fast ferries across the Messina Straits in competition with the Franzas, but we could not obtain a suitable berth. They owned the best berth close to the motorway entrance and we would have had to dock a mile away.

I also knew this part of the world well from my regular sailing trips. The Straits, just to the north of Taormina, are only three miles wide, and to get through them you must pass between Scylla and Charybdis which, as those with a classical education will remember from their Homer, is where Odysseus was forced to choose between the six-headed monster Scylla or Charybdis, a whirlpool which would have pulled his whole ship under. He chose Scylla, and lost only six members of his crew, one to each head. I love to run my yacht into Charybdis, cut the motor and twirl slowly, watching Mount Etna gently puff away. The region from Rome to Sicily is known for its volcanic activity, and one of our favourite pastimes is to sit on our boat off Stromboli at night watching the volcano erupt at fifteen-minute intervals. One night we smelled burning fabric and discovered that a particularly explosive discharge had showered the boat's awnings with hot cinders.

I had given up hope of getting the Timeo until one day in 2009 we were contacted by the Franza family, who said they had decided to sell both the Timeo and Sant' Andrea hotels and wondered if we were still interested. Obviously we were, but I was keener on the Timeo than the Sant' Andrea because the latter was smaller and more seasonal. However Maurizio Saccani, who manages all of the Orient-Express Hotels in Italy, liked both, and I could see the logic of this in that only one management and administrative structure is required, and they balance each other well: guests can stay in the grander Timeo and enjoy the town and its many restaurants and shops, and go down to Sant' Andrea for lunch on the beach and a swim – or vice versa.

I first called Giancarlo Arragona, the superb Italian ambassador in London who, with his English wife Sandra had unceasingly promoted our Italian hotel interests (and wine from my vineyard in Tuscany). Sicily is the home of the mafia and I wanted to be assured that we would not be getting into a mafia situation. Many years earlier I had appointed an agent in Palermo for Sea Containers' marine container business, which was in competition with a mafia-controlled company. After a few months, when our agent kept having his trucks' tyres shot out, I decided then that we could avoid doing business in Sicily. Giancarlo gave the Franza family a glowing reference, and said we need not fear mafia problems because Messina and Taormina did not tolerate such activity. Shirley and I then went to Taormina and met with Olga Franza, the head of the family, and inspected the properties.

Although most visitors think of Sicily in terms of its historic heritage, from a hotel perspective one of the great advantages is its ten-month season (which is obviously what appealed to D. H. Lawrence). You can lunch out of doors even at Christmas and while January and February are cold, by Easter the warm weather has returned. With the exception of Milan and Rome, Italian hotels are extremely seasonal because they depend largely on tourists who do not go to cold places in the winter, unless it's to ski. I was also impressed with Taormina because 80 per cent of all visitors to Sicily spend at least one night there. Car traffic is very restricted and the town has a busy social scene with cafés, shops and the Greek amphitheatre, one of the finest examples of its kind in the ancient world.

Saccani had little difficulty in convincing the board to buy the two hotels, but the bigger problem was how to finance them. After the financial collapse of late 2008 the big money-centre banks were running scared. We agreed a price of €81 million for the hotels, and would normally expect to obtain bank finance for 70 per cent, but many of the American and British banks were offering only 50 per cent. Fortunately other European banks were largely unscathed by the sub-prime mortgage crisis and we were able to secure a 70 per cent loan from them and the sellers. Orient-Express Hotels sold $131 million of common shares on 19 January 2010. Some of these funds were used for the equity in the transaction and the upgrade of the properties, which had to be spread over several years during the winter closings. The acquisition of the Sicilian hotels brought the number of Italian hotels in the Orient-Express Hotels portfolio to eight.

My strategy was always to work on at least ten possible acquisitions at any one time, expecting to complete one or two in any year. I tried always to identify the properties we wanted to buy rather than wait for them to be put on the market. Often it took years to shake a property loose from its owners, and sometimes I never did, but perseverance and patience often paid off. I had also built up a network of friends and contacts over the world who often opened the way into a transaction which otherwise would have been impossible – as with the Copacabana Palace or the Mount Nelson in Cape Town for instance, neither of which ever came on the open market.

From the Hotel Cipriani back in 1976 to the Timeo in 2010, it has been a grand game and for all the travails of Orient-Express Hotels in the past few years, it remains one of the great luxury hotel groups of the world. It owns a collection of properties which has been carefully put together, largely by me, over thirty-four years, each one of them individually selected and bought, some after years of patient stalking, and usually – as I have tried to show – with a story attached to them. Each is unique and all of them have been renovated and brought up to the high standard that the company set from the beginning when we bought the Hotel Cipriani.

The Venice Simplon-Orient-Express train, where this story began, has achieved everything I hoped it might when I first saw the cars for sale that fateful morning in Monte Carlo. It has revived and kept alive the romance of pre-war de luxe train travel to and from exotic places – and I'm very proud of that.

———

What Makes a Five-Star Hotel Great?

My experience of great hotels started in 1954 when, as a twenty-year-old midshipman in the Navy and a Yale student, I took a summer training cruise from Norfolk, Virginia to Havana. It was August, and you could fry an egg on the steel deck of the ship in the daytime. At night it was so hot below that we slept on the deck. When we reached Havana, I made a beeline for the air-conditioned Hotel Nacional, the best in the city, rented a suite and my chums and I luxuriated in the cool air and soft beds while the ship was in port. The only slight hiccup was one evening when a taxi-driver, bringing me back from the wild Tropicana Night Club, demanded four times what it had cost in the other direction. I refused to pay and the driver pulled a knife, but the doorman interceded and I learned the lesson to fix the fare in an unmetered taxi in advance.

That was my first introduction to the world of luxury hotels. From that day on, I always sought out the best in town. And there are some wonderful ones.

In Delhi I remember Maiden's, where the staff lived twenty-four hours a day outside my door, ready for any task at a moment's notice. It was air-conditioned as well, but in my day I have stayed at Indian hotels with punkah-wallahs who created a breeze by hand, and I have experienced Indian 'air-conditioning', which is a fan blowing through falling water.

I spent several periods in Honolulu when my ship docked there, and I took a suite in the wonderful Royal Hawaiian on Waikiki Beach where they used to serve luaus in the gracious gardens every evening.

I was greatly disappointed when Sheraton built a huge tower in the garden and the beach became so crowded that it was cheek-by-jowl. Georg Rafael subsequently developed the wonderful Halekulani which is by far the best hotel on the beach.

I took a course in architecture at Yale, and went out of my way to visit the great hotel and club buildings wherever I might be in the world. My weekends in Tokyo in the late 1950s were always spent at Frank Lloyd Wright's Imperial Hotel, where Wright had also designed the furniture, which was very uncomfortable – but I didn't mind, considering it a privilege just to sit on it. Among other historic buildings I came to love were the Hong Kong Club in the centre of Hong Kong, and the Army & Navy Club in Manila. In Paris I have always stayed at the Ritz in the Place Vendôme.

My company Sea Containers operated in eighty countries and I visited most of them, always seeking out the best hotel available, so I got to know many of the great hotels in the world from a guest's viewpoint. Thus my credentials were reasonably good even before 1976, when I bought the first hotel for what was to become Orient-Express Hotels. Five-star, the highest rating for a hotel, has been established as the peak of excellence by the governments of France, Italy and other discriminating countries. To get the rating, the hotel needs to comply with all sorts of requirements, some of which, such as having a bidet in each bathroom, are probably no longer necessary. Whenever I see hotels advertising themselves as six- or seven-star, I dismiss it as just hype, and take the view that if they exaggerate their rating they probably also exaggerate their product.

Although I had many years of staying at five-star hotels before I bought the Hotel Cipriani in 1976, that didn't mean I understood anything about the business of running them. Dr. Natale Rusconi, whom we hired to manage the hotel in Venice, was my mentor and teacher, and it was from him I learned much of what I know about luxury hotels. Within months of his becoming the general manager the hotel was in profit and he built a devoted staff, many of whom spent the remainder of their careers with the hotel. Most of the staff was laid off in mid-winter when the hotel was closed, and the younger ones often went to St. Moritz or one of the other big ski resorts, while older ones simply caught up on their holidays. The repeat guests became very attached to the front-of-house staff members, for whom no request was to be denied. Rusconi created an equally dedicated kitchen staff, and a famous artist, Arbit Blatas, did a wonderful portrait of Giovanni, the hotel's splendid chef. Rusconi has now retired, but when he comes back to the Cipriani, which he does from time to time to dine with me, the staff treats him almost as a god – which indeed he was to many of them.

That was the first lesson Rusconi taught me: the staff are the most important ingredient of any five-star hotel. After that comes a host of features which I also consider of great importance. My list is personal, and not everyone will agree with it. I cannot promise that every hotel operated by Orient-Express Hotels has all these features, but most of them do.

Noise. A bedroom must be totally quiet, both from street noise and internal noise. Street noise is usually dealt with by double-glazed windows, but internal noise can often be worse: elevator shafts whistle as the cars move up and down and air-conditioning can make a terrible noise. Today most air-conditioning is ducted away from the noisy compressors, but many hotels still have old individual fan-coil units in the rooms, which make a variety of ticking, rubbing, whacking and other offensive sounds. Fortunately, they can now be rebuilt to provide an acceptable noise level.

Many of the immediate post-war chains did not insulate their rooms properly so guests were liable to hear their neighbours talk (and worse) through paper-thin walls. Most of the Orient-Express Hotels iconic properties were built well before that period (some of them, including the Mount Nelson, Reid's, the Ritz in Madrid, the Timeo in Sicily and the Grand Hotel Europe in St. Petersburg, are more than 100 years old, and others, such as the Copacabana Palace, are getting on that way) so rarely encountered this problem, and when we did, we corrected it with insulation. There are still some hotels of other companies out there parading as five-star when they don't deserve it on noise grounds.

Reception. A guest in a five-star hotel should always be escorted to the room by a member of the reception staff, or if the porters are trained to explain the room features, by one of them as they accompany you with your luggage. However, many five-star hotels deliver the luggage after the guest enters the room, so someone from reception should accompany them. At check-in, the receptionist should ask what newspapers are wanted – it is now possible to get a print-out of any leading newspaper in the world, regardless of language, within minutes of its publication. The machines which do this are expensive so hotels usually contract out the work, but the physical newspapers should still be on the door knobs of the room at an early hour. Of course many guests now read newspapers online, but I still prefer the hard copy.

Concierge. Every five-star hotel must have a good concierge. The guest should understand that concierges often run their desks as private businesses and are sometimes paid only minimum wage. They take a percentage of all car (and boat) hires, entertainment tickets and restaurant bookings. It is also customary to tip them when one checks out, but only if they have provided special service. (I always make my restaurant bookings through the concierge well in advance of my arrival in a city, as demand for a good restaurant is often so great that you need to book well in advance. I could not go to San Francisco without booking weeks ahead at my favourite restaurant, Alice Waters' Chez Panisse in Berkeley.) A good concierge will not send you to a restaurant you will not like. If you are disappointed tell the concierge so.

Hotel food. In Asia the best food is usually served in hotels. In the Middle East alcohol can often only be obtained in them, so if you want a good bottle of wine better plan on eating in a hotel there. In December 1978, I was in Tehran trying to collect money from the Iranian government. The huge Hilton International where we stayed was nearly deserted and tanks patrolled the streets. We dined at the hotel's excellent French restaurant, and the manager told us to choose the finest Bordeaux, which we could have on the house. He said it was only a matter of weeks until the revolutionary guards would destroy the entire wine cellar. The Shah left in January and I presume the cellar met its fate soon after.

In Europe and some other places it has become fashionable to have great chefs create a multiplicity of restaurants carrying their name. It is often a rip-off. The great chefs are most unlikely to be present when you dine there, and the food is often pretentious, expensive and disappointing. Really great chefs are in their kitchen most nights. Certainly Raymond Blanc is usually present at the Manoir and his deputy knows he is always under Raymond's watchful eye.

It is possible to create fabulous independent restaurants, and I like to think that '21' Club is one of these, but even there the chefs get bored and try to change things, which I fiercely resist. We finally reached a compromise by having part of the menu devoted to classics and the rest to other dishes. My favourite independent restaurant is Joe's Stone Crab in Miami Beach, founded by Joe Weis in 1918 and still run by his daughter Jo Ann. The food standard is superb, but they don't take reservations, which means tipping the head waiter if you want to jump the queue.

Doctors. Five-star hotels must have five-star doctors (and dentists) on call. Doctors must come quickly when summoned and be able to deal effectively with any situation. Guests can be victims of altitude sickness, unfamiliar food, jet lag and worse. When Elizabeth Taylor suffered a throat complaint at the Hotel Cipriani on a Sunday the specialist roared into Venice from his country house and insisted that his payment only be an autographed picture. A five-star hotel takes care of the initial medical bill and doesn't allow a hassle to arise over money at the hospital door (of course, it puts the cost on the bill).

Entertainment. Gérard Gallet, our inspired interior designer, created the pop-up TV. This is a TV housed in a cabinet at the foot of the bed, rising to viewing position with the press of a button. If the distance from the foot of the bed to the wall is short enough, a large flat screen can be put on the wall instead but it is vital that the screen is large enough to provide theatre-like viewing. Irritatingly, some hotel general managers hide away small-screen TVs in the far corners of bedrooms, or the wall-mounted screens are too small for good viewing. I always insist on having DVD players in the bedrooms, so guests can watch decent films. I came up with the idea of having an Academy Award booklet in every room, offering every winner of the Academy Award for Best Picture since 1927 when the awards started, and the runners-up.

The first Academy Award winner (and the only silent one) was *Wings* about World War I fighter pilots. It launched the career of Gary Cooper (and also his affair with Clara Bow) and it is a wonderful movie. I don't approve of films on demand for Orient-Express Hotels, mostly because the films are rubbish but also because they sometimes offer pornography, which most of our guests find offensive and which certainly should not be accessible to children.

I am a great advocate of live music in our restaurants, but alas it is now too expensive in many countries. Natale Rusconi once hired a one-man band to play at the Cips' Club in the Hotel Cipriani. This chap was remarkably versatile and could play several electronic instruments at the same time but, alas, when he left his post for a short break his rig, which was on a slope, rolled into the lagoon. He didn't come back.

In places like Cape Town and Rio de Janeiro we are able to hire at reasonable cost some very talented musicians and they lift the dining experience wonderfully.

I despise canned music in restaurants although there are exceptions, such as Cusco where gentle Andean flute music is played.

Lighting. For me, the symbol of a cheapie hotel is always the wattage of their light bulbs. Young hotel general managers must be trained somewhere to put 40-watt bulbs in room lamps instead of 100-watt ones. Roger Collins, our vice-president of technical services, always said this is a foolish economy because lights are not left on for long. In the U.S. the three intensity light bulb is in common use, and this works well if the high intensity setting is 100 watts. Even though we are being forced by the environmentalists to move into the cold-light LED bulbs, it is the intensity which counts. Surprisingly I often find that desk lights are too dim and it would seem that some general managers have forgotten the purpose of a desk.

Some hotel managers seeking to save money on energy bills cover the windows with blue plastic film, which gives the room a sad appearance in daylight. Sheer curtains are a more elegant solution as they can be opened to lighten the room.

Wi-Fi, faxes and telephones. Wi-Fi is now obligatory in all hotel rooms. I am usually glued to my iPad but I need long documents to be printed in hard copy, so I can correct and annotate them more easily. Someday there will be Bluetooth printers in every room which can be ordered at the time of booking and be compatible with the guest's laptop or iPad. The reception or concierge desks should be able to send and receive faxes and emails and deliver them promptly to the guest.

Although guests increasingly use their cell-phones in preference to landlines, the hard-wired telephone is still needed in hotel rooms. The phones should have voicemail and the telephone number written on the instrument – how often is one asking a person to call back at the hotel but locating the number means a search for letterheads with the hotel number written on it?

The bathroom. The cookie-cutter American hotels of the immediate post-war period mostly had tiny bathrooms with no windows, a shower in the tub, single basins and poor lighting. Some of these exist even today in five-star hotels but less and less frequently, thank goodness.

A five-star hotel bathroom should have a tub and separate shower stall, twin basins, WC in a separate room with a door, and full face lighting. For reasons I cannot fathom, many decorators put extremely strong spot lights in the ceiling above the basins, which creates a shadow on the face. Four Seasons doesn't do this and I congratulate them. If you look into the mirror I think you want to see your face well lit, not in shadow.

Asian hotel bathrooms are among the best. When Mr. Nara built the Observatory in Sydney he put in wonderful tubs, showers and steam rooms, and Michael Kadoorie did the same in the tower of the Peninsula in Kowloon. It has become somewhat trendy to have shower heads directly above one's head which means you get your hair wet whether you want to or not, but in the Observatory or Peninsula you have a choice of shower at an angle, overhead or multiple body-sprays.

I always wondered why, when turning on a shower, the controls were under the shower head so you always got a burst of cold or scalding water in the face when switching on. After discussion with Roger Collins, he said it was perfectly feasible to put shower controls elsewhere on the wall so they could be activated without a splash in the face, and this is what we did in every Orient-Express Hotels bathroom when a shower stall was put in.

I also like the automatic room curtains. In cheapie hotels there are hand rods to close curtains, but in five-star hotels the curtains have more elegant drawstrings, or automatic closers.

Regent Hotels (Burns, Zecha and Rafael) pioneered the concept of having the dressing-room in the bathroom, which meant that the bedrooms would be uncluttered. I tried to encourage this approach for Orient-Express Hotels. The idea is to have a cupboard or cupboards with a partial shelf where a suitcase can be laid flat, with drawers below, and a jacket hanging rail above. Part of the cupboard is open from top to bottom for long hanging clothes. I'd love to eliminate entirely folding luggage racks in bedrooms, but it seems this is not to be because most people travel with more than the cupboards can accommodate.

The safe should be in the back of the cupboard at eye level, and it needs to be well mounted into the wall so it cannot be ripped out. I prefer Elsafes with four digits. We occasionally have a guest complain about theft of jewellery or money left in a room and – dare I say it – there have been losses reported which may have been made up for insurance purposes. When there is a safe in the room a guest can hardly complain if he or she hasn't taken advantage of it. Some hotels have installed safes near the floor, but I think that forcing guests to get down on their knees to access the safe is a bad idea.

One of my absolute requirements, not popular with hotel designers, is that the outlook from the bed should not be spoiled by a view of sinks and bathtubs. One logical reason for this is that if the bathroom door is in your line of sight from the bed, the lights going on and off in the bathroom can be very annoying. The other reason is that the opulent and comfortable décor of the bedroom should not be spoiled by a view of marble, sinks and bathtubs. The easy way to avoid this is to have the back of the bed against the wall of the bathroom with the door around the corner.

Split level rooms are usually a failure. If the bedroom is on the upper level the heat will rise and make the bedroom stuffy, and if the bathroom is on the lower level it is an invitation to break a leg in the dark. I'm a great advocate of nightlights, which avoid accidents in dark bedrooms. Shirley and I often leave the shaving mirror light on in the bathroom to cast a weak glow.

The bed and bedding. All five-star hotels now have king-size beds (and a few twins for Japanese who seem to prefer them). The minimum width of a king-size bed should be 1.83 metres. It is vital that there be good bedside reading lights. I sometimes think that interior designers have never tried to read a book when in bed in a bedroom of their design. The bedside lamp must clearly illuminate the book and cause the least disturbance to the partner sleeping in the bed.

My greatest complaint when it comes to beds is the use of duvets. The duvet is extremely warm and is great for frigid Russia, Scandinavia and Germany where it has been popular for ever. But in warmer climes it can be too warm and five-star hotels should offer sheet and blanket options. Duvets are also a generational thing with younger people preferring them, while old fogeys (like me) dislike them. I think a five-star hotel should ask its guests what sort of bedding they like at the time of booking.

Room amenities. We all have our favourites but when I check into a five-star hotel room I like, at a minimum, a bottle of premium beer in the mini-bar, some cold still water like Evian, a bar of Toblerone and a tin or bottle of salted cashews. I prefer a bottle of good still wine to sparkling wine. There is usually a fruit bowl, and the quality of the fruit can say a lot about the hotel's standards. A cheese plate with biscuits is a popular arrival offering, as is a vase of fresh flowers nicely arranged. When you are married to a botanist and the world's leading collector of botanical art, you learn to appreciate this.

I always ask for an electric kettle, a selection of teas and instant coffees, cold milk (for the tea) and cups and saucers and spoons for stirring. I get these amenities in many four-star American hotels so there is no excuse for them not being provided in five-star hotels worldwide, except when general managers try to force guests to order these things from room service at great cost. I often carry Nestlé Classic instant coffee and English Breakfast teabags, along with different plugs for every eventuality.

The soaps, shampoos and conditioners which are put in the bathrooms for the guests are another cause for concern. Each general manager seems to do his own thing, but the results can be pretty variable. I hate with a passion soaps that are tightly wrapped in plastic because it is impossible to unwrap them with moist hands, so I always prefer that the soap be in a paper wrapper.

Artwork. The Windsor Court had a splendid collection of British art and when we sold the hotel I had a few paintings valued and bought them from the company. At the Villa San Michele the indoor dining room was formerly an open cloister, which we then covered with a glass roof. It was spartan but I was able to acquire a magnificent colourful antique tapestry to adorn one side of the room, and it sets the stage for the Renaissance experience of staying there.

When we rebuilt the Caruso in Ravello we started putting decorative mosaics in bathrooms and Natale Rusconi commissioned some wonderful nudes for the spa at the Hotel Cipriani. Natale has great taste (and not just in nudes) and has filled the hotel with fine artwork by Sarah Schulte, Liselotte Hohs and other Venetian artists. La Residencia in Mallorca is decorated from top to bottom with paintings by the important artists who have lived in the village since the Robert Graves days. We have always tried to do something decorative with a local flavour in each hotel.

Swimming pools, tennis courts and spas. Every five-star hotel should have a swimming pool but sometimes (rarely) it needs to be indoors. Some hotels seem to have pools which are only a metre or so deep throughout. I don't know if these have been built for non-swimmers, children or to save money on heating, but they are no fun to swim in. A pool must have a deep end and ideally this should be two metres (absolute minimum 1.9 metres). The shallow end, which can be 1.2 metres in depth, should have steps and a hand-rail for older guests who are a bit shaky on their pins. The bigger the pool the better. The best ones, where the water comes right up to the top edge with splash gutters beyond, are called 'eye-level' pools and allow swimmers to make the most of the views from the pool. The Hotel Caruso in Ravello and The Westcliff in Johannesburg have stunning ones.

Sun beds for poolside should not have arms. People like to sun both sides and turning over when the beds have arms is very constricting. Natale Rusconi located an Italian supplier of wonderful sun beds, which were not too expensive, and they proved so successful for the Cipriani that we rolled them out at nearly every property. The sun beds need to have wheels at one end and must not be too heavy, as guests like to move them around with the sun.

I was always a keen tennis player and felt that our resort hotels should have courts when feasible. We actually went so far as to build a tennis court on the roof of the old casino rooms in the Copacabana Palace, but it is rarely used. Demand for tennis has declined, but every summer Bernard Arnault, reported to be the world's fourth richest person (CEO of LVMH), asks me for permission to play on the Hotel Splendido's tennis court when he arrives in Portofino on his yacht. The general manager is happy to oblige.

An entire spa culture seems to have grown up over the last twenty years or so, and every hotel today has to have a spa. I am not a spa person so some years ago I set about trying to understand the phenomenon. I visited Chiva-Som, the famous spa in Thailand about 100 miles from Bangkok on the shore of the Gulf of Siam, and was very impressed with their product. It wasn't a medical institution but rather a wellness one. I was told in great seriousness that the main dining room had to be painted in a malachite green as this colour depresses the appetite. Lunch is a salad-bar and while wine is offered in the evening, it is only provided in half-bottles. There are lots of massages, yoga and meditation. Translating this back to the less exotic world of Europe and North America, it seems to me that a gym with the latest exercise equipment, massage rooms with subdued and nice aromas and a hairdresser are the key components. Saunas are popular in some places but steam rooms are often not.

Balustrades. The bane of my existence has been balustrades, usually dictated by planning authorities, which are too high to see over when one is seated at a table. It is absurd to block a view of a wonderful vista, but planners have no interest in views and become obsessed with the remote possibility of guests falling over, even if no one ever has. Roger Collins has addressed this problem in a number of different ways: at the Copacabana Palace the tables and chairs are put on a platform set back from the balustrade so you can see over it, and at the Inn at Perry Cabin a stainless steel wire is strung across the open space at the legally required height. In Asia it is usually possible to build a ledge under the balustrade so that anyone tripping over would just land on that. In Cape Town there is a hotel restaurant called Salt which has clear glass panels forming the balustrade, allowing great views of the sea crashing on the rocks below.

Room service. Shirley and I always have breakfast in our suite, although I sometimes have to engage in the strictly American custom of a business breakfast served in the hotel's breakfast room. If you want to attract guests for dinner they had best be seated in a different location for breakfast, although in some cases it is just not physically possible to make the distinction. I always judge the quality of room service by the croissants, the orange juice and the coffee. If the croissants have been made with plenty of butter and are moist, they rank high. If they are hard dry lumps I suggest you go out of the hotel for meals.

Our friend Michael Winner judges hotels by their orange juice, which he insists must be freshly squeezed and come from sweet oranges if available. Cheapie hotels often use a machine to make orange juice and sometimes it cuts too close to the skin, giving the juice a slightly bitter taste.

One of my complaints is that the pots in which coffee or hot water are served often lose their heat too fast. I made an investigation and found that a Danish-designed thermos pot called Alfi was perfect for the job, but it is possibly too 'trendy' for some hotel general managers. Chinaware is another subject of differing opinions. I particularly love Limoges, but young food and beverage managers today seem to go for only white china in a variety of peculiar shapes, which in my opinion do not improve the food by a whit. It must be a sign of my age.

The style of artwork, china, linens, cutlery and glassware tells a lot about hotel owners and whether they are discriminating or not. I hope that history will record that Orient-Express Hotels had the taste, sophistication and personal touch to put it in a class of its own.

INDEX

VENICE SIMPLON
ORIENT-EXPRESS